THE STONEWALL RIOTS

Marc Stein

THE STONEWALL RIOTS

RIOTS

A DOCUMENTARY HISTORY

NEW YORK UNIVERSITY PRESS
NEW YORK

NEW YORK UNIVERSITY PRESS
New York
www.nyupress.org

References to Internet websites (URLs) were accurate at the time of writing. Neither the author nor New York University Press is responsible for URLs that may have expired or changed since the manuscript was prepared.

Library of Congress Cataloging-in-Publication Data
Names: Stein, Marc., author.
Title: The Stonewall Riots : a documentary history / Marc Stein.
Description: New York : New York University Press, [2019] |
Includes bibliographical references and index.
Identifiers: LCCN 2018041761| ISBN 9781479858286 (cloth : alk. paper) |
ISBN 9781479816859 (pbk : alk. paper)
Subjects: LCSH: Stonewall Riots, New York, N.Y., 1969. | Gay liberation movement—
United States—History. | Gay rights—United States—History—20th century. | Gays—
United States—History—20th century.
Classification: LCC HQ76.8.U5 S753 2019 | DDC 306.76/6097471—dc23
LC record available at https://lccn.loc.gov/2018041761

New York University Press books are printed on acid-free paper, and their binding materials are chosen for strength and durability. We strive to use environmentally responsible suppliers and materials to the greatest extent possible in publishing our books.

Manufactured in the United States of America

10 9 8 7 6 5 4 3 2 1

Also available as an ebook

Frontispiece: Photojournalist Diana Davies (b. 1938) visited the Stonewall Inn in September 1969, shortly after the riots in late June and early July. Credit: Photo by Diana Davies, Manuscripts and Archives Division, the New York Public Library.

CONTENTS

THREE. POLITICAL PROTESTS BEFORE STONEWALL 85

PART II. STONEWALL

PART III. AFTER STONEWALL, 1969–1973

INTRODUCTION

The Stonewall Riots of 1969, when thousands of people protested in the streets in response to a police raid on a Greenwich Village gay bar, have long been identified as the most important event in U.S. lesbian, gay, bisexual, trans, and queer (LGBTQ) history.[1] Whether they are understood as the starting point or turning point in the history of LGBTQ activism, the riots are justifiably viewed as a key moment in the mobilization of one of the most transformative social movements of the twentieth and twenty-first centuries. They also have become an iconic symbol of resistance to oppression and an inspirational example of empowerment for the dispossessed. Each year, millions of people around the world participate in pride parades and protests that commemorate the rebellion on or near its anniversary. In a distinctly memorable invocation that linked the uprising to other aspirational struggles for social justice, U.S. President Barack Obama declared in his 2013 inaugural address: "We, the people, declare today that the most evident of truths—that all of us are created equal—is the star that guides us still, just as it guided our forebears through Seneca Falls, and Selma, and Stonewall."[2]

Despite the widely recognized significance of the riots, most people know little or nothing about what happened at the Stonewall Inn in 1969. Nor do they know much about the earlier developments that contributed to the eruption of protests that summer, the changes experienced by the movement in the weeks and months that followed, and the ways in which the rebellion influenced the city, country, and world. In high school, college, and university classrooms, many teachers address the uprising, but they do so without a substantial collection of primary sources that can encourage students to explore the uprising for themselves. There are scholarly works, museum exhibits, public history websites, and oral history projects that address the rebellion, but none offers the breadth and depth of the documentary materials collected in this volume. By providing an introductory essay, transcripts of two hundred primary sources, and a selection of maps and photographs, *The Stonewall Riots: A Documentary History* hopes to promote new interpretations, innovative analyses, and original explorations by everyone who examines these materials.

WHAT HAPPENED?

So what exactly happened during the Stonewall Riots? This is an impossible question to answer—we can never re-create or revisit the past. Even if we could travel back in time and transport ourselves to the Stonewall Inn in the early morning hours of 28 June 1969, our experiences and accounts would likely differ based on our cultural identities (including our age, class, ethnicity, gender, gender identity, nationality, race, religion, and sexual orientation), social roles (as police officers, bar owners, club managers, bartenders, bouncers, patrons, neighbors, tourists, or passersby), communication networks, and physical absence or presence over the next several days. Our experiences and accounts would also be influenced by our abilities and disabilities (related, for example, to health, language, mobility, sight, and hearing); our consumption of food, water, alcohol, and drugs; and countless other factors. In addition, our narratives would vary if we were asked in the midst of the uprising, the days and weeks that followed, or the months and years that came later.

None of this means that we cannot interpret and analyze the riots. It simply means that we should have a little humility about making definitive pronouncements about what happened. It also means that we should try to remember that every account of the rebellion—whether produced at the time or later—is just that: an account. A single person's narrative does not and cannot provide us with the authoritative truth of what happened. But if we put together a collection of documents and sources, assess their plausibility and credibility, consider their standpoints and perspectives, and evaluate their value and meaning, we can develop compelling interpretations and persuasive analyses. Borrowing from the language of the courts, we can reach some conclusions that are beyond a reasonable doubt, develop other interpretations that are consistent with the preponderance of evidence, and make other meaningful comments based on standards of proof that fall short of what might be required in a court of law.

The Stonewall Inn, located at 51–53 Christopher Street, occupied two adjacent buildings constructed in the 1840s to serve as horse stables.[3] In 1914, no. 53 was converted for use as a bakery on the first floor and an apartment on the second. In 1930, the two buildings were combined, allowing for expansion of the commercial and residential spaces. Four years later, the Stonewall Inn (also known as Bonnie's Stonewall Inn), which had been operating as a speakeasy at 91 Seventh Avenue South since 1930, moved into the commercial space, where it functioned as a bar and restaurant. In 1965, real estate investor Joel Weiser purchased 51–53 Christopher Street along with several nearby properties. The original Stonewall Inn Restaurant closed shortly thereafter, following a fire that damaged the business, but in 1966 four men with organized crime affiliations, at least one of whom was gay, decided to open a gay bar at the site.

When the new Stonewall Inn opened in 1967, it did so as a bottle club. Officially, bottle clubs admitted only members and their guests; members were expected to bring their own bottles of alcohol, which would be served by waiters. In reality, this was a mechanism commonly used by organized crime to circumvent liquor laws. On most nights, the Stonewall's doorman admitted most people who wanted to enter as long as they were perceived to be gay, trans, gender-queer, and/or interested in same-sex sex; admission was $1.00

on weekdays and $3.00 on weekends. Some patrons complained about high prices, watered-down drinks, dirty glasses, and unclean facilities, but the bar's relatively large size, eclectic mix of patrons, and reputation for dancing, drugs, camping, cruising, and go-go boys made it a popular destination. Many accounts suggest that the patrons were diverse in terms of class and race. Most were probably white; a significant number were African American and Puerto Rican. Most were probably middle or working class; some were poor and/or homeless. The large majority identified as men, a small number as women. Many likely saw themselves as gay, bisexual, or homosexual; a small minority probably viewed themselves as lesbian; others may have enjoyed same-sex sex without claiming a distinct sexual identity; some probably identified as straight or heterosexual. There was a significant and visible presence of gender-queer people, some of whom identified as butches, drags, queens, transsexuals, or transvestites. Some were hustlers or prostitutes. Most patrons were in their teens, twenties, or thirties.

The pivotal raid on the Stonewall (the second in one week) began in the early morning hours of Saturday, 28 June. Some accounts suggest that the police targeted the bar because it was unlicensed, unsanitary, and suspected of violating liquor laws. Others claim that the main cause was a breakdown in the system whereby the owners paid off the police (approximately $1,200 per month) to minimize raids and closures. Still others point to official or unofficial investigations into police corruption, male prostitution, and blackmailing rings that targeted men who had sex with men. There was also the upcoming mayoral election; many public officials believed that antigay crackdowns were politically advantageous because it made them appear morally virtuous and tough on crime.

Armed with a warrant authorizing them to search the Stonewall for evidence of illegal alcohol sales, the police began their operation. Shortly after midnight, four undercover police officers—two men and two women—and an inspector from the New York City Department of Consumer Affairs entered the bar to observe the scene and gather evidence. A short while later, the two undercover policemen exited the bar and met up with four officers waiting nearby. At approximately 1:20 a.m., five of the six policemen outside the bar entered the building, announced their presence, and demanded to see identification cards. Several sources indicate that there were approximately two hundred people in the bar when the raid began. The police detained several bar employees, patrons without identification, butches, transvestites, and people who talked back or fought back; they told everyone else to leave. As the latter exited the bar, they joined others to form an angry and agitated crowd on the nearby streets and sidewalks.

When the police emerged from the bar with several patrons and employees in their custody, the multiracial crowd began to erupt. According to some accounts, a lesbian was the first to fight back; multiple accounts emphasize the distinctively aggressive defiance of trans people and street youth. Soon the

Figure I.1. President Barack Obama designated the Stonewall National Monument in 2016. Credit: National Park Service.

crowd, which included straight allies, was shouting at the police and throwing coins at the building. As the police, now joined by other officers from their precincts, attacked the protesters and the protesters fought back, several prisoners were liberated or liberated themselves from the police wagon. The officer in charge then ordered the wagon to leave with those who had been taken into custody, which it did, but the crowd forced the remaining police to retreat into the bar. The crowd subsequently shattered some of the Stonewall's windows; attacked the building with bricks, stones, cans, and bottles; tried to break down the front door with an uprooted parking meter; and attempted to light the bar on fire. Eventually police reinforcements arrived and members of the Tactical Patrol Force, specialists in riot control, tried to clear the streets. Over the next several hours, thousands of people rioted in the streets with campy courage and fierce fury. Thousands rioted again on Saturday night and Sunday morning. The situation calmed down on Sunday, Monday, and Tuesday nights, but a third night of major protests took place on Wednesday.

This is just a broad overview; after all, the point of this book is to encourage readers to develop their own interpretations. Overall, the preponderance of evidence indicates that approximately thirteen people (including several bar employees) were arrested on the first night; three or four on the second; and five on the third. Many more were detained. Police records from the first night reference six of the people who were arrested. Judging by the names, one was a woman and five were men; one was folk singer Dave Van Ronk (believed to be straight and white); one was Raymond Castro, who identified as Puerto Rican and gay. Several police officers and a larger number of protesters were injured. One protester reportedly lost two fingers when his hand was slammed in a car door; another required ten stitches from injuries sustained when he was clubbed in the knees; many more were battered and bloodied by police violence. One of the officers was hit in the eye with flying glass; another fell and broke his wrist; many more suffered bruised egos. As for the Stonewall Inn, the exterior of the building and the interior contents suffered extensive damage; the bar closed in October 1969. By this time, the riots had inspired the formation of the Gay Liberation Front and Queens Liberation Front in New York, the transformation of the LGBT movement, and the mobilization of thousands of new activists. Over the next several decades, as the rebellion was commemorated in pride protests and parades in and beyond New York, the building where the uprising began was used for various commercial purposes. In 2016, President Obama officially designated the Stonewall National Monument at the site of the Stonewall Inn.[4]

HISTORICAL TEXTS AND CONTEXTS

Keeping in mind that *there is always more to the story*, what sources have historians used when constructing their accounts of the Stonewall Riots? In history classrooms, we typically distinguish between primary and secondary sources. The former consist of materials *from* the historical moment. The latter, produced later, are materials *about* the historical moment, including studies by academic and nonacademic historians. This introduction is a secondary source; the documents that follow are primary. To be more precise, much of this chapter is a specific type of secondary source, a work of historiography, meaning that it provides an overview of different historical interpretations (a history of history). There are also sources that do not fit neatly into these categories. Depending on how they are used, for example, oral histories can be treated as primary or secondary sources; the same is true of autobiographies, memoirs, and works of popular memory, including historical landmarks, public monuments, and other types of creative work such as films and novels.

For the Stonewall Riots, the three best secondary sources are journalist Donn Teal's *The Gay Militants: How Gay Liberation Began in America, 1969–1971* (1971), academic historian Martin Duberman's *Stonewall* (1993), and public historian David Carter's *Stonewall: The Riots That Sparked the Gay Revolution* (2004). These are book-length studies, but there are also shorter discussions in a variety of works, including my book *Rethinking the Gay and Lesbian Movement* (2012). Recent works for teenagers and adults include Ann Bausum's *Stonewall: Breaking Out in the Fight for Gay Rights* (2016) and Tristan Poehlmann's *The Stonewall Riots: The Fight for LGBT Rights* (2017). Films include Nigel Finch's *Stonewall* (1995), Kate Davis and David Heilbroner's *Stonewall Uprising* (2010), and Roland Emmerich's *Stonewall* (2015).[5]

Secondary sources reveal what *others* have concluded based on *their* primary research. They also help us see that interpretations change over time and are influenced by the historical moments in which they are produced. If we want to develop our own interpretations, however, it is vital that we do primary research. For the Stonewall Riots, historians generally rely on six types of primary sources. Perhaps the most widely used are media accounts, including coverage in the mainstream media (such as the *New York Times*), the alternative press (such as the *Village Voice*), and LGBT periodicals (such as the *Mattachine Society of New York Newsletter*). Second, there are ephemeral materials, including fliers, pamphlets, posters, and graffiti. Third, there are police reports, which historians Michael Scherker, Jonathan Ned Katz, and David Carter acquired through public records requests.[6] Fourth, there are gay bar guides and other sources that reference the Stonewall Inn. Fifth, there are photographs taken on the streets of Greenwich Village before, during, and after the uprising. Sixth, there are oral histories, autobiographical works, and other oral, written, and audiovisual accounts by participants and observers.[7]

Constructing a clear and concise account of what happened during the Stonewall Riots is possible using these and other primary sources, but doing so does not provide a rich and revealing discussion of why the riots occurred when and where they did, what earlier developments influenced and shaped the rebellion, and what were the later effects and results of the uprising. In considering these questions, historians have to make choices about which contexts to emphasize and how to move back and forth between texts and contexts. The stories we tell will vary depending on which of the following (or other) contexts we emphasize:

- Greenwich Village, New York City, and other U.S. cities
- Law enforcement, organized crime, and urban policing
- Gender and sexuality (normative and nonnormative)
- Anti-LGBT discrimination, prejudice, oppression, and violence
- LGBT bars, businesses, cultures, and communities
- LGBT activism, politics, protest, and resistance
- Urban riots, social movements, and political activism, including African American, feminist, antiwar, student, and countercultural activism
- Local, state, and national political developments, electoral politics, political parties, and political cultures
- Transnational developments, influences, and inspirations

Our stories will also vary based on whether we prioritize lesbian, gay, bisexual, trans, or queer history (and how we conceptualize each of these); whether we emphasize class, race, (dis)ability, and other factors that intersect with gender and sexuality (and how we define each of these); and whether we focus on the immediate context (the summer of 1969), the medium term (the years immediately preceding and following the riots), the longer term (the decades surrounding the uprising), or the longest term (from the beginning of time to the present).

INTERPRETIVE FRAMEWORKS: INFLUENCES AND INSPIRATIONS

What best explains why the Stonewall Riots happened when and where they did? Some of the obvious factors should not be overlooked. LGBT people were structurally and systematically oppressed in American society, commonly treated as criminals by law, sinners by religion, diseased by science, defective by business, deviant by popular culture, and faulty by family and friends. Police officers routinely engaged in acts of anti-LGBT hate, harassment, discrimination, and disrespect, especially against people of color, immigrants, poor people, sex workers, and gender-queers. Police raids on gay bars, many owned, operated, and "protected" by organized crime, were common. Bars were especially vulnerable when they did not pay off the police and when politicians wanted to present themselves as paragons of virtue, opponents of vice, and proponents of law and order. New York City was home to the largest LGBT communities in the United States and an even larger world of queer desires and acts. Greenwich Village, longtime hotbed of cultural bohemianism and political radicalism, was a center of LGBT life.[8] It is thus not surprising that the rebellion occurred in the context of a police raid on a Greenwich Village gay bar. But why did the uprising begin in June 1969 rather than earlier or later? And why did the patrons and passersby riot rather than respond in other ways?

One of the most popular interpretations—often criticized as a myth by historians—is that the rebellion was a spontaneous eruption of anger and an unprecedented explosion of resistance. Furious that the police were yet again raiding a popular gay club and targeting the most vulnerable members of their communities, the Stonewall's patrons and their allies on the streets fought back and started a revolution. Those who claim that the gay movement began at Stonewall—an assertion made by gay liberationists in the aftermath of the riots, repeated subsequently during pride marches, and now invoked commonly in the mainstream media—typically view the rebellion as unprecedented. They sometimes go so far as to claim that the riots were the first time that LGBT people fought back against oppression. From this perspective, the dark and dreary world of homosexuality in the pre-Stonewall era suddenly disappeared in June 1969 and was replaced by the light and bright universe of gay liberation. A campy version of this interpretation places emphasis on the fact that the funeral of Judy Garland—the actress and singer whose triumphs and tragedies had been followed by many LGBT fans and whose rendition of "Somewhere over the Rainbow" had inspired queer hopes for better futures—took place just hours before the riots began and contributed to their emotional intensity.

The notion that the Stonewall Riots were the first time that LGBT people fought back had little support from older movement veterans in the rebellion's aftermath. Longtime activists Dick Leitsch, Jim Kepner, and Randy Wicker, for example, all rejected this idea in articles they published in 1969–73, with Wicker doing so in an article titled "The Stonewall Myth: Lies about Gay Liberation."[9] The notion that the LGBT movement began at Stonewall (or the slightly modified claim that the "modern" movement began there) also has had little support among historians. Studies of pre-Stonewall history have demonstrated convincingly that at the time of the riots there were long traditions of LGBT resistance and protest and that these traditions influenced both the rebellion and the mass mobilization that followed. It may have served the interests of Stonewall and post-Stonewall radicals to present themselves as making a revolutionary break with the past, but historians typically find both continuity and discontinuity when studying revolutions—they often see signs of change in the periods leading up to revolutions and evidence of the limits of change in postrevolutionary eras. This is what they have found when examining the Stonewall Riots, which has led to the development of alternative frameworks for thinking about why the uprising occurred when and where it did.

One of the most influential of these frameworks argues that the uprising was the culmination of two decades of organized LGBT movement activism in the 1950s and 1960s. This interpretation was first put forward by movement veterans in Stonewall's aftermath, but it was developed more fully by historian John D'Emilio in his 1983 book *Sexual Politics*.[10] According to D'Emilio, developments in the 1940s and 1950s—principally national mobilization during World War II and political repression during the McCarthy era—led to the emergence of an organized "homophile" movement in the 1950s and 1960s. Founded by

Los Angeles leftists in 1950–51, the Mattachine Society was soon joined by ONE, Incorporated, in Los Angeles (founded in 1952), the Daughters of Bilitis in San Francisco (founded in 1955), and other homophile groups elsewhere. These organizations lobbied and litigated for reform, supported research and education, and achieved important successes in the pre-Stonewall era, including a 1958 U.S. Supreme Court victory that established the constitutional rights of these groups to publish their periodicals. While they sometimes criticized gay bars and presented themselves as respectable alternatives, homophile groups also published informative bar guides, challenged discriminatory police raids, rejected unfair liquor control practices, provided valuable legal advice, and supported courageous litigation by bar patrons, workers, and owners. More generally, they laid the foundations for the riots by changing the consciousness of the community and country, challenging the gender and sexual oppression of U.S. society, and promoting the notion that LGBT people were entitled to freedom, equality, and justice.

Many who see the riots as the culmination of two decades of LGBT political organizing place special emphasis on the movement's increased militancy and radicalism in the second half of the 1960s (before Stonewall). Some accounts of homophile activism skip over this period, focusing instead on the movement's leftist origins in the early 1950s and its retreat to respectability a few years later. These narratives, which typically describe the pre-Stonewall movement as small and accommodationist, miss the fact that LGBT activism changed significantly in the mid-1960s. While the Daughters of Bilitis continued to be the country's leading lesbian organization and the Erickson Educational Foundation (founded in 1964) emerged as a key supporter of transsexual and transgender empowerment, the Mattachine Society dissolved its national structure in 1961 and stopped publishing its magazine in 1967. By the mid-1960s, much of the movement's vanguard consisted of autonomous local groups, not local chapters of national organizations. These included the Mattachine Societies of New York and Washington, D.C.; Mattachine Midwest in Chicago; the Janus Society, Homosexual Law Reform Society, and Homophile Action League in Philadelphia; Personal Rights in Defense and Education (PRIDE) in Los Angeles; and the Society for Individual Rights (SIR), Vanguard, and Committee for Homosexual Freedom (CHF) in San Francisco. In fact, CHF leaders claimed in the months following the Stonewall Riots that their Bay Area protests in the spring of 1969—against businesses that had fired known or suspected homosexuals and against police who had shot and killed a man accused of soliciting sex from an undercover officer—inspired the uprising in New York. They asserted then and continued to assert for decades that their demonstrations, rather than the Stonewall Riots, launched the new gay liberation movement.[11]

More generally, the radicalizing local LGBT groups of 1965–69—more assertive about LGBT rights and freedoms, more oriented to direct action and sexual liberation, and more supportive of "gay power" and the "gay revolution"—were responsible for a wave of more than thirty pre-Stonewall demonstrations, sit-ins, and riots. These included protests at the United Nations in New York, Independence Hall in Philadelphia, and the White House, Pentagon, and Civil Service Commission in Washington, D.C.; a sit-in at Dewey's restaurant in Philadelphia; two major demonstrations against police raids on Los Angeles gay bars (one with more than four hundred participants); and a riot at Compton's Cafeteria in San Francisco. The scale of these (measured by the number of participants) was much smaller than the Stonewall Riots; they did not receive extensive national publicity in the mainstream press; and they did not lead to mass mobilization. Still, the wave of LGBT protests from 1965 to 1969 makes it clear that the riots were not unprecedented.

There are compelling reasons to accept this interpretive framework and see the Stonewall Riots as the culmination of two decades of LGBT movement activism. Critics of this framework, however, argue that the pre-Stonewall homophiles of the 1950s and 1960s had limited success in attracting large numbers of participants, garnering significant public attention, and achieving major social reforms. They point out that much of the homophile movement—even in the second half of the 1960s—was ambivalent about gay bars and critical of disreputable clubs like the Stonewall. Most homophile activists supported the constitutional rights of gay people to gather in bars and were critical of discriminatory police raids and liquor control practices, but many embraced the politics of respectability. This led them to criticize gender and sexual practices that they commonly associated with gay bars, including casual sex, sexual promiscuity, sex work, public sex, erotic expression, and gender transgression.

Critics of this framework also point out that the demographic characteristics of homophile activists were quite different from those of the Stonewall rioters—the former were older, whiter, more middle class, less politically radical, less countercultural, and less gender-transgressive. In addition, while it is true that the LGBT movement radicalized in the years leading up to the rebellion, few homophile activists believed that rioting was an effective or desirable form of protest. These points can easily be overstated—countless homophiles were strong defenders of gay bars, many were sexual and gender liberationists, and some were demographically similar to the Stonewall protesters. Comparative analyses of pre-Stonewall homophiles and Stonewall rioters nevertheless suggest that there are good reasons to question the notion that the Stonewall uprising is best understood as the culmination of LGBT movement activism in the 1950s and 1960s.

These limitations have led to the development of a third influential framework. Instead of seeing the rebellion as the product of LGBT political organizing in the 1950s and 1960s, some historians argue that the riots are best understood as the outgrowth of a much longer tradition of bar-based resistance practices. Perhaps the most influential historical studies of LGBT bar cultures are Elizabeth Kennedy and Madeline Davis's 1993 book *Boots of Leather*, which explores lesbian bars in Buffalo from the 1930s to the 1960s, and George Chauncey's 1994 book *Gay New York*, which addresses gay bars from the 1890s to the 1930s. These works and others that consider different locations show that bar owners, managers, workers, and patrons had developed multiple ways of responding to anti-LGBT policing in the decades leading up to the riots.[12]

Bar-based resistance practices had a long history in the United States, where national alcohol prohibition from 1920 to 1933 had been replaced by new forms of local, state, and federal liquor regulation. In the context of multiple legal and extralegal obstacles, gay bar owners and managers, for example, made careful choices about where to locate their establishments, blocked or darkened their windows to minimize public scrutiny, and restricted entry and access through a variety of mechanisms. They paid off the police, collaborated with organized crime, and developed early warning systems to alert their patrons in times of trouble. They strategically permitted and policed transgressive sexual expression, including touching, kissing, and dancing, and subversive gender expression, including drag performances and transgender clothing. They made deliberate choices about segregation and integration based on race, class, and gender. And they challenged the actions of local and state authorities in court, winning partial victories, for example, in a series of California gay bar cases in the 1950s.[13] As for patrons, some argue that the very act of going to a gay bar in these circumstances was a form of resistance. Many resisted in other ways—by escaping, running, and hiding during raids, defending themselves and criticizing the police, coming together to provide mutual assistance and support, challenging the charges they faced in court, and fighting back with words and other weapons. From this perspective, the Stonewall Riots are best understood as the culmination of decades of resistance practices that LGBT people had developed in response to police repression.

Further support for this framework comes from studies that emphasize the importance of consumer culture in general and gay consumer culture in particular during this era. Civil rights historians have long noted that the sit-in movement of the 1960s started as an effort by African American youth to gain access to a Woolworth's lunch counter in Greensboro, North Carolina. Other protests by racial and ethnic minorities focused on their exclusion from, segregated access to, and discriminatory treatment by other consumer-oriented businesses, including bars, restaurants, movie theaters, amusement parks, and department stores. The United States had become, in the words of historian Lizabeth Cohen, "a consumers' republic," and historian David Johnson's recent book *Buying Gay* demonstrates that gay Americans increasingly demanded the same rights to consume that others took for granted or fought to exercise. In this context, we should not be surprised that the Stonewall's patrons, lubricated by alcohol and drugs, erupted when the police interfered with their rights to consume.[14]

There is much to recommend the notion that the Stonewall Riots were the outgrowth of bar- and consumer-based resistance practices that had developed over decades. This framework, however, does not explain the unprecedented scale, intensity, and militancy of the response to the police raid on the Stone-wall. Nor does it help us understand the mass political mobilization that occurred afterwards. The long history of bar-based resistance practices helps us appreciate one of the key historical contexts for the riots, but more is needed to understand why the rebellion erupted when and where it did and why the LGBT movement changed as much as it did in the aftermath.

The limitations of the interpretations presented thus far have led to the development of another framework, one that situates the riots in relation to the general radicalization of political activism in the late 1960s and early 1970s. This explanation, that the riots were inspired and influenced by other social movements, was favored by many post-Stonewall gay liberationists, who saw themselves as part of a broad-based social justice coalition, and it has been mentioned or emphasized by many historians who have written about Stone-wall.[15] Perhaps the greatest inspiration was the African American movement, which increasingly adopted a "black power" orientation in the mid-1960s. We see this influence in the pre-Stonewall use of slogans like "Gay Is Good" and "Gay Power," which were adaptations or appropriations of "Black Is Beauti-ful" and "Black Power," and in the LGBT movement's adoption of direct action tactics, including demonstrations, sit-ins, and riots. The 1965 Watts Rebellion in Los Angeles, when African Americans rioted in response to police racism and economic impoverishment, and subsequent riots against racism in 1966, 1967, and 1968 directly inspired the Stonewall rebellion.

LGBT radicalization in the second half of the 1960s was influenced by changes in other social movements as well. In this period, red, brown, and yellow power activism grew, radical feminism strengthened, protests against the Vietnam War escalated, and U.S. leftists increasingly saw themselves as part of a global revolution against colonialism. Countercultural activism cele-brated "sex, love, and rock 'n' roll" and critiqued bourgeois culture, capitalist consumerism, and suburban conformity. LGBT people were influenced by all of these developments and by the growth of a sexual liberation movement that challenged multiple forms of erotic repression. These influences were not just intellectual and theoretical—LGBT people moved between and among these movements, becoming agents of inspiration and vectors of transmission in the "movement of movements." From this perspective, the Stonewall Riots hap-pened because of the radicalizing effects of other social movements on LGBT activism and resistance.

There is a fifth framework that may be useful in thinking about why the riots occurred when and where they did. As was the case with the preceding framework, this one considers the larger political context and pays attention to evidence of temporal synchronicity, but rather than focus on the radicalizing influences of other movements, this framework concentrates on the radical-izing effects of rising expectations and dashed hopes. A few months after the riots, gay journalist Don Jackson addressed the politics of disillusionment in an article about the rebellion's "sociological implications." According to Jackson,

"Experts in group behavior say that tensions in a minority group become most acute at times when the minority group members see their status suddenly take a turn for the worse after a long period of improvement. This exactly describes the situation in New York, preceding the riots."[16]

Jackson did not specify what he meant by the "long period of improvement," but he might have been thinking about the reforms achieved by the LGBT movement in the years leading up to the riots. In 1966 and 1967, for example, homophile activists had convinced New York City's mayor and police commissioner to limit the use of police entrapment practices and the enforcement of sexual solicitation laws.[17] In 1967 and 1968, New York State activists had helped secure a new law that further constrained police entrapment practices and a court decision that provided increased protection to gay bars.[18] The *New York Times Magazine* in 1967 and *Wall Street Journal* in 1968 had published major articles that seemed to predict further advances in LGBT rights.[19] Just weeks before the Stonewall Riots, the city's Civil Service Commission had agreed to end its ban on hiring homosexuals in most city government jobs.[20]

There were also signs of improvement elsewhere. In 1967, a federal district court in Minnesota had ruled in favor of a major gay publisher in an obscenity case.[21] In the same year, England and Wales had decriminalized private and consensual same-sex sex among adults over the age of twenty-one, except for those in the military.[22] In the early days of 1969, the Los Angeles Police Commission dropped its prohibition on cross-gender impersonation by entertainers.[23] In the first week of June 1969, Connecticut's legislature voted to make that state the second (after Illinois) to repeal its sodomy law.[24] Around the same time, San Francisco's Committee for Homosexual Freedom declared victory in its fight to secure the reinstatement of a fired record store worker.[25] West Germany partially decriminalized sodomy three days before the Christopher Street riots began and Canada did so just hours before the police raided the Stonewall.[26] Though they could not have known this when the uprising began, the *San Francisco Chronicle* began a groundbreaking four-part series on lesbians on 30 June and gay activists won a major federal court ruling against employment discrimination by the U.S. Civil Service Commission on 1 July.[27]

If all of this sustains the notion that LGBT people had reasons for perceiving major improvements in their status in the years leading up to the rebellion (and that New Yorkers had reasons for feeling frustrated because some of this did not apply to them), are there grounds for thinking that they might have seen the raid on the Stonewall as part of Jackson's "turn for the worse"? Much of the country had grown darkly pessimistic in the preceding eighteen months. In 1968, the Tet Offensive had raised the prospects of an escalation of the Vietnam War in January and February; civil rights leader Martin Luther King was assassinated in April; Democratic presidential candidate Robert Kennedy was assassinated in June; and Chicago police violently attacked protesters at the Democratic Party convention in August. For many observers, these were bloody new chapters in the long and brutal history of American violence. In November 1968, Republican Richard Nixon won election as U.S. president on a law and order platform that promised to reverse the reforms of the Kennedy and Johnson administrations; he was inaugurated in January 1969. For New Yorkers, this was the first time since 1903 that they had a Republican mayor, governor, and president. Governor Nelson Rockefeller (elected 1959) and Mayor John Lindsay (elected 1966) may have been known as liberal or moderate Republicans, but Nixon's election seemed to threaten the future of progressive reform and Lindsay was defeated by a more conservative candidate in the Republican primary on 17 June.[28] Fears about the future of reform were confirmed in May, when Nixon nominated conservative Warren Burger to replace liberal Earl Warren as chief justice of the Supreme Court. Burger took office five days before the riots began.[29]

This was not all. In the weeks and months leading up to the Stonewall Riots, a series of police raids on New York bars and bathhouses, including one on the Stonewall Inn just a few days before the one that sparked the riots, had inspired new anger and frustration about anti-LGBT oppression. Some blamed the raids on the upcoming city elections, but the crackdown caught many by surprise, since they had come to expect better treatment from Mayor Lindsay. In May, local, state, and federal prosecutors used obscenity laws to force the closure of one of the country's most popular gay periodicals, the Philadelphia-based *Drum* magazine. In the weeks leading up to the Stonewall Riots, vigilantes in Kew Gardens (a neighborhood in Queens, one of New York City's five boroughs) initiated a campaign of harassment against men who cruised for sex in a local park; when those efforts failed, axe-wielding men chopped down several dozen of the park's trees just a few days before the riots began. Also in June, the *Mattachine Society of New York Newsletter* reported on three recent killings of gay men. In New York, police had discovered the body of a man strangled to death in March; his corpse was found in the Hudson River near a popular gay cruising spot. In Los Angeles, police had violently attacked and killed Howard Efland during a March raid on a gay hotel. In the Bay Area in April, Frank Bartley had been shot and killed by an undercover policeman who sexually entrapped him in a Berkeley cruising park.[30] Then, on 21 June, Philip Caplan died after a public toilet beating by vice squad officers in Oakland, California.[31] We cannot know whether the Stonewall rioters knew about these developments, whether they were part of a larger trend of increased hate and hostility, or whether the media stories that reported on these incidents reflected or produced increased public attention to antigay violence, but if we try to imagine the mood in the bar and on the streets during the raid on the Stonewall, the situation seems to fit Jackson's profile of a revolutionary situation, when "minority group members see their status suddenly take a turn for the worse after a long period of improvement."

All of these frameworks help us to understand why the Stonewall Riots occurred when and where they did. Some aspects of the uprising were spontaneous and unprecedented. The homophile movement of the 1950s and 1960s and its radicalization in the second half of the 1960s created the pre-conditions for revolt. The long history of bar-based resistance practices created a repertoire of rebellious responses. Other social movements provided revolutionary inspiration and influence. And the combination of heightened expectations and dashed hopes that many felt as the country transitioned from a period of liberal reform to one of conservative backlash—and that LGBT people experienced in the context of a new wave of police raids, violent killings, and local vigilantism—created an explosive situation that erupted on 28 June.

INTERPRETIVE FRAMEWORKS—RESULTS AND IMPLICATIONS

When interpreting the Stonewall Riots, historians have addressed more than just the influences and inspirations; they also have considered the results and implications. On this issue, it is useful to remember that correlation is not the same as causation. Just because something happened *after* the riots (correlation) does not mean that it happened *because* of the riots (causation). Popular discourse might suggest that virtually everything that happened in LGBT history after the rebellion happened because of it, but we could just as readily attribute these changes to pre- or post-Stonewall developments, including shifts in science, religion, law, and politics; transformations in social and cultural activism; and modifications in race, class, gender, and sexual politics. A distinctly important argument to consider is that it was not the riots themselves that led to major social change; it was the political mobilizations and cultural transformations that occurred after the riots. After all, if activists—some from the homophile movement, some from other movements, and some newly politicized—had not seized the opportunities created by the Stonewall rebellion, the results might not have been as significant as they were.

As noted above, one way of thinking about post-Stonewall history emphasizes radical discontinuities between the pre- and post-Stonewall eras:

- From oppression to resistance
- From repression to liberation
- From criminalization to legalization
- From invisibility to visibility
- From privacy to publicity
- From the closets to the streets
- From a small movement to mass mobilization
- From minor liberal reforms to major revolutionary changes
- From sexual respectability to sexual radicalism
- From gender conformity to gender transgression
- From single-issue politics to coalitional and intersectional politics
- From a white and middle-class movement to a multiracial and class-diverse movement.

Those who believe that these are helpful ways to characterize developments before and after Stonewall typically argue that the riots inspired and instigated these shifts. Critics respond that this misses important continuities and exaggerates the situation on both sides of the Stonewall divide. For example, as evidence of pre-Stonewall change and post-Stonewall stasis accummulates, it becomes more challenging to sustain arguments about radical discontinuities. Moreover, it can be difficult to demonstrate that the riots themselves—as opposed to political mobilizations after the riots—led to significant social change. And yet the impression remains that the riots marked a fundamental break in LGBT history.

Another approach—typically embraced by liberal reformers rather than radical revolutionaries—sees the Stonewall era as leading to slow, steady, and linear progress toward universally shared goals. Those who use this framework tend to see the major reforms of the post-Stonewall era—declassification of homosexuality as a psychiatric disorder, LGBT inclusion in the military, decriminalization of sodomy, legalization of cross-dressing, recognition of same-sex marriage, legitimization of LGBT families, and LGBT visibility in mainstream media—as direct outgrowths of the riots. Supporters of this approach often focus on the mass mobilization triggered by the rebellion, which led to the proliferation of LGBT organizations and their engagement in multiple forms of political activism. Critics respond that progress has not been linear; reforms have been partial, limited, qualified, and incomplete; the changes that have occurred should not necessarily be characterized as progress; and the goals that have been achieved are not universally celebrated. Many of the people who participated in the Stonewall Riots and many who joined the LGBT movement in the late 1960s and early 1970s, for example, rejected liberal inclusion in U.S. society, favoring revolutionary transformation instead.

When discussing post-Stonewall history, many radicals offer narratives of declension (decline) rather than progress. Those who favor this framework commonly see the Stonewall moment (often conceptualized as lasting from 1969 to 1973) as one of radical potential that was lost as the LGBT movement moderated, mainstreamed, bureaucratized, and institutionalized. For example, many in the Stonewall generation were opposed to the Vietnam War, critiqued organized religion, challenged corporate capitalism, and attacked the nuclear family, whereas the mainstream LGBT movement of the late twentieth and early twenty-first centuries celebrates military inclusion, religious acceptance, business support, marriage equality, and LGBT reproduction. Many in the Stonewall generation favored grassroots local organizing and direct-action protests; the mainstream LGBT movement of today is led by powerful national groups that focus on electoral politics, legislative lobbying, and court-based litigation. From these perspectives, the LGBT movement, after taming and tempering the radical politics of 1969–73, picked up where pre-Stonewall homophile activism left off, meaning that the riots only briefly interrupted a movement that generally has been defined by liberal rather than radical politics. Much of this exaggerates the radicalism of the Stonewall generation and minimizes the complexities of pre-1969 and post-1973 LGBT politics, but there are compelling reasons to adopt and accept narratives of post-Stonewall declension.

A fourth approach rejects linear narratives of progress or decline and instead sees periodic and cyclical eruptions of LGBT radicalism that have interrupted and disrupted the politics of liberal inclusion. This framework works, for example, for those who see the LGBT movement as moderating after the initial radical rush of Stonewall but radicalizing again at later moments. Supporters of this approach argue that LGBT radicalism erupted again in the late 1970s, when LGBT people of color transformed the movement with intersectional and transnational activism; in the late 1980s, when AIDS activists revolutionized LGBT politics; and in the early 1990s, when queer and trans activists reoriented the movement once again.

Since the documents collected in this book do not extend beyond 1973, they do not provide enough evidence to reach firm conclusions about the long-term effects and results of the Stonewall Riots. They can, however, provide the basis for more informed discussions about post-Stonewall developments by promoting stronger foundations of knowledge about the years from 1965 to 1973.[32]

INTERPRETIVE FRAMEWORKS: WHOSE RIOTS?

Another set of discussions about the riots concerns who can, who does, and who should lay claim to them. These are based in part on *historical* questions— who frequented the Stonewall, started the rebellion, participated in the uprising, mobilized afterward, and commemorated the uprising in pride parades and protests? They also are based on *genealogical* questions—who today claims an identity, identification, community, or culture that leads them to view the riots in ancestral terms? There are important *political* questions to consider as well—what political affinities and affiliations might lead someone to stake a claim to Stonewall and what are the political echoes and effects of such claims? As the documents in this collection make clear, these debates and discussions are not new; they began in the rebellion's immediate aftermath.

LGBT people have long staked their claims to Stonewall, but they often have done so in contested and contentious ways. On the historical questions, most accounts of the riots emphasize the participation of gay men; many highlight the roles played by trans resisters and gender queers; some note that lesbians were among the first to fight back; others mention bisexuals and people who identified as neither gay nor straight or as both gay and straight. There have been particularly intense debates about the presence, participation, and prominence of three individuals: Sylvia Rivera, commonly identified as Puerto Rican, gay, and trans; Marsha P. Johnson, commonly identified as African American, gay, and trans; and Stormé DeLarverie, commonly identified as African American, mixed race, butch, lesbian, and trans. Multiple sources on the riots reference these and other individuals, but many accounts are incomplete, inconsistent, and in conflict about key details. Some argue that it is important that credit be given where credit is due; others complain that many of these discussions are ahistorical and say more about the identity politics of later moments than they do about the Stonewall Riots; still others argue that in historicizing the riots we should place more emphasis on social and structural factors rather than individual actions and activities. In these discussions, there are justifiable concerns about the class, gender, and race politics of questioning some sources more than others. In these contexts, it is challenging to avoid both minimization and exaggeration.

A further complication is that since the words and concepts used in 1969 are not the same as the ones used decades later, it is often necessary to translate when encountering identity-based terms in primary sources about the riots. I have been referring to "gay bars" in this introduction, for example, because at the time of the riots many lesbians, bisexuals, queens, and transvestites called themselves "gay" and many LGBT people referred to places like the Stonewall as "gay bars"; this might not be the case today, when identity borders and boundaries have shifted. At the time of the riots, to take another example, several key individuals referred to themselves as gay transvestites, but today "gay" and "trans" are commonly viewed as distinct identities. Some recent accounts describe the riots as queer because of the heterogeneous character of the participants and the rebellious nature of the uprising, but the meanings of "queer" have changed over the last several decades and there is not much evidence that LGBT people called the riots "queer" then.

There have been other contests and conflicts about who has strong historical bases for claiming Stonewall. With respect to age and generation, young people can lay claim to Stonewall based on the preponderance of teenagers and twenty-somethings during the uprising, but so can Stonewall's veterans, most of whom are now in their sixties, seventies, and eighties. As for race and class, many middle-class white people lay claim to the Stonewall Riots because of their presence, participation, and prominence in the rebellion and because middle-class white people commonly lay claim to everything. At the same time, street people, poor people, working-class people, and people of color assert their claims to Stonewall based on their presence, participation, and prominence and because of persistent absences and erasures in LGBT history and politics. Careful and critical readings of the documents collected in this book might be a good starting point for assessing these competing and complementary claims, but a more comprehensive approach would require analysis of other sources, including oral histories. Meanwhile, there is a whole set of other questions to ask about when, where, and why there have been such intense conflicts about claiming Stonewall.

In the aftermath of the uprising, the rebellion was commonly invoked in debates and discussions about the movement's internal divisions. Some lesbian feminists, for example, distanced themselves from the riots as they critiqued misogyny within gay and trans activism, asking why they should commemorate an event that was dominated by people they viewed as men. Some people of color, poor people, and street youth criticized early Stonewall commemorations because they were dominated by middle-class white people and ignored or downplayed the contributions of other classes and races. Some trans activists invoked the riots—and the fierce resistance of gender queers during the rebellion—when they criticized LGB activists for downplaying trans agendas and rejecting gender-queer priorities. And some queer activists referenced the riots when they attacked the mainstream movement for rejecting radical politics and reducing queer struggles for liberation to LGBT campaigns for inclusion. In these situations, activists were fighting about history, but also using the riots to address post-Stonewall politics.

In the midst of these conversations, there also have been conflicts and contests about local, national, and international claims on Stonewall. As the documents in this book demonstrate, the riots were quickly claimed by more than just New Yorkers; they became central to the ways that the national LGBT movement narrated its history, especially in the context of pride protests and parades. Most New Yorkers did not object to this, conditioned as they were to thinking of their city as the country's most important. Nor have they objected when the riots have been claimed by the international LGBT movement—LGBT organizations and businesses around the world use the word "Stonewall" and the uprising is commemorated in parades and protests on five continents. For many, the international reach of Stonewall merits celebration, as it points to powerful possibilities for global influence, leadership, and unity. For others, it deserves critique, as it is yet another example of U.S. colonialism, Western imperialism, and international inequality.

Finally, it is important to note that as Obama's inaugural invocation demonstrates, the Stonewall Riots are now claimed by more than just LGBT people. For Obama, the riots deserve recognition not only because of their importance for LGBT Americans; they deserve recognition because of their importance for all Americans. In his formulation, the "truth" that "all of us are created equal" was the star that guided "our forebears" through Stonewall, just as it guided them through Seneca Falls and Selma. In this passage, Obama staked a national ancestral claim to the history of Stonewall and situated the riots within a broad social justice tradition that included struggles for gender and racial equality. Many LGBT people were deeply moved by this, but it is worth asking what is lost as well as what is gained when a key moment in LGBT history becomes an important moment in U.S. history.

DOCUMENT SELECTION, ORGANIZATION, AND PRESENTATION

Before turning to the primary sources, readers might want to consider some of my key decisions about document selection, organization, and presentation. First, I decided to focus on the years from 1965 to 1973. A longer time frame would have allowed for more breadth but less depth; a shorter one would have had the opposite problem. I begin in 1965 because, as discussed above, the LGBT movement began to radicalize in the mid-1960s. The coverage of 1965–69 allows readers to consider developments that directly preceded the riots. I conclude in 1973 so that the book covers roughly the same amount of time before and after the rebellion. Concluding in 1973 also allows me to address some of the influences of the riots on the LGBT movement, some of the commemorations of the rebellion in the first four years of gay pride parades and protests, and two of the greatest triumphs and tragedies of the post-Stonewall era: the 1973 decision by the American Psychiatric Association to declassify homosexuality as a mental illness and the 1973 UpStairs Lounge fire in New Orleans.

Second, I decided to concentrate primarily on the four largest U.S. metropolitan regions in this era (New York, Los Angeles, Chicago, and Philadelphia) and two other major urban centers with distinct importance for LGBT history (San Francisco and Washington, D.C.). Given the location of the riots, I could have focused more exclusively on New York, which was the approach taken in Duberman's and Carter's books, but I wanted to address the rebellion's larger influences and implications. I could have tried to cover more cities and regions, but this would have sacrificed depth for breadth. Also, notwithstanding the strong arguments that some scholars have made about the urban biases of LGBT history, there are good reasons to be concerned about anti-urban biases as well. In terms of impacts and inspirations, the largest U.S. cities were critically important and dynamically diverse in this period of LGBT history. Another choice I could have made was to offer a more transnational history of the Stonewall Riots, tracing echoes and effects that extended beyond the United States. Here, too, I worried about sacrificing depth for breadth, but I hope this book will encourage further research on the broader geographic and geopolitical dimensions of Stonewall.

Third, I decided to rely primarily on LGBT sources, with exceptions made for pre-Stonewall court decisions about gay bars (in chapter 1), mainstream and alternative press stories about the Stonewall Riots (in chapter 5), and alternative press items (from periodicals like the *Village Voice*, *Rat*, and *Berkeley Barb*) in several chapters. I wanted to include more documents from the African American press, but found few strong and available options that referenced gay bars, antigay policing, or LGBT activism, especially in the period from 1965 to 1969. This is particularly unfortunate given the limited discussion of African American gay bars, antigay policing, and LGBT activism in the homophile press. That said, there are explicit and implicit references to race and to people of color in many of the documents, which hopefully will provide a foundation for further research, and there are times when we cannot assume that a primary source is discussing white people just because there are no references to race.

Initially, I planned to include mainstream media stories (including articles from *Time*, *Life*, and *Newsweek*) in multiple chapters, partly so that readers could use these sources for thinking about straight perspectives on and biases about LGBT people in this era. In the end, however, the costs of doing so (because of U.S. copyright law and the decisions of the periodicals I contacted) proved to be prohibitively expensive. This had several unforeseen advantages. Many readers have access to the digital archives of mainstream newspapers and magazines, so they can access these materials for themselves (and I hope they will); fewer have digital or "real" access to the archives of LGBT periodicals. In addition, the focus on LGBT sources means that readers will gain access to a greater diversity of LGBT views and viewpoints. Readers also will be spared the hostile and hateful language that was used in many mainstream media reports during this period, though this is also a disadvantage in that it minimizes the harsh conditions of LGBT life. Wherever possible, I try to provide useful tips about additional sources in my endnotes and there will be a more extensive supplementary online research guide that provides further recommendations.

Fourth, I decided to exclude works of fiction and post-1973 autobiographies, memoirs, and oral histories. With respect to the former, I thought about including fictional representations of gay bars, but in the end decided to leave it to my readers to find these and wrestle with the challenges of interpreting works that do not purport to represent reality. The exclusion of the latter was perhaps my most difficult decision and was based on several factors. I had more than enough written accounts from 1965 to 1973 and found it difficult to choose among them. In addition, some Stonewall-related works of autobiography, memoir, and oral history have been challenged as inauthentic. Indeed, it sometimes seems true that if every person who claims to have participated in the riots was actually there, Manhattan would have sunk. In the context of preparing this book in a timely fashion, it did not seem possible to address the credibility of these sources. Post-1973 first-person accounts also are inevitably filtered through the lens of subsequent developments, which makes them valuable for thinking about later eras but problematic as primary sources. In many respects, they are more like secondary sources, offering retrospective reflections on the riots rather than primary sources from the riots. Finally, more and more works of oral history about the riots are available online, making it less important to present them in this volume. I hope that readers of this book will be inspired to seek out these oral histories and consider them in dialogue with the documentary sources reprinted here.

Fifth, I decided to highlight some but not other aspects of pre- and post-Stonewall LGBT history. This is envisioned as a book about the Stonewall Riots, not a book about LGBT history more generally. Beyond the two chapters that focus on the Stonewall Inn and Stonewall Riots, readers will find one chapter that addresses LGBT bars and policing in the pre-Stonewall era, two on LGBT political agendas and visions (one before and one after Stonewall), two on LGBT direct-action protests (one before and one after Stonewall), and one on post-Stonewall pride marches and parades. I privileged these aspects of LGBT history because the riots were prompted by a police raid on a gay bar;

the rebellion was part of a longer tradition of LGBT direct-action protests; and the uprising was commemorated in pride marches and parades. I was especially interested in presenting documents on direct action because this is an under-studied aspect of the LGBT movement; many historical discussions today focus on what LGBT activists thought but not on what they did. Moreover, LGBT direct-action protests in the late 1960s and early 1970s were exceptionally creative, dramatic, and numerous; they may be useful for those searching for ideas and inspirations in new political struggles. I hope the documents reprinted here will provide a strong point of departure for identifying and interpreting primary sources on other aspects of LGBT history, including sex and intimacy, community and culture, business and work, other forms of LGBT political activism, and other aspects of queer politics.

My work on this book was informed by my previous research and writing but also relied on visits to real and digital archives. By real archives I mean the GLBT Historical Society in San Francisco, the History Project in Boston, the LGBT collections of the New York Public Library, the LGBT Community Center National History Archive in New York, the John J. Wilcox, Jr. Archives at the LGBT Community Center in Philadelphia, and the Canadian Lesbian and Gay Archives in Toronto. The ONE National Gay & Lesbian Archives in Los Angeles supplied me with additional documents. For readers who have never been to one of the world's hundreds of LGBT archives, these extraordinarily valuable institutions, often highly dependent on volunteer labor and private donations, collect and preserve materials that make books like this possible.

Just as valuable were digital archives, which allowed me to review hundreds of documents that might otherwise have been inaccessible to me. Some of the most useful were EBSCO's *LGBT Life with Full Text*, Gale's *Archives of Sexuality and Gender*, Reveal Digital's *Independent Voices*, OutHistory's *Come Out!* collection, the University of Victoria's *Transgender Archives*, and the *San Francisco Bay Area Gay and Lesbian Serial Collection* at the University of California at Berkeley library. For researchers who rely on digital archives and funders who support digitization projects, it is noteworthy that none of these resources provides full searchable texts for the complete runs of several of the most widely circulating LGBT periodicals from the 1960s and 1970s, including *Drum*, *The Advocate*, and *GAY*. For these, researchers still must visit physical archives or make use of microfilm reels. Although it may not be apparent in the documents that follow, I also made use of Proquest's *Historical Newspapers* and EBSCO's *Readers' Guide Retrospective*, which provide helpful tools for searching mainstream periodicals.

The primary sources that follow are organized in three parts. The first, which focuses on the pre-Stonewall years (1965–69), includes a first chapter on gay bars and antigay policing, a second on activist agendas and visions, and a third on political protests. The second part includes a fourth chapter on the Stonewall Inn and a fifth on the riots. The third part, which addresses the post-Stonewall era (1969–73), includes a sixth chapter on activist agendas and visions, a seventh on political protests, and an eighth on pride marches and parades. This structure is meant to facilitate comparative and chronological analysis within each chapter (addressing, for example, the changing nature of protests before Stonewall), comparative analysis within each part (addressing, for example, relationships between agendas and actions), and comparative analysis across the three parts (addressing, for example, differences between the pre- and post-Stonewall eras).

Readers should think carefully and critically about my editorial work. The transcripts published here necessarily take words out of their literal context—you will not see the placement and juxtaposition of media articles on the pages of printed newsletters, newspapers, and magazines; you will not see most sub-headings and subtitles; you will not see accompanying photographic images, artwork, and captions. I have silently corrected names and other words that are misspelled and silently modified punctuation and capitalization for purposes of clarity and coherence. Ellipses in the original texts are presented as periods without spaces; my ellipses, which are used to indicate the places where I have deleted words, sentences, or paragraphs, are presented as periods with spaces between them. While most style guides no longer require the use of ellipses at the beginning and conclusion of quoted material, I have used ellipses in such cases so that readers will know when my excerpt does not begin at the beginning or conclude at the conclusion. I have tried to avoid overusing and misusing ellipses, but had I presented all texts in their entirety the book would have been more than 1,000 pages or I would have had to cut more than half of the texts. All bracketed words and endnotes are mine; they did not appear in the originals. I do not provide the birth names of trans people who used different names during the period covered by this book, but I do provide the names (in brackets) of people who otherwise used pseudonyms. In my notes, I briefly identify individuals and periodicals using relevant details from the moment when the document was produced (but not later); the notes also identify authors as people of color when other sources identify them as such. For these and other reasons, advanced researchers are encouraged to examine the original texts.

Finally, I want to offer a few words of advice about critical-reading practices for these types of documents (and more generally for all historical sources). My main suggestion is to remember that *there's always more to the story*. Historical documents are representations of reality; they are not reality (other than in the sense that "representations" are "real"). The book is designed so that in part 2 readers will be able to compare and contrast multiple accounts of the Stonewall Inn and Stonewall Riots. In parts 1 and 3, I generally provide one example of a particular viewpoint or one account of a particular event, but other examples or accounts may differ in important ways. In a few cases, I provide citations for alternative accounts; there are many more in the online supplementary guide for further research. In multiple cases, scholars have challenged the "facts" presented in the accounts reprinted here. Also keep in mind that the words and concepts of 1969 are not the words and concepts of the twenty-first century; readers will encounter terms in primary texts, including "Negro," that are commonly viewed as inappropriate and offensive today. Another example, still commonly found in histories of the Stonewall Riots, is "paddy wagon," which is an anti-Irish slur. Remember, as well, that it was and is common to misrepresent people in terms of their claimed gender, race, class, and other identities (or to erase or ignore those identities). With respect to race, in particular, many sources identified people of color as such, but others did not. My first and last advice is that in doing historical research it is always a good idea to be suspicious about all claims about "firsts" and "lasts." Keep that in mind as you read about the "first time" LGBT people fought back against oppression and the "last time" police raided a gay bar.

PART I
BEFORE STONEWALL, 1965–1969

1
GAY BARS AND ANTIGAY POLICING

IN THE YEARS LEADING UP TO THE STONEWALL RIOTS, bars, bathhouses, clubs, and restaurants were central institutions in LGBT cultures and communities. Gay bar guides listed thousands of sites where LGBT people could express their genders, enjoy their sexualities, and experience social connections. Large cities typically featured dozens of gay-oriented businesses; smaller cities and towns might have one or two. Many gay bars were predominantly or exclusively white and male; others had more diverse patronage; a smaller number were patronized primarily by women and/or people of color. Some bars welcomed gender transgressors; others excluded them.

In the 1960s, gay bars, bathhouses, clubs, and restaurants faced numerous challenges. Straight men targeted them with acts of hate and harassment. Local police conducted raids, demanded payoffs, and engaged in sexual entrapment practices (in which undercover officers enticed men to commit sex crimes and then arrested them). Organized crime owned, operated, and exploited many gay bars. State liquor regulators acted against businesses that served "homosexuals" or permitted "disorderly," "indecent," or "lewd" behavior on their premises. In spite of these challenges, many gay commercial establishments were popular and profitable.

The eighteen documents reprinted in this chapter focus on gay bars and antigay policing from 1965 to mid-1969.

DOCUMENTS 1–2, published originally in homophile magazines, address gay bars as social and sexual spaces.

DOCUMENTS 3–10, also taken from the homophile press, highlight anti-LGBT policing and resistance to police practices.

DOCUMENTS 11–15 provide further examples of resistance.

DOCUMENTS 16–18 are excerpted transcripts of state court rulings on gay bars.

DOCUMENT 1

Lily Hansen [Lilli Vincenz], "Bridge to Understanding"

Eastern Mattachine Magazine, Nov. 1965, 20–22[1]

. . . I went alone to a gay bar the other night for a glass of beer and to people-watch. As I was contemplating the clientele, both straight and gay, one of two handsome young men at an adjacent table smiled at me. When I returned the smile, he and his friend came over to me. "Are you male or female?" were the first awkward words I heard. Since I had taken them for gay boys, I was amused. "Isn't it obvious that I am female?" I asked. "In this place one can't be sure," came the cautious reply.

"This is a weird place," commented one boy as he sat down next to me. "I don't find it so at all," was my appropriate answer. As I explained, when they came here, they had known it was a homosexual bar. Such an impartial reply was apparently suspect. "How come you fix your hair that way?" I was asked as they gave my no-longer-recognizable pixie cut the once-over. "One might mistake you for a Lesbian." Should I give myself away? "I am a Lesbian," I admitted and braced myself.

They hadn't expected candor. But they had always wanted to talk to a homosexual. . . . They confessed that homosexuals were a complete riddle to them; neither could imagine how anyone could find the same sex attractive. They wanted to know whether the entertainer was a girl or boy; why some boys like to dress up as girls; why some Lesbians wore such (to them) uncomplimentary clothes and haircuts. And which of the customers in the bar was gay—this one, that one, and what about that one? I tried to answer their questions discreetly—while discouraging them from pointing with their fingers. They were quite young (one was celebrating his 21st birthday) and wavered between an eagerness to learn more about the subject, bewilderment, and contempt. One of them was tempted to call the waitress over with "Hey, butch"—but fortunately was stopped in time.

Their questions and comments demonstrated how confused they were. To a certain extent I could have sympathy with their incredulity, awkwardness, and embarrassment at not knowing how to react to a situation with no precedent. (After all, isn't it dampening to a straight man's ego to invite a girl over to his table, only to have her reply, "No, thank you. I'm waiting for a girl"? This had happened to one of my audience earlier.)

The contrast between heterosexual and homosexual attitudes stood out sharply in my mind as we talked. These uncomprehending persons in their effort to understand must have felt like astronauts floating in an inscrutable universe. Occasionally their sense of tact was definitely suspended—as if not applicable outside heterosexual respectability. Some people think "anything goes" when they are among what they consider social nonentities and outcasts—like homosexuals, Negroes, Puerto Ricans, etc. And yet, these boys would have thought twice about being loud-mouthed in even a Negro bar.

Sometimes they were coarse, but often they bent over backwards not to offend me with their questions and voiced surprise that they didn't embarrass me. How did I become a Lesbian? Did I plan to be "cured"? I tried to explain that I didn't consider myself sick and that a change to heterosexuality was no longer an issue—since in my opinion the most important thing about an individual was not his sexual orientation but the kind of human being he was and the degree of self-fulfillment he had achieved. Was this bit of philosophy too complicated? They didn't know what to say and had to "think that over."

I listened to their experiences with homosexuals who had approached them. They listened to my distinctions between solicitors and molesters who happened to be homosexual and the average, decent homosexual, who doesn't infringe on the sensibilities of others any more than the average heterosexual person. Naturally I educated them about the Mattachine Society and described our pickets. They had never heard of the homophile movement and it seemed ludicrous to them at first that the concept of civil rights was applicable in this area. Yet they finally agreed that homosexuals were a minority just like Negroes.

By the end of the evening they had become quite enthusiastic about me and apparently wanted to show me off. They expressed their intentions to have me meet their friends. . . . As a willing guinea pig I accepted the future offer, not without the ulterior motive of using this opportunity to advance the cause for a more enlightened approach to homosexuality. As a token of their esteem, they took me to a very nice restaurant and offered me "anything on the menu." When we finally parted, it seemed that through mutual recognition of our common humanity a glimmer of understanding had made communication between the heterosexual and homosexual view of life possible.

Will I ever see them again? Who knows—but one thing is certain: they will no longer be so ready to regard homosexuals as categories to be ridiculed. This is not to say that all their misunderstandings and fears had dissolved in an aura of benevolence and brotherhood. They did not lose their skepticism. But, through personal contact, they have begun to see the homosexual as other than a contemptible or dangerous outsider.

DOCUMENT 2
Clark P. Polak, "On Gay Bars"
Drum, Feb. 1966, 12–15[2]

Some facts about gay bars are almost too obvious to require mention: they are highly profitable; a disproportionately small number are owned by homosexuals; the gay bar is the only consistently and readily available homosexual gathering place; and they can be, but are not invariably, good places for sexual assignation.

Other factors are less well known. . . . There are probably more gay or semi-gay bars in any given larger city than even confirmed barniks are aware of, no less frequent; nationally, police policy towards gay bars appears to be one of containment ("Leave them alone and they won't scatter and we will know where to find them when we want."); few homosexuals go to bars with "making out" as their prime motivation; and the percentage of homosexuals who frequent bars regularly is quite small. . . .

To be sure, a small percentage of persons regard the gay bar solely in terms of potential sexual gratification—and these individuals are often those who hold bars in lowest esteem—while it is clear that the wide majority is mostly satisfied with the social aspects of bars and take sex as the cake's extra frosting. Some sexual contacts are made here, but the majority of persons leave alone many more nights than they leave with a partner.

Sexually, the world of the bars is that of the "one night stand" and short term affairs. Carnal pleasure is offered and accepted without obligation or commitment. The very nature of bars . . . mitigate[s] against all but chance and casual encounters. The amount of frustration this engenders in individual homosexuals would appear to depend on how clearly they understand gay bar ritual and how well they have been able to divorce themselves from the conventions of heterosexual morality.

Those who continue to believe in the heterosexual sanctions against promiscuous behavior and those who would like to find permanence in relationships that are almost by definition transitory are apt to consider bars and their own participation in bar activities both degrading and frustrating. Those who accept the socio-sexual advantages of bars on the terms in which they are offered often find bars a pleasant and more or less satisfying diversion. . . .

The homosexual's relatively sophisticated acceptance of sex has shifted priorities to the excitement of "the chase." The actual consummation of the sexual act many times shares the limelight with the positive pleasure derived from cruising. It is not so much that the search is unending, but that it is an enjoyable end in itself. . . .

Facts notwithstanding, the "bizarre happenings" in gay clubs is a favorite topic of reformers who are encouraged into anti-homosexual crackdowns by the traditional reluctance of bar owners to resist harassment and by public sentiment which is staunchly intolerant of displays of affection among homosexuals.

Public antipathy to gay bars was confirmed by a group of California sociologists who polled 353 middle income adults and discovered that 64.3% agreed that the "licenses of gay bars should be revoked." Such studies tend to support the view that the public will, at this time, tolerate only the abstract concept of homosexuality, while rejecting homosexuals as human beings. . . .

To the heterosexual out-group, gay bars, by their very existence, loom as a threat to the social order. The homosexual is, of course, viewed as a child-savoring, sex-starved degenerate and any large gathering of them increases the amount of panic. It is for this reason that gay bars are seldom located in straight, residential areas and are generally found in the more sophisticated or deserted sectors of cities. Business and theatre centers are generally regarded as acceptable for they are away from the inspection of the average heterosexual.

Bars are often a gay no-man's-land existing with the by-your-leave of an unseen constabulatory. Even in cities where the same bars have existed, virtually without interruption, for a large number of years, there is a lingering expectation that the next door opening might bring the police. Homosexuals often believe that the gay bar in their town stays open only by "paying-off" the local authorities. There are times bar owners are the source for such rumors to both assure their patrons that the establishment is a safe place to visit and to support otherwise unjustifiably high prices. Pay-offs other than the standard gratuity most bar and restaurant owners pay the police, however, are almost non-existent.

There is undoubtedly a high degree of sexual frustration in homosexual life—both in and out of gay bars—and the pulp fiction image of the closing-time panic over not having a partner is a partially accurate one. It is also exaggerated. Bars provide a maximum amount of sexual and social pleasure with a minimal expenditure of time and money. It is just as true to say that there are always sad and lonely people in bars as it is to say that there are always happy and socially involved people in bars. The gay bar is really a public party without any of the social disadvantages of a private party. There is no obligation to spend time with those persons found uninteresting and no prearranged protocol for leaving, being pleasant to the host, etc.

Whether the customers come "just to let their hair down" for an hour or so, or are new in town and taking a look at what the city has to offer, or are sulking in a corner, or are joking and discussing the myriad topics that occur in social settings among friends, or lost in thought, or cruising, or biding time between trains, or are there with no awareness of and less care about why, they are making highly satisfactory use of what has grown to be an international institution.

DOCUMENT 3
Kay Tobin [Lahusen], "After the Ball"
The Ladder, Feb. 1965, 4–5[3]

Dozens of police swarmed in and around California Hall in San Francisco on New Year's Day, invading a benefit costume ball organized by the Council on Religion and the Homosexual.

A line-up of police cars, one paddy wagon, plainclothes and uniformed officers, and police photographers greeted over 600 patrons of this supposedly gala event. Attending the ball were prominent ministers in the San Francisco area, as well as many members of their congregations, and members and friends of Bay Area homophile organizations.

The Mardi Gras New Year's Ball was held to raise funds for the work of the Council on Religion and the Homosexual, a group formed "to promote a continuing dialogue between the church and the homosexual." The Council is composed of representatives from six homophile organizations—Daughters of Bilitis, Mattachine Society (San Francisco), Tavern Guild, Society for Individual

Rights, The Coits, Strait and Associates—as well as ministers of the Methodist, Episcopal, Lutheran, and United Church of Christ faiths.

Police dogged the assembly from 9 p.m. to 1 a.m. in a blatant display of police power. Official police photographers snapped pictures of most of the 600 guests as they arrived. Arrested were three attorneys and a housewife who challenged inspectors from the sex-crimes detail by insisting the police needed either a warrant, or information that a crime was being committed, in order to enter the hall. The four were charged with obstructing police officers. A clergyman was threatened with arrest while escorting two guests to their car. Two men attending the ball were arrested on charges of disorderly conduct, which brought to six the number of arrests.

This flagrant harassment, surveillance, and show of force by police caused the ball to break up an hour early. Nevertheless the guests tried to enjoy the festivities as planned. No criticisms were made by police of the costumes, the dancing, or the program.

"Angry Ministers Rip Police" said one newspaper headline over a report of a press conference held by the ministers on January 2. The clergymen accused the police of "intimidation, broken promises, and obvious hostility" and claimed police had acted "in bad faith" and had "terrified" well-behaved guests.

The ministers explained they had gone to the police on December 23 to tell them in good faith about plans for the benefit event. Thereafter, police reportedly tried to get California Hall officials to cancel the Mardi Gras Ball booking.

On December 29, ministers and members of homophile groups met again with police officials, who gave assurances that guests in costume (including drag) would not be summarily arrested. Ministers described these negotiations as "strained."

The clergymen contended police had questioned them about their "theological concepts." They reported police "looked at the rings on our fingers and said 'We see you're married—how do your wives accept this?'" Police also suggested to the ministers they were being "used" by the homosexual organizations....

Del Martin, DOB Treasurer and a member of the Council, commented that "this is the type of police activity that homosexuals know well, but heretofore the police had never played their hand before Mr. Average Citizen.... It was always the testimony of the police officer versus the homosexual, and the homosexual, fearing publicity and knowing the odds were against him, succumbed. But in this instance the police overplayed their part." Miss Martin speculated that police had arrested two of the ball guests on disorderly conduct charges in order to justify police invasion of a peaceful, orderly gathering.

As this issue of *The Ladder* goes to press, San Francisco's Mayor John Shelley and Police Chief Thomas Cahill still aren't talking. . . .

What next? "Police action in this affair will be contested in court to establish the right of homosexuals and all adults to assemble lawfully without invasion of privacy...," according to a statement issued by the Committee for the Mardi Gras Ball. . . .

DOCUMENT 4

The Council on Religion and the Homosexual
"A Brief of Injustices," *ONE*, Oct. 1965, 6–17[4]

. . . Our investigation into the homosexual's behavior and his relationships to his society led us to consider the so-called "gay bars." For the harassed homosexual, there hardly seems to be any place other than the gay bar in which he may freely associate without baleful scrutiny and the need to wear a mask.

We investigated heterosexual bars and gay bars impartially, and at no time did we observe in gay bars any actions we might deem shocking or immoral. . . . In appearance, atmosphere, deportment of clientele, and the nature of any sexuality which might inadvertently find expression, the average gay bar is forced to be well above its heterosexual counterpart.

After a thorough investigation of bars we met with various bartenders, managers and others who were familiar with the problems faced by the bar owner and his patrons. This led to a confrontation with the Alcoholic Beverage Control in a meeting we held with its regional director. Unsatisfied with what we had been told there, we examined court records of such famous litigations as "Stoumen vs. Reilly," or what is popularly known as "The Black Cat Case"; "Mary's First and Last Chance," a bar which was located in Oakland; and some more recent closures affecting "Jack's Waterfront," "The D'Oak Room" and "The Jumpin' Frog" bars, which we had inspected prior to their closing. Legal matters were reviewed with several lawyers, and in some cases we talked with some of the patrons who had been arrested. . . .

Basically what we found was that an agency of government, in this case the ABC, was using prejudicial enforcement of a questionable law to justify the closing of homosexual bars under legal provisions it used much less frequently in cases involving heterosexual bars. Since the average life span of a gay bar seems to be something short of two years, while heterosexual bars usually remain open almost indefinitely, it appears that the degree of scrutiny which homosexual bars receive may greatly exceed that accorded heterosexual bars. Apparently they are usually closed on several grounds which may be summed up in this way: the licensee is running a disorderly house injurious to the public decency or morals, because within the premises and with his full knowledge he permitted lewd or lascivious acts, a public display or manifestation of aberrant sexual urges or desires, verbal solicitations indicating the intent to perform such acts, or that he allowed his bar to become a resort for dope pushers or addicts, prostitutes, pimps, panderers or sexual perverts. . . .

To close bars just because they are patronized by homosexuals, on the basis of the incorrect belief that homosexuals are sexual perverts, is incoherent reasoning. In fact, we are told by people knowledgeable in the field that even if this spurious contention were valid there is no way to determine with any certainty what persons or groups of persons in a bar are homosexual. Therefore, as written, justice and equity in applying this law are almost impossible.

There are more basic issues. Charges drawn up against gay bars are an itemization either of verbal solicitations or of acts tending to the public display or manifestation of aberrant sexual urges or desires, which are directed to, or seen by, specific ABC undercover agents whose entry into and departure from the bar are unknown to its owner. In such a sense, the act of a man placing his arm loosely around the waist of another man, in a gay bar, within the view of such an agent, indicates that the man is a homosexual publicly expressing sexual urges or desires, or the intent thereto, which are clearly against the present statutes. This sort of evidence is used to establish that the bar owner is keeping a disorderly house. . . .

The manner of application and enforcement of these statutes depends upon the personal opinions and prejudices of the ABC and its agents, a type of enforcement which fosters oppression, blackmail and discrimination. We hardly think it prudent to invest the ABC with the exclusive, unlimited and unrestrained authority to suppress or regulate the behavior of bar patrons through its right to suspend or revoke licenses. Thus ABC becomes what it should not become, the keeper of morals for bar patrons in general and for homosexuals in particular. . . .

The methods used by the ABC to gather evidence against bars are not unlike those used by the plainclothes agents of the police department. Through deceit and inducement, lure and suggestion, both police and ABC undercover agents encourage solicitations for sexual acts. . . . In reading the charges filed against several of the bars, we concluded that almost any act or conversation in a gay bar is sufficient for arrest and for use as data in revoking the license. There is also the question of the strict legality of ruses and ploys employed by these agents. . . .

If they are disorderly, bars should be closed. But such treatment should be equitable, and should be based on investigations and charges which apply uniformly and which do not violate due process. Gay bars per se are not hotbeds of unspeakable acts, or the scenes of wild orgies. Just because homosexuals gather together there is no automatic offense to public morals and decency. . . .

Our police department, ever alert in rooting out crime in our community, does its small part to intimidate the patrons of gay bars. Besides the use of entrapment and enticement inside the bars they also harass people as they enter or leave. Indeed, as we have discovered, in the last ten years arrests in and out of bars has increased sharply. . . .

In sexual matters the law should be concerned with the protection of youth and the guarding of the public against force or predatory conduct. Other sexual behavior should be rooted in personal liberty and should be legally protected. Closely related, the right to peacefully meet in places open to the public is no more than the right of assembly granted to all citizens and should not be denied to the homosexual. . . .

DOCUMENT 5

"L.A. Cops, Gay Groups Seek Peace"

The Los Angeles Advocate, Oct. 1967, 1, 2, 5[5]

"The community sets the tone of law enforcement. Law enforcement itself doesn't set the tone for the community, because if we did and it was repugnant to the community's idea, the community would suddenly change that by various means." So said Captain Charles Crumly of the Los Angeles Police Department in explaining why practices of the police toward homosexuals in Los Angeles and San Francisco are so different.

Capt. Crumly, head of the Hollywood vice detail, and Sgt. Alexander of the same unit were the star attractions at a meeting on Aug. 30 with representatives of homophile organizations at the home of PRIDE [Personal Rights in Defense and Education] president Jerry Joachim. Billed as an "historic" first meeting, the wide-ranging, four-hour, informal discussion covered a multitude of problems that are important to the homophile community—entrapment, arrests in bars, homosexual dances, crimes against homosexuals, relations with the Health Department, and a variety of other issues. . . .

A large part of the discussion involved arrests in bars. Crumly denied that vice officers pick out people to arrest indiscriminately. When vice officers go into bars and observe violations, he said, they may not arrest the law breakers on the spot. This might create a disturbance in a crowded bar, so they leave and call for assistance. When the radio cars arrive, they go back in and "pick out the ones they have observed violating the law, and those are the ones they arrest."

But when does a simple gesture of friendliness or affection become lewd conduct? A pat on the shoulder or even on the butt may not mean a thing, one questioner pointed out.

A pat on the butt may be only a friendly gesture of salutation, Crumly replied, "but when the hand lingers there over a sort of a lengthy period of time, it's no longer a salutation. He might reach clear up underneath and sort of not pat him on the rear, but pat him on the front in reverse." Also, in some bars, on the stools or benches, two people may be engaging in a little kissing. "At the same time, they're sort of rubbing their legs between each other's legs and in the general vicinity of the crotch.... They may be sitting in a booth putting on a passionate necking scene, and the hands are not entirely kept above the belt line, and so, these things all constitute violations."

Crumly puts much of the fault for the predicament of the bars on employees and bar owners themselves, many of whom he meets just before they are to go before the ABC [Alcoholic Beverage Control] on a revocation hearing. "It's his place. He has an investment there, and he certainly ought to do something about protecting it. If he permits violations to occur and arrests are made therein, and his license...is in jeopardy, it's his fault." There are gay bars, he adds, where people act as they should, "without groping and all those other things…and they make their contacts, and they go on their way, and nobody bothers them…. We have other gay bars where they're really carrying on and committing all types of illegal acts, so these are the locations where generally most of the arrests are made."

No matter how proper a person's behavior is, one participant said, there is a real fear that an arrest may take place anyway. Many of his friends have been quite careful and still "got stuck."

The police guard against cases without foundation, Crumly replied, by requiring the arresting officer to establish a good case on the arrest report. Otherwise, the arrested person may not even get booked, or the police may ask that the case be dismissed. . . .

On entrapment, Crumly denies that police use it. Entrapment is a valid defense in court, he points out, and if a case is dismissed or lost because of entrapment, he investigates to find out what happened. Sometimes it isn't entrapment, but "improper techniques" on the part of the investigator. "We would perhaps engage in some type of training to teach him the proper way to secure a violation without getting involved in this business of entrapment." Part of the training would be on the proper terminology to use, that is, the vernacular of the homosexual. . . .

On another subject, crimes against homosexuals, Crumly and Alexander denied that police treat these any differently than they would crimes against a minister. They urge homosexuals to report all such crimes and to press their cases. The chief complaint of the police in this area is that a homosexual often will not identify the person that has assaulted or robbed them. They make reluctant witnesses, thus making it very difficult for the police. . . .

DOCUMENT 6

A. B. [Ada Bello] and C. F. [Carole Friedman], Editorial

Daughters of Bilitis Philadelphia Newsletter, May 1968 (misdated Apr. 1968), 1–2[6]

On March 8, 1968, the most popular female homosexual bar in Philadelphia— Rusty's—was raided by the police. No minors were found on the premises. There were no apparent violations of existing law. We assume that the bar was operating as usual: couples dancing to the juke-box rock; people talking, trying to make themselves heard over the music; newcomers looking for familiar faces in the semi-darkness. In fact the same familiar scene to be found in any bar in the city. Just one exception: the patrons were all female. Rusty's was closed for the remainder of the evening. Approximately a dozen of the customers were taken in by the police and, after being treated to a tour of three police stations, booked on the all-purpose charge of "disorderly conduct." Several of the women were subjected to verbal abuse in connection with their sexual preferences. The women were not advised of their rights to refuse to answer questions until after those rights had been violated. They were pressured to fill out a questionnaire which extracted information which could be potentially harmful to those arrested, without being told that it was within their constitutional rights to refuse such information. The women were held in jail overnight, subjected to further harassment, and brought before a magistrate in the morning. The charges, of course, were dropped. No harm done. Except that the women's rights *were* abused. Except that they were coerced by fear. Except that they were made to feel like criminals. Except that they know that enough information was left behind to make them vulnerable to future harassment. The charges were dropped. No harm done.

Such occurrences do not seem to arouse the indignation of the community. It is taken for granted that such inconveniences are part of the price one pays for being homosexual in this society. But we are told that this society is governed by laws, not by men, and that these laws are to be applied equally to all. Show us, then, the statute which prohibits the gathering of congenial people in a place of their choosing. Show us the statute which makes it a criminal act for two women to dance or drink or engage in conversation. No, the girls were not charged with being homosexual—because that is not a crime. They were not charged with sodomy—because no such act was being committed. They were not charged with immoral conduct—because that plainly was not the case. They were charged with disorderly conduct because people in positions of authority had decided it was the opportune time to exercise their prejudices again.

What can be done about this situation? First, the homophile community must become aware of its rights, aroused by these violations, and determined to secure the full and equal protection of the law. We must not be satisfied with deploring our situation among ourselves, and trying to adjust to the limitations imposed by the arbitrary actions of the authorities. We, as a group, must find the means to make our case known to the entire community so that those traditionally concerned with protecting individual rights will lend us their support, and see our cause as their own.

DOCUMENT 7

David S. (as told to Dick Michaels [Richard Mitch]), "Anatomy of a Raid"

The Los Angeles Advocate, July 1968, 6–7; Aug. 1968, 6, 8[7]

There was nothing very unusual about the Yukon—nothing to make it stand out from dozens of other small gay bars. It was just a neighborhood beer bar on Beverly Boulevard a few blocks west of Vermont. As in any neighborhood place, most of the customers during the week were regulars who lived nearby. The bar usually wasn't jammed until Friday and Saturday nights and for the Sunday afternoon "beer bust." Even then, it took only about 35 people to make a mob in the Yukon. So, as I say, there was nothing unusual about the place—that is, not until that Friday night near the end of March 1966.

The Yukon's greatest asset was its manager and regular bartender, Tommy. He was a blond, good looking young man with a nice body and an infectiously happy personality. He probably still is, I guess. I say "was" only because I haven't seen him in almost two years. . . .

Although he made it a fun place, Tommy ran a tight bar, in the sense that he never allowed any hanky-panky that would endanger the bar's license or its customers. He was quick to warn people when they got a little out of hand but did it in such an expert way that there was never any bad feeling afterwards.

On that fateful Friday, I had picked up my lover of that time, Larry, at about seven o'clock, when he got off work. We went to the Yukon and drank beer for an hour or so. Several friends we hadn't seen for a while wandered in, and it looked like it was going to be a good fun night at the Yukon. We went to dinner and got back to the bar about 10:30. By then the place was crowded, and there was a lot of laughing and joking around. . . .

At one point, about 12:30 A.M., Tommy was passing by and stopped to talk to me. After we talked a few minutes, I noticed that he wasn't paying attention. He was looking over my shoulder toward the door. I turned and saw several uniformed policemen coming in. Two plainclothesmen were with them. One of them, whom we later referred to as Hooknose, yanked the juke box cord and ordered the lights turned up. . . .

Hooknose announced, "We're going to make a few arrests. Just stay where you are. Anyone who runs will be shot." No one ran. He went behind the bar, checked the license, stared closely at the label on a bottle of Champale, then came back out, and went about his fun task of picking victims.

I'm not sure where he started, but I think it was with two boys dressed in cowboy garb, who were obviously not cowboys. He then picked George, who was standing at the bar to Larry's right. Each tap on the shoulder was punctuated with "You're under arrest." At one point he stopped to count on his fingers. He seemed to be figuring out how many people the cars outside could take. Then he went back to his grim business. He skipped over Larry. My back was to Hooknose. I felt the dreaded tap and turned. "You're under arrest."

I walked out to the street. Several more uniformed cops were standing around. Five or six black-and-white cars lined the curb. I was put into the back seat of one of them. Others came out, usually two at a time handcuffed together. Two of these were put in the back of the car with me. Two cops sat in front.

I found out later that Tommy during the arrests went up to the Gum Chewer and said, "I'm the manager; what's going on here?" Gum Chewer arrested him, the only arrest he made that night. "What for?" Tommy demanded. "You'll find out," was the reply. . . .

Altogether they took 12 people out of the Yukon that night—about a third of the patrons. They took us to the Hollywood station. . . .

Gum Chewer, still chewing, advised us of our "rights" as we stood in a circle. Then as we passed through a door into the cell area, he pointed to each and said "Lewd conduct," except for one who was charged with being drunk.

We were all put into one cell. Then Gum Chewer called us out one by one and talked to each for a minute or so. When my turn came, we stood a half dozen feet from the cell as Gum Chewer pointed toward the cell. "See that boy in the blue shirt?" It was Lee; I've known him for years but never had sex with him in any form. "You humped him," the Man said. I told him I didn't know what he was talking about. He tried to ask several other questions ("Are you a homosexual?" "Where do you work?" "Do you have a security clearance?"), but I clammed up.

That's pretty much the way it went for each one. Lee was accused of groping someone sitting next to him, and that guy was charged with rubbing legs with Lee. Tommy was supposed to have groped one of the "cowboys."

They took us all downtown in a police bus for booking. . . .

When I was booked, I answered the questions about name and address but balked at where I worked. "That's not necessary, is it?" I asked, not knowing what they were really entitled to know. "You don't have to say a damn thing," he snapped back, obviously irritated. Probably to get even, when he took the contents of my pockets, he kept all my cigarettes and all the money except one dime. . . .

After that there was a lot of waiting in little rooms as the cops took mug shots and fingerprints of each person. I couldn't understand how some of the guys arrested with me could joke around and laugh. Maybe it was just a nervous reaction. I was worried—worried about my job and some personal matters that this arrest could make worse. I was silent most of the time and didn't feel like talking to anyone.

One young Canadian boy was in a state of near-panic. He was so frightened that the cop trying to take his fingerprints was having a rough time. The boy couldn't relax his hand enough. The cop threatened to knock him on his ass if he didn't relax. That just made things worse. The hassle went on for what seemed a long time.

All of us eventually wound up in one large cell, each waiting for a bail bondsman. Tommy got out first and seemed reluctant to leave while we were all still there. When the bondsman sent by Larry arrived for me, I had no trouble convincing him that I was solvent. I asked him to see about getting Lee and some of the others out, but Lee wasn't working at the time, and those guys don't like to take chances.

It was past 4AM when I finally left the jail. The bondsman drove me to my apartment, but just as we got there, I remembered that my car was still parked at the Yukon. I asked him to take me there, less than half a mile away. He was irritated. I was irritated, tired, scared, and depressed. And I still am whenever I think about that night. . . .

Although I was nervous as hell when [my trial date] came, I felt that we were going to put up a good fight. At the courthouse, while we awaited our turn, my lawyer had a conference with the city attorney. When he emerged from it, he told me that the charge would be reduced from 647a to 415 (disturbing the peace) if I would plead guilty to the lesser charge. He pointed out that a 415 conviction carries no morals implications and that I wouldn't have to register as a sex offender for the rest of my life, which is the case in a 647a conviction.

I had to make a decision—and right away. My attorney seemed to want me to take the deal. I knew I was innocent, yet I also knew other innocent people who had been convicted on 647a. I thought of my job—a very good job—and a dozen other things. I decided on the cop-out. To this day, I'm not proud of that decision.

Tommy, Lee, and four other fellows had the same lawyer, and their cases were consolidated for one trial, which lasted about three days. . . .

At the trial of the six, Hooknose was the prosecution's only witness. He testified as to what each defendant had allegedly done. More important, though, he also testified that he was the only vice officer in the bar the night of the raid, that he questioned us at the Hollywood station, and that he booked us downtown—all absolutely false statements made under oath.

The defense presented testimony of the defendants, of course, plus three witnesses who weren't arrested. Two of them were a straight couple, a woman and her boyfriend. All contradicted Hooknose's testimony.

Predictably, the prosecutor in his summary to the jury pointed out that the defendants had nothing to lose by lying. The lone officer, however, risked his life to protect "you and your children," he told them. The child-molesting myth works like instant prejudice on any jury.

The verdict of guilty for all six surprised no one, least of all the defendants. But some of them did notice something curious. One of the older women on the jury appeared to be crying, and she gazed sympathetically at the defendants as the verdicts were read.

The judge deferred sentencing to a later date. In the meantime, the defense attorney set out to discover why the weeping woman wept. He eventually got affidavits from her and another woman to the effect that other jurors had browbeaten them into voting guilty. It seems that some of the others had important things to do and couldn't waste any more time debating the merits of the case. When the attorney presented these facts to the court, the judge threw out the verdict and declared a mistrial. A new trial was set for several weeks later.

The case had already dragged on for two or three months, and the defendants had lost several days' work each on various court appearances. Between Trial I and Trial II, four of the six were offered cop-outs, which they took, probably in desperation to get out of the mess. That left only Tommy and Lee for the second trial. It took place before a judge (no jury this time) on the record of testimony given at the first trial. For some strange reason, the judge found Lee guilty and Tommy innocent—both of these verdicts on the same testimony of the only prosecution witness, the "lone" vice cop.

As for the Yukon itself, it didn't fare any better. Tommy lost his job as manager soon after the raid. Business dropped off quickly and drastically. The owner tried to carry on for a while and hired a new manager, but he made a hideously poor choice. At any rate, within a few months he sold out. The bar is now straight and under a new name.

Whenever I think back on all these events, two things stand out in my mind: the routine and casual way the police treated the raid and the terrible consequences of this one routine action. . . .

DOCUMENT 8

"Bathhouse Raided"

Mattachine Society of New York Newsletter, Apr. 1969, 1–2[8]

On the evening of February 20, the police raided the popular Continental Baths. According to witnesses, uniformed city police entered the place and made the customers get dressed and file out. While they were leaving, a man, naked except for a towel, pointed out the ones he alleged had either had sex, or offered sex to him. Some of the people claim that the towel-clad man (a cop) had had sex with them.

A sharp letter was sent to the Police Department from the [Mattachine] Society, criticizing the raid and the procedures used in carrying it out.

Inasmuch as the police still have not found even a lead on who killed the homosexual in the "gay" section of Central Park last fall, and cannot deal with the muggings, pickpockets and others who prey upon homosexuals in the parks, the docks, etc., we pointed out, wouldn't it be easier for them to wink at the bathhouses? After all, such places provide an indoor, protected location where assignations may be made, and don't involve the crimes against person and property that semi-public places do. . . .

According to the police, the Continental Baths got into trouble because of their advertising. CB has been running ads in various publications. The police say that someone saw an ad, thought the CB was just a bathhouse, and visited the place. When the "innocent customer" found himself in the midst of gay sex and lots of it, he called the cops and they had no choice but to raid.

Some 22 people were arrested in the raid, some of them employees and others customers, caught, say the cops, in the act of sodomy. Irwin Strauss, the attorney who drafted New York's new statute prohibiting entrapment, is defending some of the men, and we'll see how well his new law works. This is the first test, as this is the first time since May of 1966 that there has been a case involving anything like the use of plainclothes (or in this case naked) cops to make homosexual arrests. . . .

It is unfortunate that the management of CB has seen fit to carry on an advertising campaign. It was opened and planned as a gay place and word-of-mouth advertising would have been enough to make it go after an initial advertising campaign in the gay and underground press.

MSNY's Executive Director has suggested that instead of spending money on advertising, the management should use it to pay the legal expenses of the customers who were arrested in the raid and put the rest aside in case of future trouble. The gay grapevine would advertise the place to New Yorkers and the various gay guides will list it for the convenience of out-of-towners.

Public advertising is just asking for trouble, while paying the legal costs of the victims of the raid would be a gesture that would win enormous good will for the CB.

We don't know what they plan to do, but if you continue to see CB ads around town, our advice is to avoid the place. It could be raided again at any time. If, on the other hand, the ads stop and thus reduce the chances of unfriendly people entering the place, it is most highly recommended, because it is clean, beautiful and well-run.

Meantime, we will watch with interest the evidence that develops at the hearings to see if there really was police entrapment used in making the arrests. If there was, you'll hear us following Mayor Lindsay around the campaign trail next time shouting "sell-out!"

DOCUMENT 9

"Grim Reapings—Coast to Coast"

Mattachine Society of New York Newsletter, June 1969, 6–7

On April 3, the NYC police found a male body floating in the Hudson River, near the Christopher Street docks. According to the Medical Examiner's report, the body had been in the water about 10 days; that is, since about March 23.

The deceased was probably between 20 and 25, about 5' 11" tall, and weighed about 185 pounds. He had good teeth and brown hair. The corpse was clothed in golden-brown corduroy trousers (very tight-fitting), a tan and brown dress shirt, and one black shoe and one brown sock.

The man was apparently strangled to death before the body ended up in the river. The police suspect he was probably another victim of the "dock scene," just about the most dangerous gay scene in New York. . . .

While in New York we are being plagued by a series of murders of gay men and the cops are frantically looking for those who have committed the crimes, the West Coast is having trouble of a different sort. In Berkeley, just outside of San Francisco, and in Los Angeles, the cops are killing off the gay population.

In Berkeley, a 33-year-old man [Frank Bartley] had parked his car in Aquatic Park, a popular cruising spot. Two Berkeley cops, Officers Kline and Reynolds, had been keeping the area under surveillance, and Reynolds initiated what we would call an entrapment. He loitered about the car and got an invitation to enter it. He did. A sexual advance followed. On the pretext of finding his cigarettes, which he claimed to have dropped outside, the cop got out of the car, found his partner, Officer Kline, and suggested arresting the man.

The man tried to get away and in the resulting struggle was shot and died later. . . .

Meanwhile, in Los Angeles, a gay man [Howard Efland, also known as J. McCann] was savagely beaten to death by the L.A. cops in a gay hotel. According to our reports, the whole hotel was awakened at about 1:00 A.M. by a loud struggle. Most of the residents rushed to a second floor hallway where they saw two men, each about six feet tall and weighing around 200 pounds, beating the hell out of a 5' 7", 147-lb. Jewish boy. They were bouncing him back and forth between the hallway walls. The boy was bleeding from the eyes, nose and mouth, but screaming for help. The big guys kept fighting off potential good Samaritans, saying, "We're the Los Angeles police. Get the fuck away from here."

The cops then proceeded to handcuff the bloody boy and drag him along the hall, down the steps and outside to an alley. They tried to throw him into a police car, but he gathered the last reserves of his strength and resisted entering the car. According to a number of witnesses, the cops then began picking up and dropping their victim on the sidewalk. That halted his resistance, and another cop car pulled up and helped get the limp man into the other car. The victim died minutes after getting to the hospital.

At the inquest, attended by many of the homosexuals who had seen the beating, the cops proceeded to lie and distort everything that happened. Struggling with the man (he was 5' 7" and weighed 147 pounds) had "so exhausted" them that they had accidentally dropped him. That presumably explained the "contusions, lacerations, abrasions, ruptured pancreas, and massive internal hemorrhaging" that were listed as contributing causes of death.

The desk clerk of the hotel, several of the guests and others described to the coroner the savage beating the cops had inflicted on the deceased. In all, five accounts of the police brutality were given under oath.

The cops then took the stand and told how they had attempted to arrest the deceased for having made a sexual proposition to one of them, how he had resisted arrest, and had struggled with them to the point where they were so exhausted that when they tried to lift him to put him in their car, they had dropped him. One of the cops also said he had "fallen" from exhaustion and landed on top of the deceased (and had not deliberately jumped on him, as the witnesses testified).

The middle-aged coroner's jury took thirty minutes to return a verdict of "justifiable homicide."

DOCUMENT 10

[Dick Leitsch], "Gay Party at Police Station"

Mattachine Society of New York Newsletter, June 1969, 10, 12[9]

The NYC Police Department recently hosted a wild gay party which was so successful they moved it down to the Criminal Courts Building. They didn't start out to have a party, of course, but they ended up having a dilly that won't be forgotten soon by the "guests," the cops, or the courts. Here's the story as we heard it from one of the "guests."

A new gay "club" opened recently in the East Fifties. The owners were blithely selling liquor to three score customers, sans license, permit, or even the basic Certificate of Occupancy. In walked the fuzz and arrested the management (which is legal) and all the customers (which is illegal), for "disorderly conduct." The cops herded more than fifty very elegantly dressed, and very high, male homosexuals, four women, one sex-change-in-progress, and one dog (belonging to a customer) into the paddy wagons. A lot of the people, we understand, had pills, which they proceeded to swallow as fast as possible, so as not to be caught with them. By the time they got to the station house, they were flying. The cops could neither control them nor shut them up.

The arrested people had to be questioned and searched, and that was a real freak-out. The artificial gaiety of the high ones rubbed off on everybody else, and the station house was the scene of perhaps the biggest "camp-in" of all time. The more the cops tried to maintain order, the more ridiculous the whole situation got, and the more the cops lost control of the mob they had arrested.

Things hit a high point when it came time to search the sex-change. He had siliconed breasts, which were reportedly enormous. But he still had his male equipment as well. The cops were at a loss as to who should search him (her?)—a policeman or a police woman. Somebody suggested that a police woman search the top half and a policeman the bottom half. That broke up the whole crowd, and the embarrassed cop in charge decided not to search the sex-change at all.

Finally, despite great obstacles in the form of loud camping, freaky carryings on by those so high on pills they weren't sure what was happening, a yapping dog, four furious women, and a bunch of gay kids, some of whom were enjoying the whole ridiculous scene and others who were very unhappy about it all, the cops got all their paper work done, and then loaded everyone into paddy wagons again to go to jail.

That trip precipitated another crisis. The women wouldn't ride with the "queens" so the cops settled that by letting the real ladies ride up front. The sex-change, to the amusement of everyone else and the consternation of the cops, demanded the same privilege. That was eventually settled and everyone went to jail. There, isolated ones were photographed—with much posturing, posing and camping. A cop suggested fingerprints, and a squeal arose about ruined manicures and dirty fingers. Finally, rather than go through another scene, the cops forgot the fingerprinting idea.

The gay boys were herded into two cells, 25 to a cell. The women got a cell to themselves, and the sex-change (again, they couldn't decide whether it was a "he" or a "she"), got a cell alone, and the dog was impounded in a separate cell.

Every hour during the rest of the night, the cops came around and took half the gay boys out of one cell and moved them to the other, apparently with the idea of preventing sexual carrying-on. What they didn't notice was that the same crowd was moving each time, and the coupling was going on. With so many people in the cell, the cops couldn't see what was happening in the back, and there was more than a little hanky-panky.

Came the dawn, as the old movie titles say, and everyone got "breakfast"— hot tea with no sugar and bologna sandwiches. Once again they were piled into the wagons and hauled to the court house. There, they were kept in a back room and led out four at a time before the judge. Our reporter says the whole scene was too much. All those rumpled Cardin suits, hair in disarray, and pimples and beard stubble sticking out under traces of make-up.

The first four trooped before the judge, who heard the case and dismissed the charges. Another four, this time more swishy, trooped in. The courtroom began to titter, and the judge rapped for order. The charges were dismissed. The next four were called, and three gay boys and the sex-change came in. That, it is said, did it.

The judge made the mistake of asking the sex change why "she" had a man's name. He got a lecture on sex changes and how they work. The lawyers, bailiffs, criminals awaiting trial, and spectators all got involved. Courtroom discipline collapsed. For the rest of the morning, four queens at a time tripped before the bar of justice while the judge tried to be serious. The courtroom remained in an uproar, and it took a lunch recess to restore order.

The cops told our informant that they intend to arrest, on charges of disorderly conduct, any person found in a club that they bust for not having a license. We doubt if they mean that, especially after this incident, which destroyed police and court discipline for 17 hours one night.

However, we serve notice on them now that if they continue with such a campaign of illegal arrests, we will initiate a campaign to have all the people who have to go through this sue for false arrest. The police have no right to make such arrests, and if they insist upon doing so, we'll have to win a few thousand dollars for some of their victims. If justice and law will not prevail, perhaps economics will.

DOCUMENT 11

Randolfe Wicker, "The Wicker Report," *Eastern Mattachine Magazine* Sept. 1965, 10[10]

Mattachine Midwest got off to a good start with a minor victory in the courtroom. In Chicago, Friday night is often "round-up" night for homosexuals. The police, as we hear it, arrest those they think to be homosexuals and charge them with disorderly conduct. They are held overnight or over the weekend, and when they appear in the courtroom, the cases are dismissed because the arresting officer doesn't show up to testify against them.

A recent "round-up" resulted in one of the victims calling the offices of Mattachine Midwest, [which] arranged bailbondsmen and attorneys for the victims. The next day, when the cases came to trial there were no arresting officers on hand to testify. The attorney complained to the judge that this practice wasted the lawyer's time, the defendants' time and the court's time. It was simply a means of harassment and crowded the already over-crowded calendars. The judge agreed, and he sent for the arresting officers. They, being night-working cops, probably were dragged out of their warm beds.

One of the officers confessed that he and his brother officers never appeared in such cases. The judge not only dismissed the cases against the defendants, but reprimanded the cops.

DOCUMENT 12

"Cross-Currents"

The Ladder, Feb. 1966, 17

. . . Citizens Alert is a citizens' committee formed chiefly to protect individuals, especially those identified with minority groups, from the harassment, brutality, and discriminatory treatment by police which have become a matter of concern and alarm in San Francisco.

The chairman, Rev. A. Cecil Williams, said in a press release that Citizens Alert "is not an organization for the harassment of our police" and that it seeks to cooperate with law enforcement agencies. But, he said, the group will investigate all complaints about police practices and will give assistance to persons whose claims of harassment and/or brutality are justified. Rev. Williams urged all citizens who either witness or undergo police brutality or harassment to call Citizens Alert, which will maintain round-the-clock phone service and will promptly check into the legitimacy of these reports and summon whatever professional services may be needed.[11]

Citizens Alert is also concerned with cases of unequal enforcement of the law because of a person's income, skin color, racial origin, or sexual orientation. Police misbehavior has been most often associated with persons belonging to minority groups characterized by these factors.

In addition to helping individuals who are victimized by the police, Citizens Alert will also prepare reports on its findings concerning police misbehavior and will send these reports to governmental and social agencies.

Citizens Alert includes professional persons, prominent citizens, and representatives from civil rights organizations and minority groups. Its board of directors includes two representatives from the homosexual community: Lois Williams of Daughters of Bilitis and Larry Littlejohn of the Society for Individual Rights.

The courageous members of Citizens Alert aim to reduce substantially, if not eliminate entirely, the incidence of police misconduct toward citizens in San Francisco.

DOCUMENT 13

"Entrapment Attacked"

The Ladder, June 1966, 12–13

Homosexuals in New York City may no longer have to fear being entrapped by plainclothesmen, *if* the police department keeps its recent promise to end the practice of entrapment.

Months ago, the New York Post ran a 5-part series of articles about the Vice Squad, highlighting the tactics police use to lure citizens into making illegal solicitations so that the officers can then arrest them to meet vice-squad quotas. The Post reporter had consulted the Mattachine Society of New York. . . . He followed up by asking the police for a statement on their entrapment policies. A high official said the police department "will not tolerate" use of entrapment tactics to boost the number of arrests on morals charges. Still entrapment continued—and so did the disavowals by police officials.

It was early in February, for example, that First Deputy Commissioner John Walsh, speaking for then Commissioner Broderick, told the Post, "We do not approve of the police enticing someone to commit a crime." Yet later that same month, a man was arrested for inviting to his apartment for a drink a plainclothesman who had unsuccessfully tried only four days before to entice the same man in the same restaurant.

Early in April, for another example, Chief Inspector Sanford Garelik, at a public meeting, denounced entrapment and urged citizens to report cases of individuals being lured by police into a violation of law so an arrest could be made. Later the same night, two young men were entrapped by a pair of plainclothesmen in a bar only a few blocks from the church where Inspector Garelik had made his statement. And a few days later in April, a Brooklyn tailor, married and the father of two children, was arrested in a Manhattan Turkish bath for allegedly "loitering" for the purpose of committing homosexual acts. The entrapping officer reportedly had drawn this victim's attention by standing in his underwear near his locker, clutching his groin and moaning.

A New York Post columnist wrote that "there is something crawling and soiled" about such police activity, and suggested that "it would probably take a psychiatrist to examine the darker aspects of these capers: the ingenuity and patience the police work requires, the relish with which the detectives seem to go about their jobs, the fact that a lot of the cops really believe they are decontaminating the society by ferreting out and arresting these people."

How many other entrapment incidents did not get publicized, no one knows. Confronted with such discrepancies between their stated policy and their activity, the police sometimes claim, as Inspector Garelik did in April, that "we don't encourage people to commit a crime that they weren't going to commit." . . .

Protests against the police activity—including letters to New York's new mayor, John V. Lindsay, as well as to police officials—were kept up especially by the New York Mattachine Society, the New York Post, the New York Civil Liberties Union, and several prominent psychotherapists.

On April 30, the Mayor held a closed-invitation meeting to air frictions between city agencies and groups of Village citizens including homosexuals and artists. He said he was disturbed by complaints about "excesses perpetuated by the city bureaucracy during the (spring) 'clean up.'" He agreed to a suggestion that attorneys for the city conduct seminars for top city officials on ways of safeguarding individual civil liberties.

Richard Leitsch, president of New York Mattachine, represented the homosexual community at this meeting and raised the issue of entrapment. Mayor Lindsay condemned the practice, and so did the new Police Commissioner, Howard Leary, who said he had already begun to issue orders to stop it.

The police department soon issued a directive ordering plainclothesmen not to entice homosexuals into making illegal overtures. Police were reportedly also being discouraged by their superiors from making such arrests without a supporting complaint from a civilian witness. But it remains to be seen whether the New York police are only making public-relations noises for the moment and whether entrapment will be resumed.

DOCUMENT 14
"Mafia Control of Gay Bars"
The New York Hymnal, Mar. 1968, 1–2[12]

Since the founding of the Tavern Guild of San Francisco, the gay bars in that city have become models for the rest of the country of what a gay bar can and should be.

Founded in 1964, the Tavern Guild of San Francisco (TGSF) quickly became the focal point of the homosexual community in San Francisco in its fight to improve the operating conditions and atmospheres of the bars. The TGSF is composed of owners and operators of gay bars and taverns. It protects its member businesses from harassment or abuse by authorities, which has virtually eliminated the problem of payoffs. The TGSF's main contribution to the improvement in the social atmosphere in San Francisco has been its firmness in resisting infiltration efforts by organized crime (the Mafia, Cosa Nostra, Syndicate, or whatever-you-want-to-call-it).

The result of the TGSF's work is evident to anyone who visits San Francisco's gay bars. Many of the bars have benefit nights for the various homophile organizations and donate one night's profits to them. They also show old movies, have ten-cent beer nights, support the homophile publications in S.F. by advertising in them and, in general, make their customers feel welcome and "at home."

A Tavern Guild of New York is impossible at the moment for the simple fact that there is only one gay bar in the city which is not Mafia-run. However, the day is coming when there will be a number of legitimate gay bars in New York [that] will form a Tavern Guild, or something similar. Until that day, one of the major problems of the homosexual community will continue to be the lack of a healthy social atmosphere.

DOCUMENT 15

"Editorial: You're an Accomplice!"

The Los Angeles Advocate, June 1968, 8

In their never-ending effort to close gay bars, the police usually use one or both of two principal routes. One method is to make a series of arrests in a particular bar, thus piling up violations against that bar to establish that it is a disorderly place. When the bar's license comes up for renewal before the Alcohol Beverage Control Board, the fuzz present their evidence and may succeed in getting the license revoked. No license, no business.

A second method is far more sinister, is far less legal, and smacks of police state tactics. The fuzz conduct a raid, picking up 15 or more victims in a single stroke. The police well know that news of such a large action spreads throughout the gay community faster than wildfire. What they expect to accomplish usually happens: the bar's business drops off drastically. Sometimes the police may follow up the raid with routine visits by a single uniformed officer to scare off customers who have hung on. They used this gimmick with the Black Cat last year, and that bar lasted only a week after a raid before closing its doors permanently. Thus, without any semblance of due process of law, the police can and do put legitimate bars out of business.

About this second method, there is one very important point to remember: IT CANNOT WORK WITHOUT THE HELP OF HOMOSEXUALS THEMSELVES. Whenever customers stay away from a particular bar because they have heard of a raid there or perhaps only a few arrests, they are helping the vice squad. They are helping to put a padlock on that bar. The police rely on the fears of homosexuals, and all too often we let them manipulate us like puppets. Some once-popular bars have never recovered after being subjected to Method II; others have closed. We can thwart this police state tactic by continuing to patronize our favorite bars regardless of what the fuzz do.

There is another side to the coin, however. Continue to give those bars your business only if they are well run. If the bartenders or managers are too busy or just don't care enough to toss out the few unruly customers, go somewhere else. If they don't want to exercise their authority and their responsibility, they're going to go out of business eventually anyway. Everybody likes a bar that's crowded and fun, and there's nothing wrong with that. But places that are "campy" have a way of turning into places where everyone is "carrying on" unless those in charge are constantly alert. Both the managers and the customers must cooperate in showing responsibility. Let's not help the vice squad.

DOCUMENT 16

Inman v. Miami

197 So. 2d 50 (Florida District Court of Appeal, 4 Apr. 1967)[13]

. . . Appellant's complaint alleged that he is a homosexual, and that by the ordinance he is denied the right to "visit and enjoy by himself or with his friends who are similarly situated the public places of amusement within the City of Miami." The ordinance prohibits liquor licensees from knowingly employing a homosexual person, or knowingly sell to, serve, or allow a homosexual person to consume alcoholic beverages, or to knowingly allow two or more homosexual persons to congregate or remain in his place of business. Appellant did not attack a particular section or provision of the ordinance but confines himself to a prayer: "...that this court take jurisdiction of this matter and find section 4–13 of the Code of the City of Miami to be unconstitutional. . . ."

The final decree appealed holds that this section of the code of the City of Miami "has a rational relation to public health, morals, safety and general welfare." We agree. . . .

The business of the distribution of liquor is one which is particularly burdened with a public concern and which may be limited and regulated by the State as a privilege. It follows that the legislative authority may limit its distribution to conditions under which liquor will be distributed with the least possible harm to the public. . . . The object of the ordinance as a whole is to prevent the congregation at liquor establishments of persons likely to prey upon the public by attempting to recruit other persons for acts which have been declared illegal by the Legislature of the State. . . .

It therefore follows that appellant's generalized attack upon the ordinance as a whole was properly denied.

DOCUMENT 17

*One Eleven Wines & Liquors v. Division of Alcoholic
Beverage Control*

50 N.J. 329 (Supreme Court of New Jersey, 6 Nov. 1967)

. . . The Division of Alcoholic Beverage Control disciplined the appellants for permitting apparent homosexuals to congregate at their licensed premises. It suspended the licenses of One Eleven Wines & Liquors, Inc. and Val's Bar, Inc. and revoked the license of Murphy's Tavern, Inc. . . .

The disastrous experiences of national prohibition led to the adoption of the twenty-first amendment and to the return of liquor control to the states in 1933. . . . When our Legislature during that year first created the Department of Alcoholic Beverage Control, it vested broad regulatory powers in a state commissioner who immediately set about to insure that abuses which had originally contributed so heavily in bringing about national prohibition, would not be permitted to recur. . . . He concerned himself not alone with matters of lawful-ness but also with matters of public sensitivity for he firmly believed that the effectiveness of the new mode of control would turn on the extent of the public's acceptance of the manner in which licensed establishments were conducted. . . .

Among the commissioner's early regulations were Rules 4 and 5 which were adopted in 1934. Rule 4 provided that no licensee shall allow in the licensed premises "any known criminals, gangsters, racketeers, pick-pockets, swin-dlers, confidence men, prostitutes, female impersonators, or other persons of ill repute." And Rule 5 provided that no licensee shall allow "any disturbances, brawls, or unnecessary noises" or allow the place of business to be conducted "in such manner as to become a nuisance." In 1936 Rule 5 was revised to include an express prohibition of "lewdness" and "immoral activities," and in 1950 it was again revised to include an express prohibition of "foul, filthy, indecent or obscene language or conduct. . . ."

During the years prior to 1954 the department instituted proceedings under Rule 4 on the basis of evidence that apparent homosexuals had been permitted to congregate at the licensed premises. Apparently the department considered that the effeminate manifestations of the patrons brought them within the pro-hibition of "female impersonators" although that term relates more properly to transvestites who are, for the most part said to be non-homosexuals. . . .

Since 1954 and despite increasing public tolerance and understanding, departmental proceedings aimed at the congregation of apparent homosexuals have continued apace but have been brought under Rule 5 rather than Rule 4. They have not been based on any specific and individualized charges of lewd or immoral conduct but rather on general charges that by permitting the apparent homosexuals to congregate, the licensees had allowed their places of business to be conducted in such manner "as to become a nuisance. . . ."

In the very cases before us the Division of Alcoholic Beverage Control made it clear that it has not in anywise moderated its long standing position that per-mitting the congregation of apparent homosexuals, without more, is violative of Rule 5. The evidence against Murphy's Tavern disclosed many individual acts which could have been the basis of specified and individualized charges of lewd or immoral conduct at the licensed premises. But no such charges were preferred and when, during the course of cross-examination, one of the division's investi-gators was asked whether he had observed any lewdness at Murphy's Tavern, the prosecuting attorney pointed out that the division had not alleged "any immoral activity or lewdness itself" but had simply alleged that the licensee had "permit-ted the licensed place of business to become a nuisance" in that it had allowed "these persons to come in and congregate upon the premises."

In the One Eleven proceeding there was no charge and no substantial evi-dence that lewd or immoral conduct was permitted at the licensed premises. There was a charge and sufficient evidence that the licensee had permitted apparent homosexuals to congregate there. Investigators had visited the prem-ises on several occasions and had observed the patrons; the testimony included the following partial account of their behavior: "They were conversing and some of them in a lisping tone of voice, and during certain parts of their conversations they used limp-wrist movements to each other. One man would stick his tongue out at another and they would laugh and they would giggle. They were very, very chummy and close. When they drank their drinks, they extended their pinkies in a very dainty manner. They took short sips from their straws.... They were very, very endearing to one another, very, very delicate to each other.... They looked in each other's eyes when they conversed. They spoke in low tones like an effeminate male. When walking, getting up from the stools, they very politely excused each other, hold on to the arm and swish and sway down to the other end of the bar and come back. . . . Their actions and mannerisms and demeanor appeared to me to be males impersonating females, they appeared to be homosexuals commonly known as queers, fags, fruits and other names."

Similarly in the proceeding against Val's Bar there was no charge nor any substantial evidence at the hearing before the director that lewd or immoral conduct was permitted at the licensed premises. Investigators had visited the premises on several occasions and testified in detail as to the behavioral characteristics which led them to the permissible conclusion that the patrons were apparent homosexuals. . . . The investigators acknowledged that for the most part the patrons were "normally dressed" and showed "very good behavior." Dr. Wardell B. Pomeroy, called as an expert witness by the licensee, testified that, although it could not be said from mere observation that any given individual was a homosexual, he would be of the opinion that tavern patrons with the characteristics described by the investigators were apparent homosexuals.

Dr. Pomeroy was associated with the Kinsey Institute for twenty years and was the co-author of several books dealing with sexual behavior and offenses. He . . . voiced the opinion that no adverse social effects would result from permitting homosexuals to congregate in licensed establishments. He noted that non-homosexuals would not be harmed by being in the same premises with homosexuals, and that any who found their mere presence to be offensive would presumably leave. He expressed the view that permitting their congregation in taverns would tend to eliminate clandestine associations in unregulated and unsupervised places. . . .

Though in our culture homosexuals are indeed unfortunates, their status does not make them criminals or outlaws. . . . So long as their public behavior violates no legal proscriptions they have the undoubted right to congregate in public. And so long as their public behavior conforms with currently acceptable standards of decency and morality, they may, at least in the present context, be viewed as having the equal right to congregate within licensed establishments. . . .

The Division of Alcoholic Beverage Control, stressing the acknowledged constitutional and statutory breadth of its regulatory powers . . . , contends that the mere congregation of apparent homosexuals in taverns is contrary to the public welfare. . . . It points to the fact that the very term "apparent homosexuals" contemplates effeminate behavioral characteristics. . . , but apparently it concedes, as it must in the light of the times, that such behavioral characteristics without more, would not constitute overt conduct offensive to current standards of morality and decency. It expresses various fears which we have carefully considered but which lack significant support in the records before us or in the available materials on the subject.

Thus the division suggests that the presence of apparent homosexuals in so-called "gay" bars may serve to harm the occasional non-homosexual patrons who happen to stray there but it produces nothing to rebut the expert testimony or the published writings to the contrary. . . . It further suggests that offensive conduct by apparent homosexuals within the licensed premises "may lead to violence" against them by non-homosexuals but this ignores the licensee's comprehensive capacity and responsibility, at the peril of its license, for precluding offensive conduct and for conducting its establishment in lawful and orderly fashion. . . . Finally, it points out that it has consistently tried "to increase public respect and confidence in the liquor industry"...and suggests that permitting the congregation of apparent homosexuals, even though carefully supervised, will impair such public respect and confidence. But here again it furnishes nothing affirmative in support of its position which appears to disregard the burgeoning movement towards greater tolerance and deeper understanding. . . .

When in the 1930's the Department of Alcoholic Beverage Control first took its severe position, it acted on the assumption that the mere congregation of apparent homosexuals had to be outlawed to achieve effective control. It of course had no experience to support the assumption but it took the prohibitory course as the safer one for the then fledgling system. At the time, the interests of the patrons in question were given little consideration and were in any event overwhelmed by the then highly felt transitional need for sweeping restraint. Now, in the 1960's, the transitional need as such is long past and it is entirely appropriate that full sweep be given to current understandings and concepts. Under them it seems clear that, so long as the division can deal effectively with the matter through lesser regulations which do not impair the rights of well behaved apparent homosexuals to patronize and meet in licensed premises, it should do so. . . .

The division has produced nothing to support any need for continuance of its flat prohibition. Nor has it produced anything to indicate that it could not readily prepare and enforce a fair and sensible regulation which, while permitting apparent homosexuals to assemble in and patronize licensed establishments, prohibits overtly indecent conduct and public displays of sexual desires manifestly offensive to currently acceptable standards of propriety. Such a regulation might well be adopted forthwith to the end that future proceedings would rightly be based on specific charges of improper conduct. . . . In the meantime, the discipline imposed in the three cases before us must be set aside. . . .

DOCUMENT 18

In the Matter of Kerma Restaurant Corporation v. State Liquor Authority

21 N.Y.2d 111 (New York Court of Appeals, 7 Dec. 1967)

Petitioner's retail liquor license has been annulled by respondent on a charge that it suffered or permitted the licensed premises to become disorderly…"in that it permitted homosexuals, degenerates and/or undesirables to be and remain on the licensed premises and conduct themselves in an offensive and indecent manner contrary to good morals. . . ."

There were 40 customers in the bar attended by one bartender, the petitioner's president, Mrs. Weinzierl. She, as the policeman testified, "was busy tending bar." The conversation in which the policeman testified he was solicited occurred at a jukebox near the front window. There is no proof that the bartender was anywhere near this conversation or in any position to overhear it. . . . This personal conversation between two men in the front of premises crowded with patrons and serviced by one busy bartender is not enough to attribute responsible knowledge to the licensee. . . .

It is manifest from the findings of the deputy commissioner that this solicitation was an essential basis of the decision to sustain the charge. He said: "I find that the patronage was openly homosexual in nature, that the officer was solicited by one of the male patrons herein for lewd and indecent purposes, that the officer and said male then ordered two (2) glasses of beer and left."

The policeman who made the arrest after he had left the premises and who came back later to issue a criminal summons to Mrs. Weinzierl for allowing the premises "to become disorderly" based this charge entirely on the fact that he had arrested a male for violation of the Penal Law and "defendant was present and in charge." This criminal charge was dismissed. The other proof in the proceeding is insufficient to establish the premises were permitted to become disorderly. In some measure this part of the charge is based on the policeman's observations of the dress and appearance of "several of the patrons" and of "three specific cases." These several had "makeup on, eye mascara, some with lipstick." The three specific cases had "hip hugger pants, slacks…, their shirts out of their trousers" showing "a bare midriff."

Indulgence in the inference that these "several" and these "three specific" men in a grill containing 40 people were, from their dress and makeup, homosexuals does not support the additional inference that they would create disorder. It is reasonable to think that even though he dresses strangely a homosexual may be orderly in the sense in which the Alcoholic Beverage Control Law defines order.

The policeman also observed "three instances" in which one male "would be" sitting on another male's lap "at the tables." He noticed also "three instances" where the males on the laps kissed the other male on the face and neck. There is no proof that the bartender was in a position to observe, or did observe, these "three instances." For the rest: "I observed several of the males when they walked away . . . keep their hands on their hips. Several of the males' voices were very effeminate and high pitched, and talked with a lisp." These "observations" are not brought home to the licensee.

But assuming from the proof as a whole that the licensee knew some homosexuals were in the place, is this disorder in the absence of some proof tending to actual disorder? If homosexual solicitation could be brought home to the licensee that would be enough; but it is certainly not demonstrated in this case, and the rest of the proof tending to disorder is insufficient. . . .

2

ACTIVIST AGENDAS AND VISIONS BEFORE STONEWALL

THE LGBT MOVEMENT CHANGED AND GREW in the years leading up to the Stonewall Riots. In the mid-1960s, new agendas and visions emerged, displacing and replacing earlier ideologies and philosophies. Influenced by the civil rights, black power, women's rights, sexual freedom, and countercultural movements, LGBT activists struck out in new directions. Homophile militants favored the use of direct action tactics. Sexual revolutionaries wanted to liberate erotic desires. New voices championed lesbian feminism and advocated for bisexuals, hustlers, transvestites, and transsexuals. Gender and sexual radicals called for "gay power" and "gay revolution." LGBT activists increasingly saw themselves as part of a broad-based coalition that was opposed to colonialism, imperialism, militarism, racism, and war.

This chapter's twenty-seven documents capture some of the inspirational visions and influential views that contributed to changes in LGBT activism before Stonewall.

DOCUMENTS 19–26 highlight movement debates that emerged in 1965 and 1966 as radicalizing homophiles called for increased militancy and direct action tactics.

DOCUMENTS 27–31 showcase activist support for the sexual revolution, the homosexual revolution, and the Homosexual Bill of Rights.

DOCUMENTS 32–34 feature lesbian feminist perspectives on LGBT activism.

DOCUMENTS 35–36 address the concerns of poor people, street people, hustlers, and bisexuals.

DOCUMENTS 37–41 highlight transgender ideologies and philosophies.

DOCUMENTS 42–45 announce new gay power agendas and gay revolutionary visions in 1968 and the first half of 1969.

DOCUMENT 19
"The Year Ahead: A Forecast"
Mattachine Review, Jan. 1965, 19–22[1]

The New Year ahead will be a significant one in the sexual revolution now under way. . . . The forces of Victorian prudery and bigoted ignorance will have to give way. . . .

Prominent in the pioneering projects which will seek to bring a greater enlightenment and freedom for people, especially in the English speaking world, will be the . . . organizations which make up the recognized "homophile movement" in the United States, England and Canada. Some of their recommendations, along with recommendations of the American Law Institute, will become reality in our legislatures in the near future. Specifically this refers to changing law so that it is no longer criminal for two consenting adults to engage in private sexual expression of any kind so long as it does not involve force or harm. . . .

Here are some of the things predicted which will affect the so-called "homophile minority" nationally and locally in the coming year and the period we shall call the "immediate future":

1. Serious examination of present statutes and a call for revision of penal codes and sex laws will continue in states such as New York, and get underway with determined action in California and other states. . . .

2. New organizations and publications of interest to homosexual adults will appear. Already in the U.S., Canada and England, there are almost 20 organized groups, and a dozen or more significant small publications. . . .

3. Laws and policy regarding hiring of homosexuals in government and permitting them to serve in the armed forces will come under closer scrutiny and the extent of the waste of manpower and talent, when finally known, will be found intolerable. . . .

4. New attitudes in what we may now call obscenity will become evident. Man will begin to see that it was a human error to regard sex and genital organs with the revulsion which prevailed in the past, and will dare to accept the fact that God and nature provided these things for human benefit and enjoyment. In these reflections, greater freedom to use the mails, greater latitude for the arts and literature, and the basic right of the individual to express himself sexually in accepted circumstances will be demanded. . . .

5. Either the courts or state legislatures will begin repealing existing birth control laws on the grounds of population pressure and principles of human rights. It will not be surprising if numerous voices from the behavioral sciences point to the possibility that homosexual expression may be one of nature's own provisions for population control.

6. The fact that fully half of the population of the U.S. over age 16 does not live in a situation of man-and-wife marriage and therefore these sexually

mature adults presently prohibited from any legal sexual expression will be weighed. Lawmakers will be pressed to consider humane legislation granting responsible freedom for all adults in private, so long as force and harm are absent, and the young are protected.

Closer home, we will see these developments, started if not completed:

1. San Francisco will not turn into a homosexual city. . . .
2. There will be changed attitudes in law enforcement regarding dress, dancing, and the right of individuals to peaceably assemble in private and semi-private situations for mutual benefit and enjoyment. This means that the scene of two men dancing together will cause no more real upset than the scene of two women (long accepted) or a man and woman. . . .
3. Don't be surprised if a re-examination of policy toward private clubs with acceptable police supervision is called for. . . .
4. Operation of Gay Bars will continue and with less harassment from liquor and police authorities, because the prejudice of the authorities will not much longer stand up against the truth. The hypocrisy of double moral standards is rotting away rapidly.
5. But the unlimited license some adults expect in matters of sex will NOT come to pass. Heterosexual men and women cannot engage in sexual acts on the streets, in the parks, and in public places. Nor will such permission be granted to anyone else. . . .

In the year ahead we shall discover . . . that homosexuals, like all other human beings, have legal and civil rights, and when they behave responsibly and without "unlimited license," keeping their private affairs to themselves as they should, then others besides the homosexual himself will join the effort to see that these human rights are established and maintained. . . .

As we extend our view forward at the beginning of 1965, we find there may be more homosexual acts in private, but fewer persons exclusively oriented as homosexual adults. The elimination of prejudice and ignorance and the constructive rebellion against ancient sexual repression will serve to bring a greater freedom and useful application of the sexual capacity of mankind for the benefit of all adults. A recognition of the basic "ambisexuality" of human beings might result. . . .

Then we shall begin to learn once and for all that ignorance does not equal knowledge, that prejudice does not equal tolerance, and that satisfaction in love relationships does not equal degeneracy. These absurd and invalid equations will disappear as human beings learn not to fear the sexual instinct, but to use it as well.

DOCUMENT 20

Dr. Franklin E. Kameny, "Does Research into Homosexuality Matter?"

The Ladder, May 1965, 14–20[2]

. . . As little as two years ago, "militancy" was something of a dirty word in the homophile movement. Long inculcation in attitudes of cringing meekness had taken its toll among homosexuals, combined with a feeling, still widely prevalent, that reasonable, logical, gentlemanly and ladylike persuasion and presentation of reasonable, logical argument could not fail to win over those who would deny us our equality and our right to be homosexual and to live as homosexuals without disadvantage. There was—and is—a feeling that given any fair chance to undertake dialogue with such opponents, we would be able to impress them with the basic rightness of our position and bring them into agreement with it.

Unfortunately, by this approach alone we will not prevail, because most people operate not rationally but emotionally on questions of sex in general, and homosexuality in particular, just as they do on racial questions.

It is thus necessary for us to adopt a *strongly* positive approach, a *militant* one. It is for us to take the initiative, the offensive—not the defensive—in matters affecting us. It is time that we began to move from endless talk (directed, in the last analysis, by us to ourselves) to firm, vigorous action.

We ARE right; those who oppose us are both factually and morally wrong. We are the true authorities on homosexuality, whether we are accepted as such or not. We must DEMAND our rights, boldly, not beg cringingly for mere privileges, and not be satisfied with crumbs tossed to us. I have been deeply gratified to note in the past year a growing spirit of militancy on the part of an increasing number of members of the homophile organizations.

We would be foolish not to recognize what the Negro rights movement has shown us is sadly so: that mere persuasion, information and education are not going to gain for us in actual practice the rights and equality which are ours in principle.

I have been pleased to see a trend away from weak, wishy-washy compromise positions in our movement, toward ones of strong affirmation of what it is that we believe and want, followed by a drive to take whatever action is needed to obtain our rights. I do not of course favor uncontrolled, unplanned, ill-considered lashing out. Due and careful consideration must always be given to tact and tactics. Within the bounds dictated by such considerations, however, we must be prepared to take firm, positive, definite action. . . .

While as a scientist I will never derogate the value of research for its own sake in order to provide additional knowledge, as an active member of the homophile movement my position must be quite different. It is time for us to move away from the comfortingly detached respectability of research into the often less pleasant rough-and-tumble of political and social activism.

DOCUMENT 21

Florence Conrad [Jaffy], "Research Is Here to Stay"
The Ladder, July 1965, 15–21[3]

Dr. Franklin Kameny's broadside attack on research . . . needs to be answered. . . .

As preliminary, I would ask where the Negro civil rights movement would be today, militant or not, if research into racial differences had not long ago supported the Negro's claim to equality of treatment? And where would WE be today without [Alfred] Kinsey's two classic volumes on sexual behavior? Ours is a science-oriented society, and scientists are God to most people. In the long run, I do not think it can be seriously doubted that what science says *will* be important for the success of the homophile movement.

Nevertheless, I do not intend to argue that the homophile movement must await research findings before working for fair treatment for homosexuals. In this I agree with Dr. Kameny, though not for his reasons. Efforts to win changes in the law, civil liberties, employment rights, etc., CAN and SHOULD proceed independently of research results. . . .

The real reason why the homophile movement should proceed to work for equal treatment now is that STATISTICAL FINDINGS FOR LARGE AGGREGATES ARE NOT PREDICTIVE FOR THE INDIVIDUAL. Regardless of whether homosexuals as a group, or Negroes, or females, or any other group you care to name, rate higher or lower on any psychological test than heterosexuals, Caucasians, males, etc., discrimination against John Doe's with regard to a particular job is *wrong*—because John Doe is not an Average! . . . To ask—or demand, if that word is preferred—that people be judged as individuals and not as stereotypes is to appeal to a central and recognized principle of our society. . . .

Research has never played, and need not play, a primary role in the ACTIVITIES of the homophile organizations. Its importance to the *ultimate attainment* of our goals is however quite basic, always has been so, and will remain so as long as our society is science-oriented. There is no reason why we cannot support research and do other things at the same time, especially since the interests of persons in the homophile movement differ. No one has ever asked that we drop other activities to become research organizations; this would be ludicrous and disastrous. Strong support for the research of properly qualified persons and institutions should in no way diminish—and will in fact increase—the effectiveness of the homophile movement. . . .

DOCUMENT 22

"Positive Policy"
Eastern Mattachine Magazine, May 1965, 23–24

The Mattachine Society of Washington takes the position that in the absence of valid evidence to the contrary, homosexuality is not a sickness, disturbance, or other pathology in any sense, but is merely a preference, orientation, or propensity on par with and not different in kind from heterosexuality.

. . . This formal endorsement of our status as responsible, respectable, first-class citizens is evidence that the homosexual community is coming of age. Although still lagging behind the Negro in his newly won self-confidence, the homosexual has decided that he himself will take the initiative in asserting his worth and dignity—to lead society, not to follow it. And other people *will* follow, once they realize that our feelings of inferiority have vanished—just as they now respect the Negro, ever since he made up his mind to stop being apologetic. We must stand up and not be afraid to make our rightful demands—to fight for them if necessary. John Brown said that "no people could have self-respect or be respected who would not fight for their freedom." Before we can fight effectively, we, like the Negro, must affirm that we are just as good as anyone else and just as sane. . . .

By openly declaring homosexuality a healthy state of being, we have taken steps to accomplish two objectives: (1) The self-doubting homosexual will feel supported—not betrayed—by his organization (whether he is a member or not), will be less hesitant to approve of himself, and can therefore fulfil his personality with greater confidence and inner freedom; (2) The perpetrators of official prejudice will be obligated to change their immoral policies and procedures in the face of this positive affirmation of worth. We are bringing clarity and determination into the battle. Henceforth we shall expect our attackers to bear the burden of proof, without being able to rely on a victory due to unopposed brainwashing. They will find it harder to disguise their irrational condemnation as reason and their ignorance as enlightenment.

DOCUMENT 23
Franklin E. Kameny, "Editorial: On Picketing"
Eastern Mattachine Magazine, July 1965, 20–21

In recent weeks, a practice new for the homophile movement, although much used elsewhere, has been adopted—mass picketing. . . .

That this upsurge of overt militancy is a phenomenon of the greatest practical importance to the homophile movement and to the American homosexual is demonstrated by the comment of a Philadelphia television announcer who, in discussing the demonstration there, commented that we are being forced to realize that these people are human beings.

It should be made plain that this organization does not look upon picketing as a mere publicity stunt, but as an avenue of last resort, to be adopted only when it is clear that all doors are closed to us and are likely to remain so.

Negotiation and productive discussion are infinitely preferable to demonstrations. Like the tango, however, it takes two to negotiate and discuss. We remain always ready to do so.

In every instance possible, any picketing done by us—whether of public agencies or of private persons and concerns—will be preceded by a sincere effort to meet, in order constructively to discuss and to seek redress for grievances.

We feel that in a democracy, segments of the citizenry should be able to expect—as a matter of right, not of mere privilege—that they will play a meaningful role in the establishment of laws and policies which affect them. That this is widely recognized and accepted was indicated most recently by the inclusion of representatives of the poor in planning for the anti-poverty program.

For three years, we have sought, patiently, by every existing recourse short of public demonstration, to air our grievances and to seek remedy for them. Our efforts to confer with our Federal officials in regard to their policies toward the homosexual American citizen have been in vain. They have refused. . . . This is not democracy; this is not the American way!

The homosexual community, in its justified impatience, has noted the successes achieved by the activism of the Negro movement. Having exhausted all other remedies—as, indeed, the Negro had done—we now see ourselves at the cautious commencement of an attempt to emulate that activism. This Society's demonstrations will be carefully considered ones, carried out in an orderly, disciplined, dignified fashion. The prediction can be ventured that continued official intransigence will result ultimately in popular demonstrations by the homosexual community at large, which will be far less responsible, controlled, and orderly. This way lies the Washington equivalent of Birmingham! Surely this is not what the government wants. Surely this is what it will get if it continues to refuse balm to an increasingly aggrieved segment of the citizenry.

At the time of our first demonstration, only some of us were aware of what is clear in retrospect—that the homophile movement, long and slowly approaching a crossroad, has now crossed it. That it has indeed crossed is all to the good.

In a movement which has advanced rapidly in the recent past, the adoption of picketing as a mode of protest represents a most significant step forward. It is a welcome addition to the movement's arsenal—but an addition whose use we deeply hope will be rendered unnecessary.

DOCUMENT 24
East Coast Homophile Organizations, July Fourth demonstration flier, 4 July 1965
Reprinted in Kay Tobin [Lahusen], "Picketing: The Impact & the Issues," *The Ladder*, Sept. 1965, 4–8[4]

July 4, the anniversary of the signing of the Declaration of Independence, is traditionally the day for a re-statement and re-affirmation of the liberties and rights, with the proclamation of which our country was born in 1776.

July 4 is a day for serious, solemn, and probing thought. It is a day properly to ask: Are we guaranteeing to ALL of our citizens the rights, the liberties, the freedoms, which took birth and first form in the Declaration of Independence and in the documents (such as the Constitution and its Bill of Rights) which followed upon it? Or are these concepts merely being given lip-service for some of our citizens?

The Declaration of Independence says: "ALL MEN ARE CREATED EQUAL." But in no walk of life, and in none of his dealings, whether with his fellow citizens or with his governments (Federal, state, or local), is the homosexual American citizen treated as equal to others; he is always placed in a status of inferiority. Systematically and unrelentingly, he is placed into and kept in the category of a second-class citizen. That the homosexual American citizen is a homosexual is always noted; that he is also an American citizen, with all that goes with that status, is always forgotten.

The Declaration of Independence says: "ALL MEN ARE ENDOWED...WITH CERTAIN UNALIENABLE RIGHTS.... AMONG THESE ARE...THE PURSUIT OF HAPPINESS." But the homosexual American citizen, upon savage penalty of law and upon pain of loss of livelihood and other severe disadvantage, is denied the proper pursuit of harmless happiness open to other citizens.

The Declaration of Independence says: "GOVERNMENTS ARE INSTI-TUTED...DERIVING THEIR JUST POWERS FROM THE CONSENT OF THE GOVERNED." But homosexual American citizens find themselves placed under laws and regulations, their activities directed, their freedoms limited, the con-duct of their lives disposed of, all without consultation and without their con-sent. They have asked—as citizens in OUR democracy have a RIGHT to ask, in the proper expectation that their request will be granted—to meet with their officials in order to discuss those aspects of their government and their laws which directly and immediately affect them, in which they are deeply involved, and in which they have a strong interest. Consistently they have been refused.

The Declaration of Independence says: "IN EVERY STAGE OF THESE OPPRESSIONS WE HAVE PETITIONED FOR REDRESS.... OUR REPEATED PETITIONS HAVE BEEN ANSWERED ONLY BY REPEATED INJURY." Homo-sexual American citizens, too, have petitioned their government for redress of their grievances and oppressions. Their petitions, too, have been ignored, in any constructive sense, and have been answered only by repeated injury. . . .

Other of our minority groups know that they have the active assistance of their governments in their fight for their proper rights and for their proper sta-tus of full equality with their fellow citizens. The homosexual American citizen meets only with the active, virulent hostility of his governments. He finds himself a member of the only major national minority group which is systematically denied an opportunity to achieve the equality which all other citizens have. . . .

Every other possible lesser means of remedy for an intolerable situation having been tried without success, we now try to bring our case directly before the public, before our fellow citizens, on a day and at a place which are singu-larly appropriate. We do so confident that we will have a fair hearing from our fellow American citizens.

DOCUMENT 25
Richard Conger [W. Dorr Legg], Editorial
ONE, Sept. 1965, 4–5[5]

Only a few weeks ago the name Watts meant little to the great majority of people, even those living in the Los Angeles area. Today Watts stands as a symbol of social protest and uncontrolled violence, a byword in Moscow and Cape-town, Bombay and Mombasa. The Governor of a great state, the President of the United States, along with thousands upon thousands of other persons have been compelled to take note of the lessons of Watts.

What are some of these? Have they any particular meaning for the readers of this Magazine? . . .

Let it never be forgotten that whether we refer to slave masses in ancient Athens, toiling peasants under the Manchus, grimy colliers in the 19th Century English Midlands or to the underprivileged Negroes of Watts no substantial sector of society can forever be kept in meek subjection. Human nature just is not like that.

The breaking point will come in one or another way. During many historical periods this breakdown has in later perspective been termed "the decline" of a culture or civilization. Since the time of new social attitudes and new moral standards inaugurated by the American and French Revolutions, and irreversibly it would seem, cultures do not necessarily "decline" any more. Instead, they may forcibly be wrenched into new positions by evolution or revolution in response to the demands of minorities to be heard and to be heeded.

As Los Angeles will never be the same again, since "the time of Watts," nor Alabama since the days at Selma, so it may be held that the Homophile Movement represents another sort of revolt. That it is quieter, that there now appears little likelihood of such eruptions as have marked the emergence of the Negro minority, in no way alters the basic picture, i.e., that minorities no longer will tolerate suppression and repression indefinitely.

How unthinkable but a few short years ago would be an editorial such as this, or a publication in which to print it! Let those who profess themselves unable to discern the dynamics of social change ponder on that simple fact a moment. Then, let them tick off on their fingers the number of other publications (good, bad or indifferent) which now freely publish homophile views. This simple bit of arithmetic furnishes as accurate a scale as any yet devised of the degree to which homosexuality has penetrated the very fabric of our society today.

And it will go farther. No force, no fulminations of law or of pulpit will alter the onward tide of social change upon which homophiles now rise toward their higher aspirations. Let those who become impatient or discouraged take the longer view and study what the social scientists have been telling us concerning the way changes come about. Let us congratulate ourselves that, from the evidence we have before us now, no Watts explosions are going to be needed or are likely to occur.

The Homophile Movement is a fact and a force in American life these days. An alert elite already has aligned itself with the higher levels of that Movement. This elite labors to bring about those higher levels of fair play and public morality that are the cornerstone and hallmark of American ideals of social justice.

Had more of us remembered that social justice is as inevitable as the sunrise there need have been no Watts. If more homophiles, and others, stand ready to learn and benefit from this lesson our society can move smoothly on to higher levels of personal freedom than it yet affords to most of its members.

Let us think on these things.

DOCUMENT 26
"Interview with Ernestine"
The Ladder, June 1966, 4–11

(This interview with Ernestine Eckstein [Eppenger] . . . was conducted by Kay Tobin [Lahusen] and Barbara Gittings in January 1966. Miss Eckstein was at the time vice-president of the New York Chapter of Daughters of Bilitis. The opinions she expressed were her own and not necessarily those of DOB.)[6]

Q. Have you been active in the Negro civil rights movement?

A. At Indiana University I was active in the NAACP [National Association for the Advancement of Colored People] chapter there, and I was an officer of the chapter in my senior year. At the time I was there, there was no other organization, no other choice. Then suddenly more progressive groups like CORE [Congress of Racial Equality] and SNCC [Student Nonviolent Coordinating Committee] came along, and I got out of NAACP and joined CORE when I came to New York. . . .

Q. Would you give us your opinion of picketing? . . .

A. Picketing I regard as almost a conservative activity now. The homosexual has to call attention to the fact that he's been unjustly acted upon. This is what the Negro did. . . . I do regard picketing as a form of education. But one thing that disturbs me a lot is that there seems to be some sort of premium placed on psychologists and therapists by the homophile movement. I personally don't understand why that should be. So far as I'm concerned, homosexuality per se is not a sickness. When our groups seek out the therapists and psychologists, to me this is admitting we are ill by the very nature of our preference. . . .

Q. Would you say the burden of change is on society or on the homosexual, if his lot is to be improved?

A. I think to a certain extent it's on both. The homosexual has to assert himself more, and society has to give more. Homosexuals are invisible, except for the stereotypes, and I feel homosexuals have to become visible and to assert themselves politically. Once homosexuals do this, society will start to give more and more.

Q. You think more homosexuals should declare themselves and get in homophile picket lines and so forth?

A. Any movement needs a certain number of courageous people, there's no getting around it. They have to come out on behalf of the cause and accept whatever consequences come. Most lesbians that I know endorse homophile picketing, but will not picket themselves. I *will* get in a picket line, but in a different city. For example, I picketed at Independence Hall in Philadelphia on July Fourth last year and at the White House in October. . . .

Q. Do you believe in any forms of civil disobedience for the homophile movement at this time?

A. I think our movement is not ready for any forms of civil disobedience. I think this would solidify resistance to our cause. This situation will change eventually. But not now.

Q. Are there any ways in which you feel our movement should emulate other movements more?

A. I don't find in the homophile movement enough stress on courtroom action. I would like to see more test cases in courts, so that our grievances can be brought out into the open. That's one of the ways for a movement to gain exposure. . . .

Q. Do you think there's much of a parallel between the homophile movement and the Negro movement in regard to variety of organizations and approaches?

A. There's only a very rough parallel. Generally, NAACP is the most conservative of all civil rights groups. And some homophile groups are the same, with the same sort of predisposition to take things easy, not to push too fast, not stick their necks out too far. For instance, demonstrations, as far as I'm concerned, are one of the very first steps toward changing society. The NAACP never reached this stage—or at least not until it was pushed into at least giving lip-service to demonstrations by other Negro organizations. And I think that in the homophile movement, some segments will have to be so vocal and so progressive, until they eventually push the ultra-conservative segments into a more progressive line of thinking and action. . . .

DOCUMENT 27
Clark P. Polak, "The Homophile Puzzle"
Drum, Dec. 1965, 13–17, 26–27, and Jan. 1966, 8–11

. . . Largely reflecting the current "liberal" view that homosexuals are acceptable as people whose rights need support if, it might be added, there is no way to make them all heterosexual, the movement alienates the "average" or what has been called "the hip" homosexual.

Gilbert Cantor, in making this point recently, drew an analogy with the Negro rights movement: "The 'square' believes in organization, negotiation, in the manners and morals and techniques of the dominant culture which he addresses in its own language. And then we discover in Watts, California, that the hip Negro has nothing to do with the square Negro and his organizations and that those organizations do not speak for him."

It is safe to say that the present homophile movement neither addresses itself to nor speaks for the hip homosexual. . . .

All too often . . . , the "square" homosexuals of the homophile movement appear to have sold themselves out and stranded the "hip" to make his happy way without their assistance. . . .

Many unaffiliated homosexuals have the distinct impression that the movement is talking about the "goodies" and they are the "baddies" on the outside looking in. The view advanced by the organizations that homosexuals are the same as heterosexuals (like many other generalities) simply does not ring true to the overwhelming majority of homosexuals who see, even if their leaders do not, some rather specific differences which they share with their friends and companions. These differences are not the fearful sightings of poorly informed heterosexuals, but center on the total value systems of both groups. The homosexual value system (which for males is largely male and for lesbians is largely female) differs from that of the straight world that uses a compromise between male and female.

When heterosexuals object to homosexual solicitation and promiscuity, they do so more because their cultural heritage (or value system) calls for monogamy and the kind of masculine supremacy that dictates their males must be the sexual aggressors. . . . In contradistinction, homosexual behavior almost *by definition* includes promiscuity and has some certain males being aggressed upon. . . .

The Western culture places penalties even upon "conformist" sexual behavior and the "non-conformist" homosexual represents a multiple threat through being different. The differences, often a matter of priorities, are at the root of anti-homosexual prejudice. . . .

If the homosexual can be seen as the recipient of society's general antisexual attitudes, then the movement could profitably explore working with other groups concerned with the reform of sexual mores. . . . The leadership must learn to address heterosexual audiences in terms of general sex problems as opposed to just homosexual problems. . . .

DOCUMENT 28

Clark P. Polak

Janus Society Newsletter, Sept. 1966, 1–2[7]

Finding defects within the homophile movement is far less difficult than offering possible or even partial solutions to those problems. In directing myself to what I see as crippling disabilities within the movement structure, I do so with more confidence that I can see clearly than that I can find the yellow brick road to Oz. . . .

Few of the leaders in the movement have examined their innards sufficiently to be able to accept homosexuality in themselves and rid themselves of their own anti-homosexual sentiments. Anti-homosexuality is rampant within the organizations and the concern is for the "good" homosexuals—which I call Aunt Maryism—and a shudder fills the room when anyone suggests there is a connection between male homosexuality and femininity and female homosexuality and masculinity. (Parenthetically it is probably necessary to add the disclaimer that I have not addressed myself to whether or not there is any such connection.)

Your publications, besides being often illiterate and poorly edited, are also reeking with anti-homosexuality, groveling, obsequiousness and seem almost designed to maintain the homosexual's position of inferiority. . . .

To address ourselves to other areas: It is time for the movement to cease to hide behind names like Mattachine, SIR, Pride, Dionysus, Phoenix, ad nauseum. As some of you know, we are in the process of changing our unfortunate choice to the Homosexual Law Reform Society. And this brings me to another point, interrelated to the previous ones for sure: what laws are we attempting to reform? Criminal sanctions? Hardly. The chief oppression faced by the homosexual is the cultural tone which says "I despise you." For the most part, the movement either ignores or fails to appreciate this most basic of all problems.

DOCUMENT 29
Bill Beardemphl, "President's Corner"
Vector, Sept. 1965, 2[8]

Oppression demands that the oppressed defend themselves. Whatever the rationales advocated by disagreeing factions, conflict eventually arises when conditions of oppression are believed to constitute an outrage to the nature of the individuals oppressed. Certain questions must be faced. In social rights movements, is violence, such as recently erupted in Los Angeles, inevitable? Will the eventual recourse of the homophile revolution be a similar blood bath?

I do not believe it will, but I find many among our movement who are forcing all homosexuals towards this end. To me, in our age, the revolution that is bankrupt is the revolution that advocates and perpetuates violence. Such an ugly, destructive, chaotic melee is based on the failure of the leadership to understand and cope with the problems at hand. This is the failure of the "establishment" *more* than a failure within the movement's leadership, but both are at fault. . . .

The homophile revolution will be one of important change for the better when it applies itself objectively to discovering and using universal truths. We must face up to these difficult tasks in a reasonable fashion.

In the final analysis, the social man has only three choices: He joins with others and helps direct society, or he supports people who will direct society as he believes necessary, or he lives outside society and pays the awful price of playing the role defined by that society as criminal.

It is my earnest hope that the homophile movement confine its actions within the framework of social responsibility.

DOCUMENT 30
William E. Beardemphl, "A Challenge to San Francisco"
The Ladder, Oct. 1966, 14–15[9]

. . . Even while the homosexual has served his community well, his community has not served him. He has been victimized and degraded.

There is unequal enforcement of our laws. Homosexuals are selected as the objects of extra surveillance, special intimidations, entrapment and enticement procedures that are not employed against any other group. When a homosexual is placed in legal jeopardy, such guilts have been instilled in him that he is fearful of seeking redress. When those few who still have courage try to seek justice, lawyers' fees double, cases are rejected by many competent attorneys, District Attorneys' offices do not cooperate in protection of their rights. But if a just decision is reached in court, the social stigma of any arrest connected with a homosexual offense brings quick, undeserved punishments. Employment discrimination is practiced against known homosexuals; the right to hold a professional license or to obtain almost any business license is denied. The Constitutional right of assembly in this city has been historically abridged for homosexuals. Federal, State, and local governments have always discriminated against us. Professional services, and in many cases public services, have been denied to known homosexuals. Even the Christian Church has been no better. . . .

We will not accept compromise or tolerate injustice any longer. The way ahead for us has been plainly determined by the history of our country. We hear the drums of equality from the American Revolution. We hear the cannons of unity from our great Civil War. We hear the bombs of universal peace from World War I. We see the awesome mushrooming cloud of freedom, of complete individual freedom, from World War II. Our banners shall read the same as for all men—Equality, Unity, Peace, Freedom.

In our day-to-day existence, we still hear the catcalls of "fruit," "fairy," "queer," "faggot." All the reactions of subjective inequality are still practiced by our neighbors and continue to dwell in man's civilized heart.

We demand our rights. First, we shall use the framework of established order. But if existing circumstances do not answer our demands, we shall create new approaches. Our approach to social action shall be to act out our rights as legally as possible, and letting society adjust to us.

If the police do not protect homosexuals as they have not protected us in the past, then I can see in the near future a separate police force paid for and operated by the homophile community. Unless restrictive laws are changed, unless the courts uphold the rights of homosexuals, we shall have no alternative but to go to the Supreme Court and overturn these laws that state all men are treated equally in our courts except for homosexuals. If politicians do not openly address themselves to homosexuals, it will be because they do not need our 90,000 votes in San Francisco. We shall put in office public servants who will talk to homosexuals.

We ask no special favor. We want only ordinary rights like every other citizen of these United States—jobs, homes, friends, social lives, safety and security.

Here is our challenge to San Francisco: FACE REALITY—FACE HOMOSEXUALITY.

DOCUMENT 31

North American Conference of Homophile Organizations, "Homosexual Bill of Rights"

17 Aug. 1968, reprinted in *The Los Angeles Advocate*, Oct. 1968, 6[10]

BASIC RIGHTS

1. Private consensual sex acts between persons over the age of consent shall not be an offense.
2. Solicitation for any sexual act shall not be an offense except upon the filing of a complaint by the aggrieved party, not a police officer or agent.
3. A person's sexual orientation or practice shall not be a factor in the granting or renewing of Federal security clearances, visas, and the granting of citizenship.
4. Service in and discharge from the armed forces and eligibility for veteran's benefits shall be without reference to homosexuality.
5. A person's sexual orientation or practice shall not affect his eligibility for employment with federal, state, or local governments, or private employers.

AREAS FOR IMMEDIATE REFORM

1. Police and other government agents shall cease the practice of enticement and entrapment of homosexuals.
2. Police shall desist from notifying the employers of those arrested for homosexual offenses.
3. Neither the police department nor any other government agency shall keep files solely for the purpose of identifying homosexuals.

4. The practice of harassing bars and other establishments and of revoking their licenses because they cater to homosexuals shall cease.

5. The practice of reviewing less-than-honorable military discharges, granted for homosexual orientation or practice, shall be established, with the goal of upgrading such discharges into fully honorable.

6. The registration of sex offenders shall not be required.

7. City ordinances involving sexual matters shall be rescinded and these matters left to the state legislatures.

8. Conviction for homosexual offenses shall not be the basis for prohibiting issuance of professional or any other licenses nor for the revocation of these licenses.

9. No questions regarding sexual orientation or practice shall appear on application forms, personnel data sheets, or in personal interviews.

10. No government agency shall use the classification of homosexuality as an alleged illness to limit the freedom, rights, or privileges of any homosexual.

DOCUMENT 32

Shirley Willer, "What Concrete Steps Can Be Taken to Further the Homophile Movement?"

The Ladder, Nov. 1966, 17–20[11]

. . . It is difficult for me to discuss what the homophile movement should be doing. I have some very clear ideas about what the Lesbian should be doing but the problems of the male homosexual and the female homosexual differ considerably. . . .

The particular problems of the male homosexual include police harassment, unequal law enforcement, legal proscription of sexual practices and for a relatively few the problem of disproportionate penalties for acts of questionable taste such as evolve from solicitations, wash-room sex acts and transexual attire.

In contrast, few women are subject to police harassment and the instances of arrest of Lesbians for solicitation, wash-room sex or transexual attire are so infrequent as to constitute little threat. . . .

The problems of importance to the Lesbian are job security, career advancement and family relationships.

The important difference between the male and female homosexual is that the Lesbian is discriminated against not only because she is a Lesbian, but because she is a woman. Although the Lesbian occupies a "privileged" place among homosexuals, she occupies an under-privileged place in the world. . . .

Lesbians have agreed (with reservations) to join in common cause with the male homosexual. . . . There has been little evidence, however, that the male homosexual has any intention of making common cause with us. We suspect that should the male homosexual achieve his particular objectives in regard to his homosexuality he might possibly become a more adamant foe of women's rights than the heterosexual male has ever been. . . .

This background may help you understand why, although the Lesbian joins the male homosexual in areas of immediate and common concern, she is at the same time preparing for a longer struggle, waged on a broader base with the widest possible participation of the rank and file Lesbian. It shows why, to the Lesbian leader, diffusion and consensus are as important as leadership and direction. Demonstrations which define the homosexual as a unique minority defeat the very cause for which the homosexual strives—TO BE CONSIDERED AN INTEGRAL PART OF SOCIETY. . . .

Proceeding from our statement of wish[es] to offer a few constructive steps . . . :

1. To affirm as a goal of [the North American Conference of Homophile Organizations]: to be as concerned about women's civil rights as male homosexuals' civil liberties.
2. To suggest that homosexual men attempt to appreciate the value of women as PEOPLE in the movement, respect abilities as individuals, not seek them out as simple "show-pieces."
3. That those philosophical factors of homosexuality which engage both sexes be basic to our concepts of reform.
4. That the number of one sex not be a determinate factor in decisions of policy, but that a consideration of all arguments be heard and that CONSENSUS be the goal of the conference. Insofar as we do find trust and value in the male-oriented homophile organizations, we will find common ground upon which to work.

DOCUMENT 33
Del Martin, "The Lesbian's Majority Status"
The Ladder, June 1967, 23–25[12]

Lesbians tend to think of themselves as belonging to a minority group which is commonly known as the homosexual (or homophile) community. In reality and certainly for all practical purposes, this is a myth, a delusion, a bill of goods sold to us by male homosexual organizations which pretend to be co-educational in character and membership.

The news media has certainly emphasized what we had become increasingly aware of, but reluctant to admit openly. *CBS Reports*, of course, did us a favor by excluding us. . . . *Life* and *Look* have been equally kind in their omissions. There are advantages, we find, in the slanted press, in the bias of male reporters trying desperately to cling to the last vestiges of the superior male image—the Masculine Mystique, if you will—which is as hollow as the culturally learned and perpetuated Feminine Mystique, so aptly described by Betty Friedan.

There are [too] many other phases of the American Sexual Revolution to which Lesbians may address themselves . . . to get bogged down in the defense of promiscuity among male homosexuals and of public sexual activity in "tea rooms."

There are many other organizations with which the Daughters of Bilitis may align themselves in the good fight for civil rights. The Lesbian, after all, is first of all a *woman*—an individual who must earn her own livelihood, who must provide her own household. She is much more concerned with problems of inequality in job and educational opportunities than in the problems of male hustlers and prostitutes. She can much more readily identify with organizations such as the League of Women Voters [and] the Business & Professional Women's Club than the "co-educational" Society for Individual Rights, whose 500 male members are thrown into panic because of the "invasion" of 20 women.

There are two new organizations which might more successfully capture the imagination of the thoughtful and responsible Lesbian. . . .

The National Organization for Women (N.O.W.) has been formed "to take action to bring women into full participation in the mainstream of American Society NOW, exercising all the privileges and responsibilities thereof in truly equal partnership with men." . . .

Another organization which Lesbians may readily identify with is the Single Persons Tax Reform Lobby. . . . Miss [Dorothy] Shinder's group contends there is discrimination of the Internal Revenue Service against single persons by not allowing them "Head of Household" status. . . . Lesbian couples, forced by society to remain in the "single" status, could benefit by these tax proposals. . . .

It is time that the Daughters of Bilitis and the Lesbian find and establish a much broader identification than that of the homosexual community or the homophile movement. The "battle of the sexes" which predominates in American Society prevails as well in the homosexual community and the Lesbian finds herself relegated to an even more inferior status.

This is not to say, however, that DOB or the Lesbian should withdraw entirely from participation in the homophile movement, for there are many worthy mutual endeavors demanding and deserving the support of female homosexuals, such as the Councils on Religion and the Homosexual, the National Legal Defense Fund, the Tavern Guilds and Citizens Alert. But participation, which is time consuming and costly, should be limited to areas where there is some semblance of cooperation, or at least some hope thereof. . . .

It is our understanding that there are more women than men in the United States. Women thus comprise a majority of the population. Let us join that majority and assume responsibility for necessary reforms in the status of women in our society and its institutions.

DOCUMENT 34

A. B. [Ada Bello], "The Masculine-Feminine Mystique"
Daughters of Bilitis Philadelphia Newsletter, Nov. 1967, 1–2

Are we so concerned with being lesbians that we tend to forget the fact that we are also women, and, as such, members of a quite numerous "minority group"? Because women are still subjected to a great deal of discrimination in our society, laws exist that overtly place females in a position of disadvantage concerning job opportunities. One case in point is the restriction on the number of hours women can work per week. No doubt the regulation originally arose from a very valid need, i.e., to avoid the exploitation of females in jobs that were physically taxing; but today such limitations are unnecessary, and can be used as an excuse to avoid the hiring of qualified females. These laws should be revised, at least in the area concerning white collar workers. But the problem goes beyond the legal level—discrimination against females arises mainly from preconceived ideas and the fact notwithstanding that measures have been taken to keep the sex of the applicant from influencing the employer's choice, the notion still exists that female are less reliable and more difficult to work with than men. About the only areas where female employees are preferred to male are those in which the salary is rather low. Which leads to another very painful reality: that of females receiving less remuneration than males for equal work. . . .

In the last analysis, we can see the problem arising from the arbitrary classification of human beings into male and female in connection with activities that have no relation to sex. . . . The logical solution would be a whole new outlook on sex, one that would place it where it logically belongs, in the realm of the intimate relationship of two individuals. Ironically, it is in this context that society seems more reluctant to recognize it. The sexes are kept apart by an intricate arrangement of morals and taboos, and when they confront each other it is very much with the attitude of enemies on the battlefield. Small wonder that the whole structure is quite unstable and growing steadily worse: too many false assumptions were placed at the foundations.

If we rid ourselves of this masculine-feminine mystique and accept individuals as such and not as part of an artificial classification, a great deal of the tensions will disappear, tensions which are taking up precious energy that could be put to much better use. We will all benefit from it.

DOCUMENT 35

J. P. [Jean-Paul] Marat, "The Views of Vanguard"

Cruise News & World Report, Oct. 1966, 10[13]

Vanguard is an organization of "kids on the street" who feel there is no place for them within the organizational structure of the homophile organizations.

More often than not they are entirely correct. . . .

The homosexual movement will never be unified; this is an impossibility that is so obvious it seems ridiculous that it would even be mentioned.

The various types of homosexuals are so far apart that a union of them would seem no less than a miracle.

You must realize that 99% of the homosexual organizations in the U.S. are composed of and run by the middle class, well-established, hidden homosexual.

VANGUARD and one or two other organizations are composed of the other 1% of the homosexuals in the country. We are the hustlers, who are bought and paid for by the same people who will not hire us to do a legitimate job.

We are the people with long hair who (you) will neither hire to work for you nor allow us in your organizations.

We are the young homosexuals, as young as thirteen or fourteen, who are too damn young and confused to really know where else to go but to one of the well-known organizations. And when we go there, we are told, "go to this institute or that psychiatrist."

I'm sure that you all know that once one of these kids puts himself or herself in the hands of these "professionals," the information is relayed to not only the person's parents and/or relations, but to the police and other organizations which now, with this information, will harass these people.

I'm not saying that I ask the people in my organization to come forth and admit their homosexuality. Anyone in any program or demonstration in which VANGUARD has been involved have [sic] volunteered this information themselves, under no duress.

My point is this: Let each and every organization understand what the goals of the whole movement are and go about reaching these goals in any possible way they may think will help.

I'm not condoning anything that may be illegal; I am condoning anything and everything that will help to further the acceptance of homosexuals and homosexuality by the majority of the heterosexuals and the majority of homosexuals who are afraid to admit to themselves this problem of loss of identity. We are all in the same boat and it's beginning to sink. We have got to start getting rid of all the masks and costumes that are weighing us down.

When this is done, when we first admit to ourselves that we are homosexuals, and admit that we are the most prejudiced people about ourselves, then at this time there will be a possible joining of forces. But I will say again, there will never be a unity of organization.

DOCUMENT 36
Keith St. Clare, "Bisexuality"
Vanguard (1.9), 1967, 25–26, 28

It is well known that at all times there have been, as there still are, human beings who can take as their sexual partner a person of either sex without allowing one trend to interfere with the other. We call these people bisexuals and accept the fact of their existence without much wondering. But in the shade of grey wherein we all live it is, I believe, more realistic to label all those who simply can make it with either sex as bisexuals; and to encourage ourselves and others to adjust to a bisexual pattern of living as hastily as possible.

Human animal-ness is such that the individual is quite naturally endowed with a set of versatile sexual organs and several diverse erogenous zones, making it necessary for him to respond to a variety of sex stimuli and frustrating for him to deny his nature. Should he attempt to thwart his plurisexuality, his spirit becomes uneasy and his body cannot rest. During periods of particular need those parts of his nature which have been most neglected irritate his consciousness the most and make it difficult for him to think of anything else but their satiation.

Unfortunately, society, religion, and mother have conspired in our civilization to "free" man of his natural impulses, thus tying him to them. From birth the masses have been taught to discredit their nature and to adopt an unnatural set of values and inhibitions. These psychological hangups result in frustration and self-condemnation whenever we experience wholesome lusts for the "wrong" sex or the "wrong" act.

Even as children we are taught that we must choose. We must select the "good" sexual pattern or the "bad." Inevitably we will lack either the softness of women or the virility of men in our sexual affairs. Frequently, the individual later builds a terrific hatred for his own or his opposite's sexual apparatus in order to adopt a single sexual pattern as the most simple solution to his innate plurisexuality.

But all human beings can be warm and loving. Tender sensual feelings for another whether manifest or covert should not be suppressed because of the age or the color or the gender of one's partner. Neither is it really important whether these desires result in sexual acts. The desire and the acceptance of the desire define the issue. We are unnatural when we suppress love or lust because "it is not done" or it is "improper."

We can rejoice that more individuals today are freeing their social-sexual desires to flow naturally in both directions in an orderly fashion without conflict. The covert or overt anxieties produced by suppressed homo- or heterosexuality that previously affected the average man has been overcome by a sizable minority. Tolerance, free love and acceptance of the variety of our natural lusts have spread from the artisan-bohemian classes to the ranks of the philosopher, politician and educator.

Proliferation of this natural tendency will directly and indirectly reduce tensions with sexual minorities. Those who are primarily homo- or heterosexual will no longer be forced to despise their counterparts because of a seeming lack of similarity.

Great cultural advances can be made. There will be new dimensions in the fields of art, music and literature. Radical changes will occur in our armies, navies and air forces. The natural expressions of bestiality and autosexuality will be freed from acquired inhibitions, fears and remorse. We will finally be able to discard the ridiculous assumption that each person has a certain amount of pleasure allotted to his sex life—or that perhaps he has only a certainly amount of sex life allotted to his pleasure.

DOCUMENT 37

"Purpose of Transvestia"

Transvestia (no. 34), 1965[14]

The customs and attitudes of our society, while recognizing and allowing great freedom to the female in the expression of the masculine side of her personality, are largely blind to and repressive toward the male who discovers the feminine aspect of his total self. Feminine expression in the male does not imply sexual deviation. This magazine is dedicated to the needs of the sexually normal individual who has discovered the existence of his or her "other side" and seeks to express it.

Transvestia, therefore, is published by, for, and about transvestites to provide them with:

ENTERTAINMENT—EDUCATION—EXPRESSION by means of fiction, articles of opinion, true experiences, etc. Its purpose is to help its reader to promote: UNDERSTANDING—ACCEPTANCE—PEACE OF MIND. Its policy is to limit its scope of coverage and interest to the field of the heterosexual transvestite. Without condemnation or judgement of any kind, the fields of homosexuality, bondage, punishment, fetishism and domination are left to others to develop.

Transvestia has and will continue to serve as a means of gathering information in its chosen field and to aid, by any means available, the dissemination of knowledge of the field to further the understanding of it by psychiatrists, psychologists, sociologists, lawyers, jurists and police officials.

Loneliness, fear and self condemnation have too long been the lot of the transvestite. It is hoped that *Transvestia* can, through knowledge and sharing with others, bring self acceptance and happiness.

DOCUMENT 38

Susanna Valenti, "I Hate Men: A Diversion by a Male Transvestite"

The Ladder, May 1965, 24–26[15]

. . . I've always felt a sense of unfairness in the way society is arranged. The world of women has been to me as much mine as it is theirs. All the time I was a little "girl" I inwardly gnashed my teeth when I was denied the supreme joy of playing with dolls, as I was dying to do, or worse still, when I saw my sister bedecked in dresses I would have given half my life to wear. My poor parents, however, only saw me as their boy. How could they know there was a girl within me? So they kept giving me the kinds of clothes and toys society demands be given to all little boys. My parents had to follow the formula, and therefore I was made to follow it too.

There is a set pattern for men to be fitted into, and woe to those who do not want or are not able to conform. One of the theories that tries to explain transvestism is based on this society-made mold into which all male children must be poured. By pushing males into the Masculine Role, society is actually sentencing to oblivion a good percentage of each individual's personality. . . .

It makes me, as a TV, indignant to see the fabulous amount of freedom a girl (born a girl) enjoys in our present society. Let's take the matter of dress—the subject dearest to the heart of the TV. If a girl wants to wear pants, who is going to stop her from doing so? She can walk on Fifth Avenue wearing a man's shirt, slacks, socks and loafers, and nobody will say boo. But let a man walk to the corner store wearing a print blouse and a skirt—and you'll see pandemonium! Men must conform to the "definition," remember?

So how can I, born a male, satisfy this craving of the "girl-within" me? I must resort to all the props of the female impersonator. These include a wig (a good one, of course) and everything down to nylons and garter belt. Now, if my beard should be heavy and dark—which it is—I must shave so close that you can see through to the other side of my face and then I must use liberal amounts of make-up. . . .

Women have all the breaks. How many times has a woman solved an important problem just by putting on a good cry? The brainless one (man) swallows the beautiful act and gives in. By acting helpless, a woman can always get an idiot to do the work for her. Women are actually using men to make women's lives easier and softer. Woman today makes all the important decisions that affect a man's life. And I have a sneaking suspicion that it's woman who has invented today's Masculine Role. She is the one who insists on man's fitting a pattern which she herself has concocted with devilish cleverness. She has decreed that he must stay within the rigid frame of that mold, while she keeps for herself all the freedom she wants in life. . . .

So as a TV, I hate men for being so stupid and allowing themselves to be kept within the bondages of the Masculine Ideal. The transvestites are the only ones who are rebelling against this artificial definition of what man is and wants, and we feel proud of being able to show the world an honest inner self—who adores frills, loves to walk on high heels, and is happy to sign an article like this with her real "real" name.

DOCUMENT 39
Western Regional Planning Conference of Homophile Organizations, "Homophile Movement Policy Statement"
Vector, May 1967, 3[16]

Since the homosexual community is composed of all types of persons, we feel that the movement ought not [to] be constricted by any limiting concept of public image. The homosexual has no reputation to protect.

It is true that the image that an organization projects inside the homosexual community may affect the support it gets from that community. But we would support the right of individuals to do what they want and should educate the homosexual to accept himself as a homosexual and to accept all other persons.

We assert the right of individuals to be what they are and do what they wish so long as it does not infringe on the rights of others.

One purpose of homophile groups is to explain the various alternatives open to the individual and the possible consequences of such alternatives, and to help individuals achieve full personhood.

We do not feel that drag, sado-masochism, and other aspects of sexual behavior can be summarily dismissed as necessarily invalid expressions of human love. As human beings and as homosexuals, we have a special interest in understanding all sexuality.

DOCUMENT 40

Virginia Bruce [Prince], "The Expression of Femininity in the Male"
Journal of Sex Research 3, no. 2 (May 1967): 129–139

. . . The psychiatric fraternity, being a branch of medicine, is imbued with the idea that anything out of the ordinary should be "cured," that is, brought back to a condition of conformity with society's customs. Thus they seek, by various means, to make the transvestite forget his enjoyment of dressing in feminine attire and expressing his feminine side. They have, however, been eminently unsuccessful. . . . Recently, there have been several reports of success with aversion therapy utilizing either the nauseating effects of apomorphine or the discomfort of electric shock applied while the patient was attired in feminine clothing in order to condition him against his dressing. It is, to my mind, a sad commentary on the scientific integrity and medical wisdom of the physicians or psychiatrists doing this. They were apparently more interested in forcing the individual to conform, than in finding out what really motivated him. I think it would be generally agreed that such negative conditioning might remove the symptom of cross-dressing, but would do little to destroy the desires underlying it or the satisfactions attained by it. Thus, all that is done by such treatment is to dam up an outlet, which in due course is liable to result in built-up pressures which will seek outlet in other ways, often much more serious and socially undesirable than the one they replace.

I have personally met probably 150 transvestites and maintain a mail contact with 500 or 600 more and I very much doubt that any one of them would submit himself to a course of aversion therapy. I believe that the best thing one can do is to help these people accept themselves for what they are, by not feeling guilty or shameful about it; to help them realize that being interested in the gender aspects of womanhood does not necessarily imply an interest in the sexual aspects, and that they should therefore stop worrying about being a homosexual; to let them know that they are not alone, that there are thousands more who feel just as they do; and, lastly, to realize that the expression of the gentle femininity that is within them does not necessarily compromise or destroy the masculinity that is their male birthright. When there is a wife involved, as there usually is, counseling should also be provided for her to assist her in answering the questions and fears that naturally come to her mind. Understanding by a wife can provide more pleasure in the life of a transvestite than any other one thing.

So finally, a word about the social prognosis of the matter of "feminine" expression in the male. It has already been pointed out that much of what is called feminine is arbitrary and subject to social revision. Due to the advance of women into what was previously exclusively male territory, the time is fast approaching when the emancipation of the Western male will become a necessity, just as the emancipation of women has been all during the last hundred years. When men learn that gentility, compassion, passivity and tenderness are but human characteristics and no more unmasculine than directness, decisiveness and executive ability are unfeminine—and these are demonstrated daily by women in business—then the arbitrary distinctions of gender will also begin to disappear. When they do, the exterior manifestations of it will diminish also, so that the day will come when the members of each sex will be permitted, nay expected, to manifest all the abilities, traits, and qualities which they may possess for the general good of society and themselves. When this happens the selection and use of clothing, cosmetics, adornment, etc. will be entirely at an individual's discretion. When society comes to the point that a wife who is a good business executive can go out and earn the living while a husband who may be a good cook and housekeeper can stay home and look after the house and kids and nobody thinks any the less of him for doing so, society will have finally destroyed most of the artificial and false gender distinctions current today. Under these conditions every individual will achieve full personality expression.

DOCUMENT 41
"Purposes and Progress"
Erickson Educational Foundation Newsletter, Spring 1969, 1[17]

In an effort to assist where "human potential is limited by physical, mental or social conditions, or where scope of research is too new, controversial, or imaginative to encourage traditionally oriented support," the Erickson Educational Foundation has been called upon to function in gender identity areas needing service not otherwise supplied. It has initiated and is achieving progress on a number of projects in this field, including:

1. Establishment of a Central Repository of Information for research and
   reference. . . .

2. Updating or introduction of accurate definitions and information on transsexualism and transvestism is being provided for new editions of dictionarics and encyclopedias, as well as for placement in subject index listings in professional publications of abstracts.

3. Establishment of a network of concerned physicians throughout the U.S. and Canada, who will be sympathetic to transsexuals and administer tests and treatment where indicated, is under way.

4. Dissemination of information to science writers, researchers and educators, criminologists, jurists, as well as medical people, to help correct public misunderstanding.

A large order? Yes—but this is just a part of what we are trying to do. The few Gender Identity Clinics now in existence in leading hospital medical schools (less than half a dozen) are prevented by lack of funds, staff and public cooperation from doing more than token research and, where psychiatrically approved, sex reassignment surgery. Psychotherapeutic help is sometimes needed by the transsexual patient in making an adjustment after undergoing surgery. This is currently being provided at The Johns Hopkins Hospital, on a limited basis only because of lack of funds.

Family members of transsexuals must be taught to understand the condition and the great need for acceptance and love.

Leaders in the legislative, law enforcement and judicial fields should be impressed with the need to revise attitudes and actions in the protection of the civil rights of transsexuals. Furthermore, state agencies and the public in general may someday realize that conversion operations may convert persons with potential social problems into contributing members of our society.

All this, and more.

DOCUMENT 42
"Hymnal Makes Bow"
The New York Hymnal, Feb. 1968, 1–2

The February 1968 issue of *The New York Hymnal* marks the beginning of a new publishing venture directed towards the homosexual community. *New York Hymnal* is published by the Oscar Wilde Memorial Bookshop. . . .

Why was the name *Hymnal* chosen? Because *Hymnal* will have a "religious" fervor and crusading spirit in its treatment of the homosexual way of life and the homophile movement. We will make no pretense of speaking to the heterosexual in trying to persuade him to "accept" homosexuals. *Hymnal* is solely concerned with what the gay person thinks of himself. The community has the economic, political, and social potential to shape its own future. This potential only needs to be encouraged and channeled.

In a sense, *Hymnal* is bringing Gay Power to New York. On the West Coast, Gay Power has been used in various ways—supporting candidates for political office, economic boycott of firms that discriminate against the homosexual and the publicizing of abuses committed against the Community by organized crime, the police (on occasion) and other governmental and private institutions. . . .[18]

ACTIVIST AGENDAS
AND VISIONS
BEFORE STONEWALL

DOCUMENT 43

"Happiness Is a Button"
The Insider: Newsletter of the Mattachine Society of Washington, Feb. 1969, 1

MSW will join the button game soon when it receives one hundred "Gay is Good" buttons and bumper stickers from California. The North American Conference of Homophile Organizations adopted the slogan "Gay is Good" last summer at its fourth annual national conference in Chicago. The success of the "Black is Beautiful" campaign of the black movement obviously influenced its thinking.

The adoption by MSW of the slogan gives support to the so-called "gay power" approach to reform. This attitude steers several homophile organizations, among them most notably Homophile Youth Movement (HYMN) in New York under the leadership of Craig Rodwell. Mr. Rodwell cites the proposed directory compiled by New York homophile organizations of businesses as a significant step to unify the homosexual buying power.

Not all are so confident in the gay power approach as HYMN. Members of MSW have accused the slogan as [*sic*] being too weak and compromising. Others prefer "Gay is Great" to make a much stronger statement in extolling the virtues of the homosexual way of life in the face of the overwhelming attitudes to the contrary. Frank Kameny however defends the "Gay is Good" slogan as being a positive statement connoting confidence in homosexuality as an orientation on par with heterosexuality rather than implying superiority of homosexuality. . . .

DOCUMENT 44

Leo E. Laurence, "Gay Revolution"
Vector, Apr. 1969, 11, 25[19]

Homosexual organizations on the west coast are doing very little to spark the Homosexual Revolution of '69. Timid leaders with enormous ego-trips, middle class bigotry and racism, and too many middle-aged up-tight conservatives are hurting almost every major homosexual organization on the West Coast and probably throughout the nation. . . .

Only about one per cent of the homosexual leaders I've interviewed are willing to publicly say: "I'm gay and I'm proud!" About the only people with that kind of courage are the new breed of young gay kids. And that's just why organizations like SIR [Society for Individual Rights] keep them out. The old-timers are scared that these kids will come in and really create a gay revolution. . . .

Racism is as big in gay organizations as it is in our middle class straight world. Gay businesses in the Bay Area forming a group called the Tavern Guild refused to join Citizen's Alert last month, a group trying to put an end to police harassment and brutality.

"I don't like Citizen's Alert 'cause that Rev. Cecil Williams is involved. He goes too far on civil rights," said one vocal up-tight racist member. Cecil is a black militant minister. . . .

I discovered the same middle class uptightness in the gay organizations of southern California. Last month, a well proportioned, handsome Go-Go Boy was dancing at the ANUBIS headquarters far out in an isolated canyon near Los Angeles.

An ANUBIS Director stopped the performance when the fellow stripped to the waist to reveal a magnificent, muscled chest. "We can't have such things happening here," the ANUBIS official scolded. . . .

President Larry Littlejohn of SIR recently told me: "1969 is our year, it's a time to move, to be militant, to demand our rights." Unfortunately, most of his officers are not supporting such militancy. . . .

Individual homosexuals must open up and honestly accept their own homosexuality. Say you're gay at work, at home, church, wherever you go.

Come out from behind a double-life of straight at work and home, but gay at night. I'll admit it's not easy to be honest, but neither was writing this article. . . .

DOCUMENT 45
Leo E. Laurence, "Gay Power's Invincible Rise"
Berkeley Barb, 20 June 1969, 11[20]

Revolutionary forces in this country seem to be ignoring a vast source of power in this country, a power that could literally stop the industrial-military complex that is controlling the politics and ruling the people of this nation.

The power I mean is the power of homosexuals, the largest minority in the United States.

Homosexuals have the potential numbers to prove that all power is with the people. We exist in ALL segments of society and on ALL socio-economic levels. We are in the hip community, the underground, and in the Establishment.

For example:

If only ten per cent of the homosexuals employed in Bay Area businesses were attracted into the revolution, the "movement" could literally stop all big business at will.

The military machine that's running the Viet Nam war wouldn't run if only ten per cent of the homosexuals in the military simply admitted being gay and demanded discharges. . . .

Homosexuals hold a tremendous source of potential political power, heretofore either ignored or feared by the leaders of today's revolution. . . .

The revolution today is for world liberation. It is a struggle to liberate the oppressed peoples who are victims of our bigoted Establishment—the blacks, hippies, students, and the kids who enjoyed playing in the People's Park.

This is the "revolution" that we all know so well, the revolution of the streets, the revolution of politics, the war, the draft, Big Business, unions, and the campus.

That is the revolution of the Black Panthers, Resistance, the SDS, the YSA, the BSU, the Hippies, and Yippies.

These people are fighting for freedom, and I feel many of their leaders are today's super-patriots. They are the Patrick Henry's of the Second American Revolution. . . .

But why is all that manly courage missing on the homosexual freedom front? When Big Business kicked out a brother because he had the guts to say he was gay, where were all the so-called brave revolutionaries?

Were they able to face the troops in Berkeley, but unable to help homosexuals fight for freedom?

In over two years of writing and fighting for the revolution, I have unfortunately discovered in the underground discrimination against gays worse than once faced the blacks in society.

Bigotry is not exclusive with the Establishment. It has permeated the revolution as well, and is aimed at the homosexual.

Anti-homosexual prejudice is tougher than anti-black bigotry. White people can point to a black man, yet know full well that his whiteness makes him different and separate from the black man.

With a homosexual it's different. The revolutionary cannot ignore homosexual feelings since medical science has proven that there's a little homosexuality in everybody.

Those revolutionaries who feel most unsure of their own sexuality may be the first and loudest to prove their discrimination by ignoring or attacking our homosexual revolution.

They try to say the gay "thing" isn't part of the "real" revolution, just as they once said of the hippy movement, now an integral part of our revolutionary forces.

The world revolution today is also for the liberation of ourselves, freedom from up-tightness, and freedom to love—including homosexual love.

We must eliminate all vestiges of prejudice and discrimination. It must be eliminated from our revolutionary forces as well as from the Establishment.

It is otherwise not justice for all. It is not freedom for all. It is not love for all.

3
POLITICAL PROTESTS BEFORE STONEWALL

IN THE 1950S AND EARLY 1960S, LGBT activists engaged in educational activities, facilitated scholarly research, participated in electoral politics, lobbied public officials, supported court-based litigation, promoted positive media coverage, and worked with legal, religious, and scientific experts. They occasionally engaged in direct action protests, but in 1965, influenced by African American activism, this became a more central movement strategy. Historians have documented more than thirty LGBT political demonstrations before the Stonewall Riots.

LGBT demonstrations criticized multiple institutions, policies, and practices in the years leading up to Stonewall—common targets included government buildings, national monuments, police stations, religious sites, local businesses, media offices, scientific gatherings, and educational institutions. The words and tactics used by LGBT demonstrators reveal a great deal about their influences and inspirations while also highlighting their politics and priorities.

The twenty-two documents in this chapter are presented in chronological order.

DOCUMENTS 46–51 address 1965 demonstrations at the White House, Pentagon, and Civil Service Commission in Washington, D.C.; the United Nations in New York City; Dewey's restaurant and Independence Hall in Philadelphia; and Grace Cathedral in San Francisco.

DOCUMENTS 52–58 focus on 1966 protests at Compton's Cafeteria and other locations in the Tenderloin in San Francisco, Julius bar in New York City, Independence Hall in Philadelphia, a variety of locations on Armed Forces Day, and the *Sun-Times* and *Daily News* in Chicago.

DOCUMENTS 59–60 highlight 1967 demonstrations at the Black Cat bar and Redd Foxx Club in Los Angeles.

DOCUMENTS 61–64 cover 1968 protests at Columbia University in New York and the American Medical Association convention and Federal Building in San Francisco.

DOCUMENTS 65–67 address pre-Stonewall 1969 demonstrations at States Steamship Company and Tower Records in San Francisco and a funeral motorcade that traveled from Glide Memorial Church in San Francisco to the Berkeley Hall of Justice.

DOCUMENT 46

"Cross-Currents"
The Ladder, May 1965, 22

The mid-April news report that Fidel Castro's government is going to crack down on Cuban homosexuals and send them to work camps touched off picketing by homophile organizations at the White House in Washington and the United Nations in New York.

Mattachine Society of New York wanted to stage a protest at the Cuban mission to the United Nations, but police rules do not permit picketing closer than one-fifth of a mile, so arrangements were made to demonstrate at Hammarskjold Plaza at the U.N. itself. There, 29 persons picketed on Sunday, April 18. The protest was covered by a New York Times reporter.

The White House had been picketed before on behalf of homosexuals, by the same one person on two occasions about a year apart. But the official demonstration by Mattachine Society of Washington on Saturday, April 17, marked the first time for mass picketing at the White House by a homophile organization.

Since the U.S. does not have diplomatic relations with Cuba and there is no Cuban embassy in Washington, MSW decided to combine protests, in effect, and to picket at the White House in regard both to Cuba's campaign against homosexuals and to American homosexuals' grievances against their own government.

The MSW picketers, 7 men and 3 women, were given a choice spot directly in front of the White House for their hour-long demonstration late in the afternoon. Both city and White House police reportedly were courteous and helpful. Newspapers had been notified in advance. A WTOP-TV cameraman was on hand. The picketers' signs read as follows:

U.S. Claims No Second-Class Citizens. What About Homosexual Citizens?

Cuba's Government Persecutes Homosexuals. U.S. Government Beat Them
    To It.

We Want: Federal Employment—Honorable Discharges—Security
    Clearances.

Gov. Wallace Met with Negroes. Our Gov't Won't Meet with Us.

U.S., Cuba, Russia United in Persecuting Homosexuals.

Employment for Homosexuals SI! Labor Camps NO!

Jews to Concentration Camps under Nazis; Homosexuals to Work Camps
    under Castro. Is the U.S. Much Better?

Members of the Mattachine Society of Washington Protest Cuba's Crack-
    down on Homosexuals.[1]

DOCUMENT 47

Mattachine Society of Washington, D.C., Committee on Picketing and Lawful Demonstrations, Rules for Picketing

ca. May 1965, Mattachine Society of New York Records, Box 3, Folder 21, New York Public Library

. . . The following rules must be observed by those picketing under the banner of ECHO [East Coast Homophile Organizations]:

A. Dress and appearance will be conservative and conventional.
   1. Men will wear suits, white shirts and ties; women will wear dresses.
   2. When outer clothing is required, overcoats, topcoats, and raincoats must be worn, not jackets or other casual, less formal outerwear.
   3. Picketers will be well-groomed; the wearing of beards will be discouraged unless the beards are well-trimmed.
B. Signs.
   1. Legends on all signs must be approved in advance.
   2. Signs must be neatly and clearly lettered.
   3. Marchers must carry signs assigned to them.
C. Marching.
   1. The order of the marchers and the signs will be established by those in charge of the demonstration.
   2. All inquiries will be referred to a previously designated spokesman or spokesmen.
   3. There will be no exchanges of remarks between picketers and passersby. Conversation among picketers should be kept to a minimum.

DOCUMENT 48

"News: Philadelphia"

Drum, Aug. 1965, 5–6

A three hour sit-in climaxed a five day protest demonstration against Dewey's, an all-night restaurant.

According to Janus Society of America President, Clark P. Polak, the action was a result of Dewey's refusal to serve a large number of homosexuals and persons wearing non-conformist clothing.

"The problem began," Polak stated, "when a small group of rowdy teenagers began using the restaurant for a meeting and camping home. The management then instructed their employees to exclude these individuals from the premises by refusing to serve them when they came in. We saw no objection in this; however, the lower level employees became somewhat over-zealous and began excluding large numbers of persons on grounds other than improper behavior.

"On Sunday, April 25, after over 150 persons were denied service, three teenagers, one girl and two boys, refused to leave.

"The police were called and the three were arrested. We had been keeping our eye on the place all weekend and I was checking shortly after the trio was taken into custody. I walked to the patrol car in which they were seated and informed them that JSA could get them a lawyer if they desired.

"An officer came to the car and asked me what I was doing. I told him. Then, I was arrested on disorderly conduct charges."

Not surprisingly, all four persons were found guilty. . . .

"A specially written letter was printed and distributed to every person as they entered the restaurant. On Sunday, May 2, the inevitable happened and three more persons were again denied service. They refused to move, but this time when the police were called, no arrests were made."

Robert L. Sitko, coordinator of the project, said: "Before the police went into Dewey's, they asked me for a copy of our handout. One policeman read it and then went over to his partner in the car, explained it to him line by line and then decided that they had better call the sergeant. The sergeant arrived and he decided he had better call the lieutenant.

"A few minutes later, the sergeant went into Dewey's and almost in an apologetic way asked Clark if he could speak to him for a moment."

"It was a far cry from the previous Sunday," Polak picked up the story, "and I was quite politely told that we could stay in there as long as we wanted as the police had no authority to ask us to leave."

Later, the JSA Executive Board issued this statement: "It is unfortunate that the problem developed in the first place and we are appreciative of both the police's and Dewey's cooperation, but our action was successful in preventing both further arrests and capricious denials of service.

"Furthermore, to our knowledge, this was the first sit-in of its kind in the history of the United States."

DOCUMENT 49
Janus Society Newsletter
May 1965, 1–2

The objectives of the Dewey's affair were (1) to bring about an immediate cessation to all indiscriminate denials of service, (2) to prevent additional arrests, (3) to assure the homosexual community that (a) we were concerned with the day-to-day problems and (b) we were prepared to intercede in helping to solve these problems, (4) to create publicity for the organization and our objectives.

We were completely successful in all of these areas. . . .

All too often, there is a tendency to be concerned with the rights of homosexuals as long as they somehow appear to be heterosexual, whatever that is. The masculine woman and feminine man often are looked down upon by the official policy of homophile organizations, but the Janus Society is concerned with the worth of an individual and the manner in which she or he comports himself. What is offensive today we have seen become the style of tomorrow, and even if what is offensive today remains offensive tomorrow to some persons, there is no reason to penalize such non-conformist behavior unless there is direct anti-social behavior connected with it.

We in no way supported those few individuals who were loud and in other ways unreasonable in their conduct.

All in all, about 1500 pieces of literature were distributed. A local T.V. channel carried our action on Friday night. All reports heard via scuttlebutt feedback from the community at large to Janus members and friends has [sic] been most favorable, and the office has received more calls and inquiries through this activity than through any other source aside from possibly the lecture series.

There is no reason to assume that this cannot be called a job well done.

DOCUMENT 50
Franklin E. Kameny, "Homosexuals Picket in Washington and Philadelphia"
Eastern Mattachine Magazine, Sept. 1965, 19–21[2]

In recent weeks, there were three picketing demonstrations by homosexuals: one in late June, and one each in early and in late July.

U.S. Civil Service Commission building, Washington, on Saturday, June 26, from 2 PM to 4 PM.

On the picket line were 23 marchers (17 men; 6 women), including one clergyman wearing his collar. Two more participants (one man; one woman) distributed a specially written leaflet to passersby.

The demonstration had two purposes: (A) To protest the continuing refusal of the U.S. Civil Service Commission to hire homosexual American citizens for Federal employment. . . . (B) The refusal of the Civil Service Commission to meet with spokesmen for the homosexual community. . . .

Demonstrators were on hand from New York and Philadelphia, and elsewhere, as well as from Washington. All demonstrators were well-dressed—men in suits, white shirts, ties; women in dresses. The demonstration was orderly and dignified. The police had been notified in advance and were on hand to offer protection, if needed. . . .

Independence Hall, Philadelphia, on Sunday, July 4, from 2 PM to 4 PM.

Marching in this demonstration, held at the site of and on the anniversary of the signing of the Declaration of Independence, were 39 picketers (32 men; 7 women). Five more (1 man; 4 women) distributed leaflets. Marchers were present from Washington, Philadelphia, New York, Chicago, and elsewhere.

The theme of the demonstration centered around the denial to the homosexual American citizen of benefits inherent to all citizens in the philosophy of the Declaration of Independence. . . .

As in previous instances the marchers were neatly and conservatively dressed; the demonstration was orderly and dignified. The Philadelphia Police Department was notified in advance. . . .

The Pentagon (Departments of Defense, Army, Navy, Air Force), near Washington on Saturday, July 31, from 2 PM to 4 PM.

Present for this demonstration were 16 picketers (12 men; 4 women). Those marching included veterans of various branches of the service, both men and women (some with front line combat experience) with both honorable discharges as well as discharges which were less-than-fully honorable because of homosexuality. One marcher had stapled to his sign his honorable discharge from the Air Force, a certificate of distinguished service, and his MP brassard.

The purpose of the demonstration was to protest (1) issuance of less-than-fully honorable discharges to homosexuals in the Armed Forces. . . . ; (2) the disqualification of homosexuals from military service . . . ; (3) offensively-worded military regulations on homosexuals and homosexuality . . . ; (4) the continuing refusal by the Departments of Defense, Army, Navy, and Air Force to meet with spokesmen for the homosexual community. . . .[3]

DOCUMENT 51
"A Brief of Injustices"
The Ladder, Nov. 1965, 4–7

Release of a hard-hitting *Brief of Injustices*—"an indictment of our society in its treatment of the homosexual"—put San Francisco's Council on Religion and the Homosexual in the news in late September. The CRH is a group of clergymen and laymen which aims to promote a continuing dialogue between the church and homosexuals. . . .

The encouragement felt by the homosexual community as a result of wide publicity given the *Brief* changed abruptly to shock and indignation when word came that the Rev. Canon Robert W. Cromey, one of the prominent signers of the *Brief*, had just had his duties in the Episcopal Church sharply curtailed.

Canon Cromey, a Trustee of the CRH and an outspoken supporter of the homophile movement in San Francisco, held an important position as diocesan director of urban affairs. His post, according to a spokesman for the diocesan council, had not been eliminated but was dropped to sixth place in priority in the budgeting and made subject to further review in mid-December.

Supporters of Canon Cromey felt that the diocesan council's cutback of his job was tantamount to getting rid of him. Thirty picketers, including leaders of San Francisco homophile organizations, turned up at Grace Cathedral, the masterpiece of the Episcopal Diocese of California, as worshippers arrived for services on Sunday morning September 26. Signs carried by the demonstrators protested the "removal of Bob Cromey."

Stories on the council's decision and the picketing appeared in the Chronicle and the Examiner on Sept. 27. The Chronicle reported that Rev. Cromey indicated "some Episcopal leaders...felt his ardent championing of homosexual equality was 'going against the teachings of God.'" The Examiner quoted the canon as saying that the diocesan council's action "was not 'primarily to move me out, but I feel they did have a sense of relief when they once saw a gentlemanly way to get rid of me.'" He added that he would continue to work for social justice as an individual. Commenting on the picketing, he said, "'I appreciated this show of concern and support for me personally.'" . . .

While the demonstration was taking place at Grace Cathedral, an audience in New York, attending the annual conference of East Coast Homophile Organizations, heard the news from Bill Beardemphl, president of a San Francisco homophile group known as SIR (Society for Individual Rights). When he announced he had learned by phone that homosexuals in San Francisco were "picketing at this very minute" to protest apparent discrimination against Canon Cromey, there was resounding applause from those members and friends of eastern homophile groups who favor picketing as a strategy to call attention to injustices. . . .[4]

DOCUMENT 52

"Young Homos Picket Compton's Restaurant"
Cruise News & World Report, Aug. 1966, 1 and foldback

Vanguard, the organization whose membership is drawn from "kids on the street," tested out its muscle on one of the worst offenders against human dignity in the Tenderloin Area of San Francisco.

Compton's at Turk and Taylor has long treated the younger residents of that area as if they were not at all human.

On various occasions, according to spokesmen of Vanguard, the Rent-A-Cop (Pinkerton Men) have manhandled innocent customers because they did not drink their coffee fast enough to suit the Rent-A-Cop.

On the 18th of July Vanguard had about 25 persons carrying picket signs from 10 pm 'til 12 pm. The action was televised by ABC and a fair presentation of the cause of Vanguard was telecast.

Specifically Vanguard was protesting:

"We of the Tenderloin are picketing and boycotting this Gene Compton Restaurant for the following reasons:

1. We of the Tenderloin are continuously subjected to physical and verbal abuse by both the management and the Pinkerton Special Officers assigned there.
2. We feel that the 25¢ "Service" charge was put into effect to keep out those of us who have little or no money.

Therefore:

Until the management of this restaurant changes its policies of harassment and discrimination of the homosexuals, hustlers, etc., of the Tenderloin Area, we will boycott and picket this restaurant. We would appreciate your cooperation in this much needed action."

During the picketing a uniformed officer was present at all times and the picketers were well-behaved. No untoward incident occurred during the picketing and Compton's did very little business.

DOCUMENT 53

The Christopher Street West–SF Parade Committee 1972, "History of Christopher Street West–S.F."

Gay Pride–San Francisco, 25 Jun. 1972, 8–9[5]

In the streets of the Tenderloin, at Turk and Taylor on a hot August night in 1966, Gays rose up angry at the constant police harassment of the drag-queens by the police. It had to be the first ever recorded violence by Gays against police anywhere. For on that evening, when the SFPD [San Francisco Police Department] paddy wagon drove up to make their "usual" sweeps of the streets, Gays this time did not go willingly. It began when the police came into a cafeteria, still located there at Turk and Taylor, Compton's, to do their usual job of hassling the drag-queens and hair-fairies and hustlers sitting at the tables. This was with permission of the management of course. But when the police grabbed the arm of one of the transvestites, he threw his cup of coffee in the cop's face, and with that, cups, saucers and trays began flying around the place and all directed at the police. They retreated outside until reinforcements arrived, and the Compton's management ordered the place closed, and with that, the Gays began breaking out every window in the place, and as they ran outside to escape the breaking glass, the police tried to grab them and throw them into the paddy wagon, but they found this no easy task for Gays began hitting them "below the belt" and drag-queens smashing them in the face with their extremely heavy purses. A police car had every window broken, a newspaper shack outside the cafeteria was burned to the ground and general havoc raised that night in the Tenderloin. The next night drag-queens, hair-fairies, conservative Gays, and hustlers joined in a picket of the cafeteria, which would not allow the drags back in again. It ended with the newly installed glass windows once more being smashed. The Police Community Relations Unit began mediating the conflict, which was never fully resolved. . . .

DOCUMENT 54

Lucy Komisar, "Three Homosexuals in Search of a Drink"
Village Voice, 5 May 1966, 15[6]

It was a Greek scene in more ways than one. Three heroes in search of justice trudged from place to place. On the other hand, it was a highly contemporary maneuver. It was a challenge to one of the remaining citadels of bias, and a citadel of bias backed up by law, at that.

The actors in the odyssey were three homosexuals, with four reporters and a photographer as supporting players. The three men were determined to force the State Liquor Authority to clarify its regulations concerning the serving of homosexuals in places of public accommodation. Many bars that have served homosexuals have been temporarily closed by the authorities, and some have even lost their licenses.

The place of rendezvous on the day of challenge—April 21—was the Ukrainian-American Village Bar on St. Mark's Place. . . . A hand-lettered sign atop the bar carried the offending rhyme: "If you are gay, please stay away." . . .

The three central characters appeared on schedule. One was Kentucky-born Dick Leitsch, 21, president of the [New York Mattachine] society, who explained that Mattachine referred to the masked Italian court jester[s] of the 16th century who were the only people allowed to speak the truth to the king. He was conservatively dressed in a well cut gray suit with narrow blue stripes and a light blue shirt. With a black attache case in hand, he was the picture of a Madison Avenue executive.

The second man was John Timmons, a 21-year-old coding clerk from Florida, who is a member of the organization's public affairs committee. His vivid red hair and small beard were set off by a bright yellow and baby-blue striped tie.

The chairman of Mattachine's young adult group, the third man, Craig Rodwell, 25, comes from Illinois. A sober, serious young man, Rodwell is a clerical worker.

The Ukrainian American Bar presented a difficulty. It was closed. Across the street, the Dom, which also posts a sign expressing its inhospitality to homosexuals, was also closed. There was one dependable alternative, Howard Johnson's, so everyone bundled into vehicles and made for Sixth Avenue and 8th Street. . . .

Inside, the trio slipped into a corner booth. . . . The young men asked for the manager, and when he appeared delivered this statement: "We, the undersigned, are homosexuals. We believe that a place of public accommodation has an obligation to serve an orderly person, and that we are entitled to service as long as we are orderly. We therefore ask to be served on your premises. Should you refuse to serve us, we will be obligated to file a complaint against you with the State Liquor Authority."

Emil Varela, the relief manager, looked around at all of us as we patiently waited for him to play the part to which he had been assigned. . . .

"How do I know you are homosexuals?" he suddenly asked. Then he bent over and shook with laughter. "Why shouldn't they be served a drink?" he asked the abashed reporters. "They look like perfect gentlemen to me," he chortled. "I drink. Who knows if I'm a homosexual or not? I've got problems," he said grinning.

Varela, who owned up to having two children and three grandchildren, declared, "It's pretty ridiculous that anybody should determine what anybody's sex life is. I think there's plenty of lawmakers whose sex life I could challenge— and they drink too." He laughed. . . .

Challenging the State Liquor Authority was proving to be a tiring and fruitless business.

Things did not improve at the Waikiki, a Polynesian-type bar on Sixth Avenue between 9th and 10th Streets. . . . The three men were served. . . .

Still frustrated by hospitality, we then took off for Julius's on West 10th Street, long famed for the solidified dust that hangs from the ceiling. . . .

"We are homosexuals and we would like a drink," said Leitsch.

"I don't know what you're trying to prove," the bartender replied. . . .

"You can't serve us if we are homosexuals?" Leitsch asked.

"No," the man replied.

There were homosexuals drinking at the bar, and Timmons said he had been served there on about four other occasions. But, he grinned with relief, "another bourbon and water and I would have been under the table."

Everyone was relieved. The case had been made. . . .

The Mattachine Society has announced that it will file a complaint with the State Liquor Authority against Julius's contending they were unfairly discriminated against. However, they state that they bear no ill-will against the bar or management. On the contrary, Mattachine will offer to pay the bar's legal expenses.

DOCUMENT 55
Don Slater, "Protest on Wheels"
Tangents, May 1966, 4–8[7]

"Oi veh!" burst forth a tiny woman, clutching herself in disbelief at the corner of Wilshire Blvd. and Fairfax Ave., "This we don't need. My son is already a homosexual." Angel-town pedestrians and motorists, who, up to that moment were convinced they had "seen everything," were witnessing their first gay motorcade. Sponsored by the Los Angeles Committee to Fight Exclusion of Homosexuals from the Armed Forces, the caravan of cars had just swung into the heart of Los Angeles' Jewish community. . . .

The basis for the protest was simply that the exclusion of homosexual men and women from military service because of their homosexuality and for no other reason was unfair. . . .

Saturday morning began with a slight drizzle. The motorcade was scheduled to start at 2 o'clock. Everyone had agreed to meet at *Tangents'* office at 12:30. The four-sided signs had to be attached to . . . 13 cars. The number was considered lucky.

Before amazed neighbors and passing motorists, the placards were boldly attached, and with riders visibly tense, the cars pulled into formation. . . . In front of Central Market, Mexican women struggling with bulging shopping bags and wayward youngsters barely noticed or understood the signs on the passing cars: "10% of all G.I.'s are homosexual," "Get Sex Questions out of Draft Exams," "Sex Belongs to Private Conscience," "Homosexuals are the most moral men in the service," "Write L.B.J. today." . . .

The Washington Committee, sponsored by the Mattachine Society of Washington, D.C., successfully picketed the White House, and then, led by Dr. Franklin Kameny, past-president of the society, about 20 participants marched 4 miles from the White House to the Pentagon. . . . In Philadelphia, a protest meeting was held by the Greater Delaware Valley Committee to Fight Exclusion of Homosexuals from the Armed Forces, sponsored by the Janus Society. Although poorly attended, Committee members had better success in handing out 10,000 protest leaflets to the general public at the Philadelphia Navy Yard. . . . In San Francisco, a demonstration at the Federal Building Plaza was sponsored by the homophile organizations in the Bay Area. Participating in the demonstration were the Council on Religion and the Homosexual, Society for Individual Rights, Daughters of Bilitis, Mattachine Society, Citizens News, and The Tavern Guild of San Francisco. Some 20,000 leaflets were printed. . . . An estimated 40 to 50 persons paraded with signs. . . . The Phoenix Society of Kansas City—the youngest of the homophile groups—confined its activities to an organizational type of meeting in which invited friends and members discussed the issues.

DOCUMENT 56
"Sweep-In"
Vanguard, Oct. 1966, 4–5

FROM THE PRESS RELEASE: Tonight a "clean sweep" will be made on Market St.; not by the police, but by the street people who are often the object of police harassment. The drug addicts, pillheads, teenage hustlers, lesbians, and homosexuals who make San Francisco's "meat rack" their home are tired of living in the midst of the filth thrown out onto the sidewalks and into the streets by nearby businessmen. . . .

This Vanguard demonstration indicates the willingness of society's outcasts to work openly for an improvement in their own socio-economic power. We have heard too much about "white power" and "black power" so get ready to hear about "street power."

FROM THE "AP" AND "UPI" WIRE SERVICES AND K G O RADIO:

"AP": A group of teenagers and young adults from S.F.'s Tenderloin district became street sweepers for a while last night in an effort to show "that we have a sense of responsibility." J-P Marat, president of Vanguard, the sponsoring organization, said between 40 and 50 youths swept Market St. between Powell and Turk Streets shortly before 10 P.M. Said Marat: "We're considered trash by much of society, and we wanted to show the rest of society that we want to work and can work."

"UPI": Some 40 members of a group called Vanguard Incorporated...composed of so-called people of the streets...swept one of S.F.'s busiest street blocks last night. They borrowed 30 big brooms from the city and swept Market St. between Mason and Powell. A spokesman for the group says they were tired of the way the street looks.

K G O RADIO: Some 40 Tenderloin youths from a group called Vanguard swept Market St. from Powell to Turk last night using equipment donated by the city. . . .

DOCUMENT 57
Denny, "Homophile Freedom Song"
Homosexual Citizen, Sept. 1966, 14–15[8]

The following song was composed for the Second Annual Reminder Picket held in front of Independence Hall, July 4th.

> Mine eyes have seen the struggles of the Negroes and the Jews,
> I have seen the counties trampled where the laws of men abuse,
> But you crush the homosexual with anything you choose,
> Now we are marching on.
>
> CHORUS:
> Glory, glory, hallelujah,
> Glory, glory, hallelujah,
> Glory, glory, hallelujah,
> Now we are marching on.
>
> Your masquerading morals squad has twisted all we've said,
> You've put peepholes in our bathrooms, and made laws to rule our bed,
> We ask you to treat us fairly but you always turn your head,
> Now we are marching on. (Chorus)

In your so-called "Great Society" you've given us no place,
We bring to you our problems, and you stand and slap our face,
How can you boast of freedom and ignore this great disgrace,
Now we are marching on. (Chorus)

Now we've asked, and begged, and pleaded for the right to have a
    life,
Free to choose the one we love, and free from man-made strife,
But you turn around and stab us with your legislative knife,
Now we are marching on. (Chorus)
We've been drowned out by injustice till our whispers can't be heard,
You have shattered all our dreams and hopes and yet we never
    stirred,
But we're rising in a chorus and you'll soon hear every word,
Now we are marching on. (Chorus)

The civil rights you took for us we want them back again.
We will talk and write and picket, until we see you bend,
If you do not give them freely, we will take them in the end,
Now we are marching on. (Chorus)

Tune: "The Battle Hymn of the Republic"[9]

DOCUMENT 58

Mattachine Midwest, "Why Are Homosexuals Demonstrating?"
1 Oct. 1966, Craig Rodwell Papers, Box 2, New York Public Library

Homosexuals and others are demonstrating to call attention to the unjust situation brought about by a society that reacts fearfully and illogically to the
millions of homosexuals it has helped to create.

The vast majority of homosexuals lead perfectly ordinary, stable lives in
socially responsible jobs. They are found in all occupations, from laborer to
executive, and are nearly always unknown to their associates as homosexuals.
One of our concerns is what happens to them if they do become known. . . .

WHY ON OCTOBER 1? October 1, 1966 is a day of nationwide efforts
sponsored by 22 organizations across the country which are active in the
Homophile Movement—the movement to improve the status of the homosexual citizen. Some of the goals of this effort are:

- An end to police entrapment, harassment and intimidation of law-abiding
  homosexual citizens in Chicago and elsewhere.
- An end to discrimination in the field of employment, both public and
  private.
- The beginning of a meaningful and productive dialog between homosexuals
  and heterosexuals, particularly in the areas of religion, law and medicine.

- An education program directed towards the homosexual so that he or she can regain his self-respect in a seemingly hostile and unconcerned society.
- The repeal of laws governing sexual activity between consenting adults in private. (Illinois is the only state so far to repeal such laws.)

WHY AT THE SUN-TIMES & DAILY NEWS? The Chicago Daily News and Sun-Times provided a good example of the misunderstandings society has about homosexuals. Mattachine Midwest submitted an ad to them for publication today. The ad would have drawn attention to October 1. The newspapers refused the ad, stating that while homosexuality might be fit for news coverage, it was not fit for their advertising pages. We feel the papers missed the point: We did not wish to advertise in favor of homosexuality; we merely wanted to illuminate the problems homosexuals face. This is a legitimate social issue, but out of squeamishness as well as ignorance of advertising practices in other parts of the country, the Sun-Times and Daily News rejected our ad. We therefore take this limited means of publicizing that fact. . . .[10]

POLITICAL PROTESTS
BEFORE STONEWALL

DOCUMENT 59
Jim Highland, "Raid!"
Tangents, Jan. 1967, 4–7[11]

Perhaps a dozen of Los Angeles' 80-plus homosexual bars line the mile of Sunset Boulevard between Sanborn Junction and Silverlake. Most are beer bars, with pool tables, juke-boxes, coin-operated game machines. The buildings housing the bars are shabby, the rents cheap, and business failures are common.

But when one bar closes another soon opens. The New Faces had survived for five years, the Black Cat for two months, on New Year's eve, 1966. For that night, New Faces promised a costume contest, the Black Cat live entertainment by a trio of Negro girls, the Rhythm Queens.

The contest brought 15 or 20 men in elaborate female dress, wigs, makeup. By 10 o'clock, New Faces was packed. . . . But once the winner was chosen at 11:30, the crowd thinned. Most of it moved 98 feet up the street to the Black Cat.

The bar looked festive. . . . There were also police officers. Eight of them. Informally dressed. One in a bright red sweater. They drank beer at the bar. They played pool. They might have been anybody. Anonymity is a game people play in such a place. . . .

The crowd grew. After 11:30 many of the newcomers were in drag. No, impersonating a woman is no longer illegal in Los Angeles. But it is far from safe and cross-dressers know it. . . .

Midnight came. . . .

An officer who had been standing next to the Black Cat's short-order cook suddenly grabbed the cook's arm and tried to lead him out the back door. It was locked. He turned and steered the cook through the crowd toward the front. Alarmed, a man in woman's clothes clutched for the front door. The butt-end of a pool cue felled him, one ear split and bleeding.

A bartender was seized by the shoulders, dragged bodily across the bar amid splintering glass and hustled outside where uniformed police waited. A second bartender tried to run, was caught and yanked across the bar, toppling a patron who fell with him to the floor. Coming to their aid, another employee was clubbed from behind and kneed as he fell. Not gently. His bowels emptied.

Towards the rear of the room a patron was flung head-first against the juke-box. It was a heavy machine but the impact jarred it away from the wall. Stunned, handcuffed behind his back, the man was removed. To a patrol car in the parking lot. So was the third bartender. A married man with a small business of his own, moonlighting this job for a few extra dollars, he went quietly.

Maybe not so quietly, but others went too. A dozen of them. For the most part they were the transvestites. The police were trying to build a case. If drag is no longer illegal, juries tend to think it should be. To the public mind it suggests degeneracy. . . .

The raid was over. It had taken ten minutes.

Just before it began, two youths had left. To return to the New Faces. Lucky? Not very. Two vice officers followed. The boys didn't make their planned entrance. Hit from the rear by flying tackles, they sprawled inside. Shocked, the woman who owned the bar came forward. So did the bartender. He asked the plainclothes men for their identification.

A fist in the face broke his nose.

One officer brandished a revolver. "This is all the identification I need." Somehow the gun or the hand that held it struck the bar owner. She fell heavily. A waiter at the back of the room saw the trouble and ran forward to help his employer. A small man, five-feet-six, 150 pounds, he didn't get to help.

More officers had arrived. They dragged him out onto the sidewalk and beat him. Savagely. So savagely that after being booked on a felony charge of assaulting a police officer, he was taken from the Police Building to Los Angeles County General Hospital where he underwent surgery to remove a ruptured spleen.

It was seven days before he could leave the hospital, three weeks before he could return to work, six months before a court acquitted him. . . .

Arrested with the New Faces waiter was the one boy in drag who had been followed from the Black Cat. Arrested at the Black Cat were 14 others. Two were booked as common drunks. The rest were booked for lewd conduct. All were free on bail by one o'clock Sunday afternoon, January 1, 1967. The few who couldn't manage rides trudged home in their bedraggled finery, high heels tucked under their arms.

Together, during the following week, those arrested talked to attorneys. Most of those who ordinarily accept homosexual cases advised copouts. "Pay the fines and forget about it." This is bad and expensive advice. Those arrested turned to the Tavern Guild, a mutual assistance league of bar owners, and to local homosexual organizations for help.

Large jars bearing the sign TAVERN GUILD LEGAL AID FUND appeared in most of the so-called gay bars. The woman owner of a Glendale beer bar energetically organized the drive. Contributions totaled $2515. San Francisco's Tavern Guild added $300. An anonymous individual lent $585 to make up the needed total of $3400 to cover costs. It was a fine show of concerned solidarity. . . .

Not all the defendants went to trial represented by the Tavern Guild attorney. Four pled *nolo contendere*, paid fines and did not need to appear in court. One hired a noted counsellor and was acquitted after a brief hearing where the arresting officer failed to identify the individual the defendant was alleged to have kissed. The common drunk charges were dismissed. So were lewd conduct charges against a married bartender.

The remaining six defendants were tried together. . . . Eight vice officers testified that men had kissed. Their stories conflicted but the jury bought them. The defendants were found guilty.

On Saturday night, February 11, 400 demonstrators carrying placards protested outside the Black Cat against police brutality. While startled officers looked on, ministers, attorneys and officers of homosexual organizations spoke through loudspeakers. This rally, the NBC telecasts, and honest coverage of the raid by the *Los Angeles Free Press* prompted an investigation by the LAPD Internal Affairs Bureau. But those questioned by bureau representatives termed the move a whitewash attempt.

Night after night, following the raid, uniformed officers walked in and out of New Faces, checking restrooms, licenses, conduct. So testifies the owner. Customers grew uneasy. Finally even the most loyal stopped coming. The only answer was to close. It happened in less than 20 days. The Black Cat's owner held on through hearing after hearing on his entertainment and liquor licenses. In the end he lost. The licenses were suspended. The Black Cat closed its doors May twenty-first.

In the first weeks after that ten minutes of violence at midnight, New Year's eve, it looked as if this was what was needed to weld the homosexuals of one city into a unit with the purpose and the strength to make their civil rights a reality. But the excitement passed. Time passed. People forgot. If the forgetters had kept up their interest, kept up their contributions, there was the chance that a détente might have been reached with the police. Laws might even have been changed. Next New Year's eve might have been different.

Now who can say it won't be the same?[12]

DOCUMENT 60

"Sir Lady Java Fights Fuzz-y Rule Nine"

The Los Angeles Advocate, Nov. 1967, 1, 2

"The law is depriving me of my livelihood. I feel it's unconstitutional," Sir Lady Java said as she distributed picket signs to the 25 men and women who had gathered to help her protest. The rally, held outside the Redd Foxx Club on La Cienega on Oct. 21, was Sir Lady Java's opening salvo in her battle against the LA Police Commission's rule No. 9, which she says keeps her from working. Among the supporters were Lady Java's friends, her agent, and Mrs. Jean H. Martin of the American Civil Liberties Union.

Sir Lady Java is a male. But, she says, she has lived as a female for years. She has never shaved, and her long, black hair is her own. Her body, a shapely one, is also all her own. When Lady Java stepped from her car, vivacious in a simple white dress and smiling radiantly, it was obvious that she was no nelly homosexual in "drag." "What else can I do?" she asked. "This is my living.... It's my livelihood, and 9 says I can't do it."

Rule 9 states, "No entertainment shall be conducted in which any performer impersonates by means of costume or dress a person of the opposite sex, unless by special permit issued by the Board of Police Commissioners." In the Los Angeles area, most female impersonators avoid a confrontation with the law by wearing trousers, a shirt, and tie with their costumes. They're not happy about this compromise, though. As one performer put it in the *Advocate* last month, it's like working in "combat boots and overalls." This loophole doesn't suit Lady Java at all, since she always dresses in female attire. "It's discrimination," she asserts, "allowing some people this privilege, and not others."

A couple of months ago, Lady Java was booked at the Redd Foxx. After fulfilling a successful two-week engagement, she was asked back for another two weeks. The police stepped in, however, and said that the club would lose its license if she performed. According to her manager, Lee Craver, Lady Java's act consists of interpretive dancing, comedy skits, and a fashion show featuring leading women of today. While on suspension from work, she was given the Commission's "special permit" to perform for a charity benefit at the Cocoanut Grove.

Everyone should have the right to make a living as long as it doesn't infringe on the rights of others, Mr. Craver told the *Advocate* during the picketing. It's a constitutional right guaranteed to all citizens, he said. Lady Java, who has been working in the LA area for two years, added, "It's got to stop somewhere, and it won't unless somebody comes forward and takes a stand. I guess that's me." She then gathered up her picket sign and began walking again...right past the vice squad.[13]

Yes, the city saw fit to send two vice officers to observe the quiet demonstration. Three of the participants identified them as such, but when they were asked if they were indeed vice officers, the two denied it. Then someone announced that the officers were there under false pretenses, and flashbulbs began popping in their direction. The two men quickly stole away. A black-and-white car cruised past a couple of times, the officers grinning in amusement. One woman piped up, "If they take us, I'll be the first to go. I'm ready.... They don't scare me." At ten o'clock, the picketers disbanded.

Although the question of homosexuality is in no way involved in the dispute, many gay entertainers around town have been bugged by Rule 9 for a long time. The Police Commission finds itself in a peculiar position since California's anti-masquerading law was declared unconstitutional and it is no longer illegal for a male to dress as a female, unless for illegal purposes. With Rule 9, it's illegal to do on the stage what it is legal to do on the streets. . . .

POLITICAL PROTESTS BEFORE STONEWALL

DOCUMENT 61

Columbia University Student Homophile League, "We Protest the Kolb Panel"

23 Apr. 1968, Phyllis Lyon, Del Martin, and DOB Collection, Box 21, Folder 1, GLBT Historical Society (San Francisco)[14]

On behalf of the entire homosexual community, the Student Homophile League of Columbia University strongly objects to any public discussion of homosexuality without participation by informed homosexuals. The SHL requested representation upon this panel—not only were we refused, but we were also informed that representatives from the homosexual community and the homophile movement were, some time ago, explicitly excluded from participation, not only on the panel but even as members of the audience!

It must be asked why the apostles of pathological theories on homosexuality are afraid to engage in debate with informed representatives of the homosexual. . . .

The problems of the homosexual are *not* inherently medical ones. They are problems of prejudice and discrimination, all too often cloaked in the language of science. Much of what is presented this evening will be just that, and will amount to little more than disguised moral value judgements. . . .

It is time that homosexuality be pulled out of the morass of psychiatry, "abnormality" and "emotional disturbance" into which it has been thrust, and placed into its proper setting as a sociological problem of deeply entrenched prejudice and discrimination against a minority group. In this setting it is obvious that heterosexuals, alone, can no more speak with authority upon homosexuality than can whites alone speak upon the plight of the Negro, or Christians alone upon anti-semitism. Certainly it is time that we cease to look upon the psychiatric and medical professions as the authorities on homosexuality. They are not. . . .

We ask the audience this evening to be on the alert for unsupported generalizations and untested assumptions, based upon an unexamined, highly non-objective negative attitude and bias toward homosexuality. You are likely to be hearing, from some of the panelists at least, not the voice of science, but the ingrained prejudices and preconceptions of our culture. . . .

DOCUMENT 62
"Cross Currents"
The Ladder, Sept. 1968, 29–30

On Wednesday, June 19, 1968, *The San Francisco Chronicle* carried a front page article by science correspondent, David Perlman, covering the June 18, 1968 talk by Dr. Charles W. Socarides before the American Medical Association, then meeting in San Francisco.

Dr. Socarides, a psychiatrist at Albert Einstein College of Medicine in New York City, characterized homosexuals . . . as mentally ill and potentially curable. He went on to advocate a government supported "national center for sexual rehabilitation," where homosexuals desiring help would be treated "humanely." . . .

Obviously, the homophile community had no alternative to rebutting this sort of biased and inaccurate treatment, and they did a fine job, too.

The Society for Individual Rights (SIR), the Daughters of Bilitis, the San Francisco Council on Religion and the Homosexual, and Dr. Joel Fort, a psychiatrist and lecturer at San Francisco State College and founder of the San Francisco Center for Special Problems, held a joint press conference at Glide Memorial Church's Fellowship Hall on June 20, 1968,

At the same time, members of DOB and SIR handed out 2,000 leaflets to persons attending the June 20, 1968 meetings of the A.M.A.

Both *The San Francisco Examiner* and *The San Francisco Chronicle* gave coverage to the press conference in their June 21, 1968 issues.

The text of the leaflet circulated at the A.M.A. meeting follows:

"The Society for Individual Rights, the Council on Religion and the Homosexual, the Daughters of Bilitis and the National Legal Defense Fund call upon the American Medical Association:

1. To present at its next national convention an interdisciplinary seminar on homosexuality at which anthropologists, sociologists, psychologists, zoologists and psychiatrists of the non-sickness, as well as the sickness, school participate. Representatives of the homophile movement should also be invited.

2. To undertake to educate the medical profession by opening the pages of its journal to the subject of homosexuality. . . .

3. To promote the better education of future doctors by strengthening and expanding medical school courses on sexuality (including homosexuality).

4. To help educate the general public on the subject of homosexuality by speaking out informatively and acting responsibly on both the national and local levels.

5. To join with the homophile organizations and many others in:
   a. Supporting the legal changes proposed by the American Law Institute;
   b. Calling for an end to present federal policies which exclude homosexuals from the draft, which results in the undesirable discharge of homosexual servicemen followed by denial of veterans' benefits, which deny employment to homosexuals wholly because of their sexual orientation and which arbitrarily label all homosexuals sex psychopaths;
   c. Criticizing the harassment of homosexuals by police and liquor authorities, the exploitation of them by unscrupulous persons, utilization of arrest procedures which involve such unsavory tactics as clandestine observation, enticement and entrapment by vice squad decoys, and the use of homosexuality as a political weapon or as the basis for witchhunts;
   d. Requesting responsible treatment of the subject of homosexuality by all news media, all public officials and all professional persons.

6. To encourage our institutions of higher education and our professional groups to undertake an extensive program of research on the subject of homosexuality in order to replace theories and opinions with facts."

DOCUMENT 63

W. E. B. [William E. Beardemphl], "Homosexuals Call for Completion of the American Revolution"

Vector, Aug. 1968, 5

July 3, 1968, at noon, on the steps of the Federal Building in San Francisco, S.I.R. [Society for Individual Rights], C.R.H. [Council on Religion and the Homosexual], D.O.B. [Daughters of Bilitis], and N.L.D.F. [National Legal Defense Fund] staged a demonstration to remind Americans that homosexuals do not have the rights granted to all other citizens. . . . Leaflets were passed out to the many persons in that area on their lunch hour. Picket signs were carried and speeches outlining the positions of homosexuals were given by Reverend Robert Cromey, Miss Shirley Willer, Rick Stokes, Jim Bradford, Larry Littlejohn, Jim Skaggs and yours truly W. E. Beardemphl.

A press release was sent to all news media in the area who responded with one of the finest coverages of a homophile happening that we have ever seen. . . . The press release follows:

On the 192nd anniversary of the signing of the Declaration of Independence, American homosexuals call for the completion of the American Revolution. The inalienable rights of "life, liberty and the pursuit of happiness"—consistently abridged by the federal government—have now become empty rhetoric for these millions of America's "Invisible Minority." Denied equal federal employment opportunities; considered "guilty" without proof as "security risks"; branded as sex deviants and destroyed for life when called to serve in their country's armed forces; legally outlawed by the nation's Supreme Court as "sexual psychopaths"—we 8 million homosexual citizens demand fulfillment of the principles we celebrate this July 4th. Like our Founding Fathers, we reaffirm the equal station to which the laws of nature and of nature's God entitle us.

Other minorities have been at least officially recognized—attempts have been made to bring them within the scope of the Declaration of Independence. The only recognition of the homosexual minority in this country has been one of oppression—homosexuals have been the "scapegoat" for our country's sexual sickness. The time for the completion of the American Revolution is long overdue. As loyal Americans we ask that the principles of the Declaration of Independence now be extended to all Americans. Therefore we demand for homosexual citizens:

1. Equal federal employment opportunities;
2. Security clearance individually considered without reference to sexual orientation;
3. An end to discriminatory practices against homosexuals in the armed services;
4. That the federal government recognize that private consensual acts between adults are not the legitimate purview of law or of law enforcement procedures. . . .

DOCUMENT 64

Dick Michaels [Richard Mitch], "'Patch' Raids Police Station"
The Los Angeles Advocate, Sept. 1968, 5–6

The campaign of harassment against The Patch, popular gay nightclub in Wilmington, reached a peak on Saturday, Aug. 17, when the Los Angeles police decided to join local hoods who have been waging a small war against the club's patrons. If the reaction of the customers there that night is any indication, a new era of determined resistance may be dawning for L.A.'s gay community.

This reporter and features editor Bill Rand [Rau] happened to be at the club that night and were able to watch the gendarmes in action. We had gone there to talk to Lee Glaze, the manager, about some incidents a week earlier involving The Patch and some local punks. . . .

Lee had spotted a couple of vice cops and went to the stage to deliver one of his frequent and funny monologs about the local goings-on. With great wit and unparalleled grace, he taunted the LAPD for sending such "homely" vice officers. Everyone got a big kick out of it all, including apparently the vice cops, who laughed along with everyone else.

By midnight the club was packed with about 250 customers, some drinking, some milling around, and some gyrating wildly on the dance floor. Bill and I were leaning against the jukebox near the bar when we saw five or six uniformed police come through the door. They were led by the vice cops. The band kept on playing as they fanned out through the club. A few minutes later we saw them taking two guys out. . . .

As soon as Lee found out what was going on, he went to the stage and began to explain to his customers. As the cops looked on, he exhorted the gay audience not to be intimidated by the tactics of the straight society and to stand up for their rights. "It's not against the law to be a homosexual," he said, "and it's not a crime to be in a gay bar. He too is against cruising the parks, tea rooms, and streets, he told the crowd. "All we want is to be left alone in our own bars." He urged everyone to band together to fight for their rights—to put an end to the harassment.

POLITICAL PROTESTS
BEFORE STONEWALL

The scene very nearly took on the aspects of a political rally. Lee was interrupted several times by applause and cheers. "We're Americans, too!" one boy shouted. At one point, I saw a uniformed cop applauding.

After announcing that The Patch would furnish a bail bondsman and a lawyer for the two arrested, Lee left for the police station to get more information on the charge. (It turned out to be 647a, lewd conduct.) He returned with a wild idea. "Anyone here own a flower shop?" he asked from the stage. Someone did. "Go clean it out. I want to buy all your flowers," he shouted, and then he invited everyone to go down to the station with him after the club closed to welcome out the two hapless victims. There were more cheers. Everyone was enthusiastic about the prospect of a hundred or more queens descending on the Harbor Division station.

As it turned out, at closing time the local hoods caused a bit more trouble outside the club, forcing Lee to call the police. By the time peace was restored, most of the patrons had drifted off. A hard core of about 25 stayed and took off for the LAPD's modern Bastille in a small caravan, arriving there before 3 AM. They marched into the waiting room carrying bouquets of gladioli, mums, daisies, carnations, and roses (but no pansies). The stone-faced desk sergeant looked confused for a moment, then told everyone that they would have to be quiet if they wanted to stay there. From time to time, some cops wandered out to view the weird assemblage, shook their heads, smiled, then disappeared. . . .

It was about 5 AM when one of the prisoners was released. He was immediately covered with the bouquets, and pandemonium reigned once again for a few minutes. The same thing happened when victim no. 2 was released a half hour later. Happy that they had finally fulfilled their mission, the tired group drifted off home. . . .

DOCUMENT 65

"Homo Revolt Blasting Off on Two Fronts"

Berkeley Barb, 11 Apr. 1969, 11

The Homosexual Revolution of '69 started this week in San Francisco as militant homosexuals made war on both gay and straight Establishments.

Leo Laurence, deposed Editor of Vector magazine, lashed out against the repressive actions of the Society for Individual Rights on Tuesday.

He and another gay militant, Gale Whittington, organized the Committee for Homosexual Freedom; and on Wednesday the group picketed Whittington's former employer, States Steamship Company, for discrimination against homosexuals.

Tuesday night, the SIR Board of Directors took their monthly magazine, Vector, away from its revolutionary editor, Laurence, who was elected overwhelmingly by SIR membership only two months ago. . . .

"Bullshit," says Laurence, who told *Barb*, "Getting kicked out as Vector Editor by the Gay Establishment is a victory for the homosexual revolution. SIR leadership is damned worried because militant revolutionary homosexuals like myself and other members of the new Committee for Homosexual Freedom are on the attack.

The C-H-F was formed by Laurence and another gay writer, Gale Whittington, who was fired by the States Steamship Company of San Francisco after *Barb* printed a photo showing both men in an embrace.

Picketing of States Lines by the Committee for Homosexual Freedom started Wednesday noon when about thirty guys, gals, and sympathizers marched at the company's 320 California Street main offices.

Company officials told a dozen Press, Radio, and TV newsmen that they were "ignoring" the homosexual pickets.

"Ignore us, hell," Laurence said. "Our gay picket line will soon be a big noon hour feature of the financial district. Already several other radical groups are interested in helping us put a stop to discrimination against homosexuals.

"The revolution should stop every States Lines ship in the world until they rehire Gale Whittington," Laurence explained. "It could be done with help from the unions and other militant groups."

Pickets by the Committee for Homosexual Freedom will hit the 320 California Street location again next Wednesday noon.

"Our picket line jumped from ten to thirty on the first day," Laurence said. "With more help from sympathizers and freedom-loving gays, we can triple that number next week."

"The Black man found self-respect and dignity when he said: 'Black is Beautiful and I am proud.' Now Homosexuals are starting to say: 'Gay is good and I, too, am proud,'" Laurence told *Barb*.

The Committee for Homosexual Freedom is hoping to form coalitions with other non-violent, militant minorities working for freedom and love. Its membership is open to everybody willing to fight publicly for homosexual rights.

One major battle of the C-H-F is to help Assemblyman Willie Brown, who has proposed a state law (AB-743) to make sex legal in California. . . .[15]

DOCUMENT 66

"Homo Death: Group Will Act"
Berkeley Barb, 2 May 1969, 11

The Alameda County coroner has flatly denied a request to hold an inquest into the police killing of Frank Bartley, a 33-year-old Berkeley homosexual.

Bartley was shot in the head by Berkeley pig Weiker Kline April 17 in a hassle over a sex offense arrest in Aquatic Park.

Bartley died April 24 from the .38 slug wound. His family wanted to donate his body for organ transplants, but the coroner ruled that since the death was a homicide, no organs could be transplanted.

Official investigations into the shooting by Berkeley police and the District Attorney cleared Kline and his partner, Frank Reynolds, and indicated that no inquest was necessary.

The request was made by Berkeley attorney Mary Montgomery, who is representing Bartley's family. Last week, attorney Montgomery told *Barb* that murder charges would be filed against the two officers.

"Our plans haven't changed, but we are going to open with a civil suit for $200,000 in damages against the city, the police department and the two officers," attorney Montgomery told *Barb*.

Berkeley Police Inspector Jack Huston told BARB that, as far as the police department was concerned, the case of Frank Bartley is closed.

"It looks like an official cover up," Larry Littlejohn, president of the Society for Individual Rights, told *Barb*.

SIR was one of several groups that participated in a mock funeral motorcade from Glide Methodist Church in San Francisco to the Berkeley Hall of Justice in protest of the killing of Frank Bartley a week ago Friday.

Littlejohn and other SIR officials met with Berkeley Police Chief Baker Wednesday, requesting that the police make a public statement concerning the Bartley killing.

"We also wanted them to make the police investigation report on the incident public," said Littlejohn.

"Baker told us that no public statement would be made and that police reports were only available to those newspapers the department chose to recognize. . . ."

Leo Laurence, press officer for the Committee for Homosexual Freedom, told *Barb* that the demonstration did not go far enough.

"We are not interested in these absurd official reports of an official murder," said Laurence.

"CHF is demanding that the two officers involved be suspended immediately and remain off the force until murder charges against them are tried in court."

"We want these killers off the streets," he said.

CHF is also demanding that Chief Baker issue immediate orders to his men to cease harassment and entrapment of homosexuals or resign his post. . . .

DOCUMENT 67

Leo E. Laurence, "Gays Get Tougher"
Berkeley Barb, 23 May 1969, 31

Militant homosexuals struck a blow to San Francisco's famed Fisherman's Wharf district when the Committee for Homosexual Freedom hit Tower Records (at Bay & Columbus Streets) with a picket line and launched a boycott against the store last Saturday.

Tower Records recently fired a clerk, Frank Denaro, on suspicion that he was a homosexual. Their complaint was that he had winked at a customer.

"Tower's sign advertises a Joan Baez album. While Joan sings of love, freedom, and brotherhood, the management says 'We don't tolerate that free spirit around here' by our employees," says Morgan Penny of the CHF.

"We intend to hit Tower Records hard with an economic boycott every weekend," says Steve Mathews of CHF. "There is a good chance that Tower will become the first to sign a Fair Employment Pledge protecting homosexual employees if people join our boycott by refusing to cross our picket line."

"An amazing number of potential customers stopped at our line," says Jim Connolly of the CHF, "then drove away after we told them that Tower Records discriminates against gays.

"Friendly employees said our strike line was really hurting their business and creating a big hassle among the bosses," Connolly said.

CHF picketing begins at 1 PM Saturday and will continue with rotating teams until midnight closing at Tower, providing the CHF can muster the manpower needed.

Picketing remains undiminished at the States Steamship Company . . . where the CHF strike started seven weeks ago. Nearly one thousand leaflets are passed out every weekday noon hour.

The gay picketers are getting bolder and are invading the offices of States Lines and their neighbor, Merrill Lynch Pierce Fenner and Smith (stockbrokerage).

Teams of CHF leafleteers swarmed through the Merrill-Lynch offices this week, ignoring the frightened objections shouted by the up-tight money mongers.

Wednesday, CHF pickets marched into the States Lines offices and politely asked to discuss their grievances with Company officials.

States Lines flatly refused to negotiate, and instead insulted the CHF members, who then formed a circle and sang their freedom songs. . . .[16]

PART II
STONEWALL

Greenwich Village

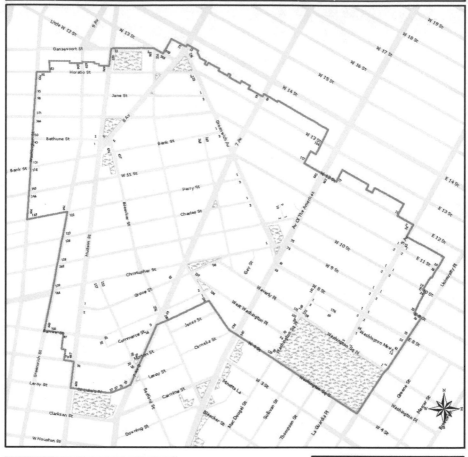

Greenwich Village Historic District
Manhattan
Designated April 29, 1969

☐ Historic District Boundaries

Figure 4.1. The City of New York Landmarks Preservation Commission designated the Greenwich Village Historic District on 29 April 1969, approximately two months before the Stonewall Riots. The Stonewall Inn was located on Christopher Street between Seventh Avenue South and Avenue of the Americas. The boundaries of the Greenwich Village Historic District were extended in 2006 and 2010. Credit: City of New York Landmarks Preservation Commission.

4
THE STONEWALL INN

AFTER THE STONEWALL INN REOPENED as a gay bar in 1967, it quickly became a popular destination for a diverse mix of people. For some, it was a liberating space for cruising, dancing, drinking, romancing, and socializing. For others, it was a sleazy and dangerous dive bar, owned by organized crime and exploited by police. For many, it was all of this and more.

After the Stonewall Riots, many former patrons offered oral and written descriptions of the bar's physical space and social dynamics. These are valuable historical sources, though they were inevitably influenced by the importance attributed to the bar after the uprising occurred. This chapter features documentary sources about the Stonewall Inn from the pre-riots era, which provide us with a sense of how the bar was perceived and experienced in the months and years leading up to the rebellion.

DOCUMENTS 68–69 are taken from 1969 gay bar guides that referenced the Stonewall Inn and other gay-oriented businesses in New York.

DOCUMENTS 70–72 are taken from a 1968 book titled *The Homosexual Handbook* and two local gay newsletters that mentioned the Stonewall.

DOCUMENT 68

International Guild Guide: Gay Listings '69
Washington, D.C.: Guild, 1969, front matter and 56–58[1]

The 1968 edition of the International Guild Guide was a major improvement over past editions. So great was the improvement that many of its users wrote in, applauding our efforts and stated that it was the *very best* Guide available on the market today—National or International. It would seem to be difficult to improve upon what we had considered to be the best in 1968. However, 1969 looks even brighter for the International Guild Guide. No effort was spared to verify the accuracy of the information presented. From all over the world came reports, suggestions, additions, deletions, and information that no other guide on the market today has been able to assemble so systematically as has been done in the 1969 International Guild Guide.

We realize that despite all efforts to curtail errors, some errors will probably occur in these pages. Because of this, we encourage all users of the Guide to send in corrections. . . .

We have introduced a coding system and some entries are already coded. . . . We ask our readers to realize that there will be differences of opinion with respect to coding, but do send in the coding that you would use for any particular bar. We will do our best to arrive at a consensus. . . .

AYOR: *"At Your Own Risk."* Designates an entry where you might like the people there, but it is highly questionable that they will like you.
B: *"Beer."* No other alcohol served.
C: *"Colored."* Predominantly, but not exclusively.
D: *"Dance."* Individuals of the same sex may do so.
E: *"Elegant."* Coat and tie.
G: *"Gay."*
GI: *"Heavy military patronage."*
H: *"Hustlers."*
L: *"Lesbian."* Not always strictly, but predominantly.
LJ: *"Leather Jacket."* Also implies S-M.
M: *"Mixed."* Appears straight but sufficiently active to make it worthwhile.
OC: *"Outside Cruising."*
P: *"Private."* Members only.
RT: *"Rough Trade."* If the atmosphere is very tense, add a hyphen and the AYOR classification!
S: *"Show."* Has drag and/or other appropriate entertainment.
WE: *"Weekends."* Not too active otherwise.
YC: *"Young Crowd."* Collegiate age. . . .

Manhattan, New York
Greenwich Village

Albert Hotel
23 E. 10th St. (cor. Univ. Place)

Aldo's Restaurant and Bar (G, M, E)
340 Bleecker St. (nr. Christopher
Street)

Asher's
114 Christopher Street

Big "D" (LJ)
49 E. Houston

Bon Soir (G, S, D)
40 W. 8th St. (bet. 5th & 6th Aves.)

Chick'n'Rib Restaurant (G)
(Hours: 9 a.m. to 3 a.m.)
39 Greenwich Ave. (nr. W. 10th St.)

Comedy Corner Coffee Shop (G)
122 Christopher St.

Crazy Horse Night Club
(formerly Louis Tavern) (M, F, S)
149 Bleecker St.

Danny's (Lefty) (LJ)
139 Christopher Street

Earle Hotel
(Tourists should use discretion)
103 Waverly Place (cor. 11th St., E. of
5th Ave.)

Eighty-two Night Club (M, E, S)
(female impersonators)
82 E. 4th St.

Fedora's Restaurant (LJ)
Sheridan Square
(Hours: 8 p.m. to 4 a.m.)

Finale Restaurant & Bar (M, E)
48 Barrow St.

Five Oaks Restaurant & Bar (M)
(Delicatessen)
49 Grove St.

Freddies (G)
411 Bleecker Street

Gallery (M)
77 Christopher St.

Gantry Bar (L)
13th St. & 6th Ave.

The Gold Bug (L)
West 3rd St. (off McDougal Street)
(Hours: 9 p.m. to 3 a.m.)

Great Society Club (P, D)
14th St. & 2nd Ave.

Hotel Lexington (G, E, D, L)
Top of the Town
33rd floor (take rear elevator)

International Bar (LJ) (Called "The
Stud")
733 Greenwich Street (Perry St. West)
(Hours: 8 p.m. to 4 a.m.)

J. B.'s Restaurant and Bar (G)
105 W. 13th Street

Julius' (M-collegiate at back tables.
G- at bar area; 98% G)
159 W. 10th St. (at Waverly Place)

Keller's Bar (G, RT, LJ)
384 W. 14th Street (at Barrow Street)
    (Mostly truck drivers)
(Hours: 8 p.m. to 3 a.m.)

Kookies Bar (L, G, D)
149 W. 14th St (nr. 7th Ave.)

The Little Den Club (P, LJ)
W. 12th St. & Greenwich St.

Loew's Sheridan Theater (AYOR)
11th and 7th Avenues
(Noon–until)

Longview Country Club (G)
(formerly Village East Rest. &
    Lounge)
232 Park Ave. South (at 19th Street)

Marlton Hotel
5 W. 8th St.

Nautilus (M, E)
267 W. 23rd St.
(Hours: 8 p.m. to 2 a.m.)

New York Motorbike Club (P, LJ–
    bottle club)
180 Christopher

Omnibus Coffee House (M)
69 W. 10th St.

Pam-Pam (M-collegiate)
95–7th Ave. (cor. Grove and
    Bleecker Sts.)

P.M. Lounge (LJ)
204 E. 18th St. (bet. 2nd &
    3rd Aves.)

Sea Colony (G, L)
8th Ave. & Horatio St.

Seventeen Barrow Street (M-
collegiate, E)
17 Barrow St. (near Sheridan Square)

St. Mark's Baths (3rd floor up)
    (AYOR, G, H, RT) (open 24 hrs.)
6 St. Mark's Place (nr. 8th St. & 3rd
    Ave.)

Silver Dollar Restaurant
(After Hours)
161 Christopher Street

Stone Wall (G, D, P)
(Hours: 9 p.m. to 3 a.m.)
53 Christopher St.[2]

Tenth of Always (M-collegiate, G)
(Hours: Midnight to 9 a.m.)
375 Bleecker Street

Tor's Restaurant (G)
(Hours: 10 a.m. to 4 a.m.)
21 Greenwich Ave. (at W. 10th St.)

Trude Heller's Restaurant (M)
418 Sixth Avenue

Village Squire (G, L)
(Haberdashery)
49 West 8th Street

Washington Square (L, G, D) (Café)
679 Broadway (cor. 3rd St.)

OC: Anywhere in the Village. Good
    on 23rd St. between 7th and 10th
    Ave. at night. Careful!

New York City Gay Scene Guide: Complete 1969 Edition
New York: Apollo, 1968, 8–11, 15–16[3]

Manhattan Bars

THE BLOW-UP, 2nd Avenue (below 81st Street, near 80th). Gay Dance bar, reportedly trying to discourage girls which is bucking the trend of guys and girls together. Dancing, food (in a limited menu), and pleasant people are making this one look like a winner. Primarily a social bar, cruising does go on.

THE BOHEMIAN, 15 Barrow Street. Relatively new gay bar, this one is for GIRLS only. Casual, after-hours bar.

BON SOIR, 40 West 8th Street (between MacDougal & 6th Ave.). Listed under "Night Clubs" in our previous issues of this guide, it has now re-opened as a gay spot, with the closing of the Moroccan Village across the street. About the most pleasant bar in town, it's a dance parlor now, and the gay crowd is really turning up in droves. They like the new look.

CANDY STORE, 44 West 56th Street (betw. 5th & 6th Aves.). Piano bar—very elegant, jacket & tie is required. (Someone recently published a comment that his nominees for bars with the most "up-tight" people are Julius' and the Candy Store.)

CANDLELIGHT LOUNGE, 309 Amsterdam Ave. (betw. 74th & 75th Sts.). Casual, informal Central Park West crowd predominates. Mixed.

CARNABY'S, 323 East 3rd St. Dancing bar, one of the newer spots in town–be sure to pay a visit. Casual.

CARR'S, 204 West 10th Street (off Bleecker). In the Village, this gay bar has a casual college-type crowd. It can be cruisy, but there's no dancing or entertainment.

CHECKERBOARD BAR, 105 Christopher St. (at the other end of block from the Theatre De Lys). Boys and girls. A small, cozy bar with friendly social atmosphere. Packed on weekends. Owner Jack Lundy has decorated it pleasantly and the dancing is among the best in town.

DANNY'S, 139 Christopher St. (corner of Greenwich St.). Formerly the location of the Buddy-Buddy Bar, check this lively spot if you haven't visited it yet. Packed on weekends, with a mixed (not straight and gay, but rather leather & some sweater) younger crowd

THE DOVER, 1201 Lexington Avenue (betw. 81st & 82nd Sts.). Dancing bar with some "trade," hustlers, etc. It has a faithful following which might seem to indicate something good about it.

FOUR SEASONS, 99 East 52nd St. (in Seagram Bldg.). MIXED, and very posh elegant, upper class clientele.

THE GOLDBUG, 3rd Street (off 6th Ave.). Sweater crowd predominates. Recently opened and is gathering a steady following. Live band, dancing, boys and girls. On Wednesday's, a $10–$50 "balloon-bursting" giveaway. Located across the street from the "Tenth of Always."

THE
STONEWALL INN

THE GOLD RAIL, 2850 Broadway. Casual, informal gay crowd.

THE GREAT SOCIETY, 14th Street and 2nd Avenue. Casual, dancing—GIRLS ONLY.

HARRY'S BACK EAST, 1422 Third Ave. (cor. of 80th St.). Boys and girls. Casual, upper East Side patronage.

THE INTERNATIONAL STUD, 733 Greenwich St. Leather bar—opens 8 p.m. on Mon.–Fri., and 2 p.m. on Sat.–Sun. Seldom do you see silk neckerchieves or Betty-Boop curls on any of its patrons.

JACK OF HEARTS, 55th Street and 2nd Ave. (next door to "Gigi's"—an after hours spot). Small gay bar with dancing. Primarily local neighborhood patronage.

JULIUS', 159 West 10th Street (at Waverly Place). One of the older and very popular bars. Clientele is generally in their 30's and up, with some show biz people and businessmen.

KELLER'S BAR, 384 West St. (near Barrow St.). "S. & M." Leather set.

KOOKIE'S, 149 West 14th Street (near 7th Avenue). GIRLS only, a lovely, gracious, well-run establishment, with nice folks.

MILANO'S LOUNGE, 267 Amsterdam Avenue. (cor. of 72nd St.). Casual, MIXED, informal neighborhood place, with little fun here.

THE NAUTILUS, 267–269 West 23rd Street. Nightclub, bar and restaurant. Reservations are needed for dinner. Dressy, mixed.

P.M., 204 East 18th St. (betw. 2nd & 3rd Ave.). Leather, "S & M."

NERO'S NOOK, 18th Street and 2nd Avenue. Fairly new gay bar. Clientele seems to be primarily in their 30's and up. Casual atmosphere. (Also serve dinner)

THE "OK" CORRAL, 835 Washington Street. Leather crowd (the "Hayloft," a private club, at same address). Popular bar for the leather set. Full course meals are served nightly from 7 to 11 PM.

OLD VIC, 309 East 60th St. (betw. 1st & 2nd Avenues). Very popular dance bar. Try to avoid on weekends, as it's very crowded.

1-2-3 BAR, 123 University Place (cor. of 14th St., west side of May's Dep't Store). One of the quieter spots in town, this dancing bar is primarily for the slightly older gay crowd.

PLAZA HOTEL MEN'S BAR, 5th Ave. & 59th St. MIXED, with some hustlers and "trade." Elegant.

THE RAT RACE, 76th St. and 1st Avenue. Piano bar downstairs, dancing upstairs, with a casual crowd.

RED VELVET SWING, 57 Lexington Avenue (cor. of 27th St.). College crowd, informal fun place, neighborhood people.

SEA COLONY, 8th Ave. and Horatio Street. GIRLS bar, survivor of every "clean-up" campaign to date. Casual, relaxed atmosphere.

SECOND FLOOR, 35 West 56th St. (one flight up) (betw. 5th & 6th Aves.). Formerly listed as "L'Intrigue," this piano bar has a steady clientele. Mostly sweater and older "suit & tie" crowd. Also has a juke-box for dancing. Elegant (rather garish) decor.

SEVENTEEN BARROW STREET, 17 Barrow St. (where else??) (nr. Sheridan Sq.). One of the nicer gay bars in the city, with a predominantly younger "fun" college-type crowd. Where the action is. If you like peanuts (the kind you eat), they're free with the drinks at 17 Barrow. No dancing, with a quiet, relaxed crowd.

STAGE 45, 305 East 45th St. (betw. Park & Lexington Avenues). A MIXED crowd, jacket & tie is required.

TENTH OF ALWAYS, 82 West 3rd Street. An after-hours, casual college crowd.

THE STONEWALL, 53 West Christopher St. (near Sheridan Sq.). It continues operating amid persistent rumors of closing. Caters to a younger crowd who seem to spend all their time perfecting their dancing. Observers note that "go-go-boys" installed on platforms have failed to attract the dwindling crowds.

(The following news item was reported in the March 1968 Mattachine (N.Y.) Newsletter, and is presented here in condensed form....) "Edward F. P. Murphy, an ex-convict who is alleged to have been the head of the national ring which recently was active in extorting money from homosexuals...has served prison terms for larceny and for carrying deadly weapons, and was arrested for impersonating an officer, and for extortion...under Federal indictment on extortion charges...permitted to plead guilty and received a five-year probation. On a number of indictments in the State courts, Murphy pleaded guilty on May 16, 1966...sentencing has been postponed six times...he could get up to 15 years in prison as a second offender, on the robbery charge alone. MSNY has also been informed that Murphy has an interest in the Stone Wall, a club on Christopher Street, and several other gay clubs in New York." *We caution our readers NEVER* to use your real name when cruising, NEVER to give your address to a questionable bar or club, and remember, that trick or hustler you've just picked up may be "working" for the management! We urge you, if you've been intimidated or blackmailed in the past, to report it to the D.A.'s office, or to M.S.N.Y.

THE TOOL BOX, 507 West St. (cor. Jane St.). Casual gay leather set. Open daily 8 p.m., Sat.–Sun. at 3 p.m.

WASHINGTON SQUARE LOUNGE, 679 Broadway at West 3rd St. Dancing, live band, entertainment, mixed.

YUKON BAR, 140 East 53rd St. (betw. 3rd and Lex. Aves.). Casual—collegiate.

Baths

CONTINENTAL BATHS, 230 West 74th Street (cor. Broadway). Opened 9/12. Open 24 hrs., pool, t.v., private rooms.

BROADWAY SAUNA & STEAM BATHS, 49 Broadway, Newark, New Jersey. It is included in this guide as it's located very near the Metropolitan N.Y. area, and has become quite popular for its clean surroundings—something that can't be said for most of the bath houses in town. A nice establishment, with friendly management. Has rooms and dormitory, open 24 hours daily.

EVERARD BATHS, 28 West 28th St. A number of Gay Guide publishers have incorrectly spelled the name of this bath house in past issues of their guides—it is Everard, not EVER HARD! Everard is one of the oldest and most popular baths houses in the city.

LUXOR BATHS, 121 West 46th St.

ST. MARK'S RUSSIAN & TURKISH BATHS, 6 St. Mark's Place (nr. 8th St. & 3rd Ave.). Most active on the third floor. Has a big swim pool. Swedish massage—open 24 hours daily. Very popular.

SAUNA BATH & HEALTH CLUB, 300 West 58th St. Recently opened at this new location (they used to be located at 18 W. 58th St.), and now consists of an entire floor, with air conditioned lounge, sauna bath, and a large dormitory. The price has been increased by only 50¢. . . .

Parks

BRYANT PARK. 5th Avenue and 42nd Street, across the street from the N.Y. Public Library. A nice place to relax, "watch the sights," and meet people. Many hustlers here also.

CENTRAL PARK. Increased emphasis by the city to use this park for community fun type entertainment makes this a nice place to stroll through in the daytime. Stay out of the park proper after dark. Central Park West is the longest cruising area in the world and should not

be missed. Particularly the area bordering the West 70's, around 72nd to 79th Sts. Most active after 6 PM to after midnight.

WASHINGTON SQUARE PARK, in Greenwich Village, near N.Y. University and 8th Avenue. Noted for impromptu speeches, this park has a predominance of college students and the Village yippy set. MIXED, but a nice place to relax and watch the cruisers on a sunny day.

Private Clubs

CORDUROY CLUB, 240 West 38th Street. A bottle club—bring your own drinks for set-ups. Nice cleanly-run establishment, which now reports well over a thousand members. It's a quiet and reserved club, crowded weekends.

THE DEN, West 12th St. & Greenwich St. Leather crowd—members only.

EL BARON CLUB, 74–02 Eliot Avenue, Middle Village, Queens, N.Y. Informal, casual crowd, very busy on the weekends. Don't miss this lively spot if you live in the area. Get a member to sponsor your membership. Predominantly a younger crowd.

THE HAYLOFT, 835-A Washington Street. Membership club—strictly for the LEATHER crowd (located at same address as the "O K" Corral). Open 10 p.m.—4 a.m. nightly. Beer bar.

92 SOCIAL CLUB, 200 West 70th Street (off Broadway). One of the newer spots in town. Dancing, boys.

THE TEL-STAR, 148 Washington Street. Membership, casual college crowd, very active on weekends. Dancing.

"9" PLUS CLUB, INC., 149 West 21st St. Formerly the location of the N.Y. Motorbike Club, it's an "S & M" bottle club—members and guests only. Open 9 p.m. to 6 a.m. (closed on Mondays). They publish the monthly "Scimitar," a bar gossip type magazine that's distributed through various bars and gay clubs.

THE NEW GALLERY, in Van Rensselaer Hotel, 15 East 11th St. Opens nightly at 10 PM. Yearly membership. A lively younger crowd, dancing, casual.

THE PENTHOUSE, in the Westover Hotel, 253 West 72nd Street. Membership, dancing, one of the liveliest and most popular of the newer places. $10 yearly membership. Bar.

THE SKULL, 421 West 13th Street. Membership. This is strictly a leather "S & M" crowd. If you dig chains, you'll like the crowd at the SKULL.

TABLE TOPS, INC., 2226 Third Ave. (betw. 121st & 122nd Sts.) Boys & girls, it's a must for our uptown readers. Open every night except Mondays. For amusement they have billiard tables, baseball games, bowling, shuffleboard games, chess, checkers, television, etc. Dancing, bottle club, casual.

THE TOP OF THE TOWN, in the Sheraton Towers Hotel (33rd Floor). Very popular dancing bar that has a predominantly younger crowd. (No wild types) and some of the "Geritol" set.

VAL'S, 421 West 13th St. Recently opened, members only. A young collegiate group, casual, dancing.

THE SEWER, 11 East 16th Street. Located in the basement. This club (which opened in late August, '68) has a dancing bar and a lively younger crowd.

CYCLE MOTOR CLUB, N.Y.C. (Membership) Leather set—publish mag.—"Wheels."

THE
STONEWALL INN

All private clubs above admit members only. A member generally must sponsor you for membership. In some instances, members may bring non-members as guests. ("Family" clubs let anyone in, as long as you fit their description of what a "fag" looks like, so they are not really private clubs or public bars.) Some private clubs serve drinks on premises, while others are "bottle clubs" (bring your own for set-ups). Contact clubs on member requirem'ts.

DOCUMENT 70

Angelo d'Arcangelo [Josef Bush], *The Homosexual Handbook*
New York: Ophelia, 1969, 128–132[4]

. . . I've been to a lot of bars. I know what they do and how they do it. And thinking it over, it seems to me to be a wise idea just to take four "typical" places here in New York and describe them. You'll probably be able to draw your own parallels in your own city. They don't change much.

I called and asked Xavier to go with me on a research project. He knew about this book and he had his little laugh about the prospect of going with me under such circumstances. . . .

"What about *The Stone Wall*?" I wanted to know if we could go there because I'd heard that it was not only a Dancing Bar, but a Dancing Bar with go-go boys. In cages, I hoped.

"Oh, you don't want to go there."

"Why not?"

"That's so tired. What do you want to watch a couple of bleached-out skinny faggots wiggling their much-used asses up on a bar for?"

I assured him that I did anyway, and that it was like "Old Faithful." If you haven't seen it you might as well; especially if you're in the neighborhood. My particular reason, which I did not confide in him, was that only a short time ago a person of my acquaintance with a growing reputation in the world of small theatricals had accompanied the playwright D. to the bar in order that they might watch his latest love, a go-go-ette. For me, there was a gritty kind of glee in the prospect of seeing this gyrating moppet, for the little fag had apparently refused to torture his admirer, thereby torturing his admirer. Treacle on my tongue! Once this D. had dared to presume on the good nature and commendable loins of my own steamy baby.

"We will begin," I said, "at *The Stone Wall*."

Sometime between that agreement and our entry into the club, another acquaintance, Wally, of whom I spoke earlier, joined us for a night on the town. There's a catch in my throat as I mention his name. That man is living proof that a man can find happiness as a pixie at the age of forty and beyond.

The bar is on Christopher Street, just off Sheridan Square, and is reputed to be a private club. The burly at the door keeps boxes that hold, or are rumored to hold, thousands of cards upon which are printed the particulars of the many thousands of customers that have come and continue to patronize this place. On the weekends, there is a price of admission which is euphemized into something else, but it's not very much actually, only a couple of dollars or so. I have often seen lines or near lines outside on a Saturday night.

In a loud voice Xaver declared himself to be "known," and the door was opened. We went inside gingerly, for even stepping out of the gloom of the evening, our eyes were not accustomed to the inky atmosphere of the noisy double bar.

There's a certain hastiness about the look of the place. It seems to have only recently been converted from a garage into a cabaret; in about eight hours and at a cost of under fifty dollars. Everything is painted black, even the windows. The long main room on the right has a bar of considerable length, and is patronized pretty well by the people who drink. Everybody doesn't, which is why the prices are so high. The younger, more agile and more sensationally demi-dressed jerk and bump on the rather large dance area at the end of the room. A space perhaps thirty by thirty. Spotlights are pointed directly down and they light the dancing youths dramatically.

This is a *young* bar. The patrons are primarily youthful and primarily good-looking. That's the premium. A haven of and for narcissists. Sex is in the air but it remains there while people preen and rubberneck about to see who is or might be watching their contortions. Median age I'd reckon to be about twenty-two.

In the room next door the scene is the same, but because the dance floor is considerably smaller, there is less dancing and so there is a great deal of that "standing around" business which is generally a sign of sexual activity, or at least the prelude to it. Occasionally people may take their eyes away from the dancers long enough to address a word or a remark to their neighbor.

Well, we did *that* for awhile, and Xavier, who seemed to know fifty per cent of the people there, danced a couple of times and then he insisted we go. OK by me and OK by Wally.

On the way out of the place I happened to notice that the light shows and projections were suddenly turned on and two boys at opposite ends of the bar were flouncing about to assorted rhythms. They wore little flesh-colored bathing trunks and seemed to be quite devoid of unwanted body hair. The lad to my left was much too languid to be anything more than a travesty of the tired stripper, but the right-hand boy was really working out with verve and energy. He was not without looks, but wore one of those unlived-in faces far too *weary of it all* for his age or even his environment. Should we ever meet, I'll thank him for being just the hard little number he is.

We left quickly and without regret. This was one of those places one goes to when one is quite young and inclined to go everywhere in coveys. More social than anything else, it is simply a place to burn off steam and to be seen. Not the kind of place for making out, though there's that possibility too, especially the later in the morning it gets. But the usual practice is to leave The Stone Wall and go on to another bar, or for a long, slow walk down Christopher or Greenwich. . . .

DOCUMENT 71
"Mafia on the Spot"
The New York Hymnal, Feb. 1968, 1–2[5]

Although it has been common knowledge among New York's homosexual community for many years, the Mafia (or "The Syndicate") control of New York City's gay bars has only recently been brought to the public's attention.

The New York Times, starting in early October of 1967, ran a number of front page articles on the Mafia and, in particular, on the Mafia's control of gay bars. The Times named John (Sonny) Franzese as kingpin of the Syndicate's gay bar operations on Long Island; and in subsequent articles they identified the heads of the Manhattan gay bar Syndicate.

The Stone Wall on Christopher St. in Greenwich Village is one of the larger and more financially lucrative of the Mafia's gay bars in Manhattan. New York *Hymnal* received a report from a reliable source over a month ago that the Stone Wall was going to be closed by the Health Department because it was alleged that a number of cases of hepatitis (which has reached epidemic proportions among the homosexual community) had been traced to the Stone Wall's bar. It was reported that the Stone Wall does not wash the glasses. . . .

The case of the Stone Wall only points up the fact that the Community cannot rely on governmental agencies to break the Mafia control of gay bars until the day comes that pay-off and collusion between the Syndicate and governmental agencies are ended.

How can you identify a gay bar as being Mafia?

1. When you walk in, there will be at least one or two "gray goons" sitting near the door checking out everyone as they enter. If it's a Mafia "private club" like the Stone Wall or the Bon Soir, and you are wearing a jacket and tie and don't fit the Mafia's stereotype of a "fairy," the goons at the door will refuse to let you in.

2. The bar will be dark—to hide the filth and to give the place an atmosphere of "anything goes."
3. On Friday and Saturday nights, it will cost you $3 or $4 to get in and they will give you 2 tickets for drinks.
4. There will very likely be dancing in a back room hidden from view when you enter the bar.
5. Policemen will make periodic and mysterious appearances to talk with the goons at the door.
6. The general atmosphere will be one of licentiousness and gloom.

Gay bars in Manhattan's Greenwich Village that fit generally the above description include the Stone Wall, Bon Soir, Danny's, The Den, The Skull, Telstar, Keller's, Checkmate, 17 Barrow and the Sea Colony.

The situation as it now exists makes it virtually impossible for a legitimate businessman to open a gay bar with a healthy social atmosphere. And the only way the situation is going to change for the better is for homosexuals to stop patronizing bars run by concealed Mafia interests. We cannot rely on governmental agencies in this fight. The Mafia monopoly on gay bars has existed in New York for decades and the City government has shown no interest. When the Department of Investigations of the City of New York was asked if they were planning any steps to break the Mafia monopoly, we received the standard "No Comment." . . .

DOCUMENT 72

"Gay Bar Closed"

Mattachine Society of New York Newsletter, Mar. 1968, 5

The police have been taking action against Mafia-operated bars and recently closed the Long Island Rail Bar and Grill in Brooklyn. The actual charges against the bar were that "homosexuals were permitted to conduct themselves in an indecent manner" in that men kissed, danced together and "solicited." The courts have ruled recently that bars cannot be closed for those acts, but a charge that men "made out" in the booths at the rear of the premises provided a reason for the closing.

In fact, the key word here is "permitted." The courts have ruled that a bartender may not refuse to serve drinks to a homosexual merely because he is a homosexual, and that indecent actions by a patron, or solicitations, are not sufficient grounds for license revocation, *unless* the bartender or manager was aware of such acts and permitted them.

The manager of the bar was Edward F. P. Murphy, an ex-convict who is alleged to have been the head of the national ring which recently was active in extorting money from homosexuals. Murphy has served prison terms for larceny and for carrying deadly weapons, and was arrested for impersonating an officer and for extortion at the New York Hilton Hotel, where he was working as a house detective.

Murphy was under Federal indictment on extortion charges and was permitted to plead guilty and received a five-year probation from Judge Constance Baker Motley on December 13. On a number of indictments in the State courts, Murphy pleaded guilty on May 16, 1966, with the consent of New York D.A. Frank Hogan's office. Sentencing has been postponed six times, most recently at a hearing on December 15 before Judge George Postel.

MSNY has been informed that Murphy's sentence has been so often postponed because he had made a "deal" to turn state's evidence, and the delays are to work out another "deal" to lighten his sentence. He could get up to 15 years in prison as a second offender, on the robbery charge alone. Other charges include attempted grand larceny, violation of the weapons law, and extortion.

MSNY has also been informed that Murphy has an interest in the Stone Wall, a club on Christopher Street, and several other gay clubs in New York. Our source claims that the membership lists of some of these clubs are used to further extortion and shake-down schemes. . . .

THE STONEWALL INN

5
THE STONEWALL RIOTS

MEDIA COVERAGE OF THE STONEWALL RIOTS was limited for an event that later assumed such national and international significance. Throughout the 1950s and 1960s, LGBT activists had criticized mainstream media for biased reporting, complaining about LGBT invisibility and negative visibility in newspapers, magazines, television programs, and radio shows. This was one of the reasons for the creation of LGBT periodicals, which provided more and different coverage than LGBT people had come to expect from other media sources. In the early 1960s, mainstream media began to pay more attention and more respectful attention to LGBT subjects, but these changes were highly uneven and inconsistent. In the late 1960s, critics continued to complain about the quantity and quality of LGBT media representations.

In New York, the Stonewall rebellion was not front-page news in the city's three main daily newspapers. Popular national magazines such as *Time* and *Newsweek* did not report on the riots until several months later. The most detailed reports were published in the *Village Voice*, an alternative New York weekly newspaper, and the *Mattachine Society of New York Newsletter*, a monthly periodical produced by the city's main gay political group.

The thirty documents reprinted in this chapter, presented in chronological order, include many of the key primary sources that have been used in research about the Stonewall Riots. They are important sources of information about the uprising and its participants, while also providing us with evidence for exploring the values and views of multiple historical actors. They additionally can be used to compare mainstream, alternative, and LGBT media reports and help us to consider the circulation of news about the rebellion in and beyond New York.

DOCUMENTS 73–75, 80, 83, 85–86, AND 91 are taken from New York's three main daily newspapers: the *Times*, *Post*, and *Daily News*.

DOCUMENTS 76–77 are the texts of fliers distributed by gay activists after the first night of rioting.

DOCUMENTS 78–79 AND 96–102 are taken from LGBT newsletters, newspapers, and magazines, including the *Mattachine Society of New York Newsletter* and *The Ladder*.

DOCUMENTS 81–82, 84, 87–90, AND 92–95 are taken from alternative, underground, and left periodicals, including the *Village Voice*, *East Village Other*, and *Rat*.[1]

DOCUMENT 73
"Village Raid Stirs Melee"
New York Post, 28 June 1969, 4

A police raid on the Stonewall Inn, a tavern frequented by homosexuals at 53 Christopher St., just east of Sheridan Square in Greenwich Village, triggered a near-riot early today.

As persons seized in the raid were driven away by police, hundreds of pass-ersby shouting "Gay Power" and "We Want Freedom" laid siege to the tavern with an improvised battering ram, garbage cans, bottles and beer cans in a protest demonstration.

Police reinforcements were rushed to the tavern to deal with the distur-bances, which continued for more than two hours. By the time calm returned to the area, at least 12 persons had been arrested on charges ranging from assault to disorderly conduct.

Among those arrested was folk singer Dave Van Ronk, 33, of 15 Sheridan Sq., who was charged with felonious assault on a police officer. Van Ronk was not in the tavern, but got into the fight when it spilled out onto the street, police said.

Police said the raid was staged because of unlicensed sale of liquor on the premises.

DOCUMENT 74
Dennis Eskow, "3 Cops Hurt as Bar Raid Riles Crowd"
New York Daily News, 29 June 1969, 30[2]

A predawn police raid on a reputed Greenwich Village homosexual hangout, the second raid within a week, touched off a two-hour melee yesterday as cus-tomers and villagers swarmed over the plainclothes cops.

Before order was restored, the cops were the targets of thrown coins, cob-blestones and uprooted parking meters, windows were smashed, a police van was nearly overturned and the front of the raided bar, the Stonewall Inn, was fire-bombed.

Three cops suffered minor injuries and 13 persons were arrested. The fire was quickly doused by a hose from the bar.

Police officials said they had raided the social club at 53 Christopher St. last week to gather evidence of illegal sale of alcohol. The club had no license to sell alcoholic beverages to the public. That raid went off without a hitch.

Yesterday, at 2 a.m., plainclothesmen, under direction of Inspectors Seymour Pine and Charles Smyth, moved in under orders to gather fresh evidence of illegal sale of alcohol, arrest offending parties and close the bar.

After 28 cases of beer and 19 bottles of liquor were confiscated, police began clearing the bar.

Figure 5.1. Freelance photographer Joseph Ambrosini documented the first night of the Stonewall Riots with this image, taken in the early morning hours of 28 June 1969 and published by the *New York Daily News*; it appeared alongside the newspaper's 29 June report on the riots. Credit: New York Daily News Archive (Getty).

The customers milled around outside. They were joined by other villagers. As the cops came out, some persons in the crowd began throwing things. The missiles gradually grew more dangerous and the brief fire followed.

Reinforcements were called and the crowd was dispersed.

Among those arrested was the doorman, Anthony Verra, 25, of 864 49th St., Brooklyn, charged with unlawful sale, consumption and storage of liquor, and Dave Van Ronk, 33, of 55 Sheridan Square, a folk singer, guitarist and song writer.

Van Ronk, who made his Town Hall debut in October 1965 before 1,000 young people, was accused of throwing an object that injured Patrolman Gil Weissman, 44, of the Charles St. station.

Judge Nicholas F. Delagi in Criminal Court paroled Van Ronk for a hearing July 15, but held Verra in $500 bail for a hearing July 14 because there was a similar warrant out for him.

Seven of those arrested were charged with unlicensed sale of liquor

Police have been keeping an eye on the inn to explore the possibility of "local syndicate involvements."

DOCUMENT 75

"4 Policemen Hurt in 'Village' Raid: Melee near Sheridan Square Follows Action at Bar"

New York Times, 29 June 1969, 33

Hundreds of young men went on a rampage in Greenwich Village shortly after 3 A.M. yesterday after a force of plainclothes men raided a bar that the police said was well known for its homosexual clientele. Thirteen persons were arrested and four policemen injured.

The young men threw bricks, bottles, garbage, pennies and a parking meter at the policemen, who had a search warrant authorizing them [to] investigate reports that liquor was sold illegally at the bar, the Stonewall Inn, 53 Christopher Street, just off Sheridan Square.

Deputy Inspector Seymour Pine said that a large crowd formed in the square after being evicted from the bar. Police reinforcements were sent to the area to hold off the crowd.

Plainclothes men and detectives confiscated cases of liquor from the bar, which Inspector Pine said was operating without a liquor license.

The police estimated that 200 young men had been expelled from the bar. The crowd grew to close to 400 during the melee, which lasted about 45 minutes, they said.

Arrested in the melee was Dave Van Ronk, 33 years old, of 15 Sheridan Square, a well-known folk singer. He was accused of having thrown a heavy object at a patrolman and later paroled in his own recognizance.

The raid was one of three held on Village bars in the last two weeks, Inspector Pine said.

Charges against the 13 who were arrested ranged from harassment and resisting arrest to disorderly conduct. A patrolman suffered a broken wrist, the police said.

Throngs of young men congregated outside the inn last night, reading aloud condemnations of the police.

A sign on the door said, "This is a private club. Members only." Only soft drinks were being served.

DOCUMENT 76

Homophile Youth Movement, "Get the Mafia and the Cops Out of Gay Bars"

ca. 29 June 1969, Craig Rodwell Papers, Box 5, New York Public Library

The nights of Friday, June 27, 1969 and Saturday, June 28, 1969 will go down in history as the first time that thousands of Homosexual men and women went out into the streets to protest the intolerable situation which has existed in New York City for many years—namely, the Mafia (or syndicate) control of this city's Gay bars in collusion with certain elements in the Police Dept. of the City of New York. The demonstrations were triggered by a Police raid on the Stonewall Inn late Friday night, June 27th. The purported reason for the raid was the Stonewall's lack of a liquor license. *Who's kidding whom?* Can anybody really believe that an operation as big as the Stonewall could continue for almost 3 years just a few blocks from the 6th Precinct house without having a liquor license? *No!* The Police have known about the Stonewall operation all along. What has happened is the presence of new "brass" in the 6th Precinct which has vowed to "drive the fags out of the Village."

Many of you have noticed one of the signs which the "management" of the Stonewall has placed outside stating "Legalize Gay bars and lick the problem." This is untrue and they know it. Judge Kenneth Keating (a former U.S. Senator) ruled in January, 1968 that even close dancing between Homosexuals is legal. *Since that date there has been nothing illegal, per se, about a Gay bar.* What is illegal about New York City's Gay bars today is the Mafia (or syndicate) stranglehold on them. Legitimate Gay businessmen are afraid to open decent Gay bars with a healthy social atmosphere (as opposed to the hell-hole atmosphere of places typified by the Stonewall) because of fear of pressure from the unholy alliance of the Mafia and the elements in the Police Dept. who accept payoffs and protect the Mafia monopoly.

We at the Homophile Youth Movement (HYMN) believe that the only way this monopoly can be broken is through the action of Homosexual men and women themselves. We obviously cannot rely on the various agencies of government who for years have known about this situation but who have refused to do anything about it. Therefore, we urge the following:

1. That Gay businessmen step forward and open Gay bars that will be run legally with competitive pricing and a healthy social atmosphere.
2. That Homosexual men and women boycott places like the Stonewall. The only way, it seems, that we can get criminal elements out of the Gay bars is simply to make it unprofitable for them.
3. That the Homosexual citizens of New York City, and concerned Heterosexuals, write to Mayor Lindsay demanding a thorough investigation and effective action to correct this intolerable situation.

DOCUMENT 77

Mattachine Society of New York, "Where Were You during the Christopher St. Riots?"
ca. 29 June 1969, Mattachine Society of New York Records, Box 11, Folder 6, New York Public Library

On the evenings of June 27th and 28th, hundreds of homosexuals violently protested the attempted closing of another gay bar in Greenwich Village. The police raided the well-known bar near Sheridan Square on the charge that

Figure 5.2. After the first night of rioting, the Mattachine Society of New York appealed to homosexuals for peace and quiet in Greenwich Village. The message was painted on a boarded-up window of the Stonewall Inn. Credit: Fred W. McDarrah (Getty).

liquor was being served without a license. This is a legitimate reason but WHY WAS THIS BAR ALLOWED TO OPERATE FOR YEARS WITH HARDLY ANY POLICE INTERFERENCE? WHY DID THE POLICE PICK THIS TIME TO CRACKDOWN ON ILLEGAL OPERATIONS? These and many other questions deserve answering.

IF YOU ARE TIRED OF—
- Police officials who have decided to harass homosexuals again
- Syndicate leaders who exploit homosexuals
- A State Liquor Authority which will not grant licenses for legitimate gay bars
- Mayoral candidates who use "Law and Order" issues to persecute minorities, including the homosexual minority
- Private citizens who form vigilante groups to rout homosexuals from their community, as has happened in Queens County
- A Governor who has failed to legalize consensual homosexual acts between adults in private due to his political cowardice

JOIN AND ACTIVELY PARTICIPATE IN MATTACHINE.... NOW IS THE TIME FOR ALL HOMOSEXUALS TO UNITE IN COMMON ACTION!

DOCUMENT 78

[Dick Leitsch], "The Hairpin Drop Heard around the World"
Mattachine Society of New York Newsletter, July 1969, 21–23[3]

The first gay riots in history took place during the pre-dawn hours of Saturday and Sunday, June 28–29, in New York's Greenwich Village. The demonstrations were touched off by a police raid on the popular Stonewall Club, 53 Christopher Street. This was the last (to date) in a series of harassments which plagued the Village area for the last several weeks.

Plainclothes officers entered the club at about 2 a.m., armed with a warrant, and closed the place on grounds of illegal selling of alcohol. Employees were arrested and the customers told to leave. The patrons gathered on the street outside, and were joined by other Village residents and visitors to the area. The police behaved, as is usually the case when they deal with homosexuals, with bad grace, and were reproached by "straight" onlookers. Pennies were thrown at the cops by the crowd, then beer cans, rocks, and even parking meters. The cops retreated inside the bar, which was set afire by the crowd.

A hose from the bar was employed by the trapped cops to douse the flames, and reinforcements were summoned. A melee ensued, with nearly a thousand persons participating, as well as several hundred cops. Nearly two hours later, the cops had "secured" the area.

The next day, the Stonewall management sent in a crew to repair the premises, and found that the cops had taken all the money from the cigarette machine, the juke box, the cash register and the safe, and had even robbed the waiters' tips!

Since they had been charged with selling liquor without a license, the club was reopened as a "free store," open to all and with everything being given away, rather than sold.

A crowd filled the place and the street in front. Singing and chanting filled Sheridan Square Park, and the crowds grew quickly.

At first, the crowd was all gay, but as the weekend tourists poured in the area, they joined the crowds. They'd begin by asking what was happening. When they were told that homosexuals were protesting the closing of a gay club, they'd become very sympathetic, and stay to watch or join in. One middle-aged lady with her husband told a cop that he should be ashamed of himself. "Don't you know that these people have no place to go, and need places like that bar?" she shouted. (Several hours later, she and her husband, with two other couples, were seen running with a large group of homosexuals from the night sticks brandished by the TPF [Tactical Police Force].)

The crowds were orderly, and limited themselves to singing and shouting slogans such as "Gay Power," "We Want Freedom Now" and "Equality for Homosexuals." As the mob grew, it spilled off the sidewalk, overflowed Sheridan Square Park, and began to fill the roadway. One of the six cops who were there to keep order began to get smart and cause hostility. A bus driver blew his horn at the meeting, and someone shouted, "Stop the Bus!" The crowd surged out into the street and blocked the progress of the bus. As the driver inched ahead, someone ripped off an advertising card and blocked the windshield with it. The crowd beat on the sides of the (empty) bus and shouted, "Christopher Street belongs to the queens!" and "Liberate the street."

The cops got the crowd to let the bus pass, but then the people began a slow-down-the-traffic campaign. A human line across the street blocked traffic, and the cars were let through one at a time. Another car, bearing a fat, gouty-looking cop with many pounds of gilt braid, chauffeured by a cute young cop, came through. The fat cop looked for all the world like a slave-owner survey-ing the plantation, and someone tossed a sack of wet garbage through the car window and right on his face. The bag broke and soggy coffee grounds dripped down the lined face, which never lost its "screw you" look.

Another police car came through Waverly Place, and stopped at the corner of Christopher. The occupants just sat there and glared at the crowd. Suddenly, a concrete block landed on the hood of the car, and the crowd drew back. Then, as one person, it surged forward and surrounded the car, beating on it with fists and dancing atop it. The cops radioed for help, and soon the crowd let the car pass.

Christopher Street, from Greenwich to Seventh Avenues, had become an almost solid mass of people—most of them gay. No traffic could pass, and even walking the few blocks on foot was next to impossible. One little old lady tried to get through, and many members of the crowd tried to help her. She brushed them away and continued her determined walk, trembling with fear and mur-muring, "It must be the full moon, it must be the full moon."

Squad cars from the 5th, 6th, 4th and 9th precincts had brought in a hun-dred or so cops who had no hope of controlling the crowd of nearly two thousand people in the streets. Until this point, the crowd had been, for the most part, pleasant and in a jovial mood. Some of the cops began to become very nasty, and started trouble. One boy, evidently a discus-thrower, reacted by bouncing garbage can lids neatly off the helmets of the cops. Others set gar-bage cans ablaze. A Christopher street merchant stood in the door of her shop and yelled at the cops to behave themselves. Whenever they would head in her direction, she'd run into the shop and lock the door.

The focus of the demonstration shifted from the Stonewall to "The Corner"—Greenwich Avenue and Christopher Street. The intersection, and the street behind it, was a solid mass of humanity. The Tactical Police Force (TPF) arrived in city busses. 100 of them debarked at The Corner, and 50 more at Seventh Ave. and Christopher.

They huddled with some of the top brass that had already arrived, and iso-lated beer cans, thrown by the crowd, hit their van and cars now and again. Suddenly, two cops darted into the crowd and dragged out a boy who had done absolutely nothing. As they carried him to a waiting van brought to take off prisoners, four more cops joined them and began pounding the boy in the face, belly and groin with night sticks. A high shrill voice called out, "Save our sister!" and there was a general pause, during which the "butch" looking "numbers" looked distracted. Momentarily, fifty or more homosexuals who would have to be described as "nelly" rushed the cops and took the boy back into the crowd. They then formed a solid front and refused to let the cops into the crowd to regain their prisoner, letting the cops hit them with their sticks, rather than let them through.

(It was an interesting sidelight on the demonstrations that those usually put down as "sissies" or "swishes" showed the most courage and sense during the action. Their bravery and daring saved many people from being hurt, and their sense of humor and "camp" helped keep the crowds from getting nasty or too violent.)

The cops gave up on the idea of taking prisoners, and concentrated on clearing the area. They rushed both ways on Greenwich, forcing the crowds into 10th Street and 6th Avenue, where the people circled the blocks and re-entered Christopher. Then the cops formed a flying wedge, and with arms linked, headed down Greenwich, forcing everyone in front of them into side streets. Cops on the ends of the wedge broke off and chased demonstrators down the side streets and away from the center of the action.

They made full use of their night sticks, brandishing them like swords. At one point a cop grabbed a wild Puerto Rican queen and lifted his arm to bring a club down on "her." In his best Mario Montez voice, the queen challenged, "How'd you like a big Spanish dick up your little Irish ass?" The cop was so shocked he hesitated in his swing and the queen escaped.

At another point, two lonely cops were chasing a hundred or more people down Waverly Place. Someone shouted out that the queens outnumbered the cops and suggested catching them, ripping off their clothes and screwing them. The cops abandoned the chase and fled back to the main force for protection.

The police action did eventually disperse the crowds, many of whom abandoned the cause and headed to the docks for some fun. By 2:30, nearly two hours after the bus had been delayed, the area was again peaceful. Apart from the two to three hundred cops standing around the area, it looked like an unusually dull Saturday night.

Then, at 3 a.m. the bars closed, and the patrons of the many gay bars in the area arrived to see what was happening. They were organized and another attempt was made to liberate Christopher Street. The police, still there in great numbers, managed to break up the demonstrations. One small group did break off and attempt to liberate the IND subway station at Sixth Avenue and Waverly Place, but the police, after a hurried consultation as to whether they could act on the "turf" of the Transit cops, went in and chased everyone out.

By 5:30 a.m., the area was secure enough that the TPF police were sent home, and the docks were packed tight with homosexuals having the times of their lives. After all, everything was perfectly "safe"—all the cops were on "The Corner"!

In all, thirteen people were arrested on Saturday morning—7 of them employees of the Stonewall. Four more were arrested on Sunday morning, and many more were detained, then released. Apparently, only four persons were injured—all of them cops. Three suffered minor bruises and scratches, and one a "broken wrist" (it was not specified whether it was the kind of "broken wrist" that requires a cast, or the kind that makes it noisy to wear a bangle bracelet—we presume it was the former).

Sunday night saw a lot of action in the Christopher Street area. Hundreds of people were on the streets including, for the first time, a large "leather" contingent. However, there were never enough people to outnumber the large squads of cops milling about, trying desperately to head off any trouble.

The Stonewall was again a "free store" and the citizenry was treated to the sight of the cops begging homosexuals to go inside the bar that they had chased everyone out of a few nights before.

Inasmuch as all the cops in town seemed to be near The Corner again, the docks were very busy, and two boys went by the Charles Street station house and pasted "Equality for Homosexuals" bumper stickers on cop cars, the autos of on-duty cops, and the van used to take away prisoners.

One of the most frightening comments was made by one cop to another, and overheard by a MSNY [Mattachine Society of New York] member being held in detention. One said he'd enjoyed the fracas. "Them queers have a good sense of humor and really had a good time," he said. His "buddy" protested: "Aw, they're sick. I like nigger riots better because there's more action, but you can't beat up a fairy. They ain't mean like blacks; they're sick. But you can't hit a sick man."

DOCUMENT 79
D. L. [Dick Leitsch], "Gay Riots"
Mattachine Society of New York Newsletter, July 1969, 24–25

The "Christopher Street Riots" marked a first in the history of homosexuals.

Shouting "Gay Power" and blocking traffic is a far cry from the old days when all homosexuals were furtive and "kept their place." The "riots" were also as far as could be imagined from what homosexuals have done before.

This was no carefully planned, super-straight picketing demonstration of 20 or 30 overdressed and severely middle-class homosexuals; nor was it a cop-out, like the "mass meeting" held by a self-styled homosexual leader under the Arch in Washington Square Park—complete with hymn-singing, speakers, and an audience of 40 or 50 tourists from Peoria.

The nearly 2,000 people who swarmed through Christopher Street between midnight and 4:00 A.M. on Sunday morning could have been an ugly mob. Only the good humor, sense of camp, and highly developed sense of the ridiculous that is characteristic of so many homosexuals kept the group from becoming a destructively raging, nasty mob.

The "riots" came about spontaneously, and were not planned by any organization or group. They were unpremeditated protests against police harassment, unfair laws, uncaring public officials, and inequality.

One bar too many had been raided, one group of homosexuals too many had been harassed, and it required more than 200 cops to restore order. Many of the demonstrators promised the cops that "it'll be a long hot summer," and it may well be. One more group in the community has had enough of inequality and unfair treatment, and the first rebellion has erupted. There could be more, and they could get nastier.

If that happens, the reasons would be easily understandable. The responsible parties would not be those who raced through Christopher Street and stopped traffic, who threw rocks and other missiles at the cops, and set trash cans ablaze. The responsible parties would be legislators who ignore the needs of the people and attempt to legislate the private morality of one or two religious groups.

Part of the blame will lie with corrupt cops who shake down gay bars for the privilege of staying open, and then when the political climate dictates, raid the bars to which they have sold protection.

Some of the blame must be borne by the community which tolerates such corruption. And a large portion of it will go to Donald S. Hostetter and the State Liquor Authority, the most corrupt agency in the State of New York and one so rotten that it makes the Cosa Nostra look like a convention of bishops.

The SLA refuses licenses to operators of gay bars, then has gay clubs closed because they don't have licenses. Licensed gay bars are held to higher standards than licensed places with other clientele. Innumerable ruses, tricks and illegal acts are employed to revoke the licenses of gay bars. Applicants for licenses are asked if they intend to permit homosexuals to use the premises, and a "yes" answer is considered grounds for not issuing a license. Even legitimate, licensed bars are harassed by cops and SLA investigators.

Because of this, no legitimate business man can survive in the business of providing a gay bar or club, and most of them are operated by shady figures, reputed to be underworld characters.

After thus making it impossible for an honest man to stay in business, the SLA and the cops close the bars that do exist, on the grounds that the owners have "underworld connections." This, the police and SLA officials, because of their bribe-taking, are de facto partners in whatever criminality does exist.

When the bars and clubs are put out of operation, the cops complain that there are too many homosexuals on the streets and start their campaigns of harassment.

Where do they expect us to go to congregate and make a social life? We can't just vanish, we certainly aren't going to kill ourselves, and moving to another town is no help—things won't be any different there.

As taxpayers and citizens, we've asked for reforms. The only person in public life who has paid any attention has been John Lindsay, and his efforts have been largely balked by other officials, most of whom are too wrapped up in their own religious and social "bags." We've gone to the courts and sued for reforms. Sometimes we win, sometimes we lose, but either way, the process takes years and costs a small fortune.

Homosexuals are tired of waiting—after all, we can't be put off with the old line that things will improve in the next generation and our children will lead better, happier lives. Most of us aren't going to have children, and we have to struggle to make our own lives better.

If the traditional means of winning reform cannot work in this age—if democracy is so dead that the citizens have no means of gaining redress by honest, straightforward means—then possibly the only place for those of us who care about reform is in the streets. Perhaps confrontation politics can win the reforms traditional politics couldn't gain for us.

The Stonewall case provided the opening shot (or, as someone on the scene said, "the dropped hairpin heard 'round the world"). What happens next is pretty much up to the SLA, the police, and the public officials.

If reforms are not made, it could indeed be a long, hot summer.

DOCUMENT 80
"Police Again Rout 'Village' Youths: Outbreak by 400 Follows a Near-Riot over Raid"
New York Times, 30 June 1969, 22

Heavy police reinforcements cleared the Sheridan Square area of Greenwich Village again yesterday morning when large crowds of young men, angered by a police raid on an inn frequented by homosexuals, swept through the area.

Tactical Patrol Force units assigned to the East Village poured into the area about 2:15 A.M. after units from the Charles Street station house were unable to control a crowd of about 400 youths, some of whom were throwing bottles and lighting small fires.

Their arms linked, a row of helmeted policemen stretching across the width of the street made several sweeps up and down Christopher Street between the Avenue of the Americas and Seventh Avenue South.

The crowd retreated before them, but many groups fled into the numerous small side streets and re-formed behind the police line. The police were not withdrawn until 4 A.M.

A number of people who did not retreat fast enough were pushed and shoved along, and at least two men were clubbed to the ground.

Stones and bottles were thrown at the police lines, and the police twice broke ranks and charged into the crowd.

Three persons were arrested on charges of harassment and disorderly conduct.

The crowd had gathered in the evening across the street from the Stonewall Inn at 53 Christopher Street, where the police staged a raid early Saturday. The police were denounced by last night's crowd for allegedly harassing homosexuals. Graffiti on the boarded-up windows of the inn included: "Support gay power" and "Legalize gay bars."

Saturday's raid took place when about 200 people were in the bar. Plainclothes men, with a warrant authorizing a search for illegal sales of alcohol, confiscated cases of liquor and beer.

A melee involving about 400 youths ensued, a partial riot mobilization was ordered by Police Headquarters, and 13 persons were arrested on a number of charges. Four policemen were injured, one suffering a broken wrist. Among those arrested was Dave Van Ronk, a folk singer.

DOCUMENT 81

Lucian Truscott IV, "Gay Power Comes to Sheridan Square"
Village Voice, 3 July 1969, 1, 18

Sheridan Square this weekend looked like something from a William Burroughs novel as the sudden specter of "gay power" erected its brazen head and spat out a fairy tale the likes of which the area has never seen.

The forces of faggotry, spurred by a Friday night raid on one of the city's largest, most popular, and longest lived gay bars, the Stonewall Inn, rallied Saturday night in an unprecedented protest against the raid and continued Sunday night to assert presence, possibility, and pride until the early hours of Monday morning. "I'm a faggot, and I'm proud of it!" "Gay Power!" "I like boys!"—these and many other slogans were heard all three nights as the show of force by the city's finery met the force of the city's finest. The result was a kind of liberation, as the gay brigade emerged from the bars, back rooms, and bedrooms of the Village and became street people.

Cops entered the Stonewall for the second time in a week just before midnight on Friday. It began as a small raid—only two patrolmen, two detectives, and two policewomen were involved. But as the patrons trapped inside were released one by one, a crowd started to gather on the street. It was initially a festive gathering, composed mostly of Stonewall boys who were waiting around for friends still inside or to see what was going to happen. Cheers would go up as favorites would emerge from the door, strike a pose, and swish by the detective with a "Hello there, fella." The stars were in their element. Wrists were limp, hair was primped, and reactions to the applause were classic. "I gave them the gay power bit, and they loved it, girls." "Have you seen Maxine? Where *is* my wife—I told her not to go far."

Suddenly the paddywagon arrived and the mood of the crowd changed. Three of the more blatant queens—in full drag—were loaded inside, along with the bartender and doorman, to a chorus of catcalls and boos from the crowd. A cry went up to push the paddywagon over, but it drove away before anything could happen. With its exit, the action waned momentarily. The next person to come out was a dyke, and she put up a struggle—from car to door to car again. It was at that moment that the scene became explosive. Limp wrists were forgotten. Beer cans and bottles were heaved at the windows, and a rain of coins descended on the cops. At the height of the action, a bearded figure was plucked from the crowd and dragged inside. It was Dave Van Ronk, who had come from the Lion's Head to see what was going on. He was later charged with having thrown an object at the police.

Three cops were necessary to get Van Ronk away from the crowd and into the Stonewall. The exit left no cops on the street, and almost by signal the crowd erupted into cobblestone and bottle heaving. The reaction was solid: they were pissed. The trashcan I was standing on was nearly yanked out from under me as a kid tried to grab it for use in the window smashing melee. From nowhere came an uprooted parking meter—used as a battering ram on the Stonewall door. I heard several cries of "Let's get some gas," but the blaze of flame which soon appeared in the window of the Stonewall was still a shock. As the wood barrier behind the glass was beaten open, the cops inside turned a firehose on the crowd. Several kids took the opportunity to cavort in the spray, and their momentary glee served to stave off what was rapidly becoming a full-scale attack. By the time the fags were able to regroup forces and come up with another assault, several carloads of police reinforcements had arrived, and in minutes the streets were clear.

A visit to the Sixth Precinct revealed the fact that 13 persons had been arrested on charges which ranged from Van Ronk's felonious assault of a police officer to the owners' illegal sale and storage of alcoholic beverages without a license. Two police officers had been injured in the battle with the crowd. By the time the last cop was off the street Saturday morning, a sign was going up announcing that the Stonewall would reopen that night. It did.

Protest set the tone for "gay power" activities on Saturday. The afternoon was spent boarding up the windows of the Stonewall and chalking them with signs of the new revolution: "We Are Open," "There is all college boys and girls in here," "Support Gay Power—C'mon in, girls," "Insp. Smyth looted our: money, jukebox, cigarette mach, telephones, safe, cash register, and the boys' tips." Among the slogans were two carefully clipped and bordered copies of the Daily News story about the previous night's events, which was anything but kind to the gay cause.

The real action Saturday was that night in the street. Friday night's crowd had returned and was being led in "gay power" cheers by a group of gay cheer-leaders. "We are the Stonewall girls / We wear our hair in curls / We have no underwear / We show our pubic hairs!" The crowd was gathered across the street from the Stonewall and was growing with additions of onlookers, East-siders, and rough street people who saw a chance for a little action. Though dress had changed from Friday night's gayery to Saturday night street clothes, the scene was a command performance for queers. If Friday night had been pick-up night, Saturday was date night. Hand-holding, kissing, and posing

Figures 5.3 and 5.4. Fred W. McDarrah (1926–2007) was a staff photographer for the *Village Voice*. These images, taken in front of the Stonewall Inn and a nearby building, are from the evening of 28 June 1969 (the second night of rioting). The photograph taken in front of the Stonewall was published alongside Lucian Truscott's article in the *Voice* on 3 July 1969. Credit: Fred W. McDarrah (Getty).

accented each of the cheers with a homosexual liberation that had appeared only fleetingly on the street before. One-liners were as practiced as if they had been used for years. "I just want you all to know," quipped a platinum blond with obvious glee, "that sometimes being homosexual is a big pain in the ass." Another allowed as how he had become a "left-deviationist." And on and on.

The quasi-political tone of the street scene was looked upon with disdain by some, for radio news announcements about the previous night's "gay power" chaos had brought half of Fire Island's Cherry Grove running back to home base to see what they had left behind. The generation gap existed even here. Older boys had strained looks on their faces and talked in concerned whispers as they watched the up-and-coming generation take being gay and flaunt it before the masses.

As the "gay power" chants on the street rose in frequency and volume, the crowd grew restless. The front of the Stonewall was losing its attraction, despite efforts by the owners to talk the crowd back into the club. "C'mon in and see what da pigs done to us," they growled. "We're honest businessmen here. We're American-born boys. We run a legitimate joint here. There ain't nuttin bein' done wrong in dis place. Everybody come and see."

The people on the street were not to be coerced. "Let's go down the street and see what's happening, girls," someone yelled. And down the street went the crowd, smack into the Tactical Patrol Force, who had been called earlier to disperse the crowd and were walking west on Christopher from Sixth Avenue. Formed in a line, the TPF swept the crowd back to the corner of Waverly Place, where they stopped. A stagnant situation there brought on some gay tomfoolery in the form of a chorus line facing the line of helmeted and club-carrying cops. Just as the line got into a full kick routine, the TPF advanced again and cleared the crowd of screaming gay powerites down Christopher to Seventh Avenue. The street and park were then held from both ends, and no one was allowed to enter—naturally causing a fall-off in normal Saturday night business, even at the straight Lion's Head and 55. The TPF positions in and around the square were held with only minor incident—one busted head and a number of scattered arrests—while the cops amused themselves by arbitrarily breaking up small groups of people up and down the avenue. The crowd finally dispersed around 3:30 a.m. The TPF had come and they had conquered, but Sunday was already there, and it was to be another story.

Sunday night was a time for watching and rapping. Gone were the "gay power" chants of Saturday, but not the new and open brand of exhibitionism. Steps, curbs, and the park provided props for what amounted to the Sunday fag follies as returning stars from the previous night's performances stopped by to close the show for the weekend.

It was slow going. Around 1 a.m. a non-helmeted version of the TPF arrived and made a controlled and very cool sweep of the area, getting everyone moving and out of the park. That put a damper on posing and primping, and as the last buses were leaving Jerseyward, the crowd grew thin. Allen Ginsberg and

Taylor Mead walked by to see what was happening and were filled in on the previous evenings' activities by some of the gay activists. "Gay power! Isn't that great!" Allen said. "We're one of the largest minorities in the country—10 per cent, you know. It's about time we did something to assert ourselves."

Ginsberg expressed a desire to visit the Stonewall—"You know, I've never been in there"—and ambled on down the street, flashing peace signs and hel-loing the TPF. It was a relief and a kind of joy to see him on the street. He lent an extra umbrella of serenity [on] the scene with his laughter and quiet commentary on consciousness, "gay power" as a new movement, and the various implications of what had happened. I followed him into the Stonewall, where rock music blared from speakers all around a room that might have come right from a Hollywood set of a gay bar. He was immediately bouncing and dancing wherever he moved.

He left, and I walked east with him. Along the way, he described how things used to be. "You know, the guys there were so beautiful—they've lost that wounded look that fags all had 10 years ago." It was the first time I had heard that crowd described as beautiful.

We reached Cooper Square, and as Ginsberg turned to head toward home, he waved and yelled, "Defend the fairies!" and bounced on across the square. He enjoyed the prospect of "gay power" and is probably working on a manifesto for the movement right now. Watch out. The liberation is under way.

DOCUMENT 82

Howard Smith, "View from Inside: Full Moon over the Stonewall"
Village Voice, 3 July 1969, 1, 25, 29

During the "gay power" riots at the Stonewall last Friday night I found myself on what seemed to me the wrong side of the blue line. Very scary. Very enlightening.

I had struck up a spontaneous relationship with Deputy Inspector Pine, who had marshalled the raid, and was following him closely, listening to all the little dialogues and plans and police inflections. Things were already pretty tense: the gay customers freshly ejected from their hangout, prancing high and jubilant in the street, had been joined by quantities of Friday night tourists hawking around for Village-type excitement. The cops had considerable trouble arresting the few people they wanted to take in for further questioning. A strange mood was in the crowd—I noticed the full moon. Loud defiances mixed with skittish hilarity made for a more dangerous stage of protest; they were feeling their impunity. This kind of crowd freaks easily.

The turning point came when the police had difficulty keeping a dyke in a patrol car. Three times she slid out and tried to walk away. The last time a cop bodily heaved her in. The crowd shrieked, "Police brutality!" "Pigs!" A few coins sailed through the air. I covered my face. Pine ordered the three cars and paddy wagon to leave with the prisoners before the crowd became more of a mob. "Hurry back," he added, realizing he and his force of eight detectives, two of them women, would be easily overwhelmed if the temper broke. "Just drop them at the Sixth Precinct and hurry back."

The sirened caravan pushed through the gauntlet, pummeled and buffeted until it managed to escape. "Pigs!" "Gaggot [sic] cops!" Pennies and dimes flew. I stood against the door. The detectives held at most a 10-foot clearing. Escalate to nickels and quarters. A bottle. Another bottle. Pine says, "Let's get inside. Lock ourselves inside, it's safer."

"You want to come in?" he asks me. "You're probably safer," with a paternal tone. Two flashes: if they go in and I stay out, will the mob know that the blue plastic thing hanging from my shirt is a press card, or by now will they assume I'm a cop too? On the other hand, it might be interesting to be locked in with a few cops, just rapping and reviewing how they work.

In goes me. We bolt the heavy door. The front of the Stonewall is mostly brick except for the windows, which are boarded within by plywood. Inside we hear the shattering of windows, followed by what we imagine to be bricks pounding on the door, voices yelling. The floor shudders at each blow. "Aren't you guys scared?" I say.

"No." But they look at least uneasy.

The door crashes open, beer cans and bottles hurtle in. Pine and his troop rush to shut it. At that point the only uniformed cop among them gets hit with something under his eye. He hollers, and his hand comes away scarlet. It looks a lot more serious than it really is. They are all suddenly furious. Three run out in front to see if they can scare the mob from the door. A hail of coins. A beer can glances off Deputy Inspector Smyth's head.

Pine, a man of about 40 and smallish build, gathers himself, leaps out into the melee, and grabs someone around the waist, pulling him downward and back into the doorway. They fall. Pine regains hold and drags the elected protester inside by the hair. The door slams again. Angry cops converge on the guy, releasing their anger on this sample from the mob. Pine is saying, "I saw him throwing somethin," and the guy unfortunately is giving some sass, snidely admits to throwing "only a few coins." The cop who was cut is incensed, yells something like, "So you're the one who hit me!" And while the other cops help, he slaps the prisoner five or six times very hard and finishes with a punch to the mouth. They handcuff the guy as he almost passes out. "All right," Pine announces, "we book him for assault." The door is smashed open again. More objects are thrown in. The detectives locate a fire hose, the idea being to ward off the madding crowd until reinforcements arrive. They can't see where to aim it, wedging the hose in a crack in the door. It sends out a weak stream. We all start to slip on water and Pine says to stop.

By now the mind's eye has forgotten the character of the mob; the sound filtering in doesn't suggest dancing faggots any more. It sounds like a powerful rage bent on vendetta. That['s] why Pine's singling out the guy I knew later to be Dan [*sic*] Van Ronk was important. The little force of detectives was beginning to feel fear, and Pine's action clinched their morale again.

A door over to the side almost gives. One cop shouts, "Get away from there or I'll shoot!" It stops shaking. The front door is completely open. One of the big plywood windows gives, and it seems inevitable that the mob will pour in. A kind of tribal adrenaline rush bolsters all of us; they all take out and check pistols. I see both policewomen busy doing the same, and the danger becomes even more real. I find a big wrench behind the bar, jam it into my belt like a scimitar. Hindsight: my fear on the verge of being trampled by a mob fills the same dimensions as my fear on the verge of being clubbed by the TPF.

Pine places a few men on each side of the corridor leading away from the entrance. They aim unwaveringly at the door. One detective arms himself in addition with a sawed-off baseball bat he has found. I hear, "We'll shoot the first motherfucker that comes through the door."

Pine glances over toward me. "Are you all right, Howard?" I can't believe what I am saying: "I'd feel a lot better with a gun."

I can only see the arm at the window. It squirts a liquid into the room, and a flaring match follows. Pine is not more than 10 feet away. He aims his gun at the figures.

He doesn't fire. The sound of sirens coincides with the whoosh of flames where the lighter fluid was thrown. Later, Pine tells me he didn't shoot because he had heard the sirens in time and felt no need to kill someone if help was arriving. It was that close.

While the squads of uniforms disperse the mob out front, inside we are checking to see if each of us [is] all right. For a few minutes we get the post-tension giggles, but as they subside I start scribbling notes to catch up, and the people around me change back to cops. They begin examining the place.

It had lasted 45 minutes. Just before and after the siege I picked up some more detached information. According to the police, they are not picking on homosexuals. On these raids they almost never arrest customers, only people working there. As of June 1, the State Liquor Authority said that all unlicensed places were eligible to apply for licenses. The police are scrutinizing all unlicensed places, and most of the bars that are in that category happen to cater to homosexuals. The Stonewall is an unlicensed private club. The raid was made with a warrant, after undercover agents inside observed illegal sale of alcohol. To make certain the raid plans did not leak, it was made without notifying the Sixth Precinct until after the detectives (all from the First Division) were inside the premises. Once the bust had actually started, one of Pine's men called the Sixth for assistance on a pay phone.

It was explained to me that generally men dressed as men, even if wearing extensive makeup, are always released; men dressed as women are sometimes arrested; and "men" fully dressed as women, but who upon inspection by a policewoman prove to have undergone the sex-change operation, are always let

Figure 5.5. *Village Voice* photojournalist Fred W. McDarrah captured this image of destroyed property inside the Stonewall Inn on 28 June 1969. Credit: Fred W. McDarrah (Getty).

go. At the Stonewall, out of five queens checked, three were men and two were changes, even though all said they were girls. Pine released them all anyway.

As for the rough-talking owners and/or managers of the Stonewall, their riff ran something like this: we are just honest businessmen who are being harassed by the police because we cater to homosexuals, and because our names are Italian so they think we are part of something bigger. We haven't done anything wrong and have never been convicted in no court. We have rights, and the courts should decide and not let the police do things like what happened here. When we got back in the place, all the mirrors, jukeboxes, phones, toilets, and cigarette machines were smashed. Even the sinks were stuffed and running over. And we say the police did it. The courts will say that we are innocent.

Who isn't, I thought, as I dropped my scimitar and departed.

DOCUMENT 83
"Hostile Crowd Dispersed near Sheridan Square"
New York Times, 3 July 1969, 19

At least four persons were arrested and charged with harassment last night in the Sheridan Square area of Greenwich Village, where the police dispersed a hostile crowd for the third time in the last week.

Figures 5.6 and 5.7. *New York Times* photographer Larry Morris (1924–1987) shot these photographs on the last night of rioting (2–3 July 1969). They were not published at the time, but were rediscovered decades later in the photography archives of the *Times*. The West Side Savings Bank was located at the intersection of Seventh Avenue South, West Fourth Street, and Christopher Street. Credit: Larry Morris/*New York Times* (Redux).

The confrontations resulted from a police raid last weekend on a local bar, the Stonewall Inn, at 53 Christopher Street, which the police said was well known for its homosexual clientele and was allegedly operating without a liquor license.

Last night a chanting crowd of about 500 persons was scattered by members of the Tactical Patrol Force and police of the Charles Street station who were the targets occasionally of bottles and beer cans. A few fires were set in trash baskets along Christopher Street.

DOCUMENT 84
Leo E. Laurence, "Gays Hit NY Cops"
Berkeley Barb, 4 July 1969, 5

Homosexuals took to the streets in New York City last weekend and joined the revolution. A two-day battle resulted after New York City Pigs busted a popular gay bar, the Stonewall Inn in Greenwich Village.

The pigs first moved in last Friday with six squad cars for a "small" raid, according to underground reports. They trapped everybody inside and began herding customers one-by-one into paddy wagons waiting outside.

Ironically, it was a chick who gave the rallying cry to fight. Pigs were loading her into the wagon when she shouted to a big crowd of bystanders: "Why don't you guys do something!"

That did it. The crowd rushed the police wagon as someone yelled: "Let's turn it over." The pig driver drove off, escaping the angry crowd.

Meanwhile, pigs inside the bar were raising hell. Reports from the scene say they looted a juke box, cigarette machine, telephone money, the safe, cash register, and tips. They also busted 13 people.

Overnight signs were chalked on the walls outside the Stonewall: "SUPPORT GAY POWER!" and "WE ARE OPEN!"

Saturday night, the action began about one a.m., according to an eyewitness, J. Marks, author of the book "Rock & Other Four-Letter Words."

The street was mobbed for about 5 blocks near the Stonewall bar. "I saw a taxi make the mistake of turning into the street when an enormous roar came from about 400 people," said Marks. "They attacked the cab, banging in the sides, and parading on the hood and top.

"The cabbie got out and began messing up a few kids and about fifteen jumped him. Meanwhile, about 15 others were trying to let the passengers get to freedom.

"A city bus ran through the street, but the mass of people wouldn't let it through. They created a thunderous sound beating on the sides of the bus before passing it through.

"Police came and the crowd pulled away for a moment, then they descended onto the prowl car. They first knocked off the red flashing light. Then they started shaking the squad car sideways as if to tip it over.

"At that point an enormous group of TPF (Tactical Patrol Force) arrived with helmets and started marching in a line and swept the crowd back.

"The kids formed a chorus line opposite the helmeted police line and started singing and dancing. The TPF advanced again and scattered them."

That ended Saturday night's battle, the eye-witness said. Sunday, the word passed for another gay demonstration. Help was expected from the SDS [Students for a Democratic Society], but they never showed up.

"The gay community in New York City has been inspired by your homosexual liberation stories in the *Barb*," Marks told me via transcontinental phone.

Allen Ginsberg visited the Stonewall bar Sunday, according to Marks, and said: "Gay Power! Isn't that great. We are one of the largest minorities in the country, ten per-cent you know. It's about time we did something to assert ourselves."

Ginsberg reportedly told the Stonewall crowd, "The guys here are so beautiful—they have lost that wounded look that fags all had ten years ago."

DOCUMENT 85

Jerry Lisker, "Homo Nest Raided, Queen Bees Are Stinging Mad"

New York Daily News, 6 July 1969, M1, M6

She sat there with her legs crossed, the lashes of her mascara-coated eyes beating like the wings of a hummingbird. She was angry. She was so upset she hadn't bothered to shave. A day old stubble was beginning to push through the pancake makeup. She was a he. A queen of Christopher Street.

Last weekend the queens had turned commandos and stood bra strap to bra strap against an invasion of the helmeted Tactical Patrol Force. The elite police squad had shut down one of their private gay clubs, the Stonewall Inn at 57 Christopher St., in the heart of a three-block homosexual community in Greenwich Village.

Queen Power reared its bleached blonde head in revolt. New York City experienced its first homosexual riot.

"We may have lost the battle, sweets, but the war is far from over," lisped an unofficial lady-in-waiting from the court of the Queens.

"We've had all we can take from the Gestapo," the spokesman, or spokeswoman, continued. "We're putting our foot down once and for all." The foot wore a spiked heel.

According to reports, the Stonewall Inn, a two-story structure with a sand painted brick and opaque glass facade, was a mecca for the homosexual element in the village who wanted nothing but a private little place where they could congregate, drink, dance and do whatever little girls do when they get together.

The thick glass shut out the outside world of the street. Inside, the Stonewall bathed in wild, bright psychedelic lights, while the patrons writhed to the sounds of a juke box on a square dance floor surrounded by booths and tables. The bar did a good business and the waiters, or waitresses, were always kept busy, as they snaked their way around the dancing customers to the booths and tables. For nearly two years, peace and tranquility reigned supreme for the Alice in Wonderland clientele.

Last Friday the privacy of the Stonewall was invaded by police from the First Division. It was a raid. They had a warrant. After two years, police said they had been informed that liquor was being served on the premises. Since the Stonewall was without a license, the place was being closed. It was the law.

All hell broke loose when the police entered the Stonewall. The girls instinctively reached for each other. Others stood frozen, locked in an embrace of fear.

Only a handful of police were on hand for the initial landing in the homosexual beachhead. They ushered the patrons out onto Christopher Street, just off Sheridan Square. A crowd had formed in front of the Stonewall and the customers were greeted with cheers of encouragement from the gallery.

The whole proceeding took on the aura of a homosexual Academy Awards Night. The Queens pranced out to the street blowing kisses and waving to the crowd. A beauty of a specimen named Stella wailed uncontrollably while being led to the sidewalk in front of the Stonewall by a cop. She later confessed that she didn't protest the manhandling by the officer[;] it was just that her hair was in curlers and she was afraid her new beau might be in the crowd and spot her. She didn't want him to see her this way, she wept.

The crowd began to get out of hand, eyewitnesses said. Then, without warning, Queen Power exploded with all the fury of a gay atomic bomb. Queens, princesses and ladies-in-waiting began hurling anything they could lay their polished, manicured fingernails on. Bobby pins, compacts, curlers, lipstick tubes and other femme fatale missiles were flying in the direction of the cops. The war was on. The lilies of the valley had become carnivorous jungle plants.

Urged on by cries of "C'mon girls, lets go get'em!," the defenders of Stonewall launched an attack. The cops called for assistance. To the rescue came the Tactical Patrol Force.

Flushed with the excitement of battle, a fellow called Gloria pranced around like Wonder Woman, while several Florence Nightingales administered first aid to the fallen warriors. There were some assorted scratches and bruises, but nothing serious was suffered by these honeys turned Madwomen of Challiot [sic].

Official reports listed four injured policemen with 13 arrests. The War of the Roses lasted about two hours from about midnight to 2 a.m. There was a return bout Wednesday night.

Two veterans recently recalled the battle and issued a warning to the cops. "If they close up all the gay joints in this area there is going to be all out war."

Both said they were refugees from Indiana and had come to New York where they could live together happily ever after. They were in their early 20's. They preferred to be called by their married names, Bruce and Nan.

"I don't like your paper," Nan lisped matter-of-factly. "It's anti-fag and pro-cop."

"I'll bet you didn't see what they did to the Stonewall. Did the pigs tell you that they smashed everything in sight? Did you ask them why they stole money out of the cash register and then smashed it with a sledge hammer? Did you ask them why it took them two years to discover that the Stonewall didn't have a liquor license?"

Bruce nodded in agreement and reached over for Nan's trembling hands.

"Calm down, doll," he said. "Your face is getting all flushed."

Nan wiped her face with a tissue.

"This would have to happen right before the wedding. The reception was going to be held at the Stonewall, too," Nan said, tossing her ashen-tinted hair over her shoulder.

"What wedding?," the bystander asked.

Nan frowned with a how-could-anybody-be-so-stupid look. "Eric and Jack's wedding, of course. They're finally tieing the knot. I thought they'd never get together."

"We'll have to find another place, that's all there is to it," Bruce sighed. "But every time we start a place, the cops break it up sooner or later."

"They let us operate just as long as the payoff is regular," Nan said bitterly. "I believe they closed up the Stonewall because there was some trouble with the payoff to the cops. I think that's the real reason. It's a shame. It was such a lovely place. We never bothered anybody. Why couldn't they leave us alone?"

Shirley Evans, a neighbor with two children, agrees that the Stonewall was not a rowdy place and the persons who frequented the club were never troublesome. She lives at 45 Christopher St.

"Up until the night of the police raid there was never any trouble there," she said. "The homosexuals minded their own business and never bothered a soul. There were never any fights or hollering, or anything like that. They just wanted to be left alone. I don't know what they did inside, but that's their business. I was never in there myself. It was just awful when the police came. It was like a swarm of hornets attacking a bunch of butterflies."

A reporter visited the now closed Stonewall and it indeed looked like a cyclone had struck the premises.

Police said there were over 200 people in the Stonewall when they entered with a warrant. The crowd outside was estimated at 500 to 1,000. According to police, the Stonewall had been under observation for some time. Being a private club, plainclothesmen were refused entrance to the inside when they periodically tried to check the place. "They had the tightest security in the Village," a First Division officer said. "We could never get near the place without a warrant."

The men of the First Division were unable to find any humor in the situation, despite the comical overtones of the raid.

"They were throwing more than lace hankies," one inspector said. "I was almost decapitated by a slab of thick glass. It was thrown like a discus and just missed my throat by inches. The beer can didn't miss, though, it hit me right above the temple."

Police also believe the club was operated by Mafia connected owners. The police did confiscate the Stonewall's cash register as proceeds of an illegal operation. The receipts were counted and are on file at the division headquarters. The warrant was served and the establishment closed on the grounds it was an illegal membership club with no license, and no license to serve liquor.

The police are sure of one thing. They haven't heard the last from the Girls of Christopher Street.

DOCUMENT 86

Jay Levin, "The Gay Anger behind the Riots"
New York Post, 8 July 1969, 36

"People are beginning to realize," said the doorman at the Stonewall Inn, "that no matter how 'Nelly' or how 'fem' a homosexual is, you can only push them so far."

With a battle cry of "gay power," the Nellies, fems, gay boys, queens—all those who flaunt their homosexuality—have been demonstrating that they have indeed been pushed too far.

For three successive nights last week, hundreds of young homosexuals flung rocks, bottles and fists at cops stationed in Sheridan Square after police twice raided the Stonewall. The charge was serving liquor without a license, despite the Christopher Street gay joint's claim that it is a private club.

"All my life," a 19-year-old blond with lacquered hair and lavender bellbottoms said, "the cops have sneered and pointed at me and my friends. We've been harassed for doing nothing more than having our fun; not hurting anybody else. Well, the 'gay riots' mean we're not going to take it any more."

The Stonewall is not the only source of gay indignation. In the past few weeks, the police have raided a number of homosexual bars and after-hours joints, especially those in the Village.

But in a precarious though enormously profitable business, the Stonewall stands as a monument to longevity and police wise management. It survived for 2½ years before being busted, making it the mecca of the gay night life. Behind its blacked out windows, the gay young men drank, danced and made attachments with a confidence that, at last, they had found sanctuary.

"It was the best place we ever had," Dick Kanon, 22, remarked as he ambled down Christopher St. Male prostitutes slouched in the doorways along the way, watching with quick eyes for potential "friends."

"Most gay people are extravagantly paranoid. If there was ever a place that cured that, it was the Stonewall. You felt safe among your own. You could come down around here without fear of being busted or of being beaten up by some punk out to prove his masculinity to himself. Around here, we outnumber the punks."

There have been frequent suggestions that the city's homosexual bars are run by the Mafia and protected by payoffs to the police. The current raids were conducted by the vice squad and kept secret from local precincts to prevent leaks.

The stated reason for the crackdown is a tough new SLA ban against "private" clubs. Denying harassment of homosexuals, police point out that licensed bars have not been bothered—only illegal saloons.

The Stonewall, though presented as a private club, charged admission of $1 on weeknights and $3 on weekends to anyone who looked or sounded as if he belonged inside. Admission is still the same, but now only soft drinks are being sold—and to a much reduced clientele.

The manager of the Stonewall refused to discuss the club's operations, or the recent troubles, with a reporter.

"You usually figure when there's a raid that someone didn't pay off the precinct," one Stonewall regular said. "But these busts were arranged higher up. So there's a feeling that it's just (Mayor) Lindsay trying to out law-and-order those other two guys."

"Ooooh, no!" his friend said. "John would never do *that*. Oh dear, no, never. I'm *sure* he's going to make the police leave us alone."

DOCUMENT 87

Ronnie Di Brienza, "Stonewall Incident"
East Village Other, 9 July 1969, 2

My name is Ronnie Di Brienza. I was born and raised in Brooklyn, twenty-six years ago. For the past seven years I have been breaking my balls from coast to coast as a musician. Most of this time I have spent eating peanut butter and pizza to survive. As a long-haired, newspaper-tabled hippy, I have had a lot of shit thrown my way, but until Friday night, June 27, I was basically a pacifist. However, pacifism is fast going out the window. How many times can one turn the other cheek. There is a limit, and Friday night was it.

Basically, I am not gay, but I am not straight either. I must consider myself a freak. My close associations are with people who are among the minorities.

I am not an expert, but homosexuality has been around since Cain and Abel. Homosexuality, however, is a reality and not just a passing thing. The establishment and their elite gestapo, the pigs, have been running things too long. First you had the Negro riots a few years back, which woke up white cats like myself to the fact that, though I am white, I am just as much considered a nigger as the black man is. From those early battles came the more intense militant organizations who like myself are sick and tired of being niggers, and want to become real and human. We have reached the bottom of the oppressed minority barrel. The gay people are the last people anyone ever suspected would violently demonstrate for equal rights. Well, let me tell you baby, you just don't fuck with the gays anymore. They, too, have turned the other cheek once too often.

On Tuesday night, June 25, the Stonewall Inn on Christopher Street was raided by the brave, stick-swinging pigs. The Stonewall has more or less become a gay institution in the Village, and has survived as such for the past three years or so. All of a sudden, however, the pigs decided to start playing political games on the fags, because when did you ever see a fag fight back? It used to be that a fag was happy to get slapped and chased home, as long as they didn't have to have their names splashed onto a court record. Now, times are-a-changin'. Tuesday night was the last night for bullshit.

On Wednesday and Thursday nights grumbling could be heard among the limp wristed set. Predominantly, the theme was "this shit has got to stop!" Come Friday night, early Saturday AM, the pigs decide they are going to do it again. So into the Stonewall goes Inspector Smyth, Inspector Pine, four fuzz and two policewomen (God knows what the hell policewomen wanted to do there), and the bust was on. The pigs proceeded to bust all the employees of the establishment, and some fags, too, for good measure. Poof, it starts. The fags have gone revolutionary. A crowd was waiting outside—possibly five hundred in all. Every time someone was released from the bar, cheers would go out along with the cry "Gay Power!"

But suddenly the mood changed. Someone began to scream, "Let them go, let them go!" From the sky came a bottle, then a stone, then a brick—all kinds of objects. The pigs then hurriedly took away the prisoners they had and barricaded themselves in the Stonewall. Not for long. A bunch of "queens," along with a few "butch" members, grabbed a parking meter, and began battering the entrance until the doors swung open. Then someone threw the meter through the plate glass windows, and it was on. Some small, scrawny, hoody-looking, cat threw a can of lighter fluid through the broken window, and set it up. The *Daily News* conveniently called this a "Fire bombing." Well, I don't know where the *News*' heads are at, but if that is their impression of a fire bombing, I can just imagine when a molotov is hurled they will headline it as an atomic attack! Shortly after a fire hose was turned on from the inside, pig reinforcements arrived on the scene, and after some brief skirmishes, it was all over... for Friday, anyway.

Saturday night was very poor. Too many people showed up looking for a carnival rather than a sincere protest. Queens were posing for pictures, slogans were being spouted out, but nothing really sincere happened in the way of protest. On Monday night, July 2, everything became more than serious. Around 10:30 P.M. some queens set fire to some trash on the corner of Waverly and Christopher. TPF and the Fire Department responded.

The fires were put out, but then the crowd began to get on the pigs. Shouts of Pig Motherfuckers, Fag Rapists and Gestapo could be heard all the way back to Hoboken. More police arrived. Then, one really fit Bircher-type pig grabbed a friend of mine, who was promptly beaten in front of two hundred people by three other pigs, and then carted off to a waiting patrol car. This was it. From nowhere the crowd swelled to an estimated thousand, and the battle was on. One head standing on the corner of Waverly was unfortunate enough to yell out "pig" just when the man was behind him. Well, in front of 1,000 witnesses, he was pummeled, dragged, kicked and lifted down the length of Christopher Street to a waiting squad car on Seventh Avenue.

Some of us tried to get him away from the man. It was heartbreaking. If more people would have helped the cat would not have been dragged off. By the way, my buddy received seven stitches over his left eye for his participation in a freedom of assembly rally.

For a while, the crowd became very warlike. I have never seen anything worse than an infuriated queen with a bottle, or long nails. Believe me, get their ire up, and you face the wrath of all the Gods that ever lived.

This all ended within an hour, and peace was restored. But the word is out. Christopher Street shall be liberated. The fags have had it with oppression. Revolution is being heard on Christopher Street, only instead of guttural MC-5 voices, we hear it coming from sopranos, and altos.

The whole thing is this. That bar, among others in the Village, has been in existence for the past three years. The pigs, if you care to see it for yourself some night, stand outside of any gay bar. They walk into that establishment with mugs on and walk out with smiling faces, and their good hands in their money pockets. They usually proceed to drive off into the night to make violent love to each other, while they goof on the dumb fags. I'm sure that if liquor was being sold without a license over the past three years, something would have been done sooner. However, a second faction is present. The Mafia has controlled these bars for years, and they have exploited the homosexual constantly by charging outrageous minimums and covers to get into their bars, and charging a dollar for a can of beer, which can be bought in a deli for 25 cents.

The strange thing about all this is that during the height of the action, you could see the fear and disbelief on the faces of the pigs, and the straight people. Yet, while I was hanging out with some eastside revolutionaries on a stoop off Waverly Place, possibly being one of ten people on the streets, the pigs suddenly had their bravado back, and threatened us with bodily harm if we were still on the street when they circled the block. Fuck them! We remained on the block. They continued to circle.

The Mafia owners of the club put up signs begging for the gay people to demonstrate peacefully tonight and whenever. Fuck them too! Why? To save their asses? To keep the public eye off them and the corrupt pigs? Horseshit, baby! WE WANT THE WORLD AND WE WANT IT NOW!

There will be more shit happening on Christopher Street. This past week is only the start. The fags, like the true revolutionaries, have become resigned to fighting for their cause, if necessary by force and with heavier weapons. On July 16 there will be another demonstration on Christopher Street.

The fags aren't just protesting the fuzz, they are protesting the fact that they must pay for the privilege of being gay. And to all of the people, the Holy Mafia, the Pigs, Smyth, Pine, and all the rest of the closet faggots in uniform, FUCK YOU. WE, THE MINORITIES, SHALL OVERCOME!

DOCUMENT 88
"Queen Power: Fags against Pigs in Stonewall Bust"
Rat, 9 July 1969, 6[4]

About 1:30 Saturday morning, I happened along Sheridan Sq. with a friend looking for a beer when we saw a crowd gathered outside the Stonewall, a famed gay bar. We walked over to see what was happening. About 3–400 guys were jammed in around a police car in front of the door, taunting several pigs in plainclothes guarding the entrance. "They raided the joint, the fucking bastards," a couple of guys told us. "Why?" we asked. "Operating without a liquor license." "Shit, man, they's out like always to chase us down and give us a good fuck. They ain't got nothin else to do during the summer," a hip spade was shouting.

We tried to find more information, just as the pigs starting hauling off in a squad car a guy they had dragged outside. The crowd protested wildly, booing, shrieking, "Up against the wall, faggots!" "Beat it off, pigs!" A few tried jumping out to disrupt the no-man's land between the door and the squad car, but most as yet were reticent about provoking any pig violence. Someone tried to sell me some speed, and another asked me for a knife. "I'm gonna slice up those motherfuckers' tires." "How many arrests?" I asked. "A few." "What happened inside?" I pursued. "About 1:15 they came, but they kept the music and dancing going so's not to get everyone up. They checked identity. If you had it they let you go. If not they held you up till they found out more."

The crowd grew larger and more agitated as the squad car drove off and a wagon pulled up. People began beating the wagon, booing, trying to see who was being hauled out and off. Several pigs were on guard and periodically threatened the crowd unless they moved back. Impossible to do. "Nobody's going to fuck around with me. I ain't going to take this shit," a guy in a dark red tee-shirt shouted, dancing in and out of the crowd. Then they hauled a couple off into the van. It was hard to see or know what was happening inside. A few plainclothesmen were surveying the crowd, obviously panicked. As yet there was no support from the riot squad, though the longer the cops took, the hotter the crowd became. They began shouting for different people that they knew were being held. "We want Tommy, the blond drag queen," shouts went up. Pennies ricocheted off the van, a beer can hit the door. Suddenly Tommy appeared in blond wig, etc. and walked cooly out the door. Shouts and screaming. "We want Tommy." Tommy, not held by the pigs, smiled and suddenly took off into the crowd to the left. The pigs were really flustered. Many went running after Tommy who took off in a taxi.

A couple more were thrown into the van. We joined in with some who wanted to storm the van, free those inside, then turn over the van. But nobody was yet prepared for that kind of action. Then a scuffle at the door. One guy refused to be put into the van. 5 or 6 cops guarding the van tried to subdue him with little success. Several guys tried to help free him. Unguarded, 3 or 4 of those in the van appeared, then quickly disappeared into the crowd. This was all anyone needed.

Several others tried [rescuing] the guy held by the cops, but the latter escaped into the Stonewall. Soon the van pulled out leaving the street unguarded. A few pigs outside had to flee for their lives inside and barricade themselves in. It was too good to be true. The crowd took the offensive. The cat in the tee-shirt began by hurling a container of something at the door. Then a can or stone cracked a window. Soon pandemonium broke loose. Cans, bottles, rocks, trash-cans, finally a parking meter crashed the windows and door. Cheers went up. A sort of wooden wall blocking out the front plate glass windows was forced down. Then with the parking meter a ram, in went the door. The cops inside were scared shitless, dodging projectiles and flying glass. The orgy was taking place. Vengeance vented against the source of repression—gay bars, busts, kids victimized and exploited by the mafia and cops. Strangely, no one spoke to the crowd or tried to direct the insurrection. Everyone's heads were in the same place. Some chanted "occupy—take over, take over" "Fag power," but kids were really scared about going too far as they saw the cops pulling guns from inside, pointed directly at the crowd. A volley of objects bounced off the walls inside. Then one cop in a fury took his gun and actually hurled it at the crowd. People couldn't believe what had happened, for the gun hit the door frame with a clunk and lay there. A miracle it hadn't gone off.

The pigs carried futility to the extreme and turned the firehose on the mob through the door. Jeers, derision. Some shouted to "grab it, grab his cock." Some then lit a trash can full of paper afire and stuffed it through the window. Flames leaped up. Then "Riot pigs" somebody was shouting. Sirens approached and kids started spilling out over the fences of Sheridan Square to flee the scene. On each side together there must have been around 1500–2000 people by this time milling about, being pushed back by about 30 or more riot cops. It was hard to tell exactly how many. But no one was ready to get their heads beat in and most of the crowds to the sides were now filled with the curious.

People hung around till after 4 am talking in little groups. People were excited and angry. In talking to a number of kids who had been inside, it was evident most understood at least rudimentarily what was happening to them. What was and should have always been theirs, what should have been the free control of the people was dramatized, shown up for what it really was, an instrument of power and exploitation. It was theatre, totally spontaneous. There was no bullshit.

DOCUMENT 89

Letters to the editor

Village Voice, 10 July 1969, 4, 49[5]

Offensive

Dear Sir:

As Jewish, Spanish-Welsh-Irish, Italian, black members of the American homosexual community, we find the use of words like "fag" and "faggot" as offensive as "kike," "spick," "mick," "wop," "nigger."

    Leo Skir

    Robert Cobuzio

    Kirk Lindsay

    George King

    John Kane

SCARED NO MORE

Dear Sir:

Re the article "Full Moon Over the Stonewall" (VV, July 3):

The Stonewall raid was not the only reason for incidents occurring on that great and glorious weekend. In the last three weeks five gay bars in the Village area that I know of have been hit by the police. Harassment of homosexuals in the Village is one of the oldest stories in the book. It's something we've come to take for granted. Well, the new age has come, and the fags have decided to expose to society another of its faults. Just as the Negroes did in 1960. Homosexuality is a part of life, no more no less. I witnessed the demonstrations that weekend and the actions by the TPF. They were all given crack courses in sadism by one of Chicago's finest, I'm sure. I witnessed many senseless brutalities which there could be no justification for. One guy walking on Sheridan Square across from the disturbances was with his chick (obviously not into it) when a TPF came from behind and just split his head open with his club (one of New York's finest).

This is a new and justified movement. Unfortunately many straights will not support us because of resentment toward fags bred into them by that "great" and "honorable" generation we emerged from or simply because, win or lose, our struggle would not affect them.

But when these people practice their whole concept of a new morality, I hope they can stop to dig the fact that we are people with something to fight for. The age of the scared little queens is gone. Hail Aquarius.

    Kevan Liscoe

    Thompson Street

VENDETTA

Dear Sir:

It is nice to read in Howard Smith's article "Full Moon Over the Stonewall" of his friendship with the police, and his synopsis of the recent State Liquor Authority bulletin. Perhaps all unlicensed places became eligible to apply for licenses on June 1, 1969, though we were under the impression anyone could apply for a license anytime. That's beside the point.

The real point of the matter is the fact that the SLA will not grant licenses to gay bars, and they will use any technicality under the law (and there are thousands of them) to refuse a license. Applicants for licenses are asked, point-blank, if they intend to use the premises to serve homosexuals, or will permit homosexuals to "congregate" on the premises. Those who say "yes" won't get a license. If they lie and get their license, they are still closed on the grounds that "homosexuals were permitted to congregate on the premises and conduct themselves in an unlawful manner."

The SLA just doesn't give a damn that the courts have held that homosexuals may assemble peaceably anywhere they choose, or that the courts have held that male-male dancing, female-female dancing, and even intra-sexual kissing does not necessarily give grounds for license revocation. The NYC cops aren't permitted to use plainclothesmen to entrap homosexuals anymore, but in other parts of the state these "decoys" are still employed to gain "evidence" of "homosexual solicitation" to be used at SLA license revocation hearings.

The point is that the SLA wages a vendetta against gay bars, and no bar has a chance of staying in business without paying off and engaging in other illegalities. This effectively keeps most decent businessmen out of the business and leaves the field wide open to underworld elements and businessmen who will make a quick buck and get out of the business.

I don't know who runs the Stonewall, and I don't care. It has run for several years now, and the cops have tried to put it out of business with raids before. They evidently couldn't substantiate the charges, and the place reopened. Now they're just harassing the place which means they're harassing the customers, as well.

It's time for the local elections and, as usual at that time in the Village, homosexuals are being harassed on the streets by the cops, the clubs are being raided, and even the legitimate, licensed bars have been bothered by the cops. This year, homosexuals are sick of being election issues. In the old days, old Ed Koch used to call the police to the Village every election campaign and many would be entrapped. Now that that's no longer possible, the bars and clubs are being bothered.

The gay crowd put up with it before because we were too weak and unorganized to do anything about it. Now we're finding our muscle and we're not going to be scapegoats and election issues any more. If Carol Greitzer doesn't shape up and protect the large gay population of the Village, she may find herself voted out of office. If the police in the Charles Street Station can't be controlled and aren't disciplined, maybe the gay set will find itself a new man to support for Mayor. And if Governor Rockefeller doesn't soon do something about reforming and cleaning up the corruption in the State Liquor Authority, the crooks are going to own the liquor business courtesy of the State of New York which every day entrenches them more deeply.

Dick Leitsch
Executive Director
Mattachine Society of New York

DOCUMENT 90
Walter Troy Spencer, "Last Call: Too Much My Dear"
Village Voice, 10 July 1969, 36

The combination of a full moon and Judy Garland's funeral was too much for them, Dick Neuweiler said the other day, assessing the cause of the Great Faggot Rebellion.

It has been good for a lot of cracks and saloon gossip, but basically, I find the Stonewall siege depressing. For a one- or even two-nighter, it was a pretty entertaining floor show—the swishy cheer-leaders; the one queen's Salome dance in front of the advancing police line, capped by the crack, as the Tactical Patrol Force prepared to step off with linked arms, "Oh, look at the lovely Rockettes."

But after a couple of nights, who needs all that tension? I go to great lengths to stay out of Times Square as much as possible, and haven't been to any demonstration since long before I turned in my police press pass. I sure don't want to have to run some gauntlet every night just to quietly slip into my friendly neighborhood saloon. . . .

One Christopher Street bar operator estimates that a single night of the indirect embargo cost him $500 business. On the other end of the economic scale, Maurice, our traveling newsstand, says that the army of tourist faggots in to watch the action are class-A deadbeats when it comes to buying literary material. On the other hand, the two guards at the door of the Stonewall gave him $1 each to find out about themselves in The Voice, which apparently isn't on the reading list of the Bayonne Social Club.

Although a lot of that weekend swishy cruising on the streets around the Stonewall had gotten annoyingly flamboyant and aggressive (nasty cracks at chicks, etc.) and although I basically dislike any restrictive club like the Stone-wall on the principle that it is anti-democratic (it's one thing if you go into any kind of place and feel uncomfortable or are unwelcome because your style doesn't mesh with that of the house; it's something else to be excluded a priori), I think basically most people's sympathy has to lie with the homosexuals. They're the guys who have been exploited for so long in the squeeze between crooks who cater to them at outrageous prices on one side and on the other by the cops, either operating to show off for the Daily News camp of public indignation or out of their own righteousness as self-appointed defenders of the public morals.

The fags, obviously, in this case are victims caught in some sort of clash between the police and whoever the people are who operate the Stonewall. (It also seems like unfairly bad timing for them, knocked out of both indoor sports at the Stonewall and outdoor recreation with all those up-in-arms Kew Gardens vigilantes harassing them out of their park. After all, my dear, if they aren't safe in Queens, what is the value of a name? Maybe the city or state should set aside something like a bird sanctuary for them.)

The Stonewall doesn't seem to be the isolated, sudden case that the publicity has made it out to be. Hasn't there been some sort of crackdown on for a while? The Snakepit, the fag after-hours joint, was raided a month ago.

An interesting sidelight to the Stonewall demonstrations, John Saroyan points out, is the bizarre alliance between the Stonewall queens, the Stonewall heavies, and street people against the cops.

More subtly disturbing is the question of what sort of friction this situation may have generated between the Village's Sixth Precinct, the First Division (who made the initial raid without telling the precinct—a standard procedure), and the TPF, who had to be called in when things got out of hand. First Division plainclothesmen just melt away, and the TPF hop on their buses and go on to bust up the next street crisis around the city, but now the Sixth Precinct has to live with the mess left behind.

The Sixth Precinct guys are as good cops as you'll find in any New York neighborhood, and during the height of the Stonewall troubles, most Village bartenders—who know them well—were muttering that the whole situation never would have boiled over if the Sixth Precinct had been allowed to handle it from the outset. . . .

Like most people who've spent time around and worked with cops, although I dislike the general idea that there has to be such a thing as police, individually I like most of them. Even TPFers can sometimes be okay if you meet them on their own terms. . . .

As Gene Gammage described his experience with the Faggot Rebellion at the height of its first Saturday night: "We walked out of the 55 to watch them taunt the police. I thought it would be a novelty to watch a gay demonstration. It was reassuring to see that they mince even under pressure. But people were getting their heads busted, and there was mostly ugliness on both sides, even if there was a lot of twittering.

"It wasn't amusing. It was just like any other violence—depressing."

DOCUMENT 91

E.W., letter to the editor

New York Post, 11 July 1969, 40

A Waste of Time

Why do the police still waste their time bothering homosexuals when there are so many better things they could be doing. The Stonewall Inn in the Village which was raided last week was for me, a person who has had difficulty in accepting what I am, an oasis where I felt safely able to meet others like myself. It had a friendly open atmosphere. Now I am afraid to go there.

I am mad that the police still choose to hound people, most of whom are good people and do not bother anybody. Why doesn't the city help instead of hinder its many homosexual citizens? Is the minority of "obvious gays" too threatening to someone's masculinity? People can't hide what they are anymore—nor should they.

DOCUMENT 92

John Gabree, "Homosexuals Harassed in New York"

National Guardian, 12 July 1969, 14[6]

Two incidents in New York City in the past several weeks have underlined both the problems and the new-found militancy of one of America's oppressed minorities, homosexuals.

On June 30 it was reported that a number of trees in a public park in Kew Gardens, Queens had been cut down 10 days earlier. Local residents described the park as a meeting place for homosexuals.

For several weeks prior to the vandalism, a vigilante neighborhood group had been harassing alleged homosexuals in the park, shining powerful flashlights in their faces and threatening them. According to Myles Tashman, a member of the vigilante committee and a lawyer, "Admittedly it was against the law, but we had police consent."

The harassment was successful for a time, according to Tashman, but eventually the homosexuals began to resist—pointing out that it was, after all, a public park. It was then that local residents retaliated by chopping off the trees, an act which probably had every Freudian in New York chuckling over his morning paper.

Although homosexuals have not been noted for molesting women and children, the vigilantes (who do not admit to cutting down the trees) insist this was the main motivation for their activities. "Nonsense," said a neighborhood woman who disagrees with the vigilante actions. "What mothers and children are out at one o'clock in the morning?"

The American Civil Liberties Union and New York City Parks Commissioner August Heckscher have called for an investigation of police department complicity in the vandalism, and the Queens district attorney has reportedly begun an inquiry. At least two persons called the 112th Precinct in Maspeth on the night of June 20 to report that someone was cutting trees in the Park.

In addition, Joan Luxemburg of Flushing has complained in a letter to Mayor John Lindsay and other city officials that she stopped a police car (No. 1176) just outside the park that evening to report seeing vandals. She said the policeman inside the car told her that neighborhood residents "were doing a job which the police were not able to do to the satisfaction of the community." Another man afraid to give his name told the New York Times last week that he had seen police chatting with persons who were chopping down the trees. Witnesses said the vandals used axes and power saws. There have been no arrests.

The Mattachine Society, an activist homosexual civil rights group, announced that it is starting a fund to replace the trees. The parks department says that will take about $15,000.

Meanwhile, police harassment of a long-established homosexual bar in Greenwich Village late last month resulted in several nights of disturbances in the Sheridan Square area.

It began June 27 when plainclothesmen, with a search warrant for illegal alcohol, raided the Stonewall Inn, 53 Christopher St., when there were about 200 customers inside. The crowd, both inside and out, was in a festive mood until a paddywagon arrived to cart off three men and a woman, all homosexuals, along with bar employes. At that point, the crowd—swelled to between four and five hundred by the addition of Sheridan Square residents, street people and tourists—began to pelt the police with small change, beer cans and bottles in a general move to liberate the Inn.

The disturbance ended with the arrival of several carloads of elite Tactical Patrol Force cops, who quickly cleared the streets.

But disturbances continued the next night and the area remained tense through the week and into the long July 4 weekend. (The calling in of the TPF had the incidental benefit of taking the heat off the Second Avenue and St. Marks Place area of the Lower East Side, the TPF's usual stomping grounds, allowing street people there an unusually relaxed July 4.)

Activism has clearly sprung up in the homosexual community. As outlaws, they have been subjected to the same radicalizing influence of the police as other street people and minorities. A standing one-liner all week was "I've become a left deviationist."

A generation gap seems to exist for homosexuals as it does for other minorities. Last week it was the younger ones who seemed most determined not to hide and who were going to get their rights, by force if necessary. "We have to fight back," said one.

Many seem to be developing a sophisticated understanding of U.S. society's motives in suppressing them. "We strike at the family," one told the Guardian, "and we undermine all the bullshit about virility that keeps most men in line." The vision of an army of aggressive militant homosexuals should give the rulers of New York something to think about. At week's end, someone chalked "I'm gay and I'm proud" on a wall near the Stonewall Inn.

DOCUMENT 93

Jefferson Fuck Poland, "Lady Inspectors"
Berkeley Barb, 16 July 1969, 17[7]

There's a curious sidelight in the Village Voice (July 3) account of Gay Power disturbances in Greenwich Village, provided by police explaining their policy on raiding gay bars:

"According to the police, they are not picking on homosexuals. On these raids they almost never arrest customers, only people working there.... It was explained to me (VV's reporter) that generally men dressed as men, even if wearing extensive makeup, are always released; men dressed as women are sometimes arrested; and 'men' fully dressed as women, but who upon inspection by a police-woman prove to have undergone the sex-change operation, are always let go."

Does it embarrass a trans-sexual to have these women always inspecting his/her crotch, looking for a telltale testicle or carefully measuring the clit to see if it's really an eentsy prick? How do ladies get the job of crotch watcher, anyway?

The situation resembles those times and countries when circumcision clearly distinguished Jew from Gentile. In ancient Rome, the Emperor Domitian's "first measure against the Jews was to make sure that neither they nor proselytes to Judaism evaded payment of the Jewish Tax. Suetonius recalls that in his youth he had seen an old man forced to expose his genitals in a crowded courtroom in order that it should be confirmed whether or not he was circumcised." (Dr. Hugh J. Schonfield, Those Incredible Christians, p. 178.)

Within the past two generations, American women have won the right to wear clothes of either sex (with the exception of male business suits). Indeed, a woman wearing blue jeans, riding boots and a man's shirt is not generally thought of as "wearing men's clothes." Almost any garment can be considered "women's wear" when a woman is actually wearing it.

Males and trans-sexuals deserve the same freedom of attire. Furthermore, all persons should have the right to impersonate whatever sex(es) they wish. When a stranger passes you on the street, it's really none of your business to know the shape of the stranger's genitals—you don't have the right to demand, as society now does, that the stranger wear certain cultural signals ("male" or "female" clothes) describing his/her crotch formation. If the stranger wants you to know, let him/her tell you voluntarily. Most folks will.

Of course, there are limits to deception. If a transvestite prostitute takes your money but delivers the wrong brand of goods, you're entitled to a refund. If a foolish bridegroom weds a blushing virgin, he may be shocked to find his bride has balls; certainly the groom is entitled to a prompt annulment. But how often does complete deception actually occur? When a sailor lets a transvestite blow him, doesn't he suspect that "she" might really be a boy—but he'd rather not actually know? Most people who deal sexually with transvestites (in this context, either homo, hetero, or bi) probably know who they're getting into. If not, let them learn by experience. No sailor ever died from getting blown by a queer. There may be a few problems here, but nothing that justifies society in forbidding sexual impersonation.

Laws forbidding transvestism should be attacked directly, in the streets in front of gay bars in bohemian areas. Gays and straights—perhaps organized jointly by Sexual Freedom League and Committee for Homosexual Freedom—should hold a Switch In. A large group of males and females, of all sexual orientations, should appear in clothing unmistakably of the opposite sex. Daring the cops to bust.

As in our public marijuana smoke-ins, the cops would have a choice between tolerating illegal activity or starting a test case which we would win.

DOCUMENT 94

Leo E. Laurence, "Mafia in the Middle"

Berkeley Tribe, 18 July 1969, 13[8]

THE
STONEWALL RIOTS

The Mafia fearing the forces of the revolution?

Maybe. The Mafia buys the pigs with payoffs, but not so the "movement." New York City gay militants are fighting both.

"Five Mafia families run the gay bars in New York City," Gay Activist Randy Wicker told me over transcontinental telephone this week.

"The police hassle the legit clubs, but avoid the Mafia. The Stonewall incident was a freak, however. Something went wrong and the cops busted the place.

"The strange thing is that the gays there thought of the raid as an attack on themselves and not the Mafia," Wicker explained.

"That's when all hell broke loose and several days of street fighting followed. I think the Mafia will slowly pull out of the gay bar business in New York City now."

Twenty-one persons were arrested in the NYC gay riots. Surprisingly, the most daring defiance to the pigs' riot clubs came from the effeminate "queens."

Like one Puerto Rican who shouted at a big bull pig: "How'd you like a big Spanish dick up your little Irish ass?"

That freaked the pig so much he hesitated swinging for just a split second and the "queen" split.

A large group of gay kids were being rushed by two young pigs in another incident. Someone shouted, "Let's grab the pigs, rip off their clothes, and screw them both!"

They too freaked and retreated fast with their pig-tails tucked between their legs.

"We can fight the Mafia if legit bars and dance halls begin to openly cater to the gay community," says Wicker. Ditto for the Establishment on the West Coast.

DOCUMENT 95
Lige [Elijah Hadyn Clarke] and Jack [John Richard Nichols],
"Pampered Perverts"
Screw, 25 July 1969, 16[9]

Lige and Jack are male lovers who dig life together and think it's a groove. They poke fun at those who would make love a crime, and hope for the day when homosexuals and heterosexuals are happily integrated. . . .

The last two weeks have been full of excitement for us. Today (July 8th) is our fifth anniversary and although we've spent all our money on a swinging vacation, we're planning a real shindig for ourselves anyway.

At the time of our first anniversary we took part in the first July 4th Annual Reminder Day picket at Independence Hall in Philadelphia. Since then the picket line has grown in size, and homosexuals from across the nation gather to protest laws, governmental hiring policies, and other inequalities.

This year's Reminder picket took place as usual, but with a new consciousness in the air. The concept of homosexual equality, it seems, is spreading among younger gay people themselves, and is no longer the province of a few die-hard revolutionaries. The revolution is taking to the streets, and it is high time that it did.

We were thrilled by the violent uprising in Sheridan Square in which homosexuals put police on notice that they'd no longer accept abuse. For many decades gay people have been afraid to stand up for themselves and have allowed policemen to run over one of their most basic civil rights: the right to assemble in public. Today, however, a new generation is angered by raids and harassment of gay bars, and last week's riots in Greenwich Village have set standards for the rest of the nation's homosexuals to follow.

The police claimed that they were only trying to close an illegally-operated bar, the Stonewall Inn. If this was so, why didn't they do it in the daytime? Why pick on customers? And why have the fuzz allowed this "illegal" establishment to operate for the last four years without raising an eyebrow? Suddenly, at election time (the proverbial time for gay bar raids in almost every large city) the police are in full swing again. Other gay bars besides the Stonewall Inn have recently been raided. On one occasion 50 patrons were arrested and thrown into cells overnight. In the morning they were brought before the judge. Why?

The Sheridan Square Riot also showed the world the homosexuals will no longer take a beating without a good fight. The police were scared shitless and the massive crowds of angry protestors chased them for blocks screaming, "Catch them! Fuck them!" Young men and women hurled bottles, stones, parking meters and coins at stunned cops, driving them into the Stonewall where they barricaded themselves in utter fear. There was a shrill, righteous indignation in the air. Homosexuals had endured such raids and harassment long enough. It was time to take a stand. A parking meter, uprooted, was used to ram the door in hope of driving the police out. So tense were the lawmen, wrote a *Village Voice* reporter who was inside the Inn with them, that they were ready to shoot "the first motherfucker" that came through the door. Then the protestors tossed a firebomb through the window and a wall of flames arose just as the sirens of police reinforcements arrived.

In the days following the first riots the prophet of the new age, Allen Ginsberg, walked past the Stonewall, and the new activists filled him in on the goings-on. And then, after years of relative silence, Ginsberg said: "Gay power! Isn't that great! We're one of the largest minorities in the country—10 per cent, you know. It's about time we did something to assert ourselves." He walked into the Stonewall, dancing and bouncing to the music. "You know," he said, "the guys there were so beautiful. They've lost that wounded look that fags all had 10 years ago."

Homosexual activists from various groups passed out leaflets and literature in the streets. Some called for an end to Mafia control of gay bars. All insisted that police stop their raids. And then, the seemingly unbelievable occurred: one of the city's largest legitimate nightclubs, The Electric Circus, called on the homosexual community to use its facilities. "If you are tired of raids, Mafia control, and checks at the front door," said the Circus, "join us for a beautiful evening on Sunday night, July 6th."

Our good friend, Randy Wicker, was asked to speak at the Circus as a "gay militant." Randy, 10 years ago, had been the first homosexual activist in New York, and had successfully brought the subject of homosexuality onto radio and TV for the first time.

Jack urged Randy to wear the American Flag shirt similar to that which he'd loaned to Abbie Hoffman when he appeared before the House [Committee] on Un-American Activities. Properly attired in the shirt, with blue and white striped bell-bottoms, Randy went to the Electric Circus to give his "gay power" speech. "In years past," he admitted, "I would have dressed more conservatively but tonight calls for a new approach!"

The Circus was packed with a groovy crowd. They too lacked the "wounded look" of ten years ago. There were hip moustaches, long hair, and hundreds of handsome young men. The acid-rock band blared forth a medley of fast tunes, and the entire audience was lost in a maze of dancing. A few straight couples mixed in with the crowd, seemingly unconcerned with the fact that most of the customers were gay. It seemed like a take-over at first, but everyone wanted the experiment to work. The officials at the Electric Circus were thrilled by the turnout, and one commented that it seemed to be the best turnout they'd had in a month. For the first time in New York's history, a huge club was experimenting with social integration between heterosexuals and homosexuals.

Shortly after midnight, an elated Randy prepared to mount the platform and give his speech in support of such ventures. The band stopped playing, and he was introduced by a well-known writer who told of Randy's many accomplishments in years past. Then, with the microphones still in disarray, Randy began to speak.

He was only able to say a few words when one rotten apple tried to spoil the barrel. An uncool creep rushed out of the audience and began swinging wildly at everyone within arm's length. "Faggots!" he shrieked. "Goddamn faggots!" For a few moments it looked as though he'd been subdued. Randy resumed his speech, but after only a few words more, the violence erupted again, and this time the creep jumped onto the platform. Several Electric Circus big-boys quelled him, however, and he was led from the premises screaming and shouting like a madman.

Next, Dick Leitsch, the Executive Director of the Mattachine Society, got up and asked for donations from homosexuals to help replant the trees that anti-homosexual vigilantes had uprooted in a public park in Queens. Much of what he said, however, was lost to the crowd, who, by this time, had had its attention riveted by the lone protestor.

Will the Electric Circus experiment work? We would like to believe that it could. Homosexuals are welcome at the Electric Circus, say officials, on any night of the week, and will be treated by the management as any other customers. They may dance, frolic, and enjoy themselves "doing their thing." The Electric Circus does not tolerate violence.

We are sure that the vast majority of those present at the Circus on Sunday night wanted the new social experiment to work too. Everyone seemed to be thoroughly enjoying themselves. There is no getting around the fact that the Circus is a first-rate nightclub with magnificent facilities for dancing or for just grooving. If only straights and gays could mix without trouble. We believe that it *is* possible. There's no reason why gay people should have to go to *segregated*, inferior clubs.

The revolution in Sheridan Square must step beyond its present boundaries. The homosexual revolution is only a part of a larger revolution sweeping through all segments of society. We hope that "Gay Power" will not become a call for separation, but for sexual integration, and that the young activists will read, study, and make themselves acquainted with all of the facts which will help them to carry the sexual revolt triumphantly into the councils of the U.S. Government, into the anti-homosexual churches, into the offices of anti-homosexual psychiatrists, into the city government, and into the state leg-islatures which make our manner of love-making a crime. It is time to push the homosexual revolution to its logical conclusion. We must crush tyranny wherever it exists and join forces with those who would assist in the utter destruction of the puritanical, repressive, anti-sexual Establishment.

DOCUMENT 96
D. L. [Dick Leitsch], "Gay Riots in the Village"
Mattachine Society of New York Newsletter, Aug. 1969, 1–2, 4

The first gay rioting in history broke out in the early morning hours of June 28, following a police raid on the Stonewall, a club on Christopher Street. Police, led by Inspectors Smythe and Pine, and armed with a warrant, arrived at about 2 A.M. and arrested the management and employees for illegal sale of alcohol. The patrons were ordered to leave, except for a few in drag who were arrested.

The patrons gathered outside, and were joined by other homosexuals and Village residents. The police started behaving with bad grace and the revolt was on. The crowd started pelting the cops with pennies ("dirty copper"), then cans, rocks, and even parking meters. The handful of cops was driven back into the bar and locked in. The crowd then set the bar afire in an attempt to cremate the police (or "cook the pigs," as someone said).

The police put out the flames after vainly searching for a fire exit. Had the place caught on fire during a busy time, the police said, most of the customers would have been doomed, as there were no fire exits. The crowd wouldn't let them out, and were throwing things into the place at them. One policeman got hit in the eye and another suffered a broken wrist. Reinforcements were summoned, and the Tactical Police Force (NY's "Riot Squad") arrived on the scene.

Street fighting followed and continued for several hours. A number of people were arrested, and more were clubbed by the cops. Some of those beaten were clubbed in the Charles Street station house after having been arrested.

The Stonewall re-opened the next night and has remained open since, serving only soft drinks, although one may bring his own bottle. Crowds gathered outside early that night chanting "Queen Power" and "Gay Power." Soon the chant changed to "Christopher Street belongs to the queens. Liberate Christopher Street." Mobs of people—gay people from all over town, tourists, Villagers, and the idly curious—swelled the crowds. Soon things got out of hand again, and the TPF was called once more. The nearly 200 cops required several hours to clear the streets, and the TPF again lived up to its reputation for violence and brutality.

The most striking feature of the rioting was that it was led, and featured as participants, "queens," not "homosexuals." "Homosexuals" have been sitting back and taking whatever the Establishment handed out; the "queens" were having none of that. The "butch" numbers who were around the area and who participated peripherally in the action remained for the most part in the background. It was the "queens" who scored the points and proved that they are not going to tolerate any more harassment or abuse. . . .

Sunday, Monday and Tuesday evenings were fairly quiet, except for small outbreaks here and there. Most of the police, except for the TPF, had taken the first two nights of rioting with some good humor. By Monday night, tempers on both sides were short, and animosity filled the air. Some of the police maintained enormous "cool," but others deliberately tried to provoke trouble. "Start something, faggot, just start something," one cop kept telling people. "I'd like to break your ass wide open." After saying that to several dozen people, one man turned and said, "What a Freudian comment, officer!" The cop started swinging and hauled the guy off to a waiting wagon.

Two cops in a car cruised the streets, yelling obscenities at people, obviously trying to start a fight. Another stood on the corner of Christopher and Waverly, swinging his nightstick (speaking of Freudian, watch the cops in the Village caressing and masturbating those billy clubs!) and making smart cracks to passersby. A wildly "fem" queen sneaked up behind him, lit a firecracker and dropped it between his feet.

It exploded and he jumped into the air in a leap that Villella would have envied, landing on a part of his anatomy that one queen called a "moneymaker." He got up screaming like a peasant woman and swinging his stick. The queen tossed another firecracker under him, and when it went off a melee followed, during which the cop's badge was lifted. The next day, the badge turned up hanging on a tree in Washington Square Park, stuck into a string of pickled pigs' feet.

When the cops found the badge-stuck pigs' feet, they didn't take them down from the tree—they beat the pigs' feet to the ground, then picked up the badge.

While there's nothing really funny about a man having a firecracker blow up under his feet, there is something eminently satisfying about seeing a cop get scared, jump and land on his backside—especially if the cop has been after you for years. And even more so as he's a symbol of the cops who used to entrap, who raided bars, and who still harass homosexuals at every opportunity.

Wednesday night, the rioting broke out in full force. Much of the good humor and high spirits of the weekend had dissipated, and the street people were no longer half-serious, half-camping. The cops, who had been caught off-guard and were on the defensive before, had taken the offensive and massive retaliation was their goal.

Some seemed quite ready to depopulate Christopher Street the moment anyone would give them permission to unholster their guns. Failing that, some of them, particularly some of the TPF men, tried to achieve the same objective with their night sticks.

At one point, 7th Avenue from Christopher to West 10th looked like a battlefield in Vietnam. Young people, many of them queens, were lying on the sidewalk, bleeding from the head, face, mouth, and even the eyes. Others were nursing bruised and often bleeding arms, legs, backs and necks.

The composition of the street action had changed. It was no longer gay frustration being vented upon unsuspecting cops by queens who were partly violent but mostly campy. The queens were almost outnumbered by Black Panthers, Yippies, Crazies and young toughs from street gangs all over the city and some from New Jersey. The exploiters had moved in and were using the gay power movement for their own ends.

A lot of them were looking for a fight, and had the police not come, they probably would have started the old game of street gangs everywhere, "beating up a queer." The blacks and students who want a revolution, any kind of revolution, were there to exploit. They swelled the crowd and tried to recruit, but "graciously" let the queens take all the bruises and suffer all the arrests. (If they have no more courage than they displayed on Christopher Street, their revolution is a long way off.)

Looting began Wednesday evening. Obviously, little of it was done by people who live in and frequent Christopher Street and environs, because all the most unlikely places were looted. The first shop to get hit was the "Gingerbread House," a toy shop run by a delightful little lady who is a friend of everyone on Christopher. The other shops broken into were also run, for the most part, by nice people, sympathetic to the gay cause and the plight of the street queen.

The really likely places, the "fag shops" that overprice their wares and bleed the gay market for exorbitant prices, were left alone. Shops whose managers complain the loudest about the cruising and swishing in the neighborhood were also, surprisingly, left alone. Observers in the know doubt if the looting was done by gay people.

A group of gay people did consider burning down the offices of the *Village Voice*. That paper's editorial policy has long infuriated most homosexuals, as the paper pretends to be "liberal" and avant-garde, but actually is conservative and uptight about homosexuality. They published two long "put down" articles about the Christopher Street incidents which contributed heavily to the anger that incited the Wednesday rioting after two relatively peaceful days.

Police and others had expected a tremendous influx of people over the long July 4 week-end that started Thursday night. People came in droves but conditions remained generally calm. Sporadic efforts were made to start trouble—by people who can best be described as "outside agitators," by gay people, and too often by uptight cops who tried to start trouble to give them an excuse to start bashing heads again.

Despite those efforts, no major outbreak erupted. It was almost as if everyone had decided that the point had been made and any further action would only bring on a backlash. As it was, everything worked out to give the homosexuals of New York City tremendous gay power. A totally spontaneous demonstration had broken out, and people who are generally considered the ultimate "sissies" had badgered the police, imprisoned some of them, and held off busses full of TPF men for hours. They had shown that they were tired of being kicked around and would no longer stand for such treatment.

The sympathy of nearly everyone in town was with the homosexuals—even the uptight *Daily News* printed a wonderfully amusing and quite long article on the situation, in which they took the side of the queens against the cops.

Had the situation continued much longer, and violence increased, the non-participants, straight and gay, would have been "turned off" and the backlash started. The police would have escalated their retaliation, and the action would have been defeated, more people would have been injured, and the police would have started getting sympathy. As it was, homosexuals have won this first battle, the government and police have been put on notice that homosexuals won't stand being kicked around, and public sympathy for the homosexual cause is growing.

DOCUMENT 97

D. L. [Dick Leitsch], "The Stonewall Riots: The Police Story"
Mattachine Society of New York Newsletter, Aug. 1969, 5–6

Naturally MSNY [Mattachine Society of New York] is sympathetic to the gay power movement—we were trying to gain gay power while many of the people who are just now becoming interested were sitting back, enjoying life, and waiting for someone else to achieve any gains the homosexual community might want.

On the other hand, it was difficult not to feel sorry for the cops who were involved in the Stonewall incident, and their associates who were obliged to explain to the [Police] Commissioner how a group of New York's "finest" could be imprisoned in a gay bar for hours and nearly cremated. Imagine the jibes they must have gotten from their brother officers, their wives, and probably even their children! What must it do to a straight guy to have his kid say, "Daddy, tell us about the time the faggots cornered you and tore up the Village"?

When the police began visiting the MSNY office on July 3, their faces and their tired eyes told the whole story. They were in trouble—real trouble—and the situation looked like it might get worse before it got better. They wanted a sympathetic ear and they wanted to know what happened. We tried to help them on both counts.

The purpose of the visits by all of the officers (and there were many of them, including the Chief of the Morals Squad and the two Deputy Inspectors, Smythe and Pine, who had been imprisoned in the Stonewall, among others), was to find out one thing: why did this happen now, and why did it happen over the Stonewall, of all places? What we told them appears in another article in this issue; what follows is their side of the Stonewall story.

At no time in recent history has there been as little police action against homosexuals as in the past three years. Plainclothes decoys are no longer used to entrap homosexuals. There has been no concentrated effort to close down gay bars as there was during the Wagner years and before.

Headquarters has tried to clamp down on any harassment of homosexuals by policemen on the beat as well, and has had speakers from MSNY address students at the Police Academy in an effort to help the police (most of whom are, after all, straight and pretty much as ignorant about homosexuality as most straight people) understand homosexuals and our needs.

There has been no harassment of legitimate gay bars, the cops all stated. (A subsequent check with a number of bars, including the Stage 45, Harry's, and others, indicated that these bars indeed had not been bothered for several years.) They do go after places that serve liquor without a license. This has nothing to do with who forms the clientele of the place, but only with the fact that it is illegal to sell liquor without a license. The State Liquor Authority had notified all unlicensed liquor-selling establishments that they must obtain a license by July 1 or stop selling. The Stonewall didn't bother, so they got raided.

Another drive is under way to attack the organized crime syndicate. Many of the gay bars in the Village are suspected of having links with the Cosa Nostra, Mafia, or whatever you want to call it. These bars will be raided if the police get enough evidence to make charges stick. The Stonewall management was also suspected, the police said, of having such ties. That, the lack of a license, and the fact that the place was a health hazard and a fire hazard were the reasons the place was raided—not that it was gay.

Why had the Stonewall been allowed to operate if it was illegal? That was the question often asked after the last raid.

The police explained that all they can do is make the raid, and impound all the liquor stock, cash registers, and other material that can be considered evidence. They arrest the management, who are booked, have bail set, and get themselves released. The next day, they get a new supply of liquor and open as usual. This happened, the police say, at the Stonewall at least ten times.

THE
STONEWALL RIOTS

The police cannot force the place to close down, because they, like everyone else, have the right to be presumed innocent until a court finds them guilty. Thus, by hiring smart lawyers, and postponing the case again and again, the bar can stay in operation for years until their case comes to trial and the court closes it.

Charges are always being made that bars have to "pay off" to stay in business, particularly if they serve a gay clientele. The police say this is possible, but not likely. They try, they said, to keep their men "clean" and check out any charges of shakedowns. Besides, they pointed out, with the legitimate bars not being harassed, there is no reason for them to "pay off" anyone. If they are approached, they should notify headquarters and turn in the culprits. Not only would they save the pay-off money, but they'd win the respect and cooperation of the command.

The Stonewall had chalked across its windows: "How Can Inspector Smythe Drive a $15,000 Car on HIS Salary?" and charges that the police had "stolen" the money in the safe, a television set, and other items. The police claim that Inspector Smythe is independently well-off ("Not all boys who grow up to be cops come from poor families") and is probably one of the most honest cops around ("He doesn't have to be crooked; he doesn't need the money.") As far as the items taken from the Stonewall are concerned, the police swear they just impounded the money, etc., and counted the money before the Stonewall management and gave receipts for the cash and other items. The television set was reclaimed by a man who said he had loaned it to the Stonewall management, showed the police a receipt, and the cops let him take it.

The police denied any campaign of harassment. They gave their word that they knew of no orders authorizing such a campaign now or in the future. (A local woman lawyer, known more for "ambulance chasing" gay cases than for her honesty, has been spreading a story about imminent crackdowns as a selling point to get bars to employ her.)

They denied that local elections had anything to do with any harassment that might have occurred. They did not deny our charge that Village political boss Ed Koch had involved them in such clean-ups in former years to help win the votes of the uptight segment of the Village, but said no pressure had been put on them this year.

They asked if we knew of any harassment. Other than that in the Village, we knew of none. A little probing on our part elicited the information that the 6th Precinct got a new commanding officer about six weeks before the rioting. That rang a bell, because that's about how long the harassment had been going on. The cops who knew the man said he seemed like a fair-minded guy who wouldn't start any harassment campaign.

"Could it be possible that the men on the beat, knowing they had a new commander, and wanting to secure points, started their own campaign to clean up the streets just in case the new boss happened to be driving by?" someone suggested. The police officials agreed that this was a real possibility.

A discussion followed of the police brutality and beatings administered during the incidents on the streets. The police unanimously declined to defend such conduct by the police, other than to remark that when tempers get high, everyone loses some of his control. They pointed out that some very nice, probably law-abiding homosexuals, carried away by the rioting, tossed beer cans and worse at cops. The police, carried away themselves, sometimes swung their clubs too hard and too indiscriminately.

The police force doesn't condone police violence any more than any other kind of violence, and does discipline police officers against whom charges of police brutality are proven. It doesn't help the police do their job if they have the citizens against them, and cops don't like to see the bloody bodies of citizens any more than anyone else does.

DOCUMENT 98

D. L. [Dick Leitsch], "The Stonewall Riots: The Gay View"

Mattachine Society of New York Newsletter, Aug. 1969, 13–14[10]

The Stonewall was very likely raided, as the police said, because it had no license and violated fire and other regulations. Yet it had been allowed to operate in this manner for about three years. It seems strange the police hadn't closed it sooner.

As it was, the Stonewall was allowed to become a Village institution, as familiar to homosexuals as the Washington Arch is to tourists or the Washington Square fountain to folk-singers. When something becomes that well established, the police cannot pretend not to know what it is (unless they want to admit that they are incompetent or plain stupid), and they cannot expect to raid it without causing hard feelings and risking a reaction.

Nor can the police be credited with much forethought in raiding a highly popular bar at the height of one of the busiest evenings of the week. Surely a more sensible plan would be to go in early in the evening, before the place is crowded, or on a night early in the week when no large crowds are on hand. Smart visits to crowded bars by police officers who order everyone around, empty out the bar, and seize the management and a few customers (only those in drag these days) may bolster the egos of the police officers and give them a sense of power and importance, but such displays of power also create hostility toward the police from citizens who find them a little pretentious, to say the least.

Coming on the heels of the raids of the Snake Pit and the Sewer, and the closing of the Checkerboard, the Tele-Star and other clubs, the Stonewall raid looked to many like part of an effort to close all gay bars and clubs in the Village. It may be true that the Checkerboard and Tele-Star died without police assistance. (It is said that the woman who managed the Checkerboard came in one night, ordered all the customers out of the place, cleaned out the cash register and called the police to get rid of those customers who stayed around.) It is very likely that the Sewer and the Snake Pit were raided because they had no licenses, as the police said.

But how are the people in the street and the customers of the places to know that? The police don't bother to explain or send press releases to the papers (and when they do, the papers make it seem that the bar was raided because it was gay). The police seem to think the citizens should just accept their actions, but homosexuals are paranoid about the police, and with good reason. They have not been out of the entrapment business long enough for anyone to trust them, and the old bar raids of the early 60s are still fresh.

Since 1965 the homosexual community of New York has been treated quite well by the City Administration and the police have either reformed or been kept in line by Lindsay and Leary. During the Wagner years we all had the old slave mentality. We didn't know what it was like not to be mistreated, expected to be mistreated, and accepted harassment when it came.

Now we've walked in the open and know how pleasant it is to have self-respect and to be treated as citizens and human beings. There's no possible way to make us accept the "old way" again, and any sign, no matter how tentative, will be vigorously fought by the homosexual community.

Should a moralist or a backroom politico succeed John Lindsay, he had better take a lesson from the Stonewall riots and eschew any "clean-ups" of the sort Robert Wagner used to gain headlines and to enforce his brand of morality (or immorality). The homosexual community has tired of the old "We Walk in Shadows" routine. We want to stay in the sunlight from now on. Efforts to force us back into the closet could be disastrous for all concerned.

The above, while a true evaluation of the situation, does not explain why the raid on the Stonewall caused such a strong reaction. Why the Stonewall, and not the Sewer or the Snake Pit? The answer lies, we believe, in the unique nature of the Stonewall. This club was more than a dance bar, more than just a gay gathering place. It catered largely to a group of people who are not welcome in, or cannot afford, other places of homosexual social gathering.

The "drags" and the "queens," two groups which would find a chilly reception or a barred door at most of the other gay bars and clubs, formed the "regulars" at the Stonewall. To a large extent, the club was for them. Should Harry's, or Julius's, for example, be closed for any reason, the middle class "respectable" customers would find another place to meet, drink and socialize before the night was over. Apart from the Goldbug and the One Two Three, "drags" and "queens" had no place but the Stonewall. (And the first two will close shortly because the buildings have been sold.)

Another group was even more dependent on the Stonewall: the very young homosexuals and those with no other homes. You've got to be 18 to buy a drink in a bar, and gay life revolved around bars. Where do you go if you are 17 or 16 and gay? The "legitimate" bars won't let you in the place, and gay restaurants and the streets aren't very sociable.

Then, too, there are hundreds of young homosexuals in New York who literally have no home. Most of them are between 16 and 25, and came here from other places without jobs, money or contacts. Many of them are running away from unhappy homes (one boy told us, "My father called me 'cocksucker' so many times, I thought it was my name"). Another said his parents fought so much over which of them "made" him a homosexual that he left so they could learn to live together.

Some got thrown out of school or the service for being gay and couldn't face going home. Some were even thrown out of their homes with only the clothes on their backs by ignorant, intolerant parents who'd rather see their kid dead than homosexual.

They came to New York with the clothes on their backs. Some of them hustled, or had skills enough to get a job. Others weren't attractive enough to hustle, and didn't manage to fall in with people who could help them. Some of them, giddy at the openness of gay life in New York, got caught up in it and some are on pills and drugs. Some are still wearing the clothes in which they came here a year or more ago.

Jobless and without skills—without decent clothes to wear to a job interview—they live in the streets, panhandling or shoplifting for the price of admission to the Stonewall. That was the one advantage to the place—for $3.00 admission, one could stay inside, out of the winter's cold or the summer heat, all night long. Not only was the Stonewall better climatically, but it also saved the kids from spending the night in a doorway or from getting arrested as vagrants.

Three dollars isn't too hard to get panhandling, and nobody hustled drinks in the Stonewall. Once the admission price was paid, one could drink or not, as he chose. The Stonewall became "home" to these kids. When it was raided, they fought for it. That, and the fact that they had nothing to lose other than the most tolerant and broadminded gay place in town, explains why the Stonewall riots were begun, led and spearheaded by the "queens."

This, then, is another problem for the whole community, and not just the gay community. These young people must be helped. Young homosexuals and "queens" need places to socialize as much as older and more "respectable" homosexuals do. The victims of society's prejudice and hostility toward homosexuality need help and must get it somewhere. If it is true that the Stonewall was run by "underworld figures," as many claim, we have seen a horrible example of society ignoring a serious social problem and handing youths with problems over to organized crime for "help."

The police may make their statements about enforcing the law and fighting organized crime, but unless the laws are made more realistic and the community accepts some responsibility for the homosexual and his needs, the poor cop is going to have to take the abuse for society's mistakes and irresponsibility.

DOCUMENT 99
A.B. [Ada Bello] and C. F. [Carole Friedman], "Give Me Liberty Or…"
Homophile Action League Newsletter, Aug. 1969, 1–2[11]

It may well be the case that years from now, when social historians write their accounts of the homophile movement, June 28, 1969 will be viewed as a turning point in the fight for equality for homosexuals. For on that date, for the first time in history, masses of homosexuals took to the streets, demanding their rights in an open confrontation with the minions of an oppressive society.

When the New York City plainclothes officers entered the Stonewall Inn at 53 Christopher Street in Greenwich Village on Friday night, June 27th, they had no reason to fear this raid would be different from all the others. The police claimed that the reason for the raid was that the bar, which operates as a private club, had been selling liquor without a license. The club was closed, the employees arrested, and the patrons ushered out. But, instead of dissolving into the night, grateful for having escaped the scene of someone else's crime anonymous and unscathed, the homosexuals congregated outside. They were joined by other Village residents and visitors, the group swelling to several hundred. Awareness of the accumulated injustices of many years electrified the crowd. The protest began to take shape.

As the police led their prisoners to the paddy wagon, they were met with a hail of coins, beer cans, rocks, and cries of "Gay Power." The police retreated into the bar, which was set afire by the angry protesters. The flames were doused, police reinforcements arrived in great numbers, and the ensuing melee raged for two hours. Thirteen persons were arrested and several policemen injured.

On Saturday night, June 28th, the crowd gathered again in Sheridan Square, augmented by hundreds more. Singing and shouting "Gay Power," "We Want Freedom Now," and "Equality for Homosexuals," the protestors, now nearly two thousand in number, filled Christopher Street, made it their own. At this point, the Tactical Police Force arrived at the scene. Night sticks were brandished indiscriminately; random individuals were dragged from the crowd and beaten. But the protestors formed a solid front, preventing the cops from gaining a foothold, allowing themselves to be hit with night sticks, rather than let the police through. Unable to wrench prisoners from the crowd, the police formed a flying wedge to clear the area, forcing all in their path into side streets. This action succeeded in fragmenting the demonstrators, and quiet was restored at about 2:30 A.M. Although crowds formed again the next evening, heavy police surveillance prevented further developments.

The exciting events of June 27–29 should not be allowed to obscure one basic issue: the relationship which exists between the police and the owners of most of New York's gay bars. To quote the East Village Other of July 9: "The pigs, if you care to see it for yourself some night, stand outside of any gay bar. They walk into that establishment with mugs on and walk out with smiling faces, and their good hands in their money pockets." Now, the Stonewall Inn has been operating in its present location, just a few blocks from the Sixth Precinct house, for almost three years. It is difficult to believe that the establishment's lacking a liquor license was unknown to the police. Therefore, the questions which must be asked are: If the Stonewall has indeed been operating illegally, what collusion between the Mafia and the police has protected it in the past? What breakdown in that unholy silent partnership prompted the police action at this time? And, must homosexuals remain helpless pawns in the hands of these de facto ruling powers? The answer to that last question has apparently been given—in the streets.

New York's homophile groups, especially the Homophile Youth Movement and the Mattachine Society of New York, have allied themselves with the protestors and are attempting to organize the total gay community in order to help channel this newly-released energy to achieve maximum effectiveness.

Whatever the outcome of what has been called the "first gay riot in history," things will never be the same again. One 19-year-old boy quoted in the New

York Post of July 8th summed up the meaning of this event with sentiments which were undoubtedly shared by many: "All my life the cops have sneered and pointed at me and my friends. We've been harassed for doing nothing more than having our fun, not hurting anybody else. Well, the 'gay riots' mean we're not going to take it any more."

DOCUMENT 100

The Insider: Newsletter of the Mattachine Society of Washington
Aug. 1969, 1–3[12]

"Now it's happening and you can't stop it happening."
–Marat/Sade

In June of 1969 two of the most significant events to occur in the history of the homosexual happened in New York City. Never before have homosexuals ever reacted to society's oppression with the militancy exhibited by the large crowd of youth who stormed the Stonewall Inn when it was closed in Manhattan. And in no time before in modern history have city residents formally organized themselves into a vigilante committee to harass homosexuals from their neighborhood as they did in Queens. The Insider prints below accounts of these two significant events, taken from the Village Voice and the New York Times, with added comment and opinion.

GAY POWER EXPLODES

During the weekend of June 27–29, Sheridan Square in Greenwich Village was the scene of unprecedented rioting by young homosexuals against the New York City Police. In a show of militancy never before exhibited in such a way by homosexuals, youth took to the streets on three successive nights in open defiance of the police.

What began as a small police raid on the Stonewall Inn, a long-standing gay bar on Christopher Street, turned into an ugly riot. For the second time in a week, cops entered the Stonewall on Friday, June 27. There were only two patrolmen, two detectives and two policewomen. The police, armed with a warrant to search for the illegal sale of alcohol, released the 200 patrons from the bar one by one. Outside a festive mood stirred amongst the onlookers as they waited for favorites to appear at the door. Then a paddywagon arrived, and the mood changed. Three drag queens, a bartender and the doorman were loaded inside. The crowd was incensed, and when a dyke put up a struggle with the police, the scene exploded with beer cans, bottles, coins, and even a parking meter being heaved at the bar and the police. Someone threw in lighter fluid and followed it with a lighted match. A firehose was used to scatter the rioters and police reinforcements arrived to disperse the remaining rioters. Thirteen people were arrested in Friday's melee, but the Stonewall announced it would re-open on Saturday night.

On Saturday night, the protest was more sharply defined as a "gay power" display. Revolutionary signs appeared on the boarded windows of the Stonewall. Gay power chants arose in streets. The Saturday night crowd came ready for action and grew restless when nothing seemed to be happening. The publicity had brought more demonstrators to swell the crowd, and they were prepared for a confrontation. The group decided to move down the street, and when it did, it suddenly encountered the Tactical Patrol Force, who had been called earlier to disperse the large crowd. The TPF swept the crowd back to the corner of Waverly Place and then a second sweep took them down Christopher to Seventh Avenue. The police held their positions, and around 3:30 A.M., the streets were cleared.

On Sunday evening the crowd returned. And so did the TPF. Most people just rapped with one another, but around 1:00 A.M., the TPF made another sweep of the area and cleared everyone out. Allen Ginsberg and Taylor Mead put in an appearance; Ginsberg called the crowd "beautiful."

**Ed. Note:* The Insider does not see this exhibition of militancy as a fluke. Militant open defiance has become the most characteristic mark of the sixties' protest movements. First used by the blacks in irrational riots, and later used more systematically by hippies and campus protestors who shut down their own universities, militancy has never been characteristic of the homophile movement. Militant protestors rationalize their destructive methods by pointing out that knocking on doors is useful only to a point. When it becomes clear that the doors are never going to open and that door knocking is only a pacifier for the masses, then it is time to knock the doors down. In these terms, the homophile movement is behind the times. It is quite possible that the homosexuals in the streets may well make obsolete much of what the present homophile is doing. For better or worse, militancy is here.

TO HELL WITH DYING ON YOUR KNEES

Things won't ever be the same.

And why should they be? Why should the homosexual be among the last vestige of American citizenship to keep his neck under the heel of the oppressor? Why should the homosexual citizen forfeit his rights to governmental responsibility as guaranteed by the Constitution of the United States? Why should a human being, who happens to be a homosexual, permit the denial of his human rights?

WHY SHOULD YOU continue to be oppressed? When the man has his foot on the back of your neck, you have several alternatives—you can wait for someone else to come along and move the man away from you—you can wait for the man to decide on his own to remove his foot from your neck—you can get up off your knees and "lay up side his head."

And that seems to be the thrust of the issue. Will the homosexual wait for the heterosexual middle-class society to magnanimously remove its value-weighted foot from the necks of those who do not conform or will the homosexual take it upon himself as an individual to remove the oppressor's foot?

It appears that the structured homophile groups have failed to motivate the homosexual community. Perhaps they have not wanted to deal with the homosexual masses.

This time something happened in the homosexual community that the homophile organizations not only can claim little credit for, but some of which refuse even to acknowledge. . . .

DOCUMENT 101

"Cross Currents"
The Ladder, Oct. 1969, 40

GAY POWER IN NEW YORK CITY: Gay power—social and political power for homosexuals—has become a reality in New York, with the inadvertent help of the Police Department. At about 2 A.M. late Saturday night of June 29, the police raided the Stonewall Inn, a gay bar at 53 Christopher Street in Greenwich Village. They had previously closed The Sewer and The Checkerboard, also gay bars within the territory of the Sixth Precinct; but this was the first raid during peak hours, when the bar was jammed.

The raid touched off a riot by approximately 400 homosexual men and women, who yelled "gay power" and threw pennies, garbage and even uprooted parking meters at the police. An unknown number of homosexuals were injured. Four policemen were sent to the hospital, one with a broken wrist. Several homosexuals, who claim that they were suddenly attacked from behind while passing through the area, are suing the Police Department for assault and battery.

THE
STONEWALL RIOTS

Homosexuals continued to riot on the streets of Greenwich Village on Sunday night, June 29, and on Wednesday, July 2nd. Both the Mattachine Society of New York and the Homophile Youth Movement began leafletting the Village in order to organize protest against the conditions which sparked the riots. The newspapers did an excellent job of coverage, particularly the New York Times. WINS radio also gave rapid impartial coverage. The Village Voice, a so-called liberal weekly which serves the Greenwich Village area primarily, but is sold all over Manhattan, did a series of articles on the riots which were noted for a liberal use of such terms as "faggot," "dike," etc., and which received violent protest from a heavily gay readership. The Village Voice has long been known to the gay community for its policy of patronizing contempt towards homosexuals.

CORRUPTION IN THE BARS. It is generally believed that the gay bars in New York City are controlled by the Mafia, in cooperation with the police.

Reputable leaders of the gay community stated as much in private during the days following the riots, and Craig Rodwell of the Homophile Youth Movement went so far as to make such charges in leaflets distributed on Greenwich Avenue. However, no solid evidence has yet been presented in court.

It is also generally believed that in order to obtain a liquor license from the State Liquor Authority, a bribe ranging from $10,000 to $30,000 must be paid. Dick Leitsch of Mattachine Society of New York states that when some friends of his attempted to get a license to run a gay bar, the SLA turned them down on technicalities, even though a recent decision of the courts has held that gay bars and intra-sexual dancing in public places are legal. Since the SLA refuses to issue licenses to gay bars, these bars are generally run without licensing, under unsanitary conditions, serving watered drinks at outrageous prices—and are therefore a perfectly legitimate target of police raids. During ordinary times, the police have allowed these bars to operate, overlooking violations in return for a percentage of the take. During election years, these bars become the target for raids and round-ups of homosexuals.

The raids in the Sixth Precinct are believed to have been triggered off by the presence of a new captain, who wishes to make his reputation as a "law-and-order" man during a conservative year by "cleaning up the Village."

DOCUMENT 102

Don Jackson, "Reflections on the N.Y. Riots"
The Los Angeles Advocate, Oct. 1969, 11, 33

The sociological implications of the gay riots in New York are of crucial importance to the homosexual community. A few observations on these events are in order.

Tensions within New York City's gay community were increased greatly following a long series of incidents beginning early in June. A park in Queens had become a popular night playground for neighborhood straight youths, who frequented the park late at night to play a popular game called "Rolling queers," which means beating and robbing night strollers in the park.

Their elders, investigating the newfound source of income of their progeny, were pleased to learn of their public-spirited activities and decided to help their young rid the park of "sex perverts" in spite of the loss of a portion of their family income.

A citizens' committee was formed for the purpose of harassing people using the park at night, ostensibly to protect these youthful paragons of virtue from seeing the "unspeakable obscenities" which allegedly were performed in the thick bushes in the park. When the vigilantes found that the gays could not be shoved around so easily, they reacted by bringing axes and pruning shears, with which they completely defoliated the park. This last incident happened on June

15 and was reported as front-page news with photographs in the *New York Times* two weeks later.

Tensions were further heightened by many incidents of police harassment of individuals and by raids on three of the most popular gay clubs in the nation. The raids and incidents were the main topic of conversation at the Stonewall Club in the early morning hours of June 28, 1969. Everyone felt angry and edgy. Many hostile and derogatory remarks about the police were overheard. A nervous anxiety seemed to pervade the usually friendly crowd. At 3 AM a force of plainclothesmen entered the club to stage a raid. . . .

Allen Ginsberg, the poet, commented on the riot, "It's time we did something to assert ourselves, after all we do comprise 10 per cent of the population." Allen's remark is quite correct. We cannot help but chuckle in our beer a bit when we read the reports, but few approve of the violent behavior arising among members of our community.

Homosexuals share a feeling of persecution arising from injustices dealt out to them and their gay friends by the straight establishment. Their suffering has been matched only by their patience. Their status has slowly improved in most areas (California being an exception). They now see their community being swept by a feeling of anger, frustration, and impatience.

Gays have waited decades before seeing any improvement in their situation. Now that they see a glint of hope for some improvement, it calls attention to how long the road to equality will be.

Social changes come slowly. Although equality seems out of reach in our lifetimes, there are many signs that the status of homosexuals is about to be substantially improved. However angry and frustrated they become at the injustices and brutalities inflicted upon them, they must remember that they are a minority.

Homosexuals simply cannot afford rioting and violence. Such incidents solidify straight opinion against them and will surely bring a reaction. Straight people do not regard homosexuals as a minority group like Negroes. The straights had moral conflicts and guilt feelings about their treatment of the Negro minority, but they have no such qualms when it comes to gays. Most Christian churches and the conservative straights regard them as disgusting and abominably wicked, while the liberals regard them as mentally ill. The Negroes had many friends in white society. The number of straights who understand homosexuals or our plight are few—very few.

Militancy in minority groups is known by behavioral scientists to arise from tension. Tension is a sort of conglomerate emotion, a mixed feeling of anger, frustration, and impatience. It becomes particularly acute when the minority see a tiny improvement in its lot.

Experts in group behavior say that tensions in a minority group become most acute at times when the minority group members see their status suddenly take a turn for the worse after a long period of improvement.

This exactly describes the situation in New York preceding the riots. The New York riots could most likely have been predicted by experts in group behavior if they had been watching the long series of incidents preceding the riots. If they would take the bother, they could perceive similar conditions in certain other cities.

We must subvert emotion to reason. It is true that the tears and pleas of homosexuals for justice have fallen on deaf ears, and that the theories of the old gay organizations that educational programs would help our cause have been discredited. . . .

There must be a compromise course of action between violence and educational programs. One is too much, the other too little. It would appear to me that organized peaceful protest is the compromise we need. It has helped the Negroes and many other minorities.

The history of minority-group conflict with the majority leaves little hope that more riots will not occur—most likely on a scale much larger than in New York. It is essential that rational leaders appear who will redirect the anger into more peaceful and successful methods.

Otherwise, history and sociology indicate, gay riots on a vast scale with needless loss of life and property damage may occur. This is not the road to equality. Such disturbances will increase the irrational hatred the straights feel toward homosexuals.

Every educated reasonable member of the gay community must aid in redirecting the anger and frustrations of the more violent and emotional members.

PART III
AFTER STONEWALL, 1969–1973

6

ACTIVIST AGENDAS AND VISIONS AFTER STONEWALL

THE LGBT MOVEMENT experienced mass mobilization and political radicalization in the weeks and months following the Stonewall Riots. In a short period of time, a movement that had consisted of dozens of organizations and hundreds of active participants was transformed by the formation of hundreds (and then thousands) of organizations with thousands (and then tens of thousands) of active participants. Older groups such as the Mattachine Society, Daughters of Bilitis, Erickson Educational Foundation, and Society of Individual Rights were challenged. Recently created organizations such as the Homophile Action League, Student Homophile League, and Committee on Homosexual Freedom welcomed the energy and enthusiasm. A new generation of LGBT groups emerged with different names, agendas, and visions. These included the Gay Liberation Front (named after the National Liberation Fronts in Algeria and Vietnam), Queens Liberation Front, Gay Activists Alliance, Street Transvestite Action Revolutionaries, Radicalesbians, and Third World Gay Revolution.

Post-Stonewall LGBT activism was colorful and diverse. In some ways, the movement picked up where the pre-Stonewall movement left off; in other ways, it was profoundly different. The movement's ideologies and philosophies were affected by the riots, but there were other influences at work and LGBT activism continued to change in the early 1970s. The documents in this chapter bear witness, for example, to the influences of anticolonial politics, antiwar protest, black radicalism, countercultural activism, and women's liberation. The agendas and visions highlighted in this chapter can also be considered in relation to the protests and parades featured in the next two chapters; in some respects, activist words and actions were aligned, but in others they were not.

This chapter's twenty documents introduce a selection of post-Stonewall movement ideologies, philosophies, manifestos, and platforms. Many of these texts were reprinted one or more times in the LGBT and alternative press, reaching more than just their original audiences.

DOCUMENTS 103–108 feature early gay liberation declarations and manifestos.
DOCUMENTS 109–113 present early articulations of radical lesbian feminism.
DOCUMENTS 114–117 highlight new directions in transgender politics.
DOCUMENTS 118–122 are LGBT vision statements by anticolonial, antiracist, black, and third world advocates.

DOCUMENT 103

"Gay Revolution Comes Out"

Rat, 12 Aug. 1969, 7

The following are excerpts from an interview held in New York City on July 31, 1969 with members of the newly formed Gay Liberation Front.[1]

Q: . . . What is the Gay Liberation Front?

A: We are a revolutionary homosexual group of men and women formed with the realization that complete sexual liberation for all people cannot come about unless existing social institutions are abolished. We reject society's attempt to impose sexual roles and definitions of our nature. We are stepping outside these roles and simplistic myths. We are going to be who we are. At the same time, we are creating new social forms and relations, that is, relations based upon brotherhood, cooperation, human love, and uninhibited sexuality. Babylon has forced us to commit ourselves to one thing...revolution.

Q: What makes you revolutionaries?

A: We formed after the recent pig bust of the Stonewall, a well known gay bar in Greenwich Village. We've come to realize that all our frustrations and feelings of oppression are real. The society has fucked with us...within our families, on our jobs, in our education, in the streets, in our bedrooms; in short, it has shit all over us. We, like everyone else, are treated as commodities. We're told what to feel, what to think, what to be...all for the needs of a money-making machine that has successfully packaged us all into antagonistic groups, keeping us divided by racism, sex, and other fears. We identify ourselves with all the oppressed: the Vietnamese struggle, the third world, the blacks, the workers...all those oppressed by this rotten, dirty, vile, fucked-up capitalist conspiracy.

Q: Can you pinpoint the oppression as it specifically relates to homosexuals?

A: Up until now the traditional homosexual has been forced to attempt to live two separate existences, which precludes his being able to live fully in either. Through a system of taboos and institutionalized repressions, society has controlled and manipulated (and in our case denied) sexual expression. And through a brutal ethos of competition and inhumane labor has alienated each of us from all our brothers and sisters. The socialization process of the society is nothing but a phony morality impressed upon us by church, media, psychiatry, and education which tells us that if we're not married heterosexual producers and pacified workers and soldiers that we are sick degenerate outcasts. We expose the institution of marriage as one of the most insidious and basic sustainers of the system. The family is the microcosm of oppression. A male worker is given the illusion of participating in the power of the ruling class through economic control of his children and through the relation he has with his wife as a sexual object and household slave.

Q: How do homosexuals react to their oppression?

A: We hope that masses of homosexuals will be open about their sexuality, and will challenge the bags the system puts people in. Unfortunately it is the repressed homosexual all too often who is willing to be an Uncle Tom or an Aunt Jamima.

Q: What does the GLF intend to do?

A: We are relating the militancy generated by the bar bust and by increasing pig harassment to a program that allows homosexuals and sexually liberated persons to confront themselves and society through encounter groups, demonstrations, dances, a newspaper, and by just being ourselves on the street. The program will create revolution of mind and body as we all confront the opposition. At this time we have specific plans to open a coffee house, a working commune, and experimental living communes. We hope to extend the coffee house idea as an alternative to the exploitative over-priced syndicate run gay bar.

Q: Why do you identify with the revolution when homosexuals are oppressed in other revolutionary cultures?

A: We feel in this respect that previous revolutions have failed, for any revolution that does not deal with the liberation of the total human being is incomplete. . . .

DOCUMENT 104

North American Conference of Homophile Organizations Committee on Youth, "A Radical Manifesto: The Homophile Movement Must Be Radicalized!"

28 Aug. 1969, reprinted in Stephen Donaldson [Robert Martin], "Student Homophile League News," *Gay Power* (1.2), ca. Sept. 1969, 16, 19–20[2]

1. We see the persecution of homosexuality as part of a general attempt to oppress all minorities and keep them powerless. Our fate is linked with these minorities; if the detention camps are filled tomorrow with blacks, hippies and other radicals, we will not escape that fate, all out attempts to dissociate ourselves from them notwithstanding. A common struggle, however, will bring common triumph.

2. Therefore we declare our support as homosexuals or bisexuals for the struggles of the black, the feminist, the Spanish-American, the Indian, the Hippie, the Young, the Student, and other victims of oppression and prejudice.

3. We call upon these groups to lend us their support and encourage their presence within NACHO and the homophile movement at large.

4. Our enemies, an implacable, repressive governmental system; much of organized religion, business and medicine will not be moved by appeasement or appeals to reason and justice, but only by power and force.

5. We regard established heterosexual standards of morality as immoral and refuse to condone them by demanding an equality which is merely the common yoke of sexual repression.

6. We declare that homosexuals, as individuals and members of the greater community, must develop homosexual ethics and esthetics independent of, and without reference to, the mores imposed upon heterosexuality.

7. We demand the removal of all restrictions on sex between consenting persons of any sex, of any orientation, of any age, anywhere, whether for money or not, and for the removal of all censorship.

8. We call upon the churches to sanction homosexual liaisons when called upon to do so by the parties concerned.

9. We call upon the homophile movement to be more honestly concerned with youth rather than trying to promote a mythical, non-existent "good public image."

10. The homophile movement must totally reject the insane war in Viet Nam and refuse to encourage complicity in the war and support of the war machine, which may well be turned against us. We oppose any attempts by the movement to obtain security clearances for homosexuals, since these contribute to the war machine.

11. The homophile movement must engage in continuous political struggle on all fronts.

12. We must open the eyes of homosexuals on this continent to the increasingly repressive nature of our society and to the realization that Chicago may await us tomorrow.

DOCUMENT 105

Preamble, Gay Activists Alliance Constitution

21 Dec. 1969, Gay Activists Alliance Records, Box 18, Folder 2, New York Public Library[3]

We as liberated homosexual activists demand the freedom for expression of our dignity and value as human beings through confrontation with and disarmament of all mechanisms which unjustly inhibit us: economic, social, and political. Before the public conscience, we demand an immediate end to all oppression of homosexuals and the immediate unconditional recognition of these basic rights:

The right to our own feelings. This is the right to feel attracted to the beauty of members of our own sex and to embrace those feelings as truly our own, free from any question or challenge whatsoever by any other person, institution, or moral authority.

The right to love. This is the right to express our feelings in action, the right to make love with anyone, anyway, anytime, provided only that the action be freely chosen by all the persons concerned.

The right to our own bodies. This is the right to treat and express our bodies as we will, to nurture them, to display them, to embellish them, solely in the manner we ourselves determine independent of any external control whatsoever.

The right to be persons. This is the right freely to express our own individuality under the governance of laws justly made and executed, and to be the bearers of social and political rights which are guaranteed by the Constitution of the United States and the Bill of Rights, enjoined upon all legislative bodies and courts, and grounded in the fact of our common humanity.

To secure these rights, we hereby institute the Gay Activists Alliance, which shall be completely and solely dedicated to their implementation and maintenance, repudiating at the same time violence (except for the right of self-defense) as unworthy of social protest, disdaining all ideologies, whether political or social, and forbearing alliance with any other organization except for those whose concrete actions are likewise so specifically dedicated.

It is, finally, to the imagination of oppressed homosexuals themselves that we commend the consideration of these rights, upon whose actions alone depends all hope for the prospect of their lasting procurement.

DOCUMENT 106
Carl Wittman, "Refugees from Amerika: A Gay Manifesto"
San Francisco Free Press, 22 Dec. 1969, 3–5[4]

San Francisco is a refugee camp for homosexuals. We have fled here from every part of the nation, and like refugees elsewhere, we came not because it is so great here, but because it was so bad there. By the tens of thousands, we fled small towns where to be ourselves would endanger our jobs and any hope of a decent life; we have fled from blackmailing cops, from families who disowned or "tolerated" us; we have been drummed out of the armed services, thrown out of schools, fired from jobs, beaten by punks and policemen.

And we have formed a ghetto, out of self protection. It is a ghetto, rather than a free territory, because it is still theirs. Straight cops patrol us, straight legislators make our laws, straight employers keep us in line, straight money exploits us. And we have pretended everything is OK, because we haven't been able to see how to change it—we've been afraid.

In the past year, there has been an awakening of gay liberation ideas and energy. How it began we don't know; perhaps we were inspired by black people and their liberation movement; we learned how to stop pretending from the hip revolution. Amerika in all its ugliness has surfaced with the war and our national leaders. And we are revulsed by the quality of our ghetto life.

Where once there was frustration, alienation, and cynicism, there are new traits among liberated gays; we are full of love for each other and are showing it; we are full of anger at what has been done to us. And as we recall all the self-censorship and repression for so many years, a reservoir of tears pours out of our eyes. And we are euphoric, high, with the initial flourish of a movement.

We want to make ourselves clear: our first job is to liberate ourselves, and that means clearing our heads of the garbage that's been poured into them. . . . It should also be clear that these ideas reflect the perspective of one person, and are determined not only by my homosexuality, but my being white, male, and middle class. It is my individual consciousness. Our group consciousness will evolve as we get ourselves together—we are only at the beginning.

I. ON ORIENTATION

1. *What Homosexuality Is*: Nature leaves undefined the object of sexual desire. The gender of that object has been imposed socially. Humans originally put a taboo on homosexuality because they needed every bit of energy to produce and raise children—survival of the species was a priority. With overpopulation and technological change, that taboo is absurd and continues only to exploit us and enslave us. . . .

   HOMOSEXUALITY IS THE CAPACITY TO LOVE SOMEONE OF THE SAME SEX.

2. *Bisexuality*: Bisexuality is good; it is the capacity to love people of either sex. The reason so few of us are bisexual is because society made such a big stink about homosexuality that we got forced into seeing ourselves as either straight or non-straight. Also, many gays got turned off to the ways men are supposed to relate to women and vice-versa, which is pretty fucked up. Gays will begin to get turned on to women when 1) it's something that we do because we want to, and not because we should; 2) when women's liberation has changed the nature of heterosexual relationships.

   We continue to call ourselves homosexual, rather than bisexual, even if we do make it with the opposite sex also, because saying "Oh, I'm Bi" is a cop out for a gay. We get told it's ok to sleep with guys as long as we sleep with women, too, and that's still putting homosexuality down. We'll be gay until everyone has forgotten that it's an issue. Then we'll begin to be complete people.

3. *Heterosexuality*: Exclusive heterosexuality is fucked up; it is a fear of people of the same sex, it is anti-homosexual, and it is fraught with frustrations. Heterosexual sex is fucked up, too; talk to women's liberation about what straight guys are like in bed. Sex is aggression for the male chauvinist; sex is obligation for the traditional women. . . .

II. *ON WOMEN*

1. *Lesbianism*: It's been a male dominated society for too long, and that has warped both men and women. So gay women are going to see things differently from gay men; they are going to feel oppression as women, too. Their liberation is tied up with both gay liberation and women's liberation.

   This paper speaks from the gay male point of view. Although some of the ideas in it may be equally relevant to gay women, it would be arrogant to presume this to be a manifesto for lesbians.

   We look forward to the emergence of a lesbian liberation voice. The existence of a lesbian caucus within the New York Gay Liberation Front has been very helpful in challenging male chauvinism among gay guys and anti-gay feelings among women's lib.

2. *Male Chauvinism*: All men are infected with male chauvinism—we were brought up that way. It means we assume that women play subordinate roles and are less human than ourselves. . . . It is no wonder that so few gay women have become active in our groups.

   Male chauvinism, however, is not central to us. We can junk it much more easily than straight men can. For we understand oppression. We have largely opted out of a system which oppresses women daily—our egos are not built on putting women down and having them build us up. Also, living in a mostly male world, we have become used to playing different roles and doing our own shit-work. And finally, we have a common enemy: the big male chauvinists are also the big anti-gays. . . .

3. *Women's Liberation*: They are assuming their equality and dignity, and in doing so are challenging the same things we are: the insufferable roles, the exploitation of minorities by capitalism, the arrogance of straight white male middle class Amerika. They are our sisters in struggle.

   Problems and differences will become clearer when we begin to work together. One major problem is our own male chauvinism. Another is the uptightness and hostility to homosexuality that many women have—that is the straight in them. A third problem is differing views on sex: sex for them has meant oppression, while it has been the symbol of our freedom. . . .

III. *ON ROLES*

1. *Mimicry of Straight Society*: We are children of a straight society. We still think straight, and that is part of our oppression. . . .

2. *Marriage*: Marriage is a prime example of a straight institution fraught with role playing. Traditional marriage is a rotten, oppressive institution. . . . Marriage is a contract which smothers both people, denies needs, and places impossible demands on both people. . . .

ACTIVIST AGENDAS
AND VISIONS
AFTER STONEWALL

3. *Alternatives to Marriage*: People want to get married for lots of good reasons, although marriage doesn't meet those needs. We're all looking for security, a flow of love, a feeling of belonging and being needed.

These needs can be met through any number of social relationships and living situations. The things we want to get away from are: 1. exclusiveness, propertied attitudes toward each other, a mutual pact against the rest of the world; 2. promises about the future, which we have no right to make and which prevent us from, or make us feel guilty about, growing; 3. inflexible roles. . . .

4. *Gay "Stereotype" Roles*: The straight's image of the gay community is defined largely by those of us who have violated straight roles. There is a tendency among "homophile" groups to deplore gays who play visible roles—the queens and the nellies. As liberated gays, we must take a clear stand: 1) gays who stand out have been the most courageous among us; they came out and withstood straight disapproval before the rest of us. They are our first martyrs; 2) if they have suffered from being open, it is straight society whom we blame. . . .

IV. *ON OPPRESSION*

It is important to catalog and understand the different facets of our oppression. There is no future in arguing about degrees of oppression. A lot of "movement" types come on with a line of shit about homosexuals not being oppressed as much as black or Vietnamese or workers or women. We don't happen to fit into their ideas of class (or caste). . . .

V. *ON SEX*

ACTIVIST AGENDAS AND VISIONS AFTER STONEWALL

1. *What Sex Is*: Sex is both creative expression and communication: good when it is either, and better when it is both. Sex can also be aggression—and usually is when those involved do not see each other as equals. . . .

2. *Objectification*: In this scheme of things, people are sexual objects, but they are also subjects, and are human beings who appreciate themselves as object and subject. This use of human bodies as objects is legitimate (not harmful) only as long as it is reciprocal. If one person is always the object and the other the subject, it stifles the human being in both. . . .

Gay liberation people must understand that women have been treated EXCLUSIVELY and DISHONESTLY as sexual objects. It is a major part of their liberation to play down sexual objectification and begin to develop other aspects of themselves which have been stifled so long. We respect this. We also understand that many liberated women will, for a while, be appalled or disgusted at the open and prominent place that we put sex in our lives—and while this is a natural response from their experience, they must learn what it means for us.

For us, sexual objectification is a focal point of our liberation. Sex is precisely that which we are not supposed to have with each other. And to learn how to be open and good with each other sexually is part of our liberation. . . .

3. *On Positions and Roles*: . . . We strive for democratic, mutual, reciprocal sex. This doesn't mean that we are all mirror images of each other in bed, but that we break away from roles which enslave us. We already do better in bed than straights do, and we can do even better.

4. *On Chicken and Studs*: Face it, nice bodies, and young bodies, are attributes, they're groovy. They are inspiration for art, for spiritual elevation, for good sex. The problem arises only in the inability to relate to people of the same age or people who do not fit the plastic stereotypes of the good body. . . .

A footnote on exploitation of children: kids can take care of themselves, and are sexual beings way earlier than we'd like to admit. Those of us who began cruising in our early teens know this, and we were doing cruising, not being debauched by our elders. . . . As for child molesting, the overwhelming amount is done by straight guys to little girls. . . .

5. *Perversion*: We've been called perverts enough to be automatically suspicious of this word. Still many of us shrink from the idea of certain kinds of sex: with animals, sado/masochism, "dirty" sex (involving piss and shit). . . . We shouldn't be apologetic to straights about gay people whose sex lives we don't understand or share. . . .

VI. *ON OUR GHETTO*

We are refugees from Amerika. So we came to the ghetto—and as other ghettos, it has its negative and positive aspects. Refugee camps are better than what preceded them, or people never would have come. But they are still enslaving, inasmuch as we are limited to being ourselves there and only there.

Ghettos breed self hatred. We stagnate here, accepting the status quo. And the status quo is rotten. We are all warped by our oppression, and in the helplessness of the ghetto we blame ourselves rather than our oppressors.

Ghettos breed exploitation: Landlords realize they can charge exorbitant rents and get away with it, because there is a limited area which is safe to live in. Mafia control of bars and baths in New York is only an extreme example of outside money controlling our institutions for their profit. In San Francisco, the Tavern Guild is in favor of maintaining the ghetto, because it is through the ghetto culture that they make a buck. . . .

SAN FRANCISCO—GHETTO OR FREE TERRITORY: Our ghetto certainly is more beautiful, larger, and more diverse and freer than most ghettos, and certainly more than Amerika—that's why we're here. But it is not ours—capitalists make money off us, police patrol us, the government tolerates us as long as we shut up, and daily we work for and pay taxes to those who oppress us.

To be a free territory, we must govern ourselves, set up our own institutions, defend ourselves, and use our own energies to improve our lives. . . .

VII. *ON COALITION*

Right now the bulk of our work has to be among ourselves—self educating, fending off attacks, and building our free territory. Thus basically we have to have a gay/straight vision of the world, until the oppression of gays is ended.

But two problems exist with that as a total vision: 1) we can't change Amerika alone; we need coalition with other oppressed groups at some point; 2) many of us have "mixed" identities—we are gay, and also we are part of another group trying to free itself—women, blacks, other minority groups; we may also have taken on identities which are vital to us: dopers, ecologists, radicals.

Who do we look to for coalition?

1. *Women's Liberation*: Without repeating earlier statements, 1) they are our closest ally—we have to try hard to get together with them; 2) a lesbian caucus is probably the easiest way to deal with gay guys' male chauvinism, and challenge the straightness of women's liberation; 3) we as males must be sensitive to their developing identities as women. . . .
2. *Black Liberation*: This is tenuous right now, because of the uptightness and supermasculinity of many black males (which is understandable). Notwithstanding, we must support their movement and demands; we must show that we mean business; and we must figure out which our common enemies are: police, city hall, capitalism. . . .
3. *Chicanos*: Basically the same problem as with blacks: trying to overcome mutual animosity and fear, and finding ways to support their movement. The extra problem of super-uptightness and machismo among Latin cultures, and the traditional pattern of Mexican "punks" beating on homosexuals, can be overcome: we're both oppressed, and by the same people at the top.
4. *White Radicals and Ideologues*: . . . We can look forward to coalition and mutual inspiration with white radical groups if they are able to transcend their anti-gay and male chauvinist patterns. . . .

   Perhaps it would be useful to approach them by helping them free the homosexual within them.
5. *Hip and Street People*: Perhaps the major dynamic of recent gay lib sentiment is the hip revolution within the gay community. Emphasis on love, drop out, be honest, stop dressing drably, hair, smoke dope. . . .

   The hip/street culture has led people into a lot of other things: encounter/sensitivity, the quest for reality, liberating territory for the people, ecological consciousness, communes. These are real points of agreement.
6. *Homophile Groups*: 1) Reformist and pokey as they might sometimes be, they are our brothers. They will grow just as we have grown and will

grow. Don't attack them, particularly in straight or mixed company. 2) Ignore their attacks on us. 3) Cooperate where cooperation is possible without essential compromise of our identity.

CONCLUSION: AN OUTLINE OF IMPERATIVES FOR GAY LIBERATION

1. Free ourselves: come out, everywhere; initiate self defense and political activity; initiate community institutions; think.
2. Turn other gay people on: talk all the time; understand, accept, forgive.
3. Free the homosexual in everyone: we'll be getting a lot of shit from threatened latents: be gentle and keep talking and acting free.
4. We've been playing an act for a long time: we're consummate actors. Now we can begin TO BE, and it'll be a good show!

DOCUMENT 107

Martha Shelley, "Gay Is Good"

Rat, 24 Feb. 1970, 11[5]

Look out, straights! Here comes the Gay Liberation Front, springing up like warts all over the bland face of Amerika, causing shudders of indigestion in the delicately-balanced bowels of the Movement. . . . We've got chapters in New York/San Francisco/San Jose/Los Angeles/Wisconsin/New England and I hear maybe even in Dallas. We're gonna make our own revolution because we're sick of revolutionary posters which depict straight he-man types and earth mothers, with guns and babies. We're sick of the Panthers lumping us together with the capitalists in their term of universal contempt—"faggot!"

And I am personally sick of liberals who say they don't care who sleeps with whom, it's what you do outside of bed that counts. This is what homosexuals have been trying to get straights to understand for years. Well, it's too late for liberalism. Because what I do outside of bed may have nothing to do with what I do inside—but my consciousness is branded, is permeated with homosexuality. . . .

We are the extrusions of your unconscious mind—your worst fears made flesh. From the beautiful boys at Cherry Grove to the aging queens in the uptown bars, the taxi-driving dykes to the lesbian fashion models, the hookers (male and female) on 42nd Street, the leather lovers...and the very ordinary very un-lurid gays.... We are the sort of people everyone was taught to despise—and now we are shaking off the chains of self-hatred and marching on your citadels of repression.

Liberalism isn't good enough for us. And we are only just beginning to discover it. Your friendly smile of acceptance—from the safe position of heterosexuality—isn't enough. As long as you cherish that secret belief that you are a little bit better, because you sleep with the opposite sex, you are still asleep in your cradle and we will be the nightmare that awakens you.

We are men and women who, from the time of our earliest memories, have been in revolt against the sex-role structure and the nuclear family structure. The roles that we have played amongst ourselves, the self-deceit, the compromises and subterfuges—these have never totally obscured the fact that we exist outside the traditional structure—and our existence threatens it.

Understand this—that the worst part of being a homosexual is having to keep it secret. Not the occasional murders by police or teenage queer-beaters, not the loss of jobs or expulsion from schools or dishonorable discharges—but the daily knowledge that what you are is something so awful that it cannot be revealed. . . .

If you are homosexual, and you get tired of waiting around for the liberals to repeal the sodomy laws, and begin to dig yourself—and get angry—you are on your way to being radical. Get in touch with the reasons that made you reject straight society when you were a kid . . . and realize that you were right. Straight roles stink.

And you straights—look down the street, at the person whose sex is not readily apparent. Are you uneasy? Or are you made more uneasy by the stereotype homosexual, the flaming faggot or diesel dyke? We want you to be uneasy, to be a little less comfortable in your straight roles. And to make you uneasy, we behave outrageously. . . .

It's difficult for me to understand how you can dig each other as human beings—in a man-woman relationship—how you can relate to each other in spite of your sex-roles. It must be awfully difficult to talk to each other, when the woman is trained to repress what the man is trained to express and vice-versa. Do straight men and women talk to each other? Or does the man talk and the woman nod approvingly? Is love possible between heterosexuals; or is it all a case of women posing as nymphs, earth-mothers, sex-objects, what-have-you; and men writing the poetry of romantic illusions to these walking stereotypes? . . .

And now I will tell you what we want, we radical homosexuals: not for you to tolerate us, or to accept us, but to understand us. And this you can only do by becoming one of us. We want to reach the homosexual entombed in you, to liberate our brothers and sisters, locked in the prisons of your skulls. . . .

We will never go straight until you go gay. As long as you divide yourselves, we will be divided from you—separated by a mirror trick of your mind. We will no longer allow you to drop us—or the homosexuals in yourselves—into the reject bin; labelled sick, childish, or perverted. And because we will not wait, your awakening may be a rude and bloody one. It's your choice. You will never be rid of us, because we reproduce ourselves out of your bodies—and out of your minds. We are one with you.

DOCUMENT 108

Steve [Kiyoshi] Kuromiya, "Come Out, Come Out, Wherever You Are!"

Philadelphia Free Press, 27 July 1970, 6–7[6]

We're sick of hearing people say, "I don't care what homosexuals do with each other in bed…as long as they don't bother me." Well, we're here. And we're going to bother you. If homosexuals bother you, it's your problem, not ours. Your oppression of us has made our homosexual consciousness permeate our whole lives. Your hypocrisy and double standards have bothered us for years. Your labels are inadequate. We're complex. We're people. We come in all sizes and shapes. Most of us have had heterosexual experiences. Personally, I don't care what heterosexuals do in bed…as long as they stop bothering ME…and start loving me as a person, fraternally, emotionally, AND physically. Then, maybe we can start dropping the labels and start treating people as people.

You don't understand us because you don't even know who we are. You've maintained that security of distance that protects your self-image of heterosexuality. You'll accept us from a distance. You hold dear that unspoken belief that you are a little bit better, a little bit more masculine or red-blooded, because you sleep with the opposite sex. . . .

You shun us because you see us as your worst fears about yourself. You see the beautiful boys and the flamboyant queens, the diesel dykes, the leather queens and the hustlers . . . and they fit your image of what we ought to be like. But most of us you won't recognize. And we're the ones you really worry about…because in every other way except for our sexual orientation, we're very much like you. . . .

One of the worst aspects of homosexuality is having to keep our sexual preferences secret. That's what we're fighting now. That's how we're going to destroy YOUR myth of homosexuality. We're tired of carrying the burden of straight society's unconscious guilt. We're ready to go to our schools and offices and factories and organizational meetings and shout out our true identities. . . .

For some of us, these self-liberating actions our movement is engaged in will cost us dearly. We may be faced with dishonorable discharges…loss of our jobs…public scorn…perhaps, beatings at the hands of young pigs or young punks or murderers. But, every revolutionary movement or movement for social action has been accompanied by repression and violence. Ours won't be unique. And like the others, our liberation is, in fact, the liberation of society as a whole.

Someday soon, you won't be calling our movement irrelevant. Or dismiss us as a "bunch of silly fairies." Someday, because of our movement, you'll no longer squirm when you see two people of the same sex holding hands or necking in public. Someday, you'll be the one holding hands with us. And that day, we'll be ready to fight the Revolution with you arm-in-arm.

Homosexuals have burst their chains and abandoned their closets to come out into the open to haunt you. Gay Liberation is on the move. And it's moving fast.

We came battle-scarred and angry to topple your sexist, racist, hateful society. We came to challenge the incredible hypocrisy of your serial monogamy, your oppressive sexual role-playing, your nuclear family, your Protestant ethic, apple pie and Mother. . . .

Twenty thousand strong we marched up Sixth Avenue in celebration of "the love that dare not speak its name." Twenty thousand sisters and brothers chanting, "Say it clear...say it loud...gay is good...gay is proud!" Twenty thousand strong we came on Christopher Street Liberation Day to make good on your guarantee to us of Life, Liberty and the Pursuit of Happiness...a guarantee you've reneged on every day of your lives.

We came to celebrate the first birthday of our movement. Gay Liberation was born one year ago on Christopher Street with six days of street fighting when the pigs raided and closed down one of our gay ghetto bars, the Stonewall in the West Village. For the first time, gay women and men, along with friendly straights, stood up and fought for homosexual rights.

For a movement born in such a fiery spirit, our birthday seems tame. But, it's a truly revolutionary act for the moderates of the Daughters of Bilitis and the Mattachine Society to join arms with the radicalesbians of the Lavender Menace and the revolutionaries of the Gay Liberation Front. . . .

We have learned from the Movement that there is power in numbers. That's why we're working to get ourselves together (and that's the reason for Christopher Street Liberation Day). We've got the numbers. We've infiltrated every smoke-filled niche of the precious bureaucracy that you call the Movement. We've infiltrated your committees and demonstrations. We infiltrated your communes and affinity groups. We've infiltrated every bastion of capitalism and the military-industrial complex. We've even infiltrated your family. Somebody you know, and love, is a homosexual. Think about it. . . .

DOCUMENT 109
Radicalesbians, "The Woman-Identified Woman"
Come Out!, June 1970, 12–13[7]

What is a lesbian? A lesbian is the rage of all women condensed to the point of explosion. She is the woman who, often beginning at an extremely early age, acts in accordance with her inner compulsion to be a more complete and freer human being than her society—perhaps then, but certainly later—cares to allow her. These needs and actions, over a period of years, bring her into painful conflict with people, situations, the accepted ways of thinking, feeling and behaving, until she is in a state of continual war with everything around her, and usually with herself. She may not be fully conscious of the political implications of what for her began as personal necessity, but on some level she has not been able to accept the limitations and oppression laid on her by the most basic role of her society—the female role. The turmoil she experiences tends to induce guilt proportional to the degree to which she feels she is not meeting social expectations, and/or eventually drives her to question and analyze what the rest of her society more or less accepts. . . . Those of us who work that through find ourselves on the other side of a tortuous journey through a night that may have been decades long. The perspective gained from that journey, the liberation of self, the inner peace, the real love of self and of all women, is something to be shared with all women—because we are all women.

It should first be understood that lesbianism, like male homosexuality, is a category of behavior possible only in a sexist society characterized by rigid sex roles and dominated by male supremacy. Those sex roles dehumanize women by defining us as a supportive/serving caste *in relation* to the master caste of men, and emotionally cripple men by demanding that they be alienated from their own bodies and emotions in order to perform their economic/political/ military functions effectively. Homosexuality is a by-product of a particular way of setting up roles (or approved patterns of behavior) on the basis of sex; as such it is an inauthentic (not consonant with "reality") category. In a society in which men do not oppress women, and sexual expression is allowed to follow feelings, the categories of homosexuality and heterosexuality would disappear.

But lesbianism is also different from male homosexuality, and serves a different function in the society. "Dyke" is a different kind of put-down from "faggot." . . . The grudging admiration felt for the tomboy, and the queasiness felt around a sissy boy point to the same thing: the contempt in which women—or those who play a female role—are held. And the investment in keeping women in that contemptuous role is very great. Lesbian is the word, the label, the condition that holds women in line. When a woman hears this word tossed her way, she knows she is stepping out of line. She knows that she has crossed the terrible boundary of her sex role. She recoils, she protests, she reshapes her actions to gain approval. Lesbian is a label invented by the Man to throw at any woman who dares to be his equal, who dares to challenge his prerogatives (including that of all women as part of the exchange medium among men), who dares to assert the primacy of her own needs. To have the label applied to people active in women's liberation is just the most recent instance of a long history; older women will recall that not so long ago, any woman who was successful, independent, not orienting her whole life about a man, would hear this word. For in this sexist society, for a woman to be independent means she *can't* be a *woman*—she *must* be a *dyke*. That in itself should tell us where women are at. It says as clearly as can be said: women and person are contradictory terms. For a lesbian is not considered a "real woman." And yet, in popular thinking, there is really only one essential difference between a lesbian and other women: that of sexual orientation—which is to say, when you strip off all the packaging, you must finally realize that the essence of being a "woman" is to get fucked by men.

"Lesbian" is one of the sexual categories by which men have divided up humanity. While all women are dehumanized as sex objects, as the objects of men they are given certain compensations: identification with his power, his ego, his status, his protection (from other males), feeling like a "real woman," finding social acceptance by adhering to her role, etc. Should a woman confront herself by confronting another woman, there are fewer rationalizations, fewer buffers by which to avoid the stark horror of her dehumanized condition. Herein we find the overriding fear of many women toward exploring intimate relationships with other women: the fear of being used as a sexual object by a woman, which not only will bring her no male-connected compensations, but also will reveal the void which is woman's real situation. This dehumanization is expressed when a straight woman learns that a sister is a lesbian; she begins to relate to her lesbian sister as her potential sex object, laying a surrogate male role on the lesbian. . . . For women, especially those in the movement, to perceive their lesbian sisters through this male grid of role definitions is to accept this male cultural conditioning and to oppress their sisters much as they themselves have been oppressed by men. Are we going to continue the male classification system of defining all females in *sexual relation* to some *other* category of people? Affixing the label lesbian not only to a woman who aspires to be a person, but also to any situation of real love, real solidarity, real primacy among women is a primary form of divisiveness among women. . . .

Women in the movement have in most cases gone to great lengths to avoid discussion and confrontation with the issue of lesbianism. . . . It is absolutely essential to the success and fulfillment of the women's liberation movement that this issue be dealt with. As long as the label "dyke" can be used to frighten women into a less militant stand, keep her separate from her sisters, keep her from giving primacy to anything other than men and family—then to that extent she is controlled by the male culture. Until women see in each other the possibility of a primal commitment which includes sexual love, they will be denying themselves the love and value they readily accord to men, thus affirming their second-class status. As long as male acceptability is primary—both to individual women and to the movement as a whole—the term lesbian will be used effectively against women. . . .

Why is it that women have related to and through men? By virtue of having been brought up in a male society, we have internalized the male culture's definition of ourselves. That definition views us as relative beings who exist not for ourselves, but for the servicing, maintenance and comfort of men. That definition consigns us to sexual and family functions, and excludes us from defining and shaping the terms of our lives. In exchange for our psychic servicing and for performing society's non-profit-making functions, the man confers on us just one thing: the slave status which makes us legitimate in the eyes of the society in which we live. This is called "femininity" or "being a real woman" in our cultural lingo. We are authentic, legitimate, real to the extent that we are the property of some man whose name we bear. To be a woman who belongs to no man is to be invisible, pathetic, in-authentic, unreal. . . .

The consequence of internalizing this role is an enormous reservoir of self-hate. This is not to say the self-hate is recognized or accepted as such; indeed most women would deny it. It may be experienced as discomfort with her role, as feeling empty, as numbness, as restlessness, a paralyzing anxiety at the center. Alternatively, it may be expressed in shrill defensiveness of the glory and destiny of her role. But it does exist, often beneath the edge of her consciousness, poisoning her existence, keeping her alienated from herself, her own needs, and rendering her a stranger to other women. They try to escape by identifying with the oppressor, living through him, gaining status and identity from his ego, his power, his accomplishments. . . .

As the source of self-hate and the lack of real self are rooted in our male-given identity, we must create a new sense of self. As long as we cling to the idea of "being a woman,'" we will sense some conflict with that incipient self, that sense of I, that sense of a whole person. It is very difficult to realize and accept that being "feminine" and being a whole person are irreconcilable. Only women can give each other a new sense of self. That identity we have to develop with reference to ourselves, and not in relation to men. This consciousness is the revolutionary force from which all else will follow, for ours is an organic revolution. For this we must be available and supportive to one another, give our commitment and our love, give the emotional support necessary to sustain this movement. Our energies must flow toward our sisters, not backwards towards our oppressors. As long as woman's liberation tries to free women without facing the basic heterosexual structure that binds us in one-to-one relationship with our own oppressors, tremendous energies will continue to flow into trying to straighten up each particular relationship with a man, how to get better sex, how to turn his head around—into trying to make the "new man" out of him, in the delusion that this will allow us to be the "new woman." This obviously splits our energies and commitments, leaving us unable to be committed to the construction of the new patterns which will liberate us.

It is the primacy of women relating to women, of women creating a new consciousness of and with each other which is at the heart of women's liberation, and the basis for the cultural revolution. Together we must find, reinforce and validate our authentic selves. As we do this, we confirm in each other that struggling incipient sense of pride and strength, the divisive barriers begin to melt, we feel this growing solidarity with our sisters. We see ourselves as prime, find our centers inside of ourselves. We find receding the sense of alienation, of being cut off, of being behind a locked window, of being unable to get out what we know is inside. We feel a real-ness, feel at last we are coinciding with ourselves. With that real self, with that consciousness, we begin a revolution to end the imposition of all coercive identifications, and to achieve maximum autonomy in human expression.

DOCUMENT 110

Lesbian Workshop, Revolutionary People's Constitutional Convention, "Lesbian Demands: Panther Constitution Convention—Sep. 5, 1970"

Come Out!, Sept. 1970, 16[8]

Women are the revolution. It must not be alluded to that women are merely an extension of a male ego game. Women are not machines that will mass produce infant revolutionaries. The entire success of the revolution does not depend on whether or not the male will "allow" the woman her liberation, but rather on the woman freeing herself of all crippling male identities and realizing the strength that is found in solidarity with her sisters.

All previous revolutions were dominated by the male mentality. In fact, previous revolutions have been incomplete. While they have served the purposes of men, there have been no revolutionary changes in the conditions of women. Women's revolution will be the first fundamental revolution because it will do what all the others aspired to.

The demands of the Lesbian workshop on September 5 in connection with the "People's Revolutionary" Constitutional Convention call for the complete control by women of all aspects of our social system. What evolved when twenty to twenty-five lesbians wrote these demands is in itself proof of the validity of these demands. Women who have asserted their autonomy, women who have severed the ties between themselves and the male power structure (even in the form of a one to one relationship with a man), women who are already learning to love and cooperate with one another, women who are not making the mistake of trying to deal with men with whom the ultimate decision always lies because women have no power base from which to speak.

The Lesbian Workshop demands will eventually lead to the equalization of all power resources, so that someday human beings of all sexes can deal with each other on a more realistic level.

DEMANDS OF THE LESBIAN WORKSHOP

1. Sexual autonomy. Prohibit sexual role programming of children.
2. Destruction of the Nuclear Family. The nuclear family is a microcosm of the fascist state, where the women and children are owned by, and their fates determined by, the needs of men, in a man's world.
3. Communal care of children. Children should be allowed to grow, in a society of their peers, cared for by adults whose aim is not to perpetrate any male-female role programming. It is advised that these adults be under the direction of women-identified women.
4. Reparations
   a) Women are a dispersed minority and we demand that amount of control of all production and industry that would ensure one hundred per-

cent control over our own destinies. This control includes commerce, industry, health facilities, education, transportation, military, etc.

b) Because women have been systematically denied information and knowledge and the opportunities for acquiring these, we demand open enrollment of all schools to all women, financial support to any woman who needs it, on the job training with pay for all women attending technical schools and under apprenticeship.

c) Women demand the time and support to research, compile and report our history and our identity.

d) The power and technology of defense are invested in men. Since these powers are used to intimidate women, we demand training in self-defense and the use of defense machinery. A Woman's Militia would be organized to defend the demands, rights and interests of women struggling towards an unoppressive social system.

DOCUMENT 111
Del Martin, "'If That's All There Is': Female Gay Blasts Men, Leaves Movement"
The Advocate, 28 Oct. 1970, 21–22[9]

. . . After 15 years of working for the homophile movement—of mediating, counselling, appeasing, of working for coalition and unity—I am facing a very real identity crisis. Like NACHO [the North American Conference of Homophile Organizations], I have been torn apart. I am bereft. For I have during the week of struggle between the men and the women, the conservatives and the Gay Liberationists, been forced to the realization that I have no brothers in the homophile movement.

Oh yes, when six of my sisters from the Daughters of Bilitis, Nova, and Gay Women's Liberation stood with me to confront the NACHO meeting on Aug. 26 (the day of the National Women's Strike) about the relevance of the homophile movement to the women within it, the delegates passed a resolution in support of the women's liberation movement. They rationalized that all of their organizations were open to women, but the women didn't join in numbers, and they just didn't know what else they could do to relate to their lesbian sisters. We suggested that their programs and their publications were not inclusive of or relevant to women. They decried the segregationist organizations which we represented but would not address themselves to the underlying reason for the existence of separate women's organizations—that the female homosexual faces sex discrimination not only in the heterosexual world, but within the homophile community.

And so, like my sister, Robin Morgan, I have come to the conclusion that I must say, "Goodbye to All That."

Goodbye to the wasteful, meaningless verbiage of empty resolutions made by hollow men of self-proclaimed privilege. . . .

Goodbye, my alienated brothers. Goodbye to the male chauvinists of the homophile movement who are so wrapped up in the "cause" they espouse that they have lost sight of the people for whom the cause came into being. . . .

Goodbye [to] all those homophile organizations across the country with an open-door policy for women. It's only window dressing for the public and in the small towns of suburbia, for mutual protection. It doesn't really mean anything and smacks of paternalism.

Goodbye, too (temporarily, I trust) to my sisters who demean themselves by accepting "women's status" in these groups—making and serving the coffee, doing the secretarial work, soothing the brows of the policy-makers who tell them, "We're doing it all for you, too." Don't believe it, sisters, for you are only an afterthought that never took place.

Goodbye to . . . the defense of washroom sex and pornographic movies. . . .

Goodbye to all the "representative" homophile publications that look more like magazines for male nudist colonies. Goodbye to the biased male point of view. The editors say they have encouraged women to contribute, but that they don't. Nor will they until the format is changed, policy broadened, and their material taken seriously.

Goodbye to the gay bars that discriminate against women. Goodbye to those that "allow" them in only if they dress up in skirts, while the men slop around in their "queer" costumes. Gay Liberationists are right when they observe that gay bars ghettoize the homophile community. They are, after all, our chief base for socialization, for meeting people of our own kind. But there is no time or place for forming friendships, for exchanging ideas, for camaraderie—only for dispensing of drinks and sex partners.

Goodbye to the Halloween Balls, the drag shows and parties. It was fun, while it lasted. But the humor has gone out of the game. The exaggerations of the switching (or swishing) of sex roles has become the norm in the public eye. While we were laughing at ourselves we became the laughing-stock and lost the personhood we were seeking. It is time to stop mimicking the heterosexual society we've been trying to escape. . . .

Goodbye to Gay Liberation, too. They applauded the lesbians who wished to establish common cause with them and the other men at the NACHO meeting. But somehow we are left with the feeling their applause was for the disruption of the meeting, not its purpose. There is reason for the splits within their own movement, why there is a women's caucus in GLF [Gay Liberation Front] in New York, and why there is a Gay Women's Liberation in the San Francisco Bay Area. Like the tired old men they berate, they have not come to grips with the gut issues. Until they do, *their* revolution cannot be ours. Their liberation would only further enslave us. . . .

Goodbye to the male homophile community. "Gay is good," but not good enough—so long as it limited to white males only. We joined with you in what we mistakenly thought was a common cause. A few of you tried, we admit. But you are still too few, and even you fall short of the mark. You, too, are victims of our culture. Fifteen years of masochism is enough. . . .

There is no hate in this goodbye—only the bitter sting of disappointment.

Momentarily, I am pregnant with rage at your blindness and your deafness—the psychosomatic symptoms of narcissism and egocentricity. But my rage will pass. Most of it has been spent already. For I realize you were programed by society for your role of supremacy. . . .

Believe it or not, there is love, too, in this farewell—just as there has always been. How could anyone hold a grudge against helpless beings who are compelled to grope for their very existence.

But I must leave you—for your good as well as mine. I refuse to be your scapegoat. By removing the target, you may no longer mock me.

Besides, I must go where the action is—where there is still hope, where there is possibility for personal and collective growth. It is a revelation to find acceptance, equality, love, and friendship—everything we sought in the homophile community—not there, but in the women's movement.

I will not be your "nigger" any longer. Nor was I ever your mother. Those were stultifying roles you laid on me, and I shall no longer concern myself with your toilet training. You're in the big leagues now, and we're both playing for big stakes. They didn't turn out to be the same.

As I bid you adieu, I leave each of you to your own device. Take care of it, stroke it gently, mouth it, fondle it. As the center of your consciousness, it's really all you have.

DOCUMENT 112
Anita Cornwell, "Open Letter to a Black Sister"
The Ladder, Oct. 1971, 33–36[10]

It's really amazing when you come right down to the nub of the thing that some of us can't seem to see just who it is that's standing very flat-footedly on our broken-down backs.

Yes, I know all about Whitey and how he's sold us down the river and up the creek back in slavery time, *and in modern times too*. But, my dear Sister, didn't it ever occur to you that if one of our good old voodoo men from "Dear Mother Africa" could make Whitey disappear from the face of the earth this precise moment, we would still be in the black man's trick bag? . . .

But to come back closer to home in these good old non-United States of male supremacy, didn't you ever wonder why you have to come home every evening after putting in ten feet-killing hours and then put in at least five more of back-breaking toil getting dinner and seeing to the kids and waiting on *him* hand and foot while he sits on his rusty-dusty giving orders and complaining up a blue streak because you don't do things to suit him?

Do you for one cotton picking moment think that Whitey has a gun on Blackey's back making him turn you into a stone workhorse while he sits there making like king of the blabber-mouths?

Well, if you want to blame Whitey for your trick bag, you go right ahead, but, in the meanwhile, you're getting mighty broken down with all that weight on your aching back. And hitting the bottle ain't going to do a damn bit of good because when you wake up tomorrow morning, at five a.m., so *you* can start getting the kids' things together, and *his* things too, all that misery is still going to be standing right there waiting for you just the way it was waiting for your Momma and her Momma. . . .

After all the kids you've had (because *he* doesn't believe in birth control and he's got *you* so screwed up until you think that having a hysterectomy, which you need in the worst sort of way, is going to take away some of your femininity—and Lord, will I ever be glad to hear the last of that slave-producing word?), well, there you are already messed up with a bushel of kids, and hitting the bottle when you should be hitting the sack and blaming your troubles on Whitey who is somewhere living it up and having forgot you ever existed, while your *true* oppressor is sitting right there at your kitchen table, sucking your blood like the only leech alive, laughing his head off and *resting* himself so's he can be looking good when he sees his *other woman.* . . .

You were a swinging, goodlooking twenty-two when you first met Blackey. You had known most of your life that Whitey was around with his foot on your back, but you were still swinging and still looking good. You had a trim figure (which now looks like a barrel with no hoops); you had a new car and money in the bank. Whitey's bank to be sure, *but it was in your name*! Remember?

Now where's it at?

Well, you know damn well where it's at. Blackey took your car, he took your identity, he took your figure (six kids in seven years sounds like a duplicating machine), and he took *your* money and spent it on that *other woman.* . . .

Now, my dear misguided Sister, aren't we ever going to stop and try to get our heads together? Aren't we ever going to stop cutting each other up while Blackey sits back whooping it up with *The Boys* and bragging about how *his* women fight over him?

And speaking of The Boys, aren't we ever going to try to put it together as to just why he likes being with them better than he likes being with us?

But even more important, aren't we ever going to get it together as to just why he's so afraid of our getting together with *The Girls*? And especially with the white girls? Which brings me right square to where I want to be which is with our white, brown and black Sisters in Women's Liberation. . . .

So don't get turned off when Blackey starts coming on with all that weird crap about Women's Liberation dividing the black community. Like when were we ever all together with *him* sitting on top of us and Whitey on top of him and everybody giving us black Sisters hell going and coming?

Now that we've got a chance to really get into the freedom bag, Blackey starts trying to snow us with that bit about we ought to stand behind him in *our* fight for black nationalism. Well, my dear Sister, just where do you think *his* black nationalism is going to leave us? . . .

Quite frankly, I was both surprised and mystified when I first learned of Blackey's hostility toward our Liberation Movement.

For on the face of it, you would think that black men, who have been oppressed for so long in this country, would be against discrimination against *everybody*.

Yet, the facts tell us otherwise. "Our" black educators and civil rights leaders (all male, of course) have repeatedly stressed the idea that black men should be advanced at the expense of black women "if full acculturation is to come about as the patriarchal family is a cherished American institution." . . .

It's as cherished as the gun and the atom bomb and twice as deadly. And, of course, if one wanted to be really nasty, you could point out that lynching black people was once a "cherished American" pastime too, but we won't go into that bag right now.

Let's stick with patriarchy, or the male-dominated family which is what that googily-sounding word really means. And patriarchy has really screwed up all of us Sisters ever since our Brothers stopped bouncing from tree to tree and came into the home and started ordering us around. For we haven't had one free-swilling breath since.

To put it bluntly, patriarchy is the root cause of all the major ills in the world today. For as long as men are able to keep half of the population in chains (us Sisters that is), they are going to be forever trying to enslave the other half. . . .

And that's why they're forever flinging that equally googily-sounding word *Matriarchy* at us. They, and Whitey too, are blaming us because we have had to go out and break our backs doing all of Whitey's crapwork for a few lousy dollars which barely kept body and soul together. But because we did manage to struggle along on those peon's wages and somehow kept our families intact, we are now being called every rancid name in the book.

As you know very well, if it hadn't been for us and our mothers and grandmothers and great, great-grandmothers, black folks in America would have gone the way of the Indian and Australian bush folk. And what thanks have we got for our back-breaking slaving? We've been slapped down by every other group of people that's ever lived in this country; that's the reward we've received.

And Whitey is bugged because we're still here and have stopped grinning and doing the buck dance, and Blackey is bombed off because having to work so hard for so long has made most of us black Sisters too strong to take his crap for very long periods at a time.

And any woman who won't take but so much guff from a man is called unwomanly by the less foul-mouthed, and is called castrating bitch by the other jackasses. But we in the Movement are no longer frightened by such terms for we realize it's just another little male trick to keep us in *our place*. . . .

But really, I don't want to go on so in this first little note. I just wanted you to start thinking about things a little, and please put the damn bottle down and drown all them frigging pills and leave the kids with *him* tomorrow and take a day off and go sporting in *your* car for a change instead of messing with them wheezing buses and dirty, thug-carrying subways.

In fact, take the whole damn week off. You've earned it. And more too, Sister!

DOCUMENT 113
Jeanne Córdova, "Lesbian Feminism & the Fourth Demand"
Gay Liberator, Apr. 1973, 4–5[11]

I am what is usually referred to as a "lesbian feminist activist." Being a lesbian feminist is somewhat like being the middle layer of bread in a triple deck sandwich. We're definitely part of the whole, but never the beginning nor end of anything. Being a lesbian feminist is living on the lunatic fringe of both the Women's Movement and the Gay Movement. . . .

Between sexist commercials on a rare night at home watching, trying to watch, sexist television, many of us ask ourselves, "Are we lesbian feminists? Feminist lesbians? Gay feminists? Or Feminist Gays?" The best answer I have heard to this dilemma was Margaret Sloan's reply to a newspaper reporter who tried to make things hard for her by asking, "Which do you consider first, a feminist or a black?" Margaret replied, "That's a typical white male stupid question. It isn't as though from Sunday thru Wednesday the man screws me over cause I'm a woman and from Thursday to Saturday I get oppressed because I'm black." The real answer to that question is that lesbian feminists represent the synthesis of women's and gay oppression. . . .

Some women might be wondering why a lesbian feminist activist is speaking at an Abortion Rally. "What are the connections between abortion and lesbianism?" One of the more obvious connections is one a sister made a year ago. When asked by a male member of the audience, "what has lesbianism got to do with abortion?" she said, "One of the things men are always saying to lesbians is, 'All you need is a good fuck by the right man. Try it, you'll like it.' Well, I tried it. I didn't like it. But now I'm pregnant."

While it is true that gay women have for the last several years struggled with their straight sisters in the Women's Movement fight for abortion law repeal, and while it is true that we celebrate our latest victory together tonight, I propose that there is another connection between lesbianism and abortion. . . . The demand for "freedom of Sexual Expression," the freedom to choose and live out our own sexuality, like the demands for abortion on demand and community controlled health care, speaks directly to our movement's fundamental demand, "A woman's right to control her own body."

The realization of abortion-law repeal gives us more control over our reproduction, but we still have no control over a yet more fundamental right—our own sexuality. Right now, women have no right to choose a sexuality that does not include men. Many women here tonight are labeled "criminal" by those outside this door. I am a criminal. You are criminals. We are not free. There is little cause for celebration for us. "Freedom of sexual expression" is on the same continuum of women's rights as abortion, no forced sterilization and free access to contraceptives. It is further down the continuum towards total liberation for women. As such, it is appropriate to realize this now as the Women's Movement prepares to take on the stronger and deeper issues that lie between us and freedom in this society. If the Women's Movement is serious about human liberation it will have to take up the issue of sexuality. . . .

It is no accident that lesbian feminists find themselves among the vanguard of both the women's and the gay movements. Lesbian feminist politics cut deeper than gay politics, which often leave gay men with their supremacist male role. It cuts deeper than feminist politics which so often make "men the primary enemy (and) fails to trace male supremacy to its real source" and therefore augments for only a larger share of what is mistakenly referred to as the male pie.

Yes, the Supreme Court's recent decision on abortion is a victory, perhaps the most fundamental victory so far of the second wave of feminism. Yet there are greater challenges. "Abortion on demand" is not the answer to racism, or even sexism. "Abortion on demand" is not the total answer to Women's Liberation.

None of us can do it alone. Most of us have tried. That is why we are here now. The sooner we begin to realize the commonalities of our oppression, the sooner we put away the politics of power plays, competitiveness, and individualism, the sooner we will begin to focus on our REAL oppressors. The politics of lesbian feminism and the oppression of lesbian feminists challenge our closest brothers and sisters, the Gay Movement and the Women's Movement, to further the business of liberation.

DOCUMENT 114
"Transvestite and Transsexual Liberation"
Gay Dealer, ca. Dec. 1970, 9[12]

The oppression against transvestites and transsexuals of either sex arises from sexist values and this oppression is manifested by homosexuals and heterosexuals of both sexes in the form of exploitation, ridicule, harassment, beatings, rapes, murders, use of us as shock troops, sacrificial victims, and others.

We reject all labels of "stereotype," "sick" or "maladjusted" from non-transvestic and non-transsexual sources and defy any attempt to repress our manifestation as transvestites and transsexuals.

Trans Lib began in the summer of 1969 when "Queens" formed in New York and began militating for equal rights, The Transvestite-Transsexual Action Organization (TAO) formed in Los Angeles, the Cockettes in San Francisco, Street Transvestites Action Revolutionaries (STAR) in New York, Fems Against Sexism, Transvestites and Transsexuals (TAT) also formed in New York, Radical Queens formed in Milwaukee—all in 1970. "Queens" became "Queens Liberation Front."

Transvestism—transsexualism—homosexuality are separate entities. Sexist values incorrectly classify any male who wears feminine attire as a homosexual, and to a lesser degree, any female who wears masculine attire is classified as a homosexual.

Demands

1. Abolishment of all crossdressing laws and restrictions of adornment.
2. An end to exploitation and discrimination within the gay world.
3. An end to exploitative practices of doctors and psychiatrists who work in the fields of transvestism and transsexualism. Hormone treatment and transsexual surgery should be provided free upon demand by the state.
4. Transsexual assistance centers should be created in all cities of over one million inhabitants, under the direction of postoperative transsexuals.
5. Transvestites and transsexuals should be granted full and equal rights on all levels of society and a full voice in the struggle for the liberation of all oppressed people.
6. Transvestites who exist as members of the opposite anatomical gender should be able to obtain full identification as members of the opposite gender. Transsexuals should be able to obtain such identification commensurate to their new gender with no difficulty, and not be required to carry special identification as transsexuals. There should be no special licensing requirements of transvestites or transsexuals who work in the entertainment field.
7. Immediate release of all persons in mental hospitals or prison for transvestism or transsexualism.

DOCUMENT 115

"Queens Liberation Front...What Is It?"
Drag (2.6), 1972, 13–14[13]

The broad objective of Queens Liberation Front is to gain the legal right for everyone who so desires to crossdress regardless of their sexual orientation or desires. . . . The voice of QLF or commonly Queens, *Drag* magazine reaches 3,500 people across the country.

In its original prospectus Queens Liberation Front, then just known as Queens, put forth two goals:

1. *Right to Congregate*: In New York the license for a drag ball or rather dance permit stated that men dressed in the female attire were not to be permitted on the premises of said dance.

2. *Right to Dress as We See Fit*: We feel that the wearing of a particular article of clothing doesn't make one a criminal. We hope to get a ruling adopting the law presently used in the state of Hawaii. It has been interpreted to mean that one may wear the clothing of the opposite sex as long as he does not deceive others. If one wears a button stating that one is a male it takes away all criminal aspects of cross-dressing.

DOCUMENT 116

Silvia [Sylvia] Lee Rivera, "Transvestites: Your Half Sisters and Half Brothers of the Revolution"
Come Out!, Winter 1972, 10[14]

As far back as I can remember, my half sisters and brothers liberated themselves from this fucked up system that has been oppressing our gay sisters and brothers—by walking on the man's land, defining the man's law, and meeting with the man face to face in his court of law. We have liberated his bathrooms and streets in our female or male attire. For exposing the man's law we are thrown into jail on charges of criminal impersonation; that dates back as far as the Boston Tea Party when the English dressed up as Indians because the motherland had raised the taxes. We have lost our jobs, our homes, friends, family because of lack of understanding of our inner-most feelings and lack of knowledge of our valid life style. They have been brainwashed by this fucked up system that has condemned us and by doctors that call us a disease and a bunch of freaks. Our family and friends have also condemned us because of their lack of true knowledge.

By being liberated my half sisters and brothers and myself are able to educate the ignorant gays and straights that transvestism is a valid life style.

Remember the Stonewall Riots? That first stone was cast by a transvestite half sister June 27, 1969 and the gay liberation movement was born. Remember that transvestites and gay street people are always on the front lines and are ready to lay their lives down for the movement. . . .

So sisters and brothers remember that transvestites are not the scum of the community; just think back on the events of the past two years. You should be proud that we are part of the community and you should try to gain some knowledge of your transvestite half brothers and sisters and our valid life style. Remember we started the whole movement that 27th day of June of the year 1969!

DOCUMENT 117

"Rapping with a Street Transvestite Revolutionary: An Interview with Marcia [Marsha] Johnson"

From *Out of the Closets: Voices of Gay Liberation*, ed. Karla Jay and Allen Young (New York: Douglas, 1972), 112–120[15]

We want to see all gay people have a chance, equal rights, as straight people have in America. We don't want to see gay people picked up on the streets for things like loitering or having sex or anything like that. STAR [Street Transvestite Action Revolutionaries] originally was started by the president, Sylvia Lee Rivera, and Bubbles Rose Marie, and they asked me to come in as the vice president. STAR is a very revolutionary group. We believe in picking up the gun, starting a revolution if necessary. Our main goal is to see gay people liberated and free and have equal rights that other people have in America. We'd like to see our gay brothers and sisters out of jail and on the streets again. . . .

We still feel oppression by other gay brothers. Gay sisters don't think too bad of transvestites. Gay brothers do. I went to a dance at Gay Activists Alliance just last week, and there was not even one gay brother that came over and said hello. They'd say hello, but they'd get away very quick. The only transvestites they were very friendly with were the ones that looked freaky in drag, like freak drag, with no tits, no nothing. Well, I can't help but have tits, they're mine. And those men weren't too friendly at all. Once in a while, I get an invitation to Daughters of Bilitis, and when I go there, they're always warm. All the gay sisters come over and say, "Hello, we're glad to see you," and they start long conversations. But not the gay brothers. . . .

Of course I can understand why. A lot of gay brothers don't like women! And transvestites remind you of women. A lot of the gay brothers don't feel too close to women, they'd rather be near men, that's how come they're gay. . . .

I'd like to see STAR get closer to GAA [Gay Activists Alliance] and other gay people in the community. I'd like to see a lot more transvestites come to STAR meetings, but it's hard to get in touch with transvestites. They're at these bars, and they're looking for husbands. There's a lot of transvestites who are very lonely, and they just go to bars to look for husbands and lovers, just like gay men do. When they get married, they don't have time for STAR meetings. I'd like to see the gay revolution get started. . . .

If transvestites don't stand up for themselves, nobody else is going to stand up for transvestites. If a transvestite doesn't say I'm gay and I'm proud and I'm a transvestite, then nobody else is going to hop up there and say I'm gay and I'm proud and I'm a transvestite. . . .

DOCUMENT 118

Huey P. Newton, "A Letter from Huey to the Revolutionary Brothers and Sisters about the Women's Liberation and Gay Liberation Movements"

Black Panther, 21 Aug. 1970, 5[16]

During the past few years, strong movements have developed among women and among homosexuals seeking their liberation. There has been some uncertainty about how to relate to these movements.

Whatever your personal opinions and your insecurities about homosexuality and the various liberation movements among homosexuals and women (and I speak of the homosexuals and women as oppressed groups), we should try to unite with them in a revolutionary fashion. I say "whatever your insecurities are" because, as we very well know sometimes our first instinct is to want to hit a homosexual in the mouth and want a woman to be quiet. We want to hit the homosexual in the mouth because we're afraid we might be homosexual; and we want to hit the woman or shut her up because we're afraid that she might castrate us, or take the nuts that we might not have to start with.

We must gain security in ourselves and therefore have respect and feelings for all oppressed people. We must not use the racist type attitude that the White racists use against people because they are Black and poor. Many times the poorest White person is the most racist, because he's afraid that he might lose something, or discover something that he doesn't have; you're some kind of threat to him. This kind of psychology is in operation when we view oppressed people and we're angry with them because of their particular kind of behavior, or their particular kind of deviation from the established norm.

Remember, we haven't established a revolutionary value system; we're only in the process of establishing it. I don't remember us ever constituting any value that said that a revolutionary must say offensive things towards homosexuals, or that a revolutionary should make sure that women do not speak out about their own particular kind of oppression. Matter of fact it's just the opposite: we say that we recognize the women's right to be free. We haven't said much about the homosexual at all, and we must relate to the homosexual movement because it's a real thing. And I know through reading and through my life experience, my observations, that homosexuals are not given freedom and liberty by anyone in the society. Maybe they might be the most oppressed people in the society.

And what made them homosexual? Perhaps it's a whole phenomena that I don't understand entirely. Some people say that it's the decadence of capitalism. I don't know whether this is the case; I rather doubt it. But whatever the case is, we know that homosexuality is a fact that exists, and we must understand it in its purest form: that is, a person should have freedom to use his body in whatever way he wants to. That's not endorsing things in homosexuality that we wouldn't view as revolutionary. But there's nothing to say that a homosexual cannot also be a revolutionary. And maybe I'm now injecting some of my prejudice by saying that "even a homosexual can be a revolutionary." Quite on the contrary, maybe a homosexual could be the most revolutionary.

When we have revolutionary conferences, rallies and demonstrations there should be full participation of the gay liberation movement and the women's liberation movement. Some groups might be more revolutionary than others. We shouldn't use the actions of a few to say that they're all reactionary or counterrevolutionary, because they're not.

We should deal with the factions just as we deal with any other group or party that claims to be revolutionary. We should try to judge somehow whether they're operating sincerely, in a revolutionary fashion, from a really oppressed situation. (And we'll grant that if they're women, they're probably oppressed.) If they do things that are un-revolutionary or counter-revolutionary, then criticize that action. If we feel that the group in spirit means to be revolutionary in practice, but they make mistakes in interpretation of the revolutionary philosophy, or they don't understand the dialectics of the social forces in operation, we should criticize that and not criticize them because they're women trying to be free. And the same is true for homosexuals. We should never say a whole movement is dishonest, when in fact they're trying to be honest; they're just making honest mistakes. Friends are allowed to make mistakes. The enemy is not allowed to make mistakes because his whole existence is a mistake, and we suffer from it. But the women's liberation front and gay liberation front are our friends, they are potential allies, and we need as many allies as possible.

We should be willing to discuss the insecurities that many people have about homosexuality. When I say "insecurities," I mean the fear that they're some kind of threat to our manhood. I can understand this fear. Because of the long conditioning process which builds insecurity in the American male, homosexuality might produce certain hangups in us. I have hangups myself about male homosexuality. Where, on the other hand, I have no hangup about female homosexuality. And that's phenomena in itself. I think it's probably because male homosexuality is a threat to me, maybe, and the females are no threat.

We should be careful about using those terms that might turn our friends off. The terms "faggot" and "punk" should be deleted from our vocabulary, and especially we should not attach names normally designed for homosexuals to men who are enemies of the people, such as [President Richard] Nixon or [Attorney General John] Mitchell. Homosexuals are not enemies of the people.

We should try to form a working coalition with the Gay liberation and Women's liberation groups. We must always handle social forces in the most appropriate manner. And this is really a significant part of the population, both women and the growing number of homosexuals that we have to deal with.

ALL POWER TO THE PEOPLE!

DOCUMENT 119
Male Homosexual Workshop, Revolutionary People's Constitutional Convention, "We Demand"
Come Out!, Dec. 1970, 15[17]

All power to the people! The revolution will not be complete until all men are free to express their love for one another sexually. We affirm the sexuality of our love. The social institution which prevents us all from expressing our total revolutionary love we define as sexism. Sexism is a belief or practice that the sex or sexual orientation of human beings gives to some the right to certain privileges, powers or roles, while denying to others their full potential. Within the context of our society, sexism is primarily manifested through male supremacy and heterosexual chauvinism. Since in the short run sexism benefits certain persons or groups, in the long run it cannot serve all people and prevents the forming of complete social consciousness among straight men. Sexism is irrational, unjust and counter-revolutionary. Sexism prevents the revolutionary solidarity of the people. We demand that the struggle against sexism be acknowledged as an essential part of the revolutionary struggle. We demand that all revolutionaries deal individually and collectively with their own sexism. We recognize as a vanguard revolutionary action the Huey P. Newton statement on gay and women's liberation. We recognize the Black Panther Party as being the vanguard of the people's revolution in Amerikkka. No revolution without us! An army of lovers cannot lose!

We Demand:

1. The right to be gay, any time, any place.
2. The right to free physiological change and modification of sex upon demand.
3. The right of free dress and adornment.
4. That all modes of human sexual self-expression deserve protection of the law and social sanction.
5. Every child's right to develop in a non-sexist, non-possessive atmosphere, which is the responsibility of all people to create.
6. That a free educational system present the entire range of human sexuality, without advocating any one form or style.
7. That language be modified so that no gender take priority.
8. That the judicial system be run by the people through the people's courts; that all people be tried by members of their peer group.
9. That gays be represented in all governmental and community institutions.
10. That organized religions be condemned for aiding in the genocide of gay people and enjoined from teaching hatred and superstition.
11. That psychiatry and psychology be enjoined from advocating a preference for any form of sexuality, and the enforcement of that preference by shock treatment, brainwashing, imprisonment, etc.

12. The abolition of the nuclear family because it perpetuates the false categories of homosexuality and heterosexuality.

13. The immediate release of and reparations for gay and other political prisoners from prisons and mental institutions; the support of gay political prisoners for all other political prisoners.

14. That gays determine the destinies of their own communities.

15. That all gay people share equally the labor and products of society.

16. That technology be used to liberate all peoples of the world from drudgery.

17. The full participation of gays in the people's revolutionary army.

18. Finally, the end of domination of one person by another. . . .

DOCUMENT 120

Third World Gay Revolution, "The Oppressed Shall Not Become the Oppressor"

Come Out!, Sept. 1970, 13[18]

Sisters and Brothers of the Third World, you who call yourselves "revolutionaries" have failed to deal with your sexist attitudes. Instead you cling to male-supremacy and therefore to the conditioned role of oppressors. Brothers still fight for the privileged position of man-on-the-top. Sisters quickly fall in line behind-their-men. By your counterrevolutionary struggle to maintain and to force heterosexuality and the nuclear family, you perpetuate outmoded remnants of Capitalism. By your anti-homosexual stance you have used the weapons of the oppressor, thereby becoming the agent of the oppressor.

It is up to Third World males to realistically define masculinity because it is you who throughout your lives have struggled to gain the unrealistic roles of "men." Third World men have always tried to reach this precarious position by climbing on the backs of women and homosexuals. "Masculinity" has been defined by white society as the amount of possessions (including women) a man collects, and the amount of physical power gained over other men. Third World men have been denied even these false standards of "masculinity." Therefore stop perpetuating in yourselves and your community the white-supremacist notions which are basic to your own oppression.

We as Third World gay people suffer a triple oppression:

1) We are oppressed as people because our humanity is routinely devoured by the carnivorous system of Capitalism.

2) We are oppressed as Third World people by the economically inherent racism of white Amerikan society.

3) We are oppressed by the sexism of the white society and the verbal and physical abuse of masculinity-deprived Third World males.

The right of self-determination over dominion of one's own body is a human right and this right must be defended with one's body being put on the line.

By the actions you have taken against your gay brothers and sisters of the Third World you who throughout your lives have suffered the torments of social oppression and sexual repression have now placed yourselves in the role of oppressor.

Anti-homosexuality fosters sexual repression, male-supremacy, weakness in revolutionary drive, and results in an inaccurate non-objective political perspective.

DOCUMENT 121

Third World Gay Revolution, "16 Point Platform and Program"

Come Out!, Dec. 1970, 16–17

Our straight sisters and brothers must recognize and support that we, third world gay women and men, are equal in every way within the revolutionary ranks.

We each organize our people about different issues, but our struggles are the same against oppression, and we will defeat it together. Once we understand these struggles, and gain a love for our sisters and brothers involved in these struggles, we must learn how best to become involved in them.

The struggles of the peoples of the world are our fight as well; their victories are our victories and our victories are theirs. Our freedom will come only with their freedom.

Together, not alone, we must explore how we view ourselves, and analyze the assumptions behind our self-identity. We can then begin to crack the barriers of our varying illnesses, our passivity, sexual chauvinism, in essence our inability to unabashedly love each other, to live, fight, and if necessary, die for the people of the earth.

As we begin to understand our place in this international revolution, and join with others in this understanding, we must develop the skills necessary to destroy the forces of repression and exploitation, so as to make it possible for a new woman and man to evolve in a society based on communal love.

While we understand that in the United States our main enemy is the socio-economic-political system of capitalism and the people who make profits off our sufferings, fights and divisions, we also recognize that we must struggle against any totalitarian, authoritarian, sex-controlled, repressive, irrational, reactionary, fascist government or government machine.

What We Want:
What We Believe:

1. We want the right of self-determination for all third world and gay people, as well as control of the destinies of our communities.

We believe that third world and gay people cannot be free until we are able to determine our own destinies. The system must be changed. Socialism is the answer.

2. We want the right of self-determination over the use of our bodies: The right to be gay, anytime, anyplace; the right to free physiological change and modification of sex on demand; the right to free dress and adornment.

We believe that these are human rights which must be defended with our bodies being put on the line. The system as it now exists denies these basic human rights by implementing forced heterosexuality. The system must be changed. Socialism is the answer.

3. We want liberation for all women: We want free and safe birth control information and devices on demand. We want free 24 hour child care centers controlled by those who need and use them. We want a redefinition of education and motivation (especially for third world women) towards broader educational opportunities without limitations because of sex. We want truthful teaching of women's history. We want an end to hiring practices which make women and national minorities

1. a readily available source of cheap labor

2. confined to mind-rotting jobs under the worst conditions.

We believe that the struggles of all oppressed groups under any form of government which does not meet the true needs of its people will eventually result in the overthrow of that government. The struggle for liberation of women is a struggle to be waged by all peoples. We must also struggle within ourselves and within our various movements to end this oldest form of oppression and its foundation—male chauvinism. We cannot develop a truly liberating form of socialism unless we fight these tendencies. The system must be changed. Socialism is the answer.

4. We want full protection of the law and social sanction for all human sexual self-expression and pleasure between consenting persons, including youth. We believe that present laws are oppressive to third-world people, gay people, and the masses. Such laws expose the inequalities of capitalism, which can only exist in a state where there are oppressed people or groups. This must end. The system must be changed. Socialism is the answer.

5. We want the abolition of the institution of the bourgeois nuclear family.

We believe that the bourgeois nuclear family perpetuates the false categories of homosexuality and heterosexuality by creating sex roles, sex definitions and sexual exploitation. The bourgeois nuclear family as the basic unit of capitalism creates oppressive roles of homosexuality and heterosexuality. All oppressions originate within the nuclear family structure. Homosexuality is a threat to this family structure and therefore to capitalism. The mother is an instrument of reproduction and teaches the necessary values of capitalist society, i.e., racism, sexism, etc. from infancy on. The father physically enforces (upon the mother and children) the behavior necessary in a capitalist system, intelligence and competitiveness in young boys and passivity in young girls. Further, it is every child's right to develop in a non-sexist, non-racist, non-possessive atmosphere which is the responsibility of all people, including gays, to create. Therefore, the system must be changed. Socialism is the answer.

6. We want a free non-compulsory education system that teaches us our true identity and history, and presents the entire range of human sexuality without advocating any one form or style; that sex roles and determination of skills according to sex be eliminated from the school system; that language be modified so that no gender takes priority; and that gay people must share the responsibilities of education.

   We believe that we have been taught to compete with our sisters and brothers for power, and from that competitive attitude grows sexism, racism, male and national chauvinism and distrust of our sisters and brothers. As we begin to understand these things within ourselves, we attempt to free ourselves of them and are moved toward a revolutionary consciousness. The system must be changed. Socialism is the answer.

7. We want guaranteed full equal employment for third world and gay people at all levels of production.

   We believe that any system of government is responsible for giving every woman and man a guaranteed income or employment, regardless of sex or sexual preference. Being interested only in profits, capitalism cannot meet the needs of the people. The system must be changed. Socialism is the answer.

8. We want decent and free housing, fit shelter for human beings.

   We believe that free shelter is a basic need and right which must not be denied on any grounds. Landlords are capitalists and, like all capitalists, are motivated only by the accumulation of profits, as opposed to the welfare of the people. Therefore, the system must be changed. Socialism is the answer.

9. We want to abolish the existing judicial system. We want all third world and gay people when brought to trial to be tried by a people's court with a jury of their peers. A peer is a person from similar social, economic, geographical, racial, historical, environmental, and sexual background. We believe that the function of the judicial system under capitalism is to uphold the ruling class and keep the masses under control. The system must be changed. Socialism is the answer.

10. We want the reparation for and release of all third world, gay and all political prisoners from jails and mental institutions.

    We believe that these people should be released because they have not received a fair and impartial trial. The system must be changed. Socialism is the answer.

11. We want the abolition of capital punishment, all forms of institutional punishment, and the penal system.

We want the establishment of psychiatric institutions for the humane treatment and rehabilitation of criminal persons as decided by the people's court. We want the establishment of a sufficient number of free and non-compulsory clinics for the treatment of sexual disturbances, as defined by the individual. We believe that the system must be changed. Socialism is the answer.

12. We want an immediate end to the fascist police force.

We believe that the only way this can be accomplished is by putting the defense of the people in the hands of the people. The system must be changed. Socialism is the answer.

13. We want all third world and gay men to be exempt from compulsory military service in the imperialist army. We want an end to military oppression both at home and abroad.

We believe that the only true army for oppressed people is the people's army and third world, gay people, and women should have full participation in the People's Revolutionary Army. The system must be changed. Socialism is the answer.

14. We want an end to all institutional religions because they aid in genocide by teaching superstition and hatred of third world people, homosexuals and women. We want a guarantee of freedom to express natural spirituality.

We believe that institutionalized religions are an instrument of capitalism, therefore an enemy of the People. The system must be changed. Socialism is the answer.

15. We demand *immediate* non-discriminatory open admission/membership for radical homosexuals into all left-wing revolutionary groups and organizations and the right to caucus.

We believe that so-called comrades who call themselves "revolutionaries" have failed to deal with their sexist attitudes. Indeed they cling to male supremacy and therefore to the conditioned role of oppressors. Men still fight for the privileged position of man-on-the-top. Women quickly fall in line behind-their-men. By their counterrevolutionary struggle to maintain and to force heterosexuality and the nuclear family, they perpetuate decadent remnants of capitalism. To gain their anti-homosexual stance, they have used the weapons of the oppressor, thereby becoming the agent of the oppressor.

It is up to men to realistically define masculinity, because it is they who, throughout their lives, have struggled to gain the unrealistic roles of "men." Men have always tried to reach this precarious position by climbing on the backs of women and homosexuals. "Masculinity" has been defined by capitalist society as the amount of possessions (including women) a man collects, and the amount of physical power gained over other men. Third world men have been denied even these false standards of "masculinity." Anti-homosexuality fosters sexual repressions, male-supremacy, weakness in revolutionary drive, and results in an inaccurate non-objective political perspective. Therefore, we believe that all left-wing revolutionary groups and organizations *must immediately* establish non-discriminatory, open admission/membership policies. The system must be changed. Socialism is the answer.

16. We want a new society—a revolutionary socialist society. We want liberation of humanity, free food, free shelter, free clothing, free transportation, free health care, free utilities, free education, free art for all. We want a society where the needs of the people come first. We believe that all people should share the labor and products of society, according to each one's needs and abilities, regardless of race, sex, age, or sexual preferences. We believe the land, technology, and the means of production belong to the people, and must be shared by the people collectively for the liberation of all.

REVOLUTIONARY SOCIALISM IS THE ANSWER.
ALL POWER TO THE PEOPLE!

DOCUMENT 122
Elandria V. Henderson, "Black and Lavender: The Black Lesbian"
Lavender Woman, Dec. 1971, 4

We are oppressed triply by society: (1) Black-Racism (2) Women-Sexism (3) Homosexual-Heterosexual bias. We naively entered the gay movement hoping to fight for common goals. In our gay movement we find ourselves subjected to racism and sexism. We find ourselves unable to relate with our gay white sisters and brothers. We cannot deal with this type of oppression. We must have a chance to work on our own oppression as black gay women. After meeting this in our gay movement, we turn to black liberation, but then find we are oppressed as gay women. We are asked to make a choice. We are Black, we are gay, we are women, we are Black Gay Women. We cannot split ourselves. We cannot fight against heterosexual bias and be subjected to racism. We cannot fight racism and be subjected to sexism. We cannot battle sexism and be subjected to heterosexual bias. It is inconceivable for us to win our battle against heterosexual bias and be placed in a role of an abnormal perverted alternative to straight society, that is Aunt Jemima. It is inconceivable for us to win equality for black people and be placed in the role of a push-button man-made woman, i.e. sick Lesbian. It is inconceivable for us to win our war against sexism and be put in the role of Uncle Tom, nigger, happy slave, i.e. Playboy-bunny. We must work on all three oppressions or not at all. I don't want to go for a job, be hired, receive lower pay because I am a woman, forced to do subordinate work because I am black and be fired because I am a Lesbian. After my clash with society because of my three-fold oppression I don't want to come to a gay meeting and have to put up with racism because whitey's problems come first. I don't want to be told to be a lady, or asked to speak softly, because I am a woman. We should be sheltered from our oppression by our own people. By our own people I mean Gay people, Black people and Women. By our own people I don't mean white, straight middle-class men. We have to fight women's liberation, because we are gay and we have to fight whitey because we are black. We have to fight men because we are women. Do we have to become completely separate in our revolution? Do we have to break off from our gay white sisters and brothers? Is there no place for us in Gay Liberation, in Black Liberation, in society? Don't think I am begging you, Mr. Oppressor, to give us a place to work on our common oppression. Don't think I am straight, Uncle-Tom pricking it. By no means. We will continue to demand our right to exist as productive, free, equal, black, gay beautiful women. We are not for a second about to forget that we are against racism, sexism and heterosexual bias. There is a place for us in this society, and we will proudly take it at all costs. Even if it means breaking off from our so-called liberal white sisters and brothers, so-called liberal gay sisters and brothers, so-called liberal black sisters and brothers. Get-it-together, because we are.

7
POLITICAL PROTESTS AFTER STONEWALL

INFLUENCED BY THE STONEWALL RIOTS, LGBT activists organized hundreds of demonstrations in the last six months of the 1960s and the first four years of the 1970s. They simultaneously engaged in other forms of activism, including lobbying public officials, litigating in court, and engaging in electoral politics, but LGBT demonstrations were distinctly dramatic, highly visible, and very successful in building the movement's momentum and promoting activist goals. The number of these actions was extraordinary, their geographic reach was exceptional, and their creativity marks them as important in the broader history of U.S. social movements.

The sixty documents featured in this chapter provide a sampling of protests and demonstrations that were inspired—directly or indirectly—by the Stonewall Riots. They also capture some of the LGBT movement's diversity, some of the changes experienced by the movement, and some of the movement's successes and failures. After the first few documents, which highlight demonstrations that occurred immediately after the Stonewall rebellion, the documents are organized to highlight the main targets of LGBT activism. Within each section, the sources are organized chronologically.

DOCUMENTS 123–126 focus on LGBT demonstrations in July and August 1969. The remaining documents highlight demonstrations and protests concerning the indicated targets.
DOCUMENTS 127–133: newspapers, magazines, and television programs.
DOCUMENTS 134–137: universities and prisons.
DOCUMENTS 138–139: war and militarism.
DOCUMENTS 140–145: sex and gender laws.
DOCUMENTS 146–153: bars and businesses.
DOCUMENTS 154–157: lesbian invisibility.
DOCUMENTS 158–160: religious institutions.
DOCUMENTS 161–164: police practices.
DOCUMENTS 165–167: anti-discrimination laws.
DOCUMENTS 168–171: government discrimination.
DOCUMENTS 172–177: electoral politics.
DOCUMENTS 178–182: psychiatry and psychology.

DOCUMENT 123

Committee for Homosexual Freedom Newsletter
8 July 1969, 1

A spirited CHF picket line of 15 to 20 people picketed the architecturally bankrupt Federal Building at 450 Golden Gate Avenue for about three hours on the afternoon of July 3rd. We were protesting the fact that homosexuals are barred from federal employment and the fact that such practices set a similar pattern among private employers. . . .

At the July 4 meeting, CHF membership decided to establish the picketing of the Federal Building on a regular basis. A noon to 1:00 line will march there each Friday, beginning Friday July 18. It was felt that CHF needed to expand its activities to attract more public attention and rekindle interest among the 100-plus "members." . . .

CHF pickets States Steamship Company every Wednesday noon till 1:00. Why? Well, sure, it may be like a flea attacking an elephant, but there are some real benefits. The thousands of people who have seen our line have been forced to think about homosexual oppression; they have seen that homosexuals aren't afraid to take a stand; they have seen that we will not quit easily; the picket line is something tangible for the media to refer to (witness the coverage by the Chronicle July 2nd). States Lines is where this new phase of homosexual freedom fighting began. . . .

DOCUMENT 124

A. B. [Ada Bello], "The Second Largest Minority"
Homophile Action League Newsletter, Aug. 1969, 2

The Fifth Annual Reminder Day demonstration in front of Independence Hall went on as planned. Groups of picketers from Washington, New York, and Philadelphia participated in the traditional Fourth of July protest, sponsored by ERCHO [Eastern Regional Conference of Homophile Organizations]. For two hours homosexuals carried, for everyone to see, signs that expressed some of our grievances and demands. It was a proud and solemn gesture, in harmony with the day's celebrations. It served as a good reminder that we are aware of our rights as American citizens and intend to attain them.

The responses that this demonstration elicited from the tourists and passersby at Independence Hall ranged from highly favorable to downright hostile. Some of them were well worth quoting:

From a young woman accompanied by her husband and child: "It is wonderful what you are doing. . . . It's about time!"

From a middle-aged lady, to a young girl: "They are nothing but troublemakers. . . . For everyone to come to Philadelphia today and see this demonstration in broad daylight is a disgrace, a disgrace!"

From an old lady walking by the line: "Good luck to you! Good luck to you! . . ."

And so the picket went on, praised or vilified, but not ignored.

Except, that is, by the press. Although the demonstration was amply covered by the Philadelphia Tribune, The Distant Drummer, and the Temple Free Press, Philadelphia's three major dailies (the Inquirer, the Bulletin and the Daily News) choose to ignore it as they ignored the New York riots of the previous week. This news blackout from the three main organs of the establishment is almost flattering. In the past they also turned a deaf ear on the noises coming from the ghetto—until they couldn't afford to do it anymore. We will just have to blow our trumpet louder and watch the walls of Jericho collapse.

DOCUMENT 125

"Cross Currents"

The Ladder, Oct. 1969, 40–41

GAY LIBERATION MEETINGS: On July 9th, the Mattachine Society of New York held a meeting at Freedom House, 20 West 40th Street, to discuss the possibilities for protest action against the police raids and corruption in the State Liquor Authority. Dick Leitsch reported on the riots and then opened the meeting to suggestions. One young man reported that police were still harassing homosexuals in Greenwich Village, picking them off the streets and beating them up in police cars. He stated that many young runaways, homeless youths who happen also to be homosexual, were especially vulnerable to these attacks, and he requested help in establishing halfway houses or a coffee shop for these youngsters.

Madolyn Cervantes suggested that a strong campaign to end corruption in the SLA be launched. Martha Shelley, of the New York Chapter of Daughters of Bilitis, suggested a gay power rally; and after about an hour's debate, this suggestion was adopted. . . .

On July 17, the New York Chapter of D.O.B. voted to co-sponsor the vigil along with the Mattachine Society. It was set for 2 P.M. on Sunday, July 27, in Washington Square Park, and leaflets were run off and distributed night after night in Greenwich Village. The committee reported that they were warmly received both by homosexuals and village residents.

Supporters of the vigil were urged to wear lavender armbands (a color symbolic of homosexuality since the era of Oscar Wilde), and a huge lavender banner was constructed, bearing two male symbols intertwined, and two female symbols intertwined. An ad was placed in the Village Voice of July 24, urging people to attend the vigil. Notices were mailed to members of the D.O.B. and the Mattachine Society.

THE GAY POWER VIGIL: The sun shone on July 27, as homosexuals gathered around the fountain in Washington [Square Park]. At 2 P.M., Martha

Shelley stood up on the rim of the fountain and complimented the hundreds who were already gathered, wearing lavender armbands, for their courage in showing up at an open meeting. "The time has come," she said, "for us to walk in the sunshine. We don't have to ask permission to do it. Here we are!"

"We will no longer be victimized by straight people who are guilt-ridden about sex," she continued. "We don't need to be told we're sick—man, if I'm sick, I know where it hurts and I go to a doctor. If I'm happily making love, I don't want a doctor to come to me and say, 'you're sick!'" She also denounced the vigilantes who had been harassing homosexuals in a park in Queens. "Why do you think they ran around at one in the morning with flashlights to chase people out of the park? To protect their children—or to get a free peep show?"

Marty Robinson of the Mattachine Society spoke about the potential of gay power. He urged homosexuals to petition their government, to organize into voting blocs, and to use the power of the boycott. "There are one million homosexuals in New York City. If we wanted to, we could boycott Blooming-dale's, and that store would be closed in two weeks." He asked those present to join with groups such as the Mattachine Society and the D.O.B. in order to continue the fight for equality. "We will not permit another reign of terror," he said. "We've got to get organized. This is our chance."

After speeches and chants of "Give me a G," "G!" "Give me an A," "A!"... "What does that spell?" GAY POWER!" the group marched down the street to rally again in front of the Stonewall Inn, scene of the initial riots. At the end of the speeches, there seemed to be about 500 in the audience, but there must have been many people sitting on the sidelines, for at least 1,000 people marched down both sides of the street to the Stonewall. Chants of "gay power" went up again, and the group sang "We Shall Overcome." . . .

DOCUMENT 126
"Kew Gardens Rally"
Mattachine Society of New York Newsletter, Sept. 1969, 4

Sunday, August 4, 1969, was possibly the most exciting day in the history of Kew Gardens, N.Y. On that day, at 2:00 in the afternoon, approximately 100 homosexuals of both sexes, and heterosexual supporters, invaded the small park where the vigilantes had cut down the trees. . . .

What was happening was a demonstration to protest the actions of the vigilantes who had harassed homosexuals and vandalized the park. A long line of male and female homosexuals (and the straight people who supported the demonstration), all wearing lavender armbands, marched for nearly an hour. They bore signs reminding the public that "Homosexuals Have Rights—and So Do Trees," and others, including a "Dishonor Roll" of countries with anti-homosexual laws. The list is rather short, consisting of the U.S.A., Russia, Cuba, China and South Africa.

Following the marching, there were some speeches (Marty Robinson's was especially stirring), and then a cleverly satirical playlet written by Martha Shelley which dealt with three Kew Gardens citizens—a cop, a real estate man and a lawyer who were card-playing, drinking "buddies"—the kind we all know— the inseparable heterosexual men whose "love exceeds that of David and Jonathan," but, presumably, never crosses the line into the sexual sphere.

The playlet developed all the stereotyped themes that had come out in the newspaper reports on the formation and actions of the vigilante committee, and how these men were concerned for the "safety" of their wives and children and so were driven to defoliate the park.

The demonstration was held in Kew Gardens to let the women and children see the "menaces" their husbands were "protecting" them from and to show that homosexuals intend to go anywhere they choose.

DOCUMENT 127

Mike Brown, Michael Tallman, and Leo Louis Martello, "The Summer of Gay Power and the Village Voice Exposed!"

Come Out!, 14 Nov. 1969, 10–11

The *Village Voice* and its writers have once again shown where their heads are really at, during this past summer of "Gay Power." They've consistently demonstrated their contempt of the Gay Community in their coverage of the long overdue rebellion of another oppressed minority. Their handling of the first Gay Riots in history read like a copy of the *New York Daily News*. Instead of being concerned about the civil rights of the Gay minority they were preoccupied with the uptight establishment's *reactions* to the riots. Their demeaning use of derogatory terms for homosexuals and lesbians was a pure demonstration of anti-humanistic liberal sentiment. Howard Smith and other *Village Voice* writers' concerns for the "harassed" police, rather than for the victims who finally fought back, was aptly pointed out. . . .

In the August 7th issue of the *Voice*, members of Gay Liberation Front placed an ad in the Public Notices section of classifieds. The substance of the ad dealt with requests for articles, photographs, art work, etc. for *Come Out*. The lead-in to the ad read "Gay Power to Gay People." Our friendly community monopoly newspaper accepted the ad with payment in full and then before printing simply deleted "Gay Power to Gay People" without the knowledge or consent of G.L.F. . . .

We decided at this point to submit another ad using the word "Gay." The opportunity presented itself again in the issue of September 4. GLF then used the *V.V.* Bulletin Board to advertise a dance for Friday night, September 5th, using the lead-in—Gay Community Dance. Again the ad was accepted when and as presented. Next day the person who placed the ad received a call from VV which explained that it was the policy of VV to refrain from printing obscure words in classifieds and *VV* thought "Gay" was obscene. When questioned why anyone would consider such a word obscene, the *Voice* said that the staff had decided "Gay" was equatable with "fuck" and other four-letter words, and that either the ad would have to be changed or the ad could not be printed. Since "homosexual" was also not acceptable, and since GLF wanted the ad for the dance placed, we accepted their only admissible substitute, "homophile" (which is a genteel bastard word not included in most dictionaries). . . . .

Undeterred, GLF began proceedings with our lawyers for suit in Federal Court. At this point we finally met Ed Fancher, when we were forced to deliver a letter stating our proposed action to his home (since Mr. Fancher was never available in his office). At this time we asked to speak to him about the *Voice* Classified policy. He refused. . . .

The day Gay Power laid itself on the line for the first time started at 9 a.m. on September 12, 1969, with much communal coffee and even more communal confusion. Ed Fancher arrived at 10 a.m., received a proclamation of our grievances, and promptly disappeared through the door into *VV* bureaucracy.

At 4:30 p.m., during the peak of the demonstration, a member of GLF submitted a classified ad saying "The Gay Liberation Front sends love to all Gay men and women in the homosexual community." The picture outside the *Voice* was characterized by a chanting picket line, a supply of 5000 leaflets being rapidly exhausted, and large numbers of people signing the petition charging the *Voice* with discrimination.

At this point, Howard Smith emerged from the door of the *Village Voice* (to boos from the crowd) and requested three representatives from GLF to "meet with Mr. Fancher." Once inside and upstairs, the representatives encountered a cry of outrage that GLF had chosen the *Village Voice* as a target (sooo liberal we are). The suggestion was made that we negotiate the three points in dispute: (1) changing classified ads without knowledge or consent of purchaser, (2) use of the words "Gay" and "homosexual" in classifieds, and (3) the contemptuous attitude of the *Village Voice* toward the Gay Community. . . . Fancher replied that the *Village Voice* exercised no censorship of its articles, and that if a writer wanted to say derogatory things about faggots, he could not in good conscience stop him. Fancher also said that we had no right to tamper with

"freedom of the press."

This GLF accepted with the absolute understanding that Gay Power has the right to return and oppose anything the *Village Voice* staff chooses to include in the paper. On the Classified Ads policy he conceded completely. . . . One of the GLF representatives in the upstairs office stepped to the window facing Seventh Avenue and flashed the V for Victory sign to the waiting crowd below. WE HAD WON!

DOCUMENT 128
"S.F. Cops Arrest 12 Pickets after Melee at Examiner"
The Los Angeles Advocate, Jan. 1970, 2, 10

What started out as a peaceful protest against the *San Francisco Examiner* [on 31 October] ended in a near-riot when S.F. police waded into the 60 gay demonstrators and arrested 12 of them.

The demonstrators were members of the Committee for Homosexual Freedom and the Gay Liberation Front. They were protesting an article that had appeared in the *Examiner*, which used terms for homosexuals such as "queers" and "semi-males with flexible wrists and hips." The writer of the offending article, Robert Patterson, also referred to the gay community as "Fairyland" and to Folsom Street as "Queer Alley."

The melee was precipitated by two men who dumped a plastic bag full of ink on the picket line from the *Examiner* building. A CHF spokesman gives this account of what followed.

"Suddenly a plastic bag full of printers ink was thrown from a second-floor *Examiner* office, soaking the pickets and splattering the walls of the building. Someone wiped his hands on the wall. In a few seconds, inked hand prints covered the wall and windows. 'Fuck the Examiner' was written by a finger dripping with ink. 'Gay is,' wrote a handsome young man just before he was dragged by the hair into the waiting police van."

The police tactical squad then "pushed aggressively into the crowd," the S.F. *Chronicle* reported. The CHF writer put it differently:

"The riot police which had been summoned charged into the picket line brandishing riot batons. Persons with cameras were the first to be attacked. Marcus Overseth, editor of the S.F. *Free Press*, was shoved against the building and dragged with his camera into the van. Leo Laurence, former editor of *Vector* Magazine and writer for the *Berkeley Tribe*, stopped to take a picture of a young guy being clubbed. A riot baton swung at Leo. By the time he was taken to the van, a line was waiting to be tossed in. Quick-minded Leo deftly removed the film from his camera and tossed it to Larry Littlejohn, SIR [Society for Individual Rights] president, who fled the scene with the film."

When the fracas ended with the police chasing the pickets down the street, 12 of them were under arrest charged with a variety of misdemeanor counts. Six of them also faced felony charges (battery on an officer, PC 243). Several of the demonstrators were injured, one reportedly hospitalized later with a broken rib and torn ear. . . .

Most of the survivors of the picket line marched through the Tenderloin district to the Glide Methodist Church. . . . Half an hour later, at 2PM, the angry Gays, still carrying their picket signs, marched to San Francisco City Hall to take their demand for justice to Mayor Alioto. . . .

At the steps of City Hall, the group stopped and began walking an oblong picket line on the sidewalk. A crowd quickly gathered in Civic Center Plaza.

POLITICAL PROTESTS
AFTER STONEWALL

"We are here to demand justice," shouted CHF co-founder Gale Whitting-ton. "We have been treated like hell for too long. . . ."

Whittington and several others left the picket line and went up City Hall steps, under the great granite dome, and up the marble staircase to the mayor's office.

"Thirteen of our brothers were savagely beaten and busted," Gale told a mayor's assistant, Mike McCone. "We demand justice." As Mayor Alioto was out of town, McCone said there was nothing he could do and suggested that they take their complaint to the police department. The group left the office and returned to the pickets outside.

The pickets started up the steps with their placards. The ring of policemen who surrounded them ran up the steps. One of them nearly knocked over a black Gay in trying to beat him through the door. The black Gay scolded, "City Hall is a public building open to everyone."

They went up the stairway into the plush office of Mayor Alioto. They sat or lay down on the carpet and began to sing.

The sit-in lasted two hours. At 5PM, the mayor's assistant told them that the building was closed. "I ask you to leave. In five minutes, I will ask the police department to arrest anyone remaining."

The Gays had agreed that each man would do as his conscience directed. Everyone left, except for three. At 5:05, the holdouts were handcuffed and taken to the waiting van.

Two weeks later, eight of those arrested at the *Examiner* were given five-day suspended jail sentences and six months' probation. They pleaded no contest to a charge of refusing to follow police orders. . . .

DOCUMENT 129
"Happy Homos Hit Harpers"
Gay Flames, 14 Nov. 1970, 7[1]

As a part of the "sexual revolution" major magazines can now publish articles about homosexuality. But these articles are inevitably written by straights and they are equally anti-gay, no matter what their pretenses. Until recently, they got away with it.

Gay Activists Alliance confronted *Harper's* after their September issue contained such an article. They informed the magazine that "Homo/Hetero: The Struggle for Sexual Identity" was offensive to gay people and said that they felt *Harper's* was under a moral obligation to give equal space to an article favorable to us. Three articles were submitted and all were rejected. Nor would the magazine commission their own.

Having exhausted all indirect channels, GAA decided to confront *Harper's*. Tuesday, 50 people arrived early in the morning. Only one receptionist was there at the time and they had no trouble in occupying all of the executive offices. They brought a coffee machine, donuts, and leaflets. Their purposes were to educate the *Harper's* staff by showing them "real" homosexuals, not the figments of their repressed minds, and to give notice to *all* the media that slander of homosexuals would not be accepted without trouble.

GAA leafleted in the building and on the street. They rapped with the employees, including heated exchanges with the woman who commissioned the article in question and the art director who chose the oppressive pictures which went along. They sang gay liberation songs, played guitars, and generally had "a beautiful time."

While *Harper's* response was only that they would "actively consider finding" an article favorable to gay people, GAA left at 4:00. They left behind them, however, one magazine which knew what hit them and would hesitate before printing trash about gay people in the future.

DOCUMENT 130

Randy Wicker and Martin St. John, "TV Show Sets Off Storm"
The Advocate, 14 Mar. 1973, 1, 23

Six persons were arrested Feb. 16 when 30 members of New York's Gay Activists Alliance occupied American Broadcasting Company executive offices in a protest of a segment of "Marcus Welby, M.D." The demonstration spread to the West Coast and forced ABC to cut part of the show's "objectionable" dialog.

The segment, titled "The Other Martin Loring," dealt with a diabetic father emotionally upset over homosexual tendencies. When his wife starts divorce proceedings, he begins drinking heavily and goes into insulin shock.

"There was more wrong with this guy than all the patients in a week of 'General Hospital,'" said an ABC spokesman in Hollywood.

The sensitive points with the gay community—among others—were when the father calls his homosexual feelings "degrading and loathsome," and says they make "my whole life a cheap, hollow fraud." Both quotes were cut.

In addition, objections centered around Dr. Welby's use of the description "a serious illness" and the advice to the father to see a psychiatrist and continue to suppress his urges so "you'll deserve the respect of your son." . . .

GAA leaflets handed out during the zap said, "Marcus Welby is a quack and a bigot. . . ."

DOCUMENT 131

"Activists in Lather over NBC Slurs"
The Advocate, 21 Nov. 1973, 3, 8

A gay activist was covered with Gillette Foamy shaving cream in Chicago, and another interrupted the NBC-TV "Today" show in New York on Oct. 26

in protest of a "Sanford and Son" program the week before which reportedly insulted Gays. . . .

"Sanford and Son," a very popular situation comedy series produced for NBC, became a new target of outrage when its Oct. 19 show paraded a number of homosexual stereotypes before its millions of viewers during a gay bar episode.

In Chicago, about 30 members of various Illinois gay groups went to the Merchandise Mart Building on the following Friday and covered Michael Bergeron, vice president of the Chicago Gay Alliance, with shaving cream while passers-by looked on.

Merchandise Mart was chosen for the protest because it not only contains regional offices of NBC, but also of Gillette, which sponsors "Sanford and Son." . . .

In New York, Mark Segal, who calls himself the head of the National Gay Raiders . . . , talked his way past NBC security guards and interrupted the "Today" show.

Announcer Frank Blair was in the middle of his newscast at 7AM New York time when Segal came out of the audience, got before the cameras and said, "Gay people are sick and tired of NBC's bigotry. . . ."

At that point the picture was cut off and security guards removed Segal to a hallway outside the studio. A moment later, co-host Barbara Walters came into the hall, followed by a producer who was ordering her to "get back in the studio." Walters said she would not return until she had heard what Segal had to say.

A few minutes later, Walters explained to the nationwide audience that Segal was protesting "the treatment of gay people on NBC." . . .

DOCUMENT 132
Karla Jay, "Lesbians Zap Dick Cavett"
Lesbian Tide, Jan. 1974, 3

About twenty-five lesbians from Lesbian Feminist Liberation along with other women from New York NOW [National Organization for Women] cleverly infiltrated the audience of the Dick Cavett Show November 30 to protest the appearance of arch-sexist George Gilder.

Gilder is the author of *Sexual Suicide*. . . . Gilder contends in his book that society is falling apart due to feminism and homosexuality. . . .

The LFL presented Gilder with an urn of ashes representing "the women who have been murdered at the altar of male supremacy..., the flesh of women burned by the thousands in the Middle Ages, the so-called witches who perished at the stake in our own New England, and the untold numbers who died beneath the knife of quack doctors performing illegal abortions." The above was read aloud on Cavett's show by two LFL spokeswomen standing with their arms around one another. Leaflets containing this statement were also distributed to the audience. Two non-LFL women later interrupted the show and were ejected from the theatre. During the remainder of the show, Gilder attempted to explain and defend his theories. His ineptness and apparent neuroses put the final threads in the noose the LFL had so beautifully set up for him.

DOCUMENT 133

Joe Kennedy, "Raiders Pull Quick Opener on Cronkite"
The Advocate, 2 Jan. 1974, 2, 12

NEW YORK CITY—The CBS evening news with Walter Cronkite, whose audience of more than 20 million persons is unequalled by any other news program or publication in the world, was disrupted briefly on Dec. 11 by the Gay Raiders, a militant homosexual group.

The Raiders were protesting alleged anti-gay incidents on CBS entertainment shows, as well as the alleged refusal of CBS officials to meet with them to discuss their grievances.

Mark Segal, 22, head of the Philadelphia-based Gay Raiders, and member Harry Langhorne were booked on charges of criminal trespass and released on their own recognizance. . . .

Segal, using the assumed name of Mark Ursa, contacted CBS news a week before the disruption and told them he was a journalism student at Camden Community College in New Jersey and would like to view a live broadcast of the Cronkite news within the studios. CBS and Cronkite agreed to his request and invited him to appear on Dec. 11.

When he showed up at the studio, he was accompanied by Langhorne, who was carrying a camera. Langhorne told CBS he was a photographer for Segal's college paper.

Both were seated about 40 feet from Cronkite, separated from him by a row of four desks. Approximately 14 minutes into the 30-minute program, Cronkite was beginning to read a story on Henry Kissinger. . . .

Segal, who had burst from his seat seconds earlier and dodged between the four desks, darted in front of the camera and held up a yellow cardboard sign with the words, "Gays Protest CBS Prejudice" and began shouting.

"Gay people are protesting against..."

The word "Gays," printed in dark letters, was clearly visible to viewers for several seconds. Cronkite stopped speaking, and it was evident to viewers that one or more persons had grabbed the intruder and that a scuffle was in progress.

At that point the screen went dark and the sound was cut off for about 10 seconds. When the picture and sound resumed, Cronkite, apparently unflapped and smiling slightly, said, "Well, that's a rather interesting development—a protest demonstration right here in our CBS news headquarters. We'll try to find out what it was all about and let you know in a few moments."

On the 7PM broadcast, the Kissinger story was redone. Cronkite came on live approximately 20 minutes into the show and said, "As we were broadcasting the live program a half hour ago, this happened," then showed the full tape of Segal's interruption.

After showing the tape, Cronkite said, "The demonstrators were from a group called the Gay Raiders, and they were protesting the unfavorable portrayal of homosexuals in CBS entertainment programs. . . ."

DOCUMENT 134
Don Jackson, "Gay Liberation Movement"
Berkeley Barb, 10 Oct. 1969, 12

Gay guerillas shouted slogans such as "Gay power" and "Gay is Good" before a crowd of around 2,000 at a rally in Sproul Plaza, Berkeley, on Sunday, October 6.

The rally was organized by the militant Committee for Homosexual Freedom as an event in the U. of California's disorientation week.

The guerillas and gay people in the crowd shouted "Gale the liberator" when Gale Whittington, co-founder of the Committee, came on center to perform a sociodramatic skit.

Gale appeared tranquil and purposeful after his release from jail on a charge of disturbing the peace. He had been arrested following an argument in a grocery store concerning the grape boycott. Gale's skit enacted a scene in which he was fired from his job by a gay employer because he wore a "Gay is good" button to work. Gale said to his employer, "I'm gay and I'm proud, but you are just a plain queer."

In real life, Gale was fired from his job at States Lines after his photograph appeared in the Berkeley *Barb* showing him embracing another man.

Gale stated that the first objective of the gay guerillas is to change the minds of gays so that they will quit hiding their homosexuality from the world. . . .

DOCUMENT 135
"Sacramento State Students Sue to Get Okay for Gay Group"
The Los Angeles Advocate, 27 May 1970, 1

Sacramento State College's student association has gone to court to get the college to officially recognize the Society for Homosexual Freedom as a student organization.

The Associated Students, with a membership of over 10,000, said in its petition to Superior Court that Dr. Otto Butz, acting college president, acted unconstitutionally March 3 when he vetoed student senate approval. . . .

"The issue is bigger than the Society for Homosexual Freedom," said Associated Students President Steve Whitmore, an admitted heterosexual. "It involves the right to freedom of expression, freedom of assembly and self-determination."

Whitmore, the Society's executive coordinator, asked for its recognition Feb. 27. The student senate gave its approval March 2, but Dr. Butz sent a letter to Whitmore the next day saying recognition of the Society "could conceivably... seem to endorse" homosexual activity—"which most American jurisdictions today...hold to be a crime." . . .

DOCUMENT 136
"Gays Protest Brutality in N.Y.C. Prisons"
The Advocate, 14 Apr. 1971, 20

About 75 people from various gay groups in the city held a picketing demonstration outside the Men's House of Detention in lower Manhattan on Saturday, Feb. 28. The protest was one of the first public actions by the recently formed "Gay Community Prisoner Defense Committee," an informal group which is attempting to draw public attention to the plight of homosexual prisoners in the city's detention facilities.

In addition to routine brutality, which the demonstrators said gay prisoners are usually subjected to, the committee is also concerned about bringing the facts to light in the case of Raymond Lavon Moore. Moore, a black gay prisoner, was found dead in his cell last November. Correctional authorities claimed his death was the result of suicide. However, there have been conflicting reports from other inmates and one guard concerning the death. An FBI investigation into the case is now under way.

After the demonstration at the men's facility, many of the participants marched up to the Women's House of Detention and joined other groups for a protest action there.

DOCUMENT 137
"Women Hit Jail Treatment"
The Advocate, 19 July 1972, 14

The Women's Center Prisoners' Collective picketed the Sybil Brand Institute for Women on Father's Day. SBI is the Los Angeles County Jail for women, and the lesbian feminists were complaining about discriminatory treatment of lesbian prisoners.

A spokesman said the "Daddy Tank" into which lesbians are segregated is "three or four times worse" than conditions in other sections of the women's jail.

An official of the Sheriff's Department did admit that women who wore masculine clothing and admitted homosexuality were segregated but denied their treatment was different than for heterosexual females incarcerated at SBI.

A lesbian spokesperson told the *Advocate* that the lesbian prisoners are given only the "filthiest" jobs and are even segregated during the institution's church services.

DOCUMENT 138

Don Jackson, "Gay Liberation Peace March"
Gay Power (1.7), ca. Dec. 1969, 16

Around 15,000 Gay people joined in marching for peace on moratorium day Nov. 15. Some 400 of them gathered at Mission Park, San Francisco at 8 A.M. and marched as a group to the Polo Field in Golden Gate Park. The group, which had been organized by the Gay Liberation Front of Berkeley and the Committee for Homosexual Freedom of San Francisco, followed behind a large banner reading "Homosexuals Against the War." As they marched they sang and shouted unison slogans such as "Say it clear, say it loud, We're Gay and we're proud." Other nearby marching groups and bystanders were visibly dismayed when the slogan shouted was changed to "Suck Cock to beat the draft." Members of the Sexual Freedom League, who by coincidence were marching next to the Gays, picked up the slogan and started shouting it themselves and added another, "Fight Fascism with Fetishism." . . . Many suddenly realized that they had a common cause in fighting erotic oppression. . . .

The group resumed the march to the Polo Fields after breakfast. Four soldiers waiting at a bus stop conspicuously lowered their eyes and looked away to pretend not to see the large sign reading "Soldiers—Make each other—Not war." At the polo field they passed out literature to the crowd, including a poem ending "Beautiful Vietnamese man, Let's suck and fuck, Let's not kill each other anymore." . . .

DOCUMENT 139

David L. Aiken, "Thousands Protest War: Activists Turn Out in D.C."
The Advocate, 26 May 1971, 1, 7

Thousands of Gays marched, protested, camped, and frolicked during the two weeks of anti-war demonstrations here. Estimates of the number who took part publicly as homosexuals ranged from several hundred up to 10,000. . . .

Nearly 80 Gays were arrested out of an overall arrest total of over 9000.

From the Apr. 24th march on the Capitol here to the attempt on May 3–4 to shut down the government, gay contingents were visible and vocal. There were charges, however, that principal organizing groups, after encouraging gay participation, had in some cases attempted to sweep them under the carpet.

Tina Mandel, a New York Daughters of Bilitis member who made the estimate of 10,000 participants, charged that trade union officials had attempted to squeeze her and recent congressional candidate Frank Kameny out of the list of speakers at the Apr. 24th rally on the Capitol steps. She said they succeeded in relegating them to the tail-end of the program after all media coverage was gone. . . .

Protest activity began with the Apr. 24th march and rally, in which a delegation of gay men and women joined almost 200,000 persons who were here to protest the war, poverty, politically motivated imprisonment, and dozens of fringe causes.

Between 50 and 100 gay people marched down Pennsylvania Avenue, carrying banners and shouting such popular chants as, "Ho, ho homosexual, the ruling class is ineffectual!" . . .

No gay people were arrested . . . until May 4, when about 65 members of the gay contingent were arrested while sitting in front of the Justice Department.

Four other Gays were arrested on charges of jaywalking and obstructing traffic. . . .

Seven members of the Washington GLF were arrested May 6 at a demonstration in front of the South Vietnamese Embassy. . . .

DOCUMENT 140
"'Not Afraid Any More': Rev. Perry Leads 200 in Protest against Sex Laws"
The Los Angeles Advocate, Jan. 1970, 1, 2

About 200 proud homosexuals marched through Los Angeles Civic Center on Sunday, Nov. 16, to protest California laws that make homosexual acts felonies.

Sponsored by the Committee for Homosexual Law Reform and led by Rev. Troy Perry, the line of demonstrators, three abreast, stretched for more than two blocks. . . .

The group marched slowly and confidently, many of them arm-in-arm as a sign of solidarity. They carried about 50 placards with slogans such as: "We're Not Afraid Anymore," "The Lord Is My Shepherd and He Knows I'm Gay," "20 Million Americans Do It Differently," "Oral Can Be Moral," and "Gay Is Groovy." . . .

The Committee for Homosexual Law Reform chose the California State Building for the destination and rally because that is where the California Supreme Court meets. That same week the court was scheduled to consider a request by L.A. attorney Walter Culpepper to grant a hearing on the constitutionality of California laws on sexual acts.

At the State Building, the marchers, still holding their signs high, sat on the steps below a speaker's podium to hear ministers, attorneys, civil rights leaders, and leaders in the homosexual community.

Jerry Joachim, former president of PRIDE, introduced Rev. Clay Colwell, who led the group in an opening prayer. Rev. Colwell founded the Council on Religion and the Homosexual in San Francisco six years ago. Two weeks before the rally, he was fired by a Southern California congregation, in Manhattan Beach, because of his activities in support of homosexuals. . . .

Although few heterosexuals witnessed the rally in the deserted downtown area, the day's event had a pronounced effect on the homosexuals that took part. Observers noted a new sense of pride, a new determination, and a new feeling of relief on the part of those who had come farther out of their "closets" than ever before. There was the feeling that this time they had started something that will not die.

DOCUMENT 141
"Hail to Queens"
New York Mattachine Times, Nov. 1970, 1, 2

Queens, an organization for transvestites and drag queens, has effectively legalized drag balls in New York City. Lee Brewster, Executive Director of Queens, announced that the organization's October 30th Hallowe'en Ball was the first "legal" drag ball in the city.

Sec. 250.15 of the N.Y Penal Law prohibits anyone's being "masked or in any manner disguised by unusual or unnatural attire or facial alteration... except...when it occurs in connection with a masquerade party or like entertainment if...permission is first obtained from the police or other appropriate agency."

New York City permitted masquerading only in connection with licensed masquerade balls but the application for the license specifically stated that "males dressed in female attire" were not to be admitted. . . . Lee Brewster, in his presentation to Bess Myerson Grant, asked that the restriction barring men from dressing as women be dropped for the following reasons:

1. The regulation was not enforced by the department;
2. The public gained the impression that the police were accepting "pay offs" to ignore the existence of such balls;
3. The regulation discriminated against men as there was no provision restricting the type of costume women might wear.

Queens graciously shares credit with MSNY [Mattachine Society of New York] for the victory. Several years ago, when Lee was organizing drag balls for MSNY, Dick Leitsch signed the license application. At that time he contacted

Mrs. Grant about anti-drag regulation, claiming it placed an undue burden on the licensee.

"Drag queens and transvestites assume, quite rightly, that they will be welcome at any function given by a homosexual organization," Leitsch wrote in his presentation. "Even if we wanted to exclude them, as the law says we should, we wouldn't know how to. Most drag queens and transvestites, when they choose to mimic women, do it so well that it is impossible to know their genital sex without making a physical examination. Obviously, we cannot ask every apparent female who attends our parties to submit to a check of their genitalia."

When Lee Brewster formed Queens (now Queens Liberation Front), he pressed the matter and won the first major victory for that most oppressed of all homosexuals, the drag queen. . . .

DOCUMENT 142

Breck Ardery, John Francis Hunter, and Joe Murray, "At Least 2500 March on N.Y. State Capitol"
The Advocate, 14 Apr. 1971, 1, 3

ALBANY, N.Y.—Between 2500 and 3000 persons marched on the state Capitol in bright sunshine Sunday, Mar. 14, to demand civil rights for homosexuals. It was the second or third largest gay demonstration ever held in the United States.

"I bring you peace, love, and homosexuality from New York. We all know why we're here today," New York Gay Activists Alliance President Jim Owles told the crowd from the Capitol steps. "We're here to demand our rights from the state legislature." . . .

"It's a beautiful day to hear this chant for justice coming up over and over against all these crazy buildings," said Women's Liberation leader and author Kate Millett in a spontaneous ad-libbed speech. "That justice, that call for justice, I felt it like a little voice inside my gut, hurting, wailing, for years and years. And today, it feels so damn good to say it out loud."

The big rally, hosted by and largely organized by the Tri-Cities Gay Liberation Front of Albany-Troy-Schenectady, was to back up six gay demands in pending legislation: (1) scrapping of the sodomy law; (2) repeal of the solicitation law; (3) an end to the statutes against cross-dressing and impersonation; (4) fair employment-equal opportunity legislation for Gays; (5) legislation outlawing discrimination against Gays in housing and public accommodations; and (6) repeal of the loitering laws. . . .

DOCUMENT 143

Lee G. Brewster, "To Cross-Dressers Everywhere"

Drag (2.7), ca. July 1972

Two Miami [Beach] city ordinances outlawing female impersonation were struck down during June, 1972, prompting cheers from gay activist leaders who feared arrest at the national political conventions in Miami Beach. U.S. District Court Judge William O. Mehrtens ruled the two laws invalid on grounds they were vague, overbroad and discriminated against men.

The National Coalition of Gay Organizations is directly responsible for this court ruling. Queens Liberation Front has often stated that we must cooperate with the gay organizations if we wish to get any laws changed across the country regarding transvestism or cross-dressing. Queens Liberation Front is a member and supporter of the National Coalition of Gay Organizations and appeals to ALL transvestites, on behalf of their Miami sisters, to show their appreciation for this action by sending in a donation. . . .

We would also like to show our strength to some members of the NCGO. It seems that some of these homosexuals want to strike the transvestite-cross-dressing issue from the Gay Platform which is to be introduced at the National Democratic Convention in Miami as a Minority Report. . . .

DOCUMENT 144

"Cross-Dressing OK"

Gay Liberator, Nov. 1973, 5

Chicago—A city ordinance which prohibits men and women from wearing clothes of the opposite sex has been ruled unconstitutional here by Circuit Court Judge Jack Sperling. The law violates equal protection guarantees of the US constitution, Sperling said, citing federal court opinions that persons have a right "to present themselves physically to the world in the manner of their own individual choice."

The case involved the arrest of four young Chicanos who had gone to a police station to file a complaint of assault and battery against several other men who allegedly attacked them in a tavern. Instead of pursuing the assailants, police arrested the four for cross-dressing.

All four youths attended their trial in drag, and heard Judge Sperling declare that the only danger they had caused was to themselves. "Where this may be a laughing matter to some people, it is a very serious matter to these defendants," he said. . . .

DOCUMENT 145

"Activist Invites D.C. Officials to Have Sex with Him"

The Advocate, 5 Dec. 1973, 12

Gay activist Frank Kameny has publicly invited the local chief of police, federal prosecutor, and District of Columbia corporation counsel to engage in sodomy with him.

It's not that he expects them to accept or even that he particularly wants them to. In fact, what he hopes they'll do is arrest him for soliciting for an illegal act so he can bring a test case up through the courts and, he hopes, have the city's sodomy law thrown out.

The invitations came in the form of five-page single-spaced letters to Chief of Police Jerry V. Wilson, U.S. Attorney Harold H. Titus Jr., and Corporation Counsel C. Francis Murphy.

After a lengthy statement of why the sodomy law is unconstitutional and void, Kameny's letters make this invitation:

"I hereby invite, suggest, and propose to solicit, encourage, and urge you to engage with me in an act or acts of oral and/or anal sodomy of your choice, in the role or roles of your choice, in a mutually agreeable, indisputably private place in the District of Columbia, at an early time of our mutual convenience. Try it; you'll like it. R.S.V.P."

He followed this up with a different sort of invitation:

"I demand that you take steps to institute and pursue prosecution of me for what—by your stated view of the law (but not mine)—is a crime, consummated by my delivery to you of the solicitation for sodomy set forth just above."

Just to put the recipients of his invitation on the spot, Kameny sent copies of the letter and a press release describing it to all news media in the area. . . .

The letters were sent Nov. 6. A few days later, Kameny received a 1½-page reply from Chief Wilson, declining his invitation.

Wilson observed that Kameny's invitation was probably not sincere. In any case, he wrote, "I am unable to test your intent, firstly because I find the notion unappealing, and secondly because sodomy is against the law, and thirdly because my wife would never allow it."

"But," Wilson concluded, "if either Frank (Murphy) or Harold (Titus) undertakes to verify your sincerity, be sure to let me know and I will consider whether or not any police department action is warranted. . . ."

DOCUMENT 146

"Gays Picket ABC Station"

The Los Angeles Advocate, Mar. 1970, 9

Bay Area homosexuals were joined by a wide variety of non-homosexual organizations for a picket line, Jan. 16, of KGO-TV, San Francisco's ABC affiliate.

Despite torrential rain most of the day, 150 pickets turned out to protest the station's firing of news editor Leo Laurence for his activities in the gay militant movement.

Laurence was notified of his dismissal on Nov. 1, the day after he and several others were arrested in front of the *S.F. Examiner* ("The day of the Purple Hand"). The National Association of Broadcast Employees and Technicians has been fighting the dismissal, although the union was apprehensive about the planned street action.

Two persons participating in the demonstration were arrested for allegedly shouting through megaphones, "I'd rather suck cock than go to Vietnam! . . ."

DOCUMENT 147
Don Jackson, "Barneys Turns Gay"
Gay Power (1.11), ca. Feb. 1970, 10, 21, 22

Around 150 noisy Gays turned up for the picketing of Barney's Beanery in Hollywood last Saturday night, Feb. 7. The peaceful demonstration was sponsored by the Gay Liberation Front.

Gays were protesting Barney's "Fagots stay out" sign, which they say is as offensive as a "Niggers not allowed" sign. Barney's has refused repeated demands from GLF to remove the bigoted sign. . . .

It was a "fun" demonstration. Everyone was smiling and in a happy mood (including the bystanders and cops). . . .

The . . . signs were beautiful, many psychedelically colored. "The Fart heard around the world," "Blow for Freedom" and "Queens like beans," read a few.

A considerable crowd of bystanders and drive by traffic were evident, possibly because the event was well publicized by the underground press and by frequent announcement of the event on KPWS. Barney's, usually crowded on Saturday night, was almost empty. They will no doubt make up for it later; Barney's hasn't had so much free publicity in its history.

Four cars of cops showed up. They were gentlemen this time, so the usual word we use for cops will be omitted. . . .

The demonstration broke up shortly after 10 P.M. by singing "Good night Barney," and promising to return to picket again. . . .

DOCUMENT 148
"S.F. Gays Picket Macy's over Busts"
The Advocate, 19 Aug. 1970, 1

An ad hoc committee from the homosexual community here set up picket lines at Macy's big downtown department store July 25 to protest the store's failure to work with responsible gay organizations to get charges lowered and to stop arrests in its restrooms.

About 40 arrests were reported in a recent three-week period—all, according to SIR's [Society for Individual Rights] past president Larry Littlejohn, by store security personnel. Macy's says the arrests were made by San Francisco police. Police spokesmen . . . say that in at least some instances, store personnel apprehended the suspects and then called police.

As near as can be determined, felony charges—oral copulation—were lodged against most of those arrested, instead of the more common lewd conduct charge, a misdemeanor. . . .

Representatives of SIR had met with store officials earlier and asked for warning signs in the restrooms and other measures to cure the problem without arrests. They said the store had promised to post the signs.

A store spokesman told the *Advocate* that signs had been posted "that the people would be arrested for loitering and thing like that, and the signs had been pulled down."

He said that doors on the toilet stalls had been cut down to discourage the activity and "No Loitering" signs would be stenciled on the walls.

"We certainly don't want to cause anybody any problems."

Some small signs were subsequently put up, but Littlejohn said they were inadequate.

Pickets marched on Saturday, the 25th, and on the following Monday and Tuesday. On Tuesday, the store complained to police, but no action was taken against the pickets.

The committee, which includes representatives from SIR, the Tavern Guild, and the Gay Liberation Front, plans to continue the picketing until it gets results. . . .

DOCUMENT 149
Ralph S. Schaffer, "GLF Hits Exploitation"
Los Angeles Free Press, 14 Aug. 1970, 54, 62

One of the widespread and difficult problems lingering from the old days in homosexual life is the exploitation of the gay community by the ghetto establishments characteristic of the old gay lifestyle. This includes the bars, baths and male film houses.

With few exceptions, those who run gay bars, many of them straights, feed off the pocketbooks of gay people without taking any interest in the welfare of the gay community. Many of these bars actually resist improvement and liberation. This is plainly due to the fact that the profiteers in these establishments are ghetto profiteers equivalent to their counterparts in the black community or other ghettos who practice the fine capitalistic art of becoming wealthy by milking the poor and oppressed.

The policies of many of these establishments are particularly obtuse. Some bars refuse to admit women, straight or gay, and will actually discourage their presence by spilling beer on them or what have you. Some bars admit only those wearing leather and other bars will reject the leather queens. Some bars, such as the Sewers of Paris, discriminate against different groups at different times. At the Sewers, transvestites will be admitted if business is poor that night. But if business is good they will be excluded. In the Arena one patron reports that women are not allowed because they "make trouble." He cited as an instance a night in which a woman made trouble by getting herself struck on the head with a beer bottle. . . . The Canyon Club discriminates against blacks. The Aquarius Baths discriminates against older men by charging a higher admission to those over 40. The sexism, racism and capitalistic exploitation in the gay community is rampant and outrageous, taking myriad different forms in different places.

The Gay Liberation Front has begun an attack on these ghetto establishments through two actions now under way.

The first is the Continental Theaters who own and operate five skin flick movie houses, most of which are all male. The demonstration is taking place at the Park Theater. In addition to supporting the projectionists union's grievances against the nonunion hiring policies of Continental, the GLF is demanding that the $1 membership charged patrons be discontinued and the $5 admission be substantially reduced. . . .

The second wing of GLF's attack is at the Sewers of Paris. On every Friday and Saturday night there is a demonstration at both entrances of this unbelievable establishment. Investigation continues during the demonstration to detect any improvement in the poor attitudes of the owners and managers of the establishment. GLF is demanding that (1) the Sewers of Paris cooperate with the gay community, (2) the Sewers of Paris cease charging $1 admission arbitrarily to some people but not to others during nonclub hours, (3) the Sewers of Paris discontinue their policy of discrimination, particularly against transvestites, hustlers and straight women, (4) the Sewers of Paris provide bail for any person arrested as a consequence of patronizing their establishment. . . .

DOCUMENT 150
"Bull from the Bar"
Chicago Gay Liberation Newsletter, Sept. 1970, 3

Members of Gay Lib, who had picketed the Normandy Bar earlier this year, were back in front of the swinging doors July 31st protesting a two-dollar minimum designed to keep out the "riff-raff"—namely the blacks. This was in direct violation of a previous agreement with the owners of the Normandy to allow dancing and not to raise prices or set a cover or minimum.

The minimum had been established by the Normandy the previous Friday, July 24th, and was discussed heatedly by Gay Lib at the following Sunday meeting. It was then decided to leaflet on Thursday and picket the Normandy on Friday, after the dance at Circle Campus.

The picket line was led by members of the recently formed black caucus of Gay Liberation. On Saturday, the Normandy agreed to drop the minimum if we would drop the picketing. As of this writing the minimum has not been reestablished and the Normandy is well-patronized by both black and white gay people.

DOCUMENT 151
"Zapping the Zephyr"
Gay Dealer, ca. Dec. 1970, 20

Once again gay people have been oppressed and discriminated against. In Washington, D.C., Friday night November 28th, during the Revolutionary Peoples' Constitutional Convention, gay brothers were ripped-off by the owners and patrons of the Zephyr Restaurant. Four brothers, a Puerto Rican from D.C., a Black from Boston, a white from Virginia, and myself, a White from Berkeley, were refused service because we were gay.

The Puerto Rican brother was wearing a pink beret and a little makeup. He and I were holding arms.

The owner refused to serve us and told us to leave as a couple of his butch fraternity-bouncer types backed him up. After an argument we left to return to relate what had happened to our brothers at the Convention.

Forty of us returned to sit in the bar to demand we be served. The manager refused and told us all to get out. . . .

After the manager called the police, a couple of the football-player-type patrons at the bar started throwing bottles and punches at the people there. Gay people fought back to defend ourselves. The place exploded: tables turned, windows smashed, and a couple straights were hurt. We split, figuring the pigs would support the owner.

As we did, the bar pigs were ganging up on one brother in the street. I went back to help him but the uniformed pigs arrived and threw us up against the car (wall). We managed to escape, as they didn't have things too together and the press was arriving. We returned to our van around the corner, made sure everyone was accounted for, then drove away. We were pulled over a few blocks away and were brought in.

The pigs drew guns, took us to the pigpen, and began hours of harassment, threats, and insults. We were caged so that the pigs could come by, point at the queers, and exercise their oppressive attitudes. We were transferred to another jail before the trial, where we were further harassed.

At the hearing, the judge made evident his racism by allowing the two whites, who had university jobs, to return to the schools until the trial. Two Puerto Ricans and two Black brothers were detained in Washington, D.C. until the trial.

This incident is just another example of how pigs and pig courts continue to arrest and prosecute the oppressed, blame them for anything that happens, and close their eyes to the real sources of trouble. . . .

DOCUMENT 152
"Snooper's Office Invaded: Quack, Who's a Duck?"
The Advocate, 17 Feb. 1971, 1, 2

The theatre district around Times Square in midtown Manhattan has seen many a turkey in its time, but on Monday afternoon, January 18, the ducks took over.

Chanting "Duck Power" and carrying signs with such slogans as "I'm proud to be a duck," about 65 members of the Gay Activists Alliance, New York's militant but nonviolent gay organization, staged a demonstration on 42nd Street outside of Fidelifacts of Greater New York and invaded the office of the founder and president of the investigatory agency, Vincent Gillen.

The quacking, chanting, angry Gays were protesting Fidelifacts' role as a collector of information on the private sexual lives of individuals and then selling that information to prospective employers. The duck motif was GAA's way of dramatizing a stereotyped pattern of behavior that Gillen has ascribed to all Gays.

"Establishing that someone is a homosexual is often difficult," Gillen told executives of the Association of Stock Exchange Brokers some time ago, "but I like to go on the rule of thumb that if one looks like a duck, walks like a duck, associates only with ducks, and quacks like a duck, he is probably a duck."

And so, responded GAA, what's wrong with being a duck? Quacking mightily under the leadership of Chief Duck Marty Robinson, the activists set up a sidewalk picket line and passed out leaflets on fair employment legislation pending in the New York City Council, while President Jim Owles and other members of the organization confronted Gillen in his office.

Gillen's position—televised later the same evening as part of WOR-TV's coverage of the event—was that "we are only in the business of making reports. We have nothing to do with the way the employer uses the information we provide."

Owles noted afterward that this argument might well have been made also by the manufacturers of gas ovens for Auschwitz or of Napalm for use in Vietnam. . . .

DOCUMENT 153

"'Syndicate' Lesbian Bar Zapped by N.Y. DOB"

The Advocate, 1 Sept. 1971, 2

In yet another public protest at exploitation of gay customers in allegedly syndicate-controlled bars here, some 75 Gays of both sexes heavily zapped Kooky's, one of Manhattan's only two exclusively lesbian bars, at midnight July 31. . . .

Kooky's, at 149 W. 14th St., was singled out for the latest zap because of its reputedly high-handed treatment of its "captive" lesbian clientele.

Customers familiar with its operation said the management charged a minimum $1 for a "watered-down" drink or a beer and that patrons were required to check their coats (for a 50-cent "gratuity") even if they didn't wish to.

DOB members were joined by others of the Gay Women's Liberation Front and by males of the Gay Activists Alliance. Their expressed purpose was to persuade customers inside Kooky's to leave. Amid a brief scuffle between the bar's bouncer at the door and protesters outside, many did. . . .

DOCUMENT 154

Elsa Gidlow, "Sisters Take a Stand"

Ain't I a Woman, 25 Sept. 1970, 12[2]

In February the Second Bay Area Women's Coalition Conference brought together a dozen or more groups and organizations concerned with different aspects of women's liberation. About 200 women participated. . . .

Of particular interest was the late afternoon panel discussion of lesbianism with representatives of NOVA, DOB [Daughters of Bilitis], and Gay Women's Liberation participating. This inclusion on the program was an advance over the first Caucus held last autumn when lesbians were kept invisible so far as the program was concerned. . . .

The lesbian panel climaxing the Conference's afternoon session...proved to be highly dramatic. More than one woman avowedly "straight" said she found the frank talks of the panelists and subsequent audience interchange the profoundest part of the program. . . .

Closing her talk, Alice Malloy said, "I was going to do something here, but was told it might not be advisable." As she paused and smiled over her audience one could sense a feeling of expectation: the women present wished her to go on. After a silence, Alice said, "I'll tell you what I had in mind and leave it to you. I was going to ask if every woman in the hall who had ever felt she could be erotically attracted to another woman would care to stand up."

After the electric statement the silence was tensely felt. Several women stood. A few more slowly followed. Then, like a dam bursting, practically every woman of the 200 or so in the hall was on her feet. Since the majority undoubtedly thought of themselves as "straight" and were living heterosexual lives, this could be seen as an expression of acceptance and sisterly solidarity, beautiful in its spontaneity. Perhaps also it was something of a group confession, for the atmosphere of relief was evident, and reflected in the frank give-and-take of the platform-audience interchange that followed.

DOCUMENT 155
"The Lavender Menace Strikes"
Come Out!, June 1970, 14

On Friday, May 1st, at 7:15 P.M. about 300 women were quietly sitting in the auditorium of intermediate School 70 waiting for the Congress to Unite Women to come to order. The lights went out, people heard running, laughter, a rebel yell here and there and when the lights were turned back on those same 300 women found themselves in the hands of the Lavender Menace.

"Lavender Menace," a taunt of the white male press rose incarnate in the persons of the Radicalesbians of New York who because of the discrimination and sexism with Women's Liberation took matters into their own hands to bring their affirmative and compelling awareness to the women at the Congress. For the first time since women's liberation began, the subject of lesbianism was brought into the open. Significantly the only way this could be done was forcefully, transcending established format—but although the take-over was decisive it was done with good feelings and humor.

Seventeen of the Radicalesbians wore lavender teeshirts with Lavender Menace stenciled across the front. These women were the first wave of the action and the ones who took over the auditorium. The second wave of the action was vocal support from about twenty sisters who hid their true lavender selves and blended into the audience. What we didn't expect was a third wave which came out of the general audience. Women responded variously—a very few left, the planning committee made a few tentative efforts to restore the "program," some women were pleasantly questioning the action but what was so incredible was the enthusiastic acceptance of most of the women. . . .

The action was so successful (we held the auditorium and the attention for two hours) because the issue is of such meaning and relevance at a gut level to all women and because the presentation was done in a humorous and non-threatening way. As the Menaces surrounded the audience and liberated the microphone, rose-colored signs sprang up on the walls and podium: SUPERDYKE LOVES YOU; TAKE A LESBIAN TO LUNCH; WOMEN'S LIBERATION IS A LESBIAN PLOT. Freed from a boring panel and able to come up to the microphone and talk to each other, women asked each other questions, confronted each other and gave testimony. Perhaps the most significant communication came in the form of the enthusiasm and joy felt by those present. . . .

DOCUMENT 156
Judy Burns and Robyn Lutzky, "LFL Zaps Museum of Natural History"
The Lesbian Feminist, Oct. 1973, 1, 2, 6, 7[3]

On Sunday, August 26, LFL [Lesbian Feminist Liberation] sponsored a demonstration at the Museum of Natural History. 200 women were present to protest the museum's sexist and racist labelling of exhibits, and lack of feminist anthropologists, research into the matriarchal era, and Lesbian history. Demonstrators marched around a 250 lb. lavender, plaster, female dinosaur, and the Victoria Woodhull Women's Marching Band serenaded protestors and passersby. Media coverage of the zap was fairly good.

On August 27, the Museum informed LFL that a female anthropologist was joining their staff as of September 16. Museum officials also agreed to a follow-up meeting with LFL on September 18. . . .

At approximately 10 A.M. on August 26, a group of women from Lesbian Feminist Liberation arrived at a basement on 99th Street and Broadway to pick up one 250 lb., lovingly made Dinosaur, to be hand delivered to the Museum of Unnatural History.

As we started down Columbus Avenue, with "Dinah," our Dykosaur, I thought back to that Wednesday night, one month earlier, when Cathy Williams and Midge Flynn told the Political Committee that they'd just come from the Museum and were appalled by how sexist and anti-feminist most of the exhibits were. They also stated that there were not enough feminist anthropologists on the staff, and that they felt our first zap for L.F.L. should be on that museum. Political Committee agreed.

Cathy and Midge had already written up a set of demands. . . . I suggested building a dinosaur in order to call as much attention as possible to our zap. Originally Dinah was to be 20 feet long and 8 feet wide, but considering that she had to be built in an apartment basement and carried out a narrow alley, she was scaled down to 4 feet wide and 15 feet long. . . .

As we approached 81st Street and Columbus Avenue, one block from the museum, we all started singing "Hail, Hail the Dykes are Here." There was tremendous spirit in all of us, despite having to carry the Dinosaur some twenty-two blocks. As we rounded the corner of the Museum the Victoria Woodhull Women's Marching Band accompanied our singing. We all felt good, because it was LFL's first zap, and a good choice too!

DOCUMENT 157
Joanie Millard, "First Nat'l Lesbian Kiss-In"
Lesbian Tide, Dec. 1973, 3–4

October 20, 1973 marked the first National Lesbian Kiss-In held on the steps of the Los Angeles County Museum of Art, and sponsored by lesbians from the

Westside Women's Center and the Gay Community Service Center of Los Angeles. Approximately 75 Southern California lesbians proudly gathered together in anticipation of that big moment at noon when, as gay sisters, they would openly hug and kiss. . . .

In our struggle we are always talking about the absolute need for sisterhood and one woman proved that sisterly love is alive and well and flourishing at Lesbian Demonstrations. This woman approached me and said "I'm straight and I'm a feminist and I really think I should be heard because I think it's important that straight women come out and support their gay sisters since they are so oppressed."

In response to this oppression the lesbian sisters, at exactly 12:00, kissed and hugged and seemed almost oblivious to the sounds of cameras from major L.A. radio and television stations clicking in their ears.

When asked how she felt about making her feelings public, Jan Field, of U.C.L.A.'s Gay Sisterhood, replied:

"If I didn't express my feelings in public, and I do continually, it's like forgiving or apologizing for my love and I won't do that as I feel very good about it. So this is a very strong statement for me and I think for all the lesbians. It means an awful lot to openly say to our parents and to the public that this is right and this is good."

Jan also answered the question as to whether or not today's actions would be antagonizing to heterosexual observers.

"Straight people often perceive two women who kiss in public or hold hands in public or walk arm in arm, just as a heterosexual couple would do, as crusading and pushing their ideas off on the rest of the public where in effect, it's a common right. They don't stop to think that they do this all the time in their lives but if we do it we antagonize them and are denied our self-rights." . . .

The women who sponsored the Kiss-In had this to say in their statement, an attitude shared by lesbians everywhere.

"We are Lesbians. We are the people who have firsthand knowledge of the beauty and righteousness of love between women.

"Today is the beginning. The beginning of a new world based on the premise that we, as working, supporting members of a society, are entitled to the basic rights of life, liberty and the open expression of happiness.

"Our evolving pride will no longer allow us to hide among the substrata of socially acceptable robots going through the motions of living in a 'free' society. Nor will it allow us to settle for an amenable tolerance based on the agreement to stay out of your sight and your minds.

"Instead we are motivated by and dedicated to the vision of a future radically different from the past, a future which will accommodate the wildest dreams of the Lesbian people and all other people.

"We as Lesbians are taking charge of our own destinies. For your own sake, support us in our struggle to build the future. If you can't be of help, step aside. Either way, there will be no turning back."

DOCUMENT 158

"Gay 'Pope' Steps Up Campaign"

GAY, 20 Apr. 1970, 15

Calling himself Pope Morris I and calling March 1 "Lavender Sunday," Morris Kight of the L.A. Gay Liberation Front confronted more L.A. churches with demands for reparations.

About 30 GLF marchers were with him on the designated Lavender Sunday and they set out to picket three churches. The group told churchgoers as they left services, "Christ never condemned us," and "Love thy neighbor," and "The church is guilty of genocide." They also proclaimed "Gay is Good!"

Catholics at St. Basil Cathedral didn't take the confrontation too well. They made rebuttals such as "You will all burn in hell, perverts," or "God hates you," or "You should all be killed." "Commie Faggot" came across too.

Members of Christ Unity were warm and receptive. "Wonderful!" one churchgoer said. Another said, "Christ is with you," and another said "Thank you!"

But most uptight was the First Congregational Church, whose members went to police to ask their help in discouraging picketers. GLF and Pope Morris I decided it might be best to leave this congregation alone with their guilt, and called off the picket. . . .

DOCUMENT 159

Sister Cocaine, "Vatican Rags at Grace Cathedral"

Gay Sunshine, Jan. 1971, 14

Every Christmas at Grace Cathedral, located in the Pacific Heights area of San Francisco, there is a traditional midnight mass. This year there was a complete mind-fuck when the congregation turned around to find The Angel of Light. The performing troupe consisted of forty children dressed in home-made angel wings and phallic halos (biblical drag?) and the Cockettes. The Cockettes are a Gay theatrical collective located in the Haight. . . .

The many costumes used in the shows are re-cycled rags and clothes retrieved from junk stores and from donations. Hibiscus of the Cockettes produced the street theatre re-enactment of the birth of Christ.

When we arrived at the church, the troupe and an entourage of onlookers were assembled on the cathedral steps, while the performers were caroling.

Soon we moved into the main chamber of the church. When we entered, communion rites were being performed. Several Gay couples walked hand in hand to the altar. Heretofore, the people sitting in the pulpit area had no knowledge of our presence. Our exhibition nicely set the stage for what Hibiscus had planned. Tahara, one of the Cockettes, lit some incense to further create the atmosphere we wanted. Suddenly there appeared a rear guard in the main archway. About twenty San Francisco pigs positioned themselves in attack formation. Out of nowhere a pig appeared next to Tahara, and demanded that the incense be extinguished; when Tahara explained that it could not be put out after it was lit, the pig confiscated our theatrical sacrament and poured water over it.

As soon as the scheduled mass concluded we were informed that we were to leave the church immediately. FAR OUT. On Xmas Eve the parishioners had us thrown out of a church. . . .

DOCUMENT 160
"DOB Pickets St. Patrick's"
The Advocate, 28 Apr. 1971, 9

NEW YORK CITY—Twenty women and two men picketed St. Patrick's Cathedral here Mar. 22 in a demonstration organized by the Daughters of Bilitis.

The demonstration was in support of Women's Lib leader Ti-Grace Atkinson, who set off a furor in a speech at Washington's Catholic University Mar. 10 in which she charged the church with oppressing women.

Patricia Bozell, sister of columnist William Buckley and conservative Sen. James Buckley of New York and wife of Brent Bozell, editor of the Catholic magazine *Triumph*, ran to the podium and tried to slap Miss Atkinson, 32, when Miss Atkinson said the Virgin Mary had been "knocked up" so she could be used as a "vessel."

Miss Atkinson later said her speech had drawn a violent reaction because "for the first time in 2000 years, a woman had stood up to the church."

Ruth Simpson, president of the New York DOB, said the picketing of St. Patrick's was also intended "to make the statement that the Catholic Church has been one of the major oppressors of homosexuals." . . .

DOCUMENT 161
"500 Angry Homosexuals Protest Raid"
GAY, 13 Apr. 1970, 3, 10

POLITICAL PROTESTS
AFTER STONEWALL

Outraged and horrified by the bizarre events connected with a pre-dawn raid on a well-known gay bar, approximately 500 homosexual men and women surged through the streets of Greenwich Village in a massive show of strength on the night of March 8. As they moved, shouts and chants of GAY POWER! filled the air. . . .

The G.A.A. leaflet that inspired the demonstration told the gruesome story concisely: "SNAKEPIT RAIDED. 167 ARRESTED. ONE BOY NEAR DEATH AT ST. VINCENT'S. Police raided the Snakepit at corner of Bleecker and West 10th last night. 167 were arrested and given summonses for disorderly conduct. One boy either fell or jumped out precinct window, landed and was *impaled* on a metal fence! Any way you look at it, that boy was PUSHED!! We are all being pushed! Fighting Gays and any of you who call yourselves HUMAN BEINGS with guts to stand up to this horror—gather at Sheridan Square tonight at 9 to march on the 6th precinct. Stop the Raids! Defend your Rights!"

The leaflet stated there would also be a death watch vigil at the hospital, an assumption based on dire reports of the condition of the individual who tried to leap to freedom. Six fourteen-inch iron prongs had pierced his body and leg, thigh, and pelvis. To avoid further injury, firemen had had to use a blowtorch to cut a section of the fence, and then he had been taken to the hospital operating room with the spikes still in his body. Surgeons had labored for hours that morning to save his life. Pictures of his impaled body were spread across the *Daily News*. As of this writing, nearly two weeks later, he is still listed as critical. During the demonstration he lay in a coma.

The G.A.A. demonstration picked up support from members of the Gay Liberation Front . . . , the Homophile Youth Movement, Homosexuals Intransigent and many, many members of the gay community who are not affiliated with any organization. Village residents straight and gay emerged from their apartments and swelled the ranks of the crowd as it swept through the streets. Others gaped from their windows and doorways. Men who had been arrested in the raid also joined the demonstration. Father James Weeks of the Church of the Holy Apostles also marched. . . .

At the police barricades spread before the 6th precinct house, the crowd angrily and insistently called for the police captain: "WE WANT SALMEIRI . . . !"

When this individual refused to appear, the chants changed again. "WHO GETS THE PAY-OFF? THE POLICE GET THE PAY-OFF. . . !" Then, "THERE'S THE MAFIA IN BLUE. . . !"

Dozens of police in pale blue helmets were amassed in the street and on the station house steps, behind the barricades. Jim Owles, president of G.A.A., and Father Weeks approached the officer in charge of their defensive line.

Owles contended that three or four representatives should be allowed to enter the station and to confront verbally Captain Salmeiri or whoever was in command at that hour. He argued that the crowd would be mollified, however slightly, and the potential for rioting then and there would be substantially reduced if the police would listen to representatives. The police refused. . . .

Jim Owles turned to the frustrated demonstrators. "Our brother lies near death at St. Vincent's Hospital! We've made our point to the police by our numbers! Now we will march in solemn procession to the hospital."

The crowd cooled and headed for St. Vincent's. Some carried lighted candles. Before the large hospital, and occupying every inch of sidewalk space, the demonstrators halted to hear a prayer offered by Father Weeks for the recovery of the man inside who lay in critical condition in the intensive care unit. They proceeded to march in silence around the block containing the hospital, resuming chants of GAY POWER only after heading back to their starting point, Sheridan Square. . . .

At the close, hoarse from angry shouting and chanting, the demonstrators were scarcely able to handle the singing of WE SHALL OVERCOME, upon their return to Sheridan Square. G.A.A. officers, who had worked to organize the demonstration since being telephoned by one of the arrested men at 7:30 that morning, wearily called the demonstration to a close. Jim Owles, nearly unable to speak, announced that blood was needed by the hospital for the critically injured man and urged its donation. He expressed his appreciation for the fact that despite political and ideological differences, members of a variety of homophile groups had been able to join together and work together in what was to be the largest and angriest planned gay demonstration thus far in the history of the homosexual movement in this country. . . .

DOCUMENT 162
Douglas Key, "Gays Plan Marches, Leather Sunday"
Los Angeles Free Press, 13 Mar. 1970, 3, 15

. . . About 200–250 Gays rallied in downtown Los Angeles Sunday evening, held a memorial service for homosexual martyr Howard Efland and marched on the police headquarters. . . .

A floral wreath was placed at the entrance of the Dover Hotel where Efland (who was also known as J. McCann) was taken from his room one year ago and beaten to death by police.

The wreath was then taken to a spot in an alley and a service was held by Reverend Troy Perry of the Committee for Homosexual Law Reform.

Standing in a flat-bed truck, Perry shouted emotionally, "It disgusts me to know that in this country someone could have the license to kill another human being simply because of what a person does in bed. In no way can the actions of the persons responsible be called "excusable homicide." Perry attacked the coroner's hearing on Efland's death as false and obscene.

Morris Kight of the Gay Liberation Front also spoke and stressed non-violent methods.

About a fourth of the marchers were black, and there were many female homosexuals.

The Gays then marched a mile and a half to the police headquarters building, and picketed the entrance while Reverend Perry went inside and delivered a letter to a representative of police chief Davis. The letter demanded an immediate end to police entrapment of Gays and an immediate end to arrests of persons for sex acts. . . .

DOCUMENT 163

"New Gay Riots Erupt in Greenwich Village: Demonstration Ends in Violent Melee"

GAY, 21 Sept. 1970, 1, 16

Eighteen persons were arrested when over 1000 homosexuals and onlookers were drawn into a riot situation in Greenwich Village on August 29. The melee followed a peaceful demonstration in Times Square called by Gay Liberation Front and Gay Activists Alliance to protest the new wave of police harassment in which over 300 homosexuals were arrested during August.

Over 350 demonstrators marched on 42nd Street between 7th and 8th Avenues demanding an immediate end to police harassment. The Saturday night crowd in the Times Square area was quite obviously surprised to see angry homosexuals shouting "Gay Power!" and "2-4-6-8, Gay Is Just as Good as Straight!" Police were out in large numbers and by their presence prevented any untoward incidents from occurring in the crowded area.

The GAA leaflet for the occasion read in part, "Police are illegally arresting homosexuals on charges of loitering, disorderly conduct, unlawful assembly, and solicitation. These cases are thrown out of court when brought before a judge. . . . We demand an end to police harassment of homosexuals." . . .

By contrast, the GLF leaflet for the occasion read in part: "The time for gays to take matters into their own hands is now. Talking to police commissioners is doing no good. We will be oppressed as long as we do not have the power to fight back.... THE TIME OF THE PIG IS OVER, THE TIME OF THE PEOPLE IS HERE." . . .

After marching around the key block on 42nd Street a half dozen times, the protesters then marched past the 14th Precinct Police Station on West 35th Street, the station where homosexuals who are arrested in Times Square are booked. Police were massed in front of the building as demonstrators filed by shouting "End Police Harassment, End Police Harassment!"

The gay crowd then chose 7th Avenue as its route to Greenwich Village. . . . As the marchers came to the Village proper, GLF passed the word that it would march around the Women's House of Detention to protest that controversial institution's very existence. Because GAA is a nonviolent organization working exclusively for the gay cause, GAA folded its banner and officially ended its participation in the march at Greenwich and Christopher Streets. GLF moved on to the House of Detention shouting "Hey, Hey, Ho, Ho, House of D Has Got to Go!" GAA members began to disperse, but streets became clogged as more and more Village residents, gay and straight, gathered in the streets to lend support or watch the happenings. Streets were soon filled with over 1000 people shouting "Gay Power" and "End Police Harassment!" The crowd moved toward Sheridan Square.

At that moment, police were discovered to be harassing The Haven, a partly straight and partly gay night club in the Square. The crowd surged forward, with scores of men and women shouting and yelling at the doorway of the establishment. Police reacted, emerging in a flying wedge from the night club, their night sticks raised. The crowd scrambled back, dispersing in every possible direction. A few were actually struck by police. . . .

GLF members regrouped and led another march on the Women's House of Detention. As they demonstrated in the street and urged the abolishment of that institution, the women in the House of Detention began to riot. They yelled down to the crowd; they threw burning rags and papers from the windows. Demonstrators urged them on, as sirens wailed.

Police swarmed into the area to quell the riot inside the House of Detention and to break up the massive crowd. Gay extremists began hurling bottles at police. One source said bottles were also hurled from a roof-top in the area. Police reacted and attacked the demonstrators. A group of police brutally beat one demonstrator and dragged him away face down. Many demonstrators began yelling, "Off the Pig, Kill the Pigs!" Fires were started in litter baskets, store windows were smashed, two GLF lesbians kissed each other in front of a bank window that was smashed. A record shop was looted, and two cars were reportedly overturned.

In all, eighteen arrests were made and several gay people and several police were injured. . . .

Sunday night, many homosexuals were on the same streets again. Hundreds of gays marched in a spontaneous parade through the Village that began about 10:30 p.m. By 1:00 a.m., six gays had been taken into custody by police. . . .

The righteous rage of the homosexual community has surfaced once again. However, this time extremists stood ready to escalate the situation and turn it to sure violence. They came ready with bottles, which they called ammunition.

Conditions which prompted the spontaneous Stonewall riot last summer, police harassment and bar raids, have not been corrected. Leaders of Gay Activists Alliance said that city officials had been told of the growing indignation in the community over police harassment, but had done nothing. GAA is seeking another meeting with Police Commissioner Howard Leary to repeat its demand for a cessation of harassment. Until police harassment of the gay community is ended, a highly explosive situation will continue. . . .

POLITICAL PROTESTS
AFTER STONEWALL

DOCUMENT 164
"New Orleans Mayor Sees Irate Gays"
The Advocate, 17 Feb. 1971, 1, 12

Representatives of the two-month-old Gay Liberation Front here were to meet with Mayor "Moon" Landrieu Jan. 28 in the wake of six days of demonstrations at City Hall against police brutality and harassment of Gays.

The demonstrations began Jan. 23, when about 75 GLF members picketed City Hall. . . .

The demonstrators carried such signs as "Stop Police Brutality," "2-4-6-8, Gay Is Just as Good as Straight," and "Lesbians Are Loveable."

GLF literature put out at the time of the initial demonstration listed three separate incidents of police entrapment of Gays at Cabrini Playground on Barracks Street in the French Quarter.

At least 13 arrests and four beatings of Gays by police had been reported in the Quarter the week of Jan. 10.

The organization was making three demands:

"(1) An immediate end of all hostility, brutality, entrapment and harassment by New Orleans police of gay men and women, and of their places of gathering.

"(2) Formation of a governor's panel empowered to conduct a complete and thorough investigation of the police methods and actions against gay people. On this panel shall sit one gay man and one woman.

"(3 The immediate suspension from duty of Police Superintendent Clarence Giarrusso and Vice Squad head Sgt. Robert Frey until the governor's panel has completed its investigation. Should the panel find against these men, they shall be terminated immediately." . . .

DOCUMENT 165
"GAA Confronts Lindsay at Museum"
GAY, 4 May 1970, 3

New York, N.Y.—On April 12th, Mayor John Lindsay was treated to several confrontations with gay men and women at a gala celebration of the 100th anniversary of the Metropolitan Museum of Art. Members of the Gay Activists Alliance distributed leaflets which read as follows:

"Mr. Mayor, we are now initiating the introduction into the City Council a bill prohibiting job discrimination (in private industry as well as civil service) on the basis of sexual preference. We again ask you to speak out in support of the principles of this proposed legislation. Last month we went to City Hall. At that time, your counsel, Michael Dontzin, promised to bring this matter to your attention. WHY HAVEN'T YOU RESPONDED?"

Several confronters told the press that they had exhausted quieter means of getting the Mayor to address himself publically to their drive to extend New York's fair employment regulations to protect homosexuals in private industry.

Lindsay was first confronted when he took the podium in front of the Museum to deliver a welcoming address to several hundred persons gathered in the bright sunshine for the centennial celebration. Marty Robinson, GAA delegate-at-large, was able to approach the Mayor and ask him when he would speak out, but didn't get to finish. Police pulled Robinson back from the area.

After the address, the Mayor strolled around the new water fountain in front of the Museum, smiling constantly as he walked through the crowd. Security was surprisingly light. A leaflet was thrust into his hand; the Mayor looked it over, smiled, shrugged, and handed it to an aide.

As he climbed the steps to enter the Museum, GAA president Jim Owles stepped to his side and said, "You have our leaflet. Now when the hell are you going to speak to homosexuals?" The Mayor smiled impassively.

Activists who joined the reception line at the Museum entrance each gave Lindsay a long, firm handshake and demanded that he speak out. Some held the Mayor's grip so long that police had to pull them away. . . .

DOCUMENT 166

Guy Charles, "Intro 475 Controversy: Won't Be Sacrificial Lambs, Drags Vow"
The Advocate, 22 Dec. 1971, 12

NEW YORK CITY—In the wake of the second hearing on Intro 475 on Nov. 15, transvestites have emerged as a possible major complication in efforts to obtain passage of the measure outlawing discrimination in the hiring of homosexuals by city agencies.

Lee Brewster of Queens Liberation Front, speaking for the transvestites, has angrily accused "straight homosexuals" of trying "to sell your sister away and offer her up as a political sacrificial lamb."

"We won't go," he warned.

No one wants to admit it publicly, but many of those in the more conservative organizations—including a faction in the Gay Activists Alliance, see the transvestites as a needless embarrassment and are afraid that any insistence on specifically including them under the umbrella of the beleaguered bill may be all that it takes to kill it. . . .

Brewster, given the floor at a GAA meeting Nov. 18, pointed out that it had been the transvestites and queens who had turned on New York police at the Stonewall Club in June 1969.

"We gave you the most precious gift of all," he said, "a gift no law, no politician, no nothing could give you, at the Stonewall. With fires blazing, sirens blaring, hurling bricks and bottles, in our most unladylike fashion, we gave you and us *pride*! We founded the Gay Liberation Movement."

He also pointed out that the recent Department of Consumer Affairs action knocking out ordinances excluding homosexuals from New York cabarets and dance halls was the result of legal pressure by his group.

"We won these rights for the entire gay community," he told the GAA meeting. "And now we demand, in the name of justice and fair play, the same treatment. However, I must warn you that in the absence of your support, you will feel that heaven *and* hell hath no fury like a drag queen scorned." . . .

DOCUMENT 167
"S.F. Hiring Law Goes into Effect"
The Advocate, 24 May 1972, 3, 17

The amendment adding the words "sex and sexual orientation" to the city council civil rights ordinance became law in San Francisco Apr. 27.

The historic action, which one of its prime movers, Larry Littlejohn, called "the most far-reaching civil rights legislation affecting homosexuals in employment to date," was signed by Mayor Joseph Alioto without comment on Apr. 21.

San Francisco lost the distinction of being the first city in the nation with a ban on job discrimination against homosexuals actually on the books when East Lansing, Mich., amended its personnel rules Mar. 7 to bar such bias by city agencies.

The San Francisco ordinance, however, is more far-reaching. It includes all firms doing business with the city and county. . . .

Littlejohn and Del Martin of the Daughters of Bilitis, along with the National Organization for Women, first proposed the ordinance change in the Fall of 1969. At that time, Littlejohn was president of the Society for Individual Rights. . . .

Supervisor Dianne Feinstein, then president of the board, introduced the proposal as an amendment to the San Francisco Administrative Code last year. It languished in committee until Mrs. Feinstein brought it out for a vote Apr. 3. . . .

DOCUMENT 168
Rob Cole, "Two Men Ask Minnesota License for First Legal U.S. Gay Marriage"
The Los Angeles Advocate, 10 June 1970, 1, 4

Two young men in Minneapolis have applied for a license to marry each other. If the application is granted, their marriage next Dec. 31 will be the first legally recognized gay marriage in the United States.

The *Advocate* noted in a story in its May 13–26 edition that the marriage law in Minnesota—and possibly in California—is vague as to whether partners must be of the opposite sex, and all that remained was a test by some bold gay couple.

Jim McConnell, a librarian, and Jack Baker, a first-year law student at the University of Minnesota Law School—both 28, are making that test. They frankly expect to have to go to court before it's over.

Jim and Jack made their license application May 19. . . .

POLITICAL PROTESTS
AFTER STONEWALL

DOCUMENT 169

"Two L.A. Girls Attempt First Legal Gay Marriage"

The Los Angeles Advocate, 8 July 1970, 1, 5

The first marriage in the nation designed to legally bind two persons of the same sex was performed in Los Angeles June 12.

Two young women, Neva Joy Heckman and Judith Ann Belew, pledged their troth "until death do us part" in a simple double-ring ceremony conducted at their home by the Rev. Troy D. Perry, pastor of Metropolitan Community Church.

The occasion lent fresh significance to the minister's traditional admonition, "What God hath joined together, let no man put asunder."

A legal test of the marriage is expected.

The rites were conducted under a provision of California law that allows a common-law marriage to be formalized by a church ceremony and issuance of a church certificate when the couple have been together two years or more....

DOCUMENT 170

Pete Fisher, "Gay Couples Celebrate Engagement at Marriage License Bureau"

GAY, 5 July 1971, 1, 14

> *The Honorable Herman Katz,*
> *City Clerk, invites you*
> *to an engagement reception for*
> *Messrs. John Basso & John G. Bond*
> *Messrs. Steve Krotz & Vito Russo*
> *at his office,*
> *Room 265, Municipal Bldg.,*
> *Friday, June 4, 1971*
> *at 10:00 a.m.*
> *All welcome. Dress optional*
> *Sponsored by*
> *Gay Activists Alliance.*

New York, N.Y.—Shortly after 10:00 a.m. on Friday, June 4, approximately thirty-five GAA members hurried up the stairs to the second floor of the Municipal Building on Centre Street to the City Clerk's office, where applications for marriage licenses are available to those who meet the requirements of New York State's marriage laws. While twenty-five of the colorfully dressed gays occupied City Clerk Herman Katz's office, set up doughnuts and a coffee machine, and unveiled a multi-layer wedding cake, the others moved through the building in pairs, distributing "invitations" to the engagement party at

Katz's office. The cake, topped by a gold lambda and two tiny gay couples, two men and two women, bore the inscription: GAY POWER TO GAY LOVERS.

The unprecedented gay engagement party was the result of Mr. Katz's great interest in the propriety of gay relationships. A month earlier, after the *New York Post* had run an article on Father Robert Clement's Church of the Beloved Disciple and the ceremonies of Holy Union performed there for gay couples, Katz had phoned the *Post* to make an angry statement. . . .

Katz had expressed disgust at the idea of gay marriages and had stated that they were illegitimate. Furthermore, he intended to file suit against Clement for performing "illegal" marriage ceremonies.

GAA, which takes no stand on the issue of gay marriages or on that of homosexuals and religion, felt that Katz's action represented a clear-cut case of discrimination against homosexuals and the gay community. Father Clement, the activists pointed out, had never claimed that the ceremonies of Holy Union which he performed were legally binding under the laws of New York State. The ceremonies were an expression of private religious faith and personal love and commitment—they had nothing to do with the state. . . .

It was decided that Mr. Katz must be confronted and told to "keep his nose out of gay relationships." Two couples in GAA who planned to be married over the summer said they would enjoy nothing more than a lively engagement party in Mr. Katz's office. . . .

The engagement party started off in a light vein. The gays simply moved into the office, set up their coffee, cake, and doughnuts, and engaged the city employees there in friendly raps about the issues involved. Mr. Katz was not at work that day, and when one of his assistants inquired as to just what was going on, he received an apology for not having been given an invitation. This failed to improve his spirits.

If the gays had no appointment, he said, they were trespassing on private property and were subject to arrest. "Mr. Katz has been trespassing in private lives!" shouted an angry activist, and asked since when a city office was considered to be private property, barred to tax-paying citizens. Unable to come up with an appropriate answer, the assistant hastily called for reinforcements in the form of First Deputy City Clerk Thomas Lelane, Katz's second-in-command.

Lelane was not about to speak to the visiting homosexuals about the reasons for the zap. "You're not allowed in a public office without an appointment!" he bellowed. "Why not, because we're gay?" retorted a protester. The rhetoric on both sides quickly escalated, and while GAY POWER chants rang out through the office, Lelane hurriedly placed a call to the police, claiming he needed immediate assistance because the demonstrators were "getting violent." Meanwhile, the gays continued to serve coffee and doughnuts to the office workers.

A truly gay atmosphere prevailed for the next half hour until the police arrived. One of the demonstrators, armed with a guitar and the lyrics to several gay lib songs, led some of the visitors in gay folk-singing, while others danced between the desks. People from other offices in the building arrived and began to enjoy the unprecedented spectacle. Arthur Evans helped out by answering the office phone each time it rang: "Hello, Gay Activists Alliance. A marriage license? Yes, this is the place. We're specializing in gay marriages today. Are you gay? Stop by and have a piece of cake at our engagement party."

When the police arrived, they were hard put to find any signs of violence. Mr. Lelane quickly denied that he had claimed that the gays were getting violent. The police seemed to find it hard to take the situation seriously. They were friendly and courteous, although they said they would have to ask the gays to leave or else face arrest, due to Lelane's complaint. One police officer remarked, "I don't see how any thinking person can object to what you're asking." . . .

DOCUMENT 171
"Federal Building 'Work-In' Protests U.S. Hiring Policy"
The Advocate, 7 July 1971, 4

SAN FRANCISCO—Gay activists succeeded in corralling the attention of the media June 7 when they staged an all-day "Work-In" protest at the Federal Building here.

Two of the demonstrators were arrested but almost immediately released without being charged.

Sponsored by the Society for Individual Rights with the aid of the newly formed Gay Activists Alliance here, the demonstration was designed as a piece of theatre to protest federal policy which generally prevents known or suspected homosexuals from working for their country.

About 20 demonstrators infiltrated the Federal Building early in the morning. Wearing badges that read "Homosexual Working for the Government," the Gays swept corridors and operated elevators in the building.

When guards asked them to leave, the demonstrators considered themselves "fired" and reported to an "unemployment office" that had been set up outside, basically to attract the attention of photographers and cameramen.

Meanwhile, other protestors passed out leaflets inside the building which read, in part, "Hello, my name is ————. I am here today as an openly identified homosexual to work for the Federal Government."

The statement claimed that "hundreds" of homosexuals already worked in the building, but they "would immediately lose their jobs if the nature of their private sexual lives were known to the Civil Service Commission."

The playlet appeared to throw security guards in the building into total confusion. When Lyle Gerard, a Montana Blackfoot Indian with long black hair, and other demonstrators began acting as elevator operators— though the elevators in the building are automatic, the guards did not immediately react.

But after a few minutes, the security forces, guards of the General Services Administration, the federal housekeeping agency, began to rally. Joe Abrev, one of the demonstrators who was pushing a broom in the lobby, was determinedly escorted out of the building by one guard, who then proceeded to rope off that entrance.

Meanwhile, other guards were attempting to deal with the "elevator operators," leading to the only major confrontation of the protest.

Former SIR [Society for Individual Rights] president Larry Littlejohn and Gay Liberation activist Leo Laurence, who had been handing out leaflets, stepped into an elevator to take some of the leaflets up to the 11th floor offices of the Civil Service Commission. Guard Captain Houston Smith appeared.

"He blocked the door and wouldn't let us use the elevator or leave it," Littlejohn said. "I asked him if we were being arrested, and he just said, 'You'll have to get out.'"

As television cameras zeroed in on the scene, Smith appeared to become flustered. He closed the door and took Littlejohn and Laurence to the 16th floor, after saying he was arresting them on charges of trespassing and illegally distributing handbills.

The "suspects" were searched and fingerprinted and put briefly in a holding cell. Then they were taken to the basement of the building.

"I thought, now comes the beating," Littlejohn said later, half-seriously.

But in the basement, he said, the two were given a brief lecture and turned loose. They rejoined the demonstrators and answered questions about their "arrest" from television reporters, taking the opportunity to deplore job discrimination by the federal government. . . .

DOCUMENT 172
Cary Yurman, "GAA Protests Rocky's Silence"
GAY, 24 Aug. 1970, 3, 12

New York, N.Y.—Over 100 people carrying signs and proudly shouting, "2-4-6-8, gay is just as good as straight," and "3-5-7-9, sodomy is mighty fine," enthusiastically picketed outside the Criminal Court building and rallied in Foley Square Park on August 5. The demonstrators demanded that Governor Nelson A. Rockefeller end his long hostile silence towards his homosexual constituents and speak out on homosexual issues. The demonstrators also showed their strong support of the Rockefeller 5.

The Rockefeller 5 are five members of the Gay Activists Alliance who were arrested for sitting-in at the Republican State Committee offices last June when Republicans refused to hear GAA's six demands. The demands are the repeal of New York state sodomy and solicitation laws, an end to police enticement and entrapment throughout the state, an end to the harassment of gay bars statewide, a state fair employment law outlawing discrimination on the basis of sexual orientation, an end to the bonding companies' practice of denying bonds to homosexuals, and an investigation of the State Liquor Authority.

Outside the Criminal Court building, where the Rockefeller 5 were ordered to appear, sixty homosexuals angrily picketed and loudly demanded civil rights for homosexuals. GAA had called for the support of homosexuals and homosexual groups throughout the city, and the picket line indicated the positive response. Members of the Gay Liberation Front and the Daughters of Bilitis joined the picket line. . . .

At the rally in Foley Square Park, speeches were made by Morty Manford of GAA, Arthur Evans, one of the Rockefeller 5, Hank Ferrari of the New York GLF, Hiram Ruiz of the Florida State University chapter of the GLF, and Isabel Miller, a member of D.O.B. . . .

After the rally, the crowd, still enthusiastic, returned to picket in front of the Criminal Court building to reach as many people as possible during the lunch hour. The picketing continued throughout the lunch hour with chants, songs, and determination. . . .

DOCUMENT 173
"McCarthy, Kennedy Support Gay Rights; Muskie Reneges"
Gay Activist, Dec. 1971, 6[4]

In what is only the beginning of long-overdue demands from the gay community on 1972 Presidential hopefuls, New York Gays began confrontations of [U.S. Senators] Muskie, McCarthy, and Kennedy in November.

McCarthy and Kennedy issued favorable statements. McCarthy, in a street dialogue with the president of Gay Youth, said he would support an amendment to the 1964 civil rights act which would make it illegal to discriminate on the basis of one's sexual orientation.

Kennedy, when pressured, was quoted as saying: "I'd endorse and support civil rights of homosexuals. It's time that discrimination on the basis of security grounds ended and I can see no reason for keeping people from having jobs solely because of their homosexuality." Stating that all citizens are entitled to their basic civil rights, Kennedy spoke in favor of the idea of a Presidential executive order "if necessary" in order to bar discrimination against homosexuals in the government.

Senator Muskie was confronted by Hal Offen, GAA's newly-elected Delegate-at-Large, during a speech by the Senator at NYU. Offen demanded to know Muskie's views on repeal of the sodomy laws. The Senator replied that he hadn't thought the question over. With a possible 20 million Americans participating in homosexual acts, according to the Kinsey statistics, and the 1972 elections drawing closer every day, Muskie as well as other "uncommitted" candidates had better start thinking.

DOCUMENT 174

Guy Charles, "A New National Gay Rights Platform"

The Advocate, 15 Mar. 1972, 1, 34

CHICAGO—The National Gay Conference on Political Strategy here Feb. 11–13 drew some 200 delegates from 86 groups around the country and produced a 1972 gay rights platform and a national structure to implement it.

The new structure, the National Coalition of Gay Organizations, is the first attempt to draw in the many diverse groups in the country since the demise of the North American Conference of Homophile Organizations. . . .

The text of the gay rights platform follows:

Millions of gay women and men in this country are subject to severe social, economic, legal and psychological oppression because of their sexual orientation.

We affirm the right of all persons to define and express their own sensibility, emotionality and sexuality and to choose their own life-style, so long as they do not infringe upon the rights of others. We pledge an end to all social, economic and legal oppression of gay women and men.

We demand the repeal of all laws forbidding voluntary sex acts involving consenting persons in private.

Laws prohibiting loitering for the purpose of soliciting for a homosexual liaison are vague and unconstitutional. Nevertheless, they are frequently used as the legal cover for police entrapment of gay women and men.

We demand the repeal of all laws prohibiting solicitation for a voluntary private sexual liaison.

Prejudice and myth have led to widespread discrimination against gay women and men.

We demand the enactment of civil rights legislation which will prohibit discrimination because of sexual orientation, in employment, housing, public accommodations and public services.

DEMANDS:

Federal:

1. Amend all federal Civil Rights Acts, other legislation and governmental controls to prohibit discrimination in employment, housing, public accommodations and public services because of one's sexual orientation.
2. Issuance by the President of an executive order prohibiting the military from excluding persons who of their own volition desire entrance to the Armed Forces for reasons of their sexual orientation and from issuing less-than-fully honorable discharges for homosexuality and the upgrading to fully honorable of all such discharges for homosexuality previously issued with retroactive benefits.

3. Issuance by the President of an executive order prohibiting discrimination in the Federal Civil Service because of sexual orientation in hiring and promoting, and prohibiting discrimination against gay women and men in security clearances.

4. Elimination of tax inequities victimizing single persons and same-sex couples.

5. Elimination of bars to the entry, immigration, and naturalization of homosexual aliens.

6. Federal encouragement and support for sex education courses prepared and taught by qualified gay women and men, presenting homosexuality as a valid, healthy preference and life-style and as a viable alternative to heterosexuality.

7. Appropriate executive orders, regulations, and legislation banning the compiling, maintenance, and dissemination of the information on individual sexual preferences, behavior and social and political activities for dossiers and data banks and ordering the immediate destruction of all such existing data.

8. Federal funding of aid projects by gay women's and men's organizations designed to alleviate the problems encountered by gay women and men which are engendered by an oppressive sexist society.

9. Immediate release of all gay women and men now incarcerated in detention centers, prisons and mental institutions, because of sexual offenses relating to victimless crimes or their sexual orientation and that adequate compensation be made for the mental and physical duress encountered and that all existing records relating to the incarceration be immediately expunged.

State:

1. All federal legislation and programs enumerated in Demands 1, 6, 7, 8, and 9 above should be implemented at the state level where applicable.

2. Repeal of all state laws prohibiting private sexual acts involving consenting persons; equalization for homosexuals and heterosexuals of the enforcement of all laws.

3. Repeal all state laws prohibiting solicitation for private voluntary sexual liaisons and those laws prohibiting prostitution, both male and female.

4. Enactment of legislation prohibiting insurance companies and any other state-regulated enterprises from discriminating because of sexual orientation, in insurance and in bonding or any other control of one's personal demeanor.

5. Enactment of legislation so that child custody, adoption, visitation rights, foster parenting and the like shall not be denied because of sexual orientation or marital status.

6. Repeal of all laws oppressing transvestism and cross-dressing.

7. Repeal of all laws governing the age of sexual consent.
8. Repeal of all legislative provisions that restrict the sex or number of persons that enter into a unit of marriage, and the extension of all legal benefits to all persons who cohabit regardless of sex and number.

DOCUMENT 175

"Democratic Convention Airs Gay Lib Proposals"

GAY, 7 Aug. 1972, 1, 10

Miami Beach, Florida—Two homosexual McGovern delegates to the Democratic National Convention were allotted ten minutes on the convention floor here to present the gay liberationists' minority rights plank. . . . Their bid was defeated, but both gay liberationists, according to those who watched them present the homosexual plank, spoke movingly and effectively of the need for such a plank.

Scheduled for early morning discussion, during a time (5:00 a.m.) when most Americans would be asleep, the gay delegates presented their case, nevertheless, on national television networks.

First on the agenda was Jim Foster, a McGovern delegate from California, and the Political Chairman for the Society for Individual Rights, one of the nation's largest gay lib organizations, with headquarters in San Francisco.

Next Madeline Davis, a New York McGovern delegate, and President of the Mattachine Society of the Niagara Frontier (Buffalo) explained to her fellow delegates that she was "someone's sister, someone's daughter." "I am a woman, I am a lesbian," said the 32-year-old communications worker. She called homosexuals "the untouchables of American society" and asked for a proposal affirming "the right of all persons to define and express their own sensibility, emotionality, and sexuality."

After the gay liberationists had presented their case to the Convention, a 21-year-old McGovern delegate, Mrs. Kathy Wilch (Ohio) argued negatively for ten minutes, contending that the acceptance of such a plank would open the Democratic Party to child molesters, prostitutes, pimps, and panderers. The Party, she said, would go down to a great defeat.

Although the gay liberation plank (as well as all of the minority planks) was defeated, there was considerable audible support for it from delegates in the convention hall. Those opposing the plank shouted louder, however.

DOCUMENT 176

John P. LeRoy, "Activists Invade McGovern Hqtrs."
GAY, 18 Sept. 1972, 1, 13

At about 11 a.m., Monday, August 21, a delegation of 25 or 30 members of the New York Gay Activists Alliance paid an unexpected visit to the McGovern for President headquarters at 605 Fifth Avenue in order to protest the Democratic Party's presidential nominee's apparent disavowal of his previous stand in support of gay rights. They spilled out onto the fourth, fifth and sixth floors, brought all campaign operations to a grinding halt, seized the switchboards, blocked all incoming and outgoing calls, and staged a good-natured sit-in. . . .

Three GAA members, Martin Clabby, Bruce Voeller and Jimmy Green, chained themselves to the phones at the main switchboards, told all incoming callers that the place was under the control of the gay liberationists, and hung up. A demonstration was formed outside McGovern Headquarters, leaflets were passed out, and singing and chanting for gay rights took place extemporaneously while reporters and TV cameramen from all major newspapers and networks took it all in. A minor scuffle broke out as the gays inside tried to seize the switchboard and presented the McGovern people with their demands. Bruce Voeller got knocked down, but as he lay there, the bright lights of the GAA videotape crew (GAA videotapes all major zaps and demonstrations in order to deter brutality through eyewitness evidence and to keep a historical record) beamed down on him. Someone shouted "Let him go," and Voeller proceeded to chain himself to the phone.

An anonymous call for the police went out, and several patrolmen arrived shortly thereafter, ready to make mass arrests. Ethan Geto . . . , on a leave of absence as press secretary to Bronx Borough President Abrams in order to handle the public relations for New York's McGovern campaign, asked the police to leave and discussed gay rights with the activists. . . .

According to GAA, the reason why they were occupying McGovern's New York Headquarters was to induce the Senator to publicly repudiate a speech made by Kathy Wilch at the Democratic National Convention, which was a vitriolic attack on gay rights. . . .

On February 12, during the primaries, McGovern had issued to various gay organizations a strong pro-homosexual position. After the convention, letters were received by Richard Wandel and Ernest Reaugh, GAA President and Tri-Cities GLF President, respectively, apparently from McGovern, stating that the Senator had not changed his position, and that the views of Ms. Wilch were not his. GAA members doubt that the letters are authentic. . . . That, coupled with a story in *The Advocate* which leads one to doubt the Senator's sincerity together with the fact that Sargent Shriver, McGovern's present running mate, has barred gays from the Peace Corps, had led the activists to demand that

McGovern or one of his top aides make a strong public statement immediately in support of his original stand. . . .

Geto . . . released the following statement to the press:

"Senator George McGovern has repeatedly affirmed his commitment to civil rights and civil liberties for all Americans. He has specifically addressed himself to discrimination directed against men and women based on sexual orientation, and has pledged to alleviate such discrimination in the federal government and in other areas of public life.

"Senator McGovern believes that discrimination based on sexual orientation should be eliminated."

But the gays did not find the press release of Geto's assurances acceptable, and resolved to keep the office under siege. . . .

Around five o'clock, the office had to be closed for the day, and Geto finally had to call the police. The gays were given a choice: either leave the premises or be arrested for trespassing. After a quick vote, the gays said they weren't leaving, and the police promptly arrested six activists. . . .

DOCUMENT 177
"Target Was Nixon: He's Angry"
The Advocate, 22 Nov. 1972, 1

PHILADELPHIA—Young Mark Segal of Philadelphia now has the dubious distinction of being the first gay activist to be denounced from the White House.

Segal and his little band called "Segal's Raiders" earned the wrath of the President by invading the annual GOP $100 a plate dinner here a few days before Nixon's victory over George McGovern in the Nov. 7 election.

At the Nov. 1 dinner, politics was still the order of the day. Clark MacGregor, chairman of the Committee to Re-Elect the President, was a few minutes into a speech when Segal left a table, walked boldly to the podium, and pulled out a large sign that had been folded in his pocket. On the sign in big black lettering were the words "Gay Power." With this held high above his head, Segal shouted, "Mr. MacGregor, Mr. MacGregor, there are over 20 million homosexuals in this country. What about their civil rights? What is President Nixon going to do for them?" MacGregor, shaken, stared down in disbelief as did most of the 3000 guests.

Segal was grabbed by a GOP committeeman who had been seated at a nearby table. The committeeman got a headlock on the young activist, and with the help of another dinner guest, led him from the room. Outside, things became a little nasty as several people began to beat up Segal. Although the beating wasn't serious, Segal intends to sue. . . .

News of the incident quickly reached to the White House, where President Nixon denounced Segal as well as demonstrators in other cities who disrupted appearances by Mrs. Nixon and Vice President Agnew.

In a press release Segal warned, "This is the first of many disruptions of Nixon and his administration throughout the country by gay raiders. This promise by Mark Segal will be kept until Nixon meets our demands."

DOCUMENT 178
"GLF and Women's Lib Zap Shrinks"
GAY, 8 June 1970, 3, 12

San Francisco, Calif.—On May 14th, a coalition of Gay Liberation Front and Women's Lib invaded the meeting of the American Psychiatric Association to protest the reading of a paper by an Australian psychiatrist on the subject of "aversion therapy," a system of treatment which attempts to change gay orientation by keying unpleasant sensations (such as electric shocks) to homosexual stimuli. . . .

One woman leaped to the stage and demanded to use the microphone. Without identifying herself, she lashed out against [Nathaniel] McConaghy's paper.

"There is an alternative to this horrible, barbaric, disgusting, sadistic technique," she said. "That is, that people who are upset about something get together and talk about their problems among themselves."

Dr. John Paul Brady of Philadelphia, chairman of the session, allowed the woman to be heard out and then asked for the meeting to continue. Shouts and boos greeted him from the front rows, which the demonstrators had largely taken over, and from further back came shouts of counterprotest.

"Shut up," cried a psychiatrist near the front of the hall, and others joined in with ill-concealed hostility: "Get out," "Be quiet," "We don't want to hear you."

One man dressed as a priest, who identified himself as Michael Itkin of San Francisco, a Ph.D., psychologist and ordained clergyman of the Evangelical Catholic Church, protested against "oppression," which, he said, "has been going on for five fucking thousand years."

The GLF and Women's Lib demonstrators continued to shout down the meeting, whereupon Dr. Brady adjourned the session. . . .

DOCUMENT 179
"Gay Raiders Seize Stage at D.C. Psychiatric Meet"
The Advocate, 26 May 1971, 3

A coalition of Gay Activist Alliance members in business suits and Gay Liberation members in war paint and skag drag successfully pulled off a zap action at the annual convention of the American Psychiatric Association here May 3.

Many psychiatrists were sent into near hysterics in the process.

With careful planning, several GAA members from New York obtained phony credentials for the convention and stationed themselves near a door of the auditorium in the plush Shoreham Hotel, where an awards assembly was being held by the APA.

At a prearranged time, the GAA people swung open the doors, and about 50 other Gays rushed in and headed, shouting, toward a rostrum where a psychiatrist was giving a talk about shock treatment.

Several GAA people, all of whom had copies of a prepared talk, attempted to push their way up to the rostrum. Psychiatrists in the audience pushed and shoved at the Gays in an attempt to stop them from getting down the aisle. But there were no reports of injury.

After several minutes of pandemonium, a gay psychiatrist began to speak, challenging the conventioneers to turn their discussion toward the war and toward the thousands of anti-war protesters arrested here during Mayday action.

He was shouted down after a short while, but Frank Kameny, founder and head of the Mattachine Society of Washington, grabbed the microphone and proceeded to deliver a fiery, eloquent denunciation of the psychiatrists.

He denied their right to discuss homosexuality as a "problem" and exclude homosexuals from convention workshops.

"Psychiatry is the enemy incarnate," Kameny said. "Psychiatry has waged a relentless war of extermination against us. You may take this as a declaration of war against you." . . .

DOCUMENT 180
John P. LeRoy, "Shrinks Asked to Join Gay Liberation"
GAY, 12 June 1972, 1, 12

Leading gays descended on a meeting of the American Psychiatric Association in Dallas, Texas (May 1–5), set up a booth entitled "Gay, Proud and Healthy: The Homosexual Community Speaks" at the Dallas Memorial Auditorium, took part in a panel discussion, "Psychiatry, Friend or Foe of Homosexuals," before a standing-room crowd of 300, appeared on a 90-minute talk show, and danced together at the psychiatrists' banquet and ball as part of the "desensitization" program. Comment was minimal when Dr. Franklin Kameny took Steve Johnson in his arms and shuffled around the dance floor as doctors and their wives looked on.

The display booth was in the scientific area of the conference, having been constructed by Dick, of Philadelphia's GAA, Barbara Gittings, Kay Tobin and other gays from Philadelphia, and showed pictures of male and female gay couples enjoying fulfilling, obviously healthy lives. Literature was distributed consisting of material from S.I.R. [Society for Individual Rights] of San Francisco, copies of various articles and papers expressing a prohomosexual viewpoint, and copies of *GAY* and other publications. Over 3,000 psychiatrists visited the booth—about half of those present at the meeting. Several members of the gay community of Dallas volunteered to keep the booth well staffed.

The panel discussion was part of the formal program of the meeting. The panelists, Frank Kameny, Barbara Gittings, Judd Marmor, Robert Siddenberg, and an anonymous psychiatrist wearing a mask to dramatize the oppression of gays inside and outside the medical profession debated the issues at great length. . . .

DOCUMENT 181

"Psychiatric Association May Drop 'Sickness' Label"
GAY, 18 June 1973, 1, 6

A thousand assembled psychiatrists meeting at the annual American Psychiatric Association convention this year applauded and approved a statement by a lay gay liberationist that homosexuality is not an illness and should not be classified as such.

The convention, held in May in Honolulu at the Hilton Hawaiian Village, had held on May 9th a panel discussion on the subject "Should Homosexuality Be In The American Psychiatric Association Nomenclature?" It was chaired by Dr. Robert Spitzer, a member of the nomenclature committee, and had five psychiatrists address themselves to the question. Three were against the "illness" label; two recommended that it be retained. The three doctors who were against the label were Dr. Richard Green, Dr. Judd Marmor of the University of Southern California and Dr. Robert Stoller of UCLA. The two psychiatrists who adhered to the sickness theory were Drs. Charles Socarides and Irving Bieber of New York.

The gay liberationist who represented the homosexual viewpoint, Ron Gold of New York's Gay Activists Alliance, led the discussion with an address entitled "Stop It, You're Making Me Sick." In a moving personal account, he examined the general traditional psychiatric views on homosexuality and how they had entered into his own life, preventing him for a long time from having a healthy view of his own sexuality. He placed the burden of present civic disabilities suffered by homosexuals squarely on the shoulders of the American psychiatric establishment. . . .

DOCUMENT 182

"Sick No More"
The Advocate, 16 Jan. 1974, 1, 2

The 20 million homosexuals in the United States achieved a sort of instant "cure" as the American Psychiatric Association removed homosexuality from its list of psychiatric disorders.

The action came Dec. 15 in a 13–0 vote of the association's board of trustees meeting at its headquarters here. Two members abstained, and four were not present at the time of the vote.

The board also passed a resolution urging repeal of all state and local sodomy laws and deploring discrimination against Gays.

Dr. Robert L. Spitzer, a member of the APA's Task Force on Nomenclature, said homosexuality was removed because the APA decided it does not fit the two criteria of mental disorder: that it either "regularly cause emotional distress or regularly be associated with generalized impairment of social functioning."

In place of homosexuality as such, the APA inserted a newly defined disorder, which it labelled "sexual orientation disturbance."

This was defined as follows: "This category is for individuals whose sexual interests are directed primarily toward people of the same sex and who are either disturbed by, in conflict with, or wish to change their sexual orientation. This diagnostic category is distinguished from homosexuality, which by itself does not necessarily constitute a psychiatric disorder. . . ."

Spitzer, who drafted the two resolutions adopted by the board, said the statements did not mean the APA feels homosexuality is "normal" nor that it is "as desirable as heterosexuality."

"Many people will interpret this to mean we're saying it's normal," he noted. "We're not saying that; we're also not saying it's abnormal. The terms normal and abnormal are not really psychiatric terms."

Leaders of several gay organizations noted the limitations of the APA move but nonetheless hailed it as an historic step. . . .

8

PRIDE MARCHES AND PARADES

BEGINNING IN THE SUMMER OF 1970, the Stonewall Riots have been commemorated with demonstrations, marches, parades, protests, and other events on or near the anniversary of the rebellion. The first sizable marches, with thousands of participants, took place in New York, Los Angeles, and Chicago. Within a few years, tens of thousands of people were participating in Stonewall commemorations in and beyond the United States. Fifty years later, millions of LGBT people and their supporters celebrate the anniversary every year.

The first four years of gay pride events generated hundreds of mainstream, alternative, and LGBT media stories, many accompanied by fabulous, fascinating, and fun photographs. These sources can help us explore how the Stonewall Riots were reconstructed, represented, and remembered in the early 1970s; they also provide us with valuable evidence for thinking about post-Stonewall developments, debates, and divisions in LGBT communities.

The eighteen documents reprinted in this chapter highlight the largest Stonewall commemorations from 1970 to 1973.

DOCUMENT 183 reports on the decision to replace the July Fourth Annual Reminders at Philadelphia's Independence Hall with Christopher Street Liberation Day demonstrations on or near the anniversary of the Stonewall Riots.

DOCUMENTS 184–187 feature LGBT press coverage of the three largest gay pride marches in 1970, which took place in New York, Los Angeles, and Chicago.

DOCUMENTS 188–191 return to these cities for LGBT media accounts of the three largest pride events in 1971.

DOCUMENTS 192–196 focus on the largest pride marches in 1972, which took place in New York, Philadelphia, San Francisco, and Chicago.

DOCUMENTS 197–200 highlight the New York, San Francisco, and Chicago marches in 1973; the last item juxtaposes the joys of gay pride with the sorrows of a destructive fire that killed thirty-two people at a New Orleans gay bar.

DOCUMENT 183

C. F. [Carole Friedman], "In the Movement: ERCHO Report"
Homophile Action League Newsletter, Jan. 1970, 5–7

A meeting of the Eastern Regional Conference of Homophile Organizations was held here in Philadelphia on November 1 and 2. At those sessions, ERCHO was confronted with the challenge being presented to the homophile movement by the Gay Liberation Front and other radical groups. . . . Much of the meeting was spent in verbal tugs-of-war between the radical faction and what must be called here, for want of a more descriptive term, the liberals. But these debates, which often shaded over into some very entertaining theater, were by no means a waste of time. They offered all of us who are involved in the movement the challenge of re-evaluating our thinking; they spurred us to action as well as thought; and they presented us with alternative philosophies which will ultimately be useful whether they are accepted, rejected, or adopted in part. . . .

The Annual Reminder day, traditionally a picket line demonstration opposite Independence Hall on July 4, was found to be wanting as a means of impressing our countrymen with the denial of human rights which the homosexual faces. Therefore the following resolution was adopted:

"That the Annual Reminder, in order to be more relevant, reach a greater number of people and encompass the ideas and ideals of the larger struggle in which we are engaged—that of our fundamental human rights—be moved both in time and location.

"We propose that a demonstration be held annually on the last Saturday in June in New York City to commemorate the 1969 spontaneous demonstrations on Christopher Street and this demonstration be called Christopher Street Liberation Day.

"We also propose that we contact homophile organizations throughout the country and request that they hold parallel demonstrations on that day. We propose a nationwide show of support.

"No dress or age regulations shall be enforced in this demonstration." . . .

DOCUMENT 184

Kay Tobin [Lahusen], "Thousands Take Part in Gay Marches"
GAY, 20 July 1970, 12

Thousands of gay men and women marched joyously through the streets of Manhattan Sunday, June 28th, to celebrate the first birthday of homosexual liberation. The unprecedented march was the culmination of Gay Pride Week. The ranks of festive participants stretched out over twenty city blocks as they moved from Sheridan Square in Greenwich Village up Sixth Avenue to Sheep Meadow in Central Park.

PRIDE MARCHES AND PARADES

Thus homosexuals from all over the Eastern United States commemorated the first anniversary of the first homosexual uprising in history: that which took place in Sheridan Square in June of 1969 when homosexuals fought back after the police raided a once-popular but now-shuttered gay bar, the Stonewall Inn. On the West Coast on the same day this year a similar commemorative march was held in Los Angeles. Estimates of the New York crowd varied from 5,000 to 10,000, with the higher figure being applied to the final, huge gathering for a Gay-In in Central Park. In addition, thousands of spectators lined the three mile parade route.

Groups participating in the demonstration, many with resplendent banners, included: Daughters of Bilitis, Gay Activists Alliance, Gay People at Columbia, Gay Liberation Front, Homophile Action League, Homosexuals, Intransigent!, Mattachine Society of New York, Mattachine Society of Washington, and Philadelphia New Gay Alliance, to name a few.

The flyer from the umbrella committee of sponsoring groups stated: "We are united today to affirm our pride, our life-style and our commitment to each other. Despite political and social differences we may have, we are united on this common ground: For the first time in history, we are together as *The Homosexual Community*."

Press coverage was extensive and included the following media: *New York Times* (which put the story on page 1 the following day), *French News Agency*, U.P.I., *WNEW-TV*, *Canadian Broadcasting Corporation*, *WCBS-TV*, *WABC-TV*, *WINS*, etc.

Throughout the parade, marchers shouted various chants: We are gay all the way—Two, four, six eight, gay is just as good as straight—Three, five, seven, nine, lesbians are mighty fine!; Out of your closets and into the streets!; Ho-ho-homosexuals! Stop the population with gay liberation! Gay and proud, say it loud, gay and proud!

The thousands of marchers filed into Central Park's Sheep Meadow, moving past two gay couples at work (?) breaking the world's kissing record. . . .

The only planned activity in the Park was sponsored by Gay Activists Alliance, which provided an abundance of body contact by conducting sensitivity games in the soft grass of the meadow. Their gay love pile—composed of dozens of warm, wiggling bodies in one fantastic heap—let forth the most spontaneous, if inarticulate, yelp for liberation heard all day.

Throughout the meadow, gay couples cuddled, kissed, laughed, and listened to themselves being described by announcers across the band of their transistor radios. Television cameras ogled at the open show of gay love and affection and solidarity. The Gay-In went on until well after sundown, after which *GAY*'s reporter was told love knew no bounds.

Said one Lesbian, "We've just experienced the world's greatest consciousness raising event for homosexuals!" Said the flyer from the umbrella committee of sponsoring groups: "We are showing our strength and our love for each other by coming here today. We are all participants in the most important Gay event in history."

DOCUMENT 185

"1200 Parade in Hollywood; Crowds Line Boulevard"

The Advocate, 22 July 1970, 1, 6

The gay community of Los Angeles made its contribution to Americana on June 28.

Over 1000 homosexuals and their friends staged not just a protest march, but a full-blown parade down world-famous Hollywood Boulevard.

Flags and banners floated in the chill sunlight of late afternoon; a bright red sound truck blared martial music; drummers strutted; a horse pranced; clowns cavorted; "vice cops" chased screaming "fairies" with paper wings; the Metropolitan Community Church choir sang "Onward Christian Soldiers"; a bronzed and muscular male model flaunted a 7 1/2–foot live python.

On and on it went, interspersed with over 30 open cars carrying *Advocate* Groovy Guy contestants, the Grand Duchess of San Francisco, homophile leaders, and anyone else who wanted to be seen, and five floats, one of which depicted a huge jar of Vaseline, another a homosexual "nailed" to a cross.

Christopher Street West, they called it.

Sensation-sated Hollywood had never seen anything like it. Probably the world had never seen anything like it since the gay days of Ancient Greece. . . .

Laconic police estimates put the number of participants in the parade at anywhere from 400 to 1500, depending on which police source you took, and the number of spectators at 4000 to 5000.

More realistic estimates put the number of spectators at 15,000 to 20,000. Parade officials, using a mechanical counter, obtained a total of 1169 participants.

The turnout appeared to catch the Los Angeles Police Department largely unprepared. Although the police had opposed the parade on the grounds that hostile spectators might turn it into a riot, they had blocked off only one side of the boulevard, as specified in the permit, and permitted traffic to proceed on the other side.

As a result, cars were trapped in the crush of spectators who surged into the street all along the parade route, despite the efforts of a few squad car units and motorcycle-mounted patrolmen to force them back to the sidewalks. Shortly after the parade started, they gave up and began diverting all traffic except the paraders off the boulevard.

There was no violence of any kind, and police would acknowledge only three arrests, those of MCC [Metropolitan Community Church] Pastor Troy Perry, Daughters of Bilitis Los Angeles Chapter President Carole Shepherd, and

Kelly Weiser of HELP [Homophile Effort for Legal Protection], who were hustled away as they began a protest fast at Hollywood and Las Palmas after the parade. However, reports reached the *Advocate* of up to 47 parade participants and spectators taken to the police station and then released, and a few actual arrests on such things as traffic warrants.

The spectators appeared for the most part to be either friendly or neutral. There was a light scattering of boos, catcalls, and derisive shouts along the parade route, but applause and cheers followed the convertible in which Rev. Perry and his lover, Steve Jordan, were riding, the *Advocate* staff car, and a number of other parade units.

Laughter and applause also followed the Gay Liberation Front Guerrilla Theatre entry, a gaggle of shrieking "fairies" wearing gauzy pastels and being chased in all directions by stick-wielding "cops" sporting huge "vice" badges, the "Vaseline" float also entered by a GLF group, the several clowns in costume and white-face, and a nodding and bowing "witch doctor" in grass robes and African mask entered by the Society of Pat Rocco Enlightened Enthusiasts. . . .

As successful as the parade was, there was general agreement that it would have been much bigger without the long battle to get a Police Commission permit, which was finally resolved only two days before.

County Superior Court Judge Richard Schauer issued an injunction on June 19 forbidding the commission from imposing any and all special police costs on the parade planners. . . .

The parade was in celebration of the homosexual uprising which followed a police raid on the Stonewall Inn on Christopher Street in New York's Greenwich Village June 27 last year. . . .

DOCUMENT 186

Bob Stanley, "Gay Pride Week, 1970: That Was the Week That Was"
Mattachine Midwest Newsletter, July 1970, 1

When the New York police entered and closed the Stonewall Club during the early morning hours of June 28 a year ago, it must at first have seemed like a rerun of a segment of that old, worn-out Official Harassment Story. But this time things were different; the evicted gay patrons didn't follow the usual script. Instead, throwing rocks and bottles and chanting "Gay Power," they reacted against the years of harassment with an explosion of pent-up, angry frustration. This—history's first gay riot—and the demonstrations which followed it marked the first time that large numbers of gay people stood up against repression. For this reason the Stonewall Riot is regarded as the birth of the Gay Liberation Movement.

In commemoration of these events, the week of June 21 through 28 was declared Gay Pride Week in Chicago. Workshops were held each evening, Monday through Thursday, at the Chicago Circle Campus of the University of

Illinois on such topics as Gay Lib Ideology, the Gay Manifesto, Gay Women, Legal Action, and the Medical Situation. Communal dinners on Friday and Saturday nights at the Second Unitarian Church were associated with other workshops and discussions.

At noon on Saturday, June 29, about 200 gay people gathered in Bughouse Square with flags, signs, and high spirits. The crowd included representatives of Gay Lib and the Women's Caucus, Mattachine Midwest, and also some out-of-towners like the head of Detroit's Gay Liberation and some people from FREE [Fight Repression of Erotic Expression] of the Minneapolis–St. Paul area. After a round of speeches, the group headed down Dearborn Street to Chicago Avenue, symbolically leaving Bughouse Square and all it stands for behind. Marching and chanting, the demonstrators moved east on Chicago Avenue, turned south at the Water Tower and added a little color to Michigan Avenue. With flags flapping in the breeze and chants of "Gay Power," the group drew a lot of attention as it progressed down Wacker, State, and Randolph to the Civic Center. We were, of course, served and protected along the entire route by six or seven carloads of our very own Blue Meanies (and even a few plainclothesmen). After more speeches, chanting, and a little dancing, the group gradually dispersed. . . .

DOCUMENT 187

"Drag Queens Demonstrate"

Drag (1.1), ca. Aug. 1970, 5

Queens, a homophile organization concentrating on issues concerning drag queens, officially began operations by participating in the Christopher Street Liberation Day Parade. The parade was a result of the homosexual uprising, caused by a raid on a gay bar, the Stonewall, also a drag hang-out. The entire gay liberation movement started as a result of that raid. For the first time in history, the homosexual stood up and said, "Hands Off!" It was the effeminate or drag queen who stood up and yelled first and the loudest. It was their place! The so-called "straight" looking, manly homosexual stood back and watched the police hammer the effeminate boys.... Finally, they joined in. Gay Pride was founded.

Queens contributed financial support to the parade and officers of the organization marched the entire three mile hike in high heels! One carried a sign, "WE'RE ONLY NUMBER TWO; BUT WE TRY HARDER!" On the opposite side it read: "SECOND CLASS CITIZENS, THAT IS."

DOCUMENT 188

Breck Ardery, "Gay Pride '71: New York"

The Advocate, 21 July 1971, 1, 3, 8

Thousands of Gays from all over the Eastern Seaboard celebrated the second annual Christopher Street Liberation Day in New York City.

The day, featuring a mass march and gay-in, was the climax of Gay Pride Week which included workshops, demonstrations and social events. Up to 20,000 persons may have participated in the march.

The week's activities got under way on Friday, June 18, with the official opening of the Gay Activists Alliance Firehouse on Wooster Street. . . .

At the grand opening, many Gays who are not members of GAA arrived to inspect the new facilities. Also present were City Councilman Saul Sharison (D-Manhattan), who represents the district where the Firehouse is located. Sharison is also chairman of the general welfare committee of the City Council where the bill which would end employment and housing discrimination against Gays is bottled up.

The councilman assured the gathering that he is firmly committed to passage of the bill and urged them to put pressure on council majority leader Thomas Cuite (D-Brooklyn) in order to get the bill on the floor.

Saturday featured dances at the Daughters of Bilitis Center and the GAA headquarters. . . .

Two events late in the week caused considerable interest and publicity. A group of about 500 persons staged a candlelight march from the GAA Firehouse to City Hall to demand passage of the Human Rights Bill.

The demonstration was planned by the GAA but received wide support from women's groups and unaffiliated members of the community. At the park in front of City Hall, the marchers listened to speeches by several people from the gay movement and City Councilman Eldon Clingan (Liberal-Manhattan), one of the chief sponsors of the bill. . . .

GAA decided to escalate the pressure on Friday afternoon when another demonstration outside City Hall erupted into a melee in which nine members of the organization were arrested. The police had set up a guard around the building and did not allow demonstrators inside. When some of them reportedly attempted to push through police lines, the arrests began. . . .

There was much speculation that the reason for the heavy police presence at City Hall on Friday was a news story in the *New York Post* the previous Monday. In an article detailing the activities of Gay Pride Week, the paper mentioned that the GAA was planning some kind of militant action inside City Hall. . . .

Another worrisome rumor which spread during Gay Pride Week was that the police planned to raid a number of gay bars on the Friday and Saturday before the march. Behind-the-scenes troubleshooting with the city government and community authorities was carried out by gay leaders who feared that such raids could touch off another riot in Greenwich Village.

Whether the raids were actually planned is still unknown, but they did not occur. . . .

Thousands of Gays attended the GAA Street Fair on Saturday afternoon. One block of Wooster Street in front of the Firehouse was closed and scores of booths were set up. There were the traditional beer and food stands, along with booths unique to a gay street fair. Among them were tables for gay artists, authors and crafts people who displayed and sold their wares.

There were also booths where participants could throw darts at their favorite anti-gay public official or psychiatrist. There was a special dart booth for Dr. David Reuben, the well-known anti-gay psychiatrist.

Throughout the fair there was dancing in the streets. A voter registration table was set up and over 50 people reportedly registered.

In addition, the GAA showed video tapes of various demonstrations and zaps and a series of workshops on a variety of subjects were conducted inside the Firehouse. . . .

The June 27 mass demonstration along the Avenue of the Americas was scheduled to begin at 2PM but many participants began arriving in the assembly area well before noon, and it was soon clear that the number of marchers would be greater than last year. Many who had been present for the first Christopher Street parade agreed that the atmosphere was much more relaxed this year than last. Even some of the police seemed to be enjoying themselves. . . .

The crowd estimates varied wildly. The *New York Times* reported 5,000 demonstrators. A police official told a member of the Christopher Street Committee it looked like about 20,000 to him. Most observers believe the police estimate is closer to actuality.

In any case the crowd size was easily double and perhaps triple the number of participants last year. As the crowd moved up the avenue, the traditional chants of Gay Power, "Two, four, six, eight, Gay is just as good as straight, three, five, seven, nine, lesbians are mighty fine," were heard. There was also the periodic chant of "Justice! Justice!" accompanied by the raised fist used extensively in the demonstration in Albany last March. The reaction of most of the spectators seemed to be amusement, support or indifference.

At one point, the demonstrators passed a construction site where several hard-hats were at work about 10 stories up. Some of the construction workers looked on and waved at the marchers while others seemed to display mild disgust. One worker danced on the steel beams of the building and threw kisses at the crowd. A group of demonstrators stopped and began shouting for him to take his clothes off. It was later reported that as the last contingents of marchers were passing by, the worker did remove his trousers—revealing red undershorts. . . .

When the marchers reached Sheep Meadow in Central Park, they found many had gone directly there, skipping the long, hot march.

There were no formal events at the park. . . .

Balloons carrying the word "Gay" and commemorative buttons put out by the Christopher Street Committee were sold or given away along the march route and in the park. Some of the balloons were sold by the private vendors who capitalize on all large public events. There were also many food vendors in the park, indicating in their own way that the gay movement is beginning to enter the mainstream of public life.

News coverage of the event was widespread. Substantial reportage was provided by the *New York Times*, *New York Post*, and most radio and television stations.

DOCUMENT 189
"Gay Pride '71: Hollywood"
The Advocate, 21 July 1971, 1, 4

The Second Annual Christopher Street West Parade in Hollywood June 27 had more of the aspect of a Shriners parade—complete with clowns, outlandish costumes, and a deft baton twirler—than of a militant civil rights march.

Over 2000 persons participated in the 10-block-long parade, which drew about 15,000 spectators and lasted an hour and a half.

The parade had several large, colorful floats, the most striking of which was a giant former Rose Parade float entered by Metropolitan Community Church. . . .

There were plenty of signs and banners asserting gay pride and determination . . . , and at least two allegedly "vulgar" items that set storm signals flying. . . .

The MCC float, 55 feet long, 18 feet wide, and about 20 feet high, was adorned with 7000 fresh roses donated by a church member—John Bullock—who owns a florist shop. . . .

The two largest floats in the parade in addition to this one were the MCC May Festival float in pale lavender and green, and the lavender, green, gold, and white float entered by the Society of Pat Rocco Enlightened Enthusiasts (SPREE)—the fan club of moviemaker Pat Rocco.

The May Festival float, almost as large as the locomotive float, and like it, self-powered, carried the festival king and queen and their court. The queen wore a low-cut, white ball gown with a white ruffled cape. The bearded King was also in white with a brilliant yellow silk cloak.

The SPREE float, which had the legend on the side, "GROOVY GUYS MAKE GROOVY STARS," carried 10 young men in swim trunks against a backdrop of gold stars. At the front of the float was a life-sized statue of a palomino pony. The float had its own sound system over which beat music was played.

"We tried to get a really masculine-looking float, with really good-looking guys presenting a masculine representation of SPREE," Rocco said. "No limp wrists." . . .

DOCUMENT 190
"Long, Well-Rounded Entry Clouds Parade Aftermath"
The Advocate, 21 July 1971, 411

Rumblings of dismay spread through much of the Los Angeles gay community in the wake of the Second Annual Christopher Street West Parade, touched off mainly by two items out of hundreds of signs, banners, floats, and special entries in the 10-block-long procession which had over 2000 participants by official estimate.

Los Angeles police turned over information on one of the special entries—and possibly the entry itself—to the city attorney's office for a study of possible obscenity charges. . . .

At least one, and possibly both, of the two offending entries seemed likely to develop into a *cause célèbre*, much as did the outsized Vaseline jar float entered by the Gay Liberation Front in the first parade last year.

The entry being studied for possible obscenity charges was a 35-foot-long tubular affair of blue-and-white striped cloth, with feet and legs provided by seven otherwise anonymous young men. On one end was a pink head, two enormous eyes adorned by great fluttering black eyelashes, and a little vertical pink slit of a mouth. On the other end swung a red sac with two large lumps bulking at the bottom.

Morris Kight, a member of the Christopher Street West Committee and unofficial principal organizer of the parade, carefully referred to it as a "caterpillar," or "worm," while disclaiming any specific advance knowledge or responsibility for it.

Stan Williams, a young member of the "old guard" of GLF/LA, cheerfully admitted that the whole thing was his idea, and just as cheerfully conceded that the blue-and-white affair "could be described as a surrealistic cock." He stressed, however, that it was meant as a work of pop art, and was never intended to be obscene.

The other offending item was a large, colorful banner bearing the words, "SUCKING IS BETTER THAN WAR," whose creators chose to remain anonymous. It led one of several GLF contingents in the parade. . . .

Whether by design or simply because those powering it lost control, the caterpillar-cock staggered directly into a police car on crowd control duty at one point during the parade. Spectators burst into laughter and applause as its pink head butted against the car's windows.

"Anyone who finds a penis to be obscene," said Williams, "is forgetting where they came from. Or they must feel that their source of being is obscene. And that's a very sad thing."

He also defended the "SUCKING" banner.

"If anybody feels that war is better than sucking, he would, perhaps, be upset. I don't feel that either of these things was obscene. But I guess there were bound to be a few people who would be upset by almost anything. I'm sure there were a lot of people who were offended by the basic fact of the parade." . . .

DOCUMENT 191

John Tackaberry and Bob Fish, "Gay Pride '71: Chicago"

The Advocate, 21 July 1971, 1, 2

Some 1200 persons, many of them non-Gays who came originally just to watch, braved record-breaking 100-degree temperatures here to march through two miles of downtown Chicago streets in a Gay Pride Parade climaxing 12 days of Gay Pride Week festivities.

The celebrations were slightly marred by the arrests of two participants at a Gay Pride Picnic.

The turnout was by far the largest of its kind in Chicago history. Only 200 took part in last year's parade.

The unique display of camaraderie was characterized by band music blaring from sound trucks, a small sea of waving flags and legally acceptable incidents of body contact between marchers and sometimes between marchers and onlookers.

The city's first gay-in was celebrated in Lincoln Park at the end of the parade route. Speechmaking and dancing were occasionally disrupted by heckling and minor harassments from groups of straights on the sidelines. But no violence was reported and Mayor Daley's police did not appear in force.

The unexpectedly heavy participation in the Gay Pride Parade appeared to take the usual North Side Summer crowds by surprise. At some points along the line of march—west on Diversey Parkway from Lake Michigan, then south on Clark Street to Lincoln Park's Free Forum—it was unclear as to which persons were participants and which were the merely curious.

Floats sponsored by a few bars and by gay organizations in Chicago took part, along with well-decorated cars and motorcycles. In all, Gays from four states appeared in the line of march.

Two days before, a mass kiss-in at Civic Center Plaza was conducted by more than 100 members of the Gay Liberation Front, Men Against Cool, Women's Liberation, and other gay groups. It was specifically intended to protest the trial, set for that day, of Richard Chinn and John Cantrall, gay activist youths arrested Apr. 30 for kissing in public. Their trial, on charges of disorderly conduct and public indecency, was subsequently continued until late July.

Friday night's Gay Pride Week dance attracted nearly 1000 participants and Saturday's Gay Pride picnic in a suburban forest preserve several hundred. . . .

Jack Baker, student body president at the University of Minnesota and a leader in FREE: Gay Liberation of Minnesota, addressed marchers at a rally before the start of the climactic June 27 parade.

Baker asked tolerance by gay militants for those homosexuals "who are unable to sail along with us on the crest of social change. We must be careful not to topple the closet when some of our gay sisters and brothers are still hiding in it. Nothing is solved when we vent our anger against Gays who are only reacting to the un-Christian intolerance of non-Gays. Let's keep our anger pointed in the right direction."

DOCUMENT 192

Randy Wicker, "Thousands Parade under Sunny Skies in Damp New York"

The Advocate, 19 July 1972, 2

What newscasters termed "the East Coast's first monsoon" put a damper on nine days of Gay Pride celebrations by New York area gay groups, but the sun broke through to shine on the Third Annual Christopher Street Liberation Day March June 25. . . .

Marchers filled Christopher Street, where the march began, from Sheridan Square to beyond Bleeker Street. Veterans of the two previous marches nevertheless said the weather had cut the turnout, recalling that last year, on a warm, sunny day, the line had stretched to Hudson Street and beyond—two or three times as far.

But as the sun broke through the clouds, surges of newcomers joined the marchers as they moved chanting under multi-colored banners down past the shuttered Stonewall, where it all began. From the windows above the long-closed bar, heterosexual couples and children waved.

At the Avenue of the Americas, the procession headed uptown toward Central Park.

By the time it had reached 23rd Street, it filled half the avenue and stretched back 11 blocks. When it reached the Hilton Hotel at 56th Street, it stretched for 15 blocks.

Police estimated the number of marchers at 3500. Parade marshals insisted the total, based on an estimate of 400 or 500 persons a block, was double that.

The Christopher Street Liberation Day Committee had decided to let the women's group lead off the parade and just behind the large net banner emblazoned "Christopher Street Liberation Day," an even larger banner, "Lesbians Unite," stretched above hundreds of gay women, many walking with their arms about one another or holding hands and singing "When the Gays Go Marching In." . . .

The largest contingents marched behind the banners of the Gay Women's Liberation Front, the New York Gay Activists Alliance, and the New Jersey GAA.

Police escorts which had led the way were bolstered considerably by a line of uniformed officers in front of the Hilton, the scene of an attack on gay activists leafleting there April 15 in which Michael Maye, head of the Uniformed Firefighters Association, had been charged.

Parade marshals linked hands to create a human chain between the march-ers and policemen as the first contingent of the parade swept by chanting, "Jail Maye! Jail Maye! Justice! Justice! Justice!" Hundreds of fists were raised in the air.

At one point a small group of marchers mounted the wall behind police lines and unfurled a banner declaring "Gay Revolution." Concurrently, another small group sat down in the street in front of the Hilton, stopping the parade.

"Let's sit for just five minutes," the ringleader pleaded after getting 20 or so cohorts to seat themselves. Parade marshals, however, quickly intervened and ordered those seated to continue marching. All complied, including the ring-leader, who was outraged that the marshals wouldn't allow him "to continue sitting and be arrested."

The marchers were generally in good spirits, and humor was frequently evi-dent. "Two-four-six-eight, is your husband really straight?" intermingled with "Try it! You'll like it!" and "2-4-6-8, we don't overpopulate."

One woman's sign read: "She kissed me once. Will she kiss me again? Be sure with lesbian revolution."

Here and there, individuals dressed in full drag, half drag, and camp drag ran up and down the sidelines, miming for the photographers. One sported a white gown with fairy wings. Another wore complete clown makeup and costume.

Although forbidden to have floats, the One Potato, Roadhouse, and Peter Rabbit bars were represented with banners held by employees and patrons.

Celebrities included Dr. Benjamin Spock marching in his first gay parade with the "Gay Vets Against the War" contingent.

Michael Peace, who won the Democratic nomination for the State Assembly in the Brooklyn Heights area by less than 300 votes the previous Tuesday, was the only other political candidate present.

Morty Manford, one of the Gays attacked by Maye at the Hilton, was accompanied on the march by his mother, who carried a sign urging, "Parents of Gays, unite in support of your children." . . .

DOCUMENT 193
Gerald Hansen, "San Francisco Hosts Gay Parade"
GAY, 24 July 1972, 1, 3, 14

An estimated 2,000 to 8,000 persons marched in this city's first Gay Liberation Day parade while some 15,000 to 75,000 watched the event.

The actual number of participants and spectators on the 22-block route was open to speculation. Rev. Ray Broshears, marshal of the Christopher Street West–San Francisco extravaganza, said 5,000 to 8,000 marched and 50,000 to 75,000 persons viewed the parade. Police estimated 2,000 and 15,000, respectively.

Grand prize for the best entry was awarded to Metropolitan Community Church, San Francisco. An award for the most original entry went to the Hot Moon Commune, San Francisco. The best marching unit award was given to the Jolley Times, a group from Bakersfield which came the farthest to march in the parade.

Special honored guest was William Johnson, 26, who was ordained later this historic day as the first openly declared homosexual in the United Church of Christ. He was made a minister in a moving, dignified and joyous service in the traditional "laying on of hands," by both clergy and laity, including his brother Wayne at the Community United Church of Christ in San Carlos. He won the best male entry award at the parade. A Gay guerilla theatre group, Angels of Light, bumped and grinded away throughout the parade which proceeded from the financial district to Civic Center while a Jewish contingent carried signs proclaiming "chutzpah" (gutsiness) and sang a Hebrew folk song, "Hava Nagillah."

Grand marshals were Morris Kight, founder of Gay Liberation Front, Los Angeles, and Ms. Frieda Smith, assistant pastor at Harmony Metropolitan Community Church, Sacramento and gay women's liberationist. . . .

The parade was criticized beforehand by two homophile publications. "Demonstrations have become a monotonous part of our daily life and few people really pay much attention to them anymore," intoned an editorial in *Vector*, the Society for Individual Rights magazine. "We wish that those who are giving many hours to making the parade a success had instead given their time and effort to activity that would more surely and directly benefit the homosexual. Unfortunately, typing letters, answering telephones, stuffing envelopes, appearing before public hearings, speaking to civic clubs, etc. is not very exciting.... S.I.R. is not 'endorsing' this parade...but it does have a float in it. We urge your support because for us not to take part might clearly indicate to the public...that we are not a strong force in the community." Several S.I.R. board members said the contradictory editorial, written by managing editor George Mendenhall, did not reflect their thinking and the organization went on to quasi-endorse the parade. The S.I.R. float depicted a Gay wedding with the groom throwing flowers to the crowd.

The event was boycotted, on the other hand, by the Gay Sunshine Collective which described it as a "co-optation by commercial, capitalist gay interests." In an editorial written by coordinator Winston Leyland as "the opinion of the collective," *Gay Sunshine* said "it's becoming fashionable for those same gay pigs who, a year ago, were denigrating the Gay Liberation Movement to now use the terms 'gay brothers and sisters, Gay Liberation' without any sense of what that means."

It added that an Imperial Ball was scheduled at the exclusive Fairmont Hotel on the eve of the parade. "An Imperial Ball to celebrate the anniversary of a movement which began with a riot. Of course straight, capitalist businessmen...are only too happy to cater to affairs of this kind. It reinforces all their stereotyped thinking of homosexuals." Gay Sunshiners also objected that "of nine or ten parade committee members, none are women. The parade is basically a male chauvinist trip." In addition, "the parade is being coordinated for the most part by people (S.I.R., Tavern Guild) who have no commitment to Gay liberation." . . .

The event was marred by one other incident. Mayor Joseph Alioto refused to sign a resolution which had been on his desk for two weeks proclaiming June 25 "Gay Freedom Day" in the city. Last year Alioto vetoed a Board of Supervisors approved resolution backing Assembly bill 437, the "Brown bill," which would permit sex in private between consenting adults. "Hell, the mayor has signed resolutions calling for begonia days, and snapping turtle days," noted Broshears. "I suppose he doesn't think Gay people are as significant as begonias or snapping turtles."

The parade was climaxed on the steps of City Hall with Broshears declaring, "We're going to have our equal rights and to hell with you, Alioto! . . ."

DOCUMENT 194

Gay Sunshine Collective, "C.S.W. Fracas (Round 1)"

Gay Sunshine, ca. July 1972, 1.

San Francisco's Christopher Street West Parade, held Sunday, June 26, was marred by two incidents of violent conflict between parade organizers and a group of lesbians from San Jose. The first incident took place before the start of the march near Pine and Montgomery Street in the city's financial district. The women, members of the San Jose Radical Lesbians, reported that they approached Rev. Raymond Broshears and an unidentified man in a grey suit. Broshears, a G.A.A. member of the parade organizing committee, argued loudly with the women that the sign they were carrying ("Off Prick Power") was obscene and that they would not be permitted to carry it in the parade. After verbal altercation, the women walked away.

Later, as the women were standing on the sidewalk deciding what to do, Broshears and the grey-suited man came up to them and warned them not to carry their sign in the parade. When they attempted to discuss the matter, the two men grabbed the sign and tore it to shreds, shoving one of the sisters in the process. Broshears called over four policemen who confirmed his opinion on the sign's obscenity and told the women they would not be permitted to carry the sign. One of the women reported that the grey-suited man told her that his briefcase contained a knife which he was prepared to use on troublemakers if necessary. The sisters did later make a second sign on their own which they carried in the parade.

The second incident occurred on the steps of City Hall after the parade, when dignitaries were being introduced and awards given out. One of the lesbians, Chris Nunez, attempted to gain access to the microphone to ask why the sister had been shoved previously. She was prevented access by Broshears in spite of demands by many in the crowd that she be permitted to speak.

After the completion of the ceremonies, Broshears was approached by several of the San Jose sisters who wanted to discuss the question of their treatment. Broshears attempted to evade the questioning by leaving the area. But a large crowd had pressed around to see what was happening, thus hindering his departure. To the *Gay Sunshine* reporter who witnessed this incident Broshears appeared extremely agitated. He shouted stridently that the women had not participated in the planning stages of the parade and knew nothing of the rules laid down. Suddenly, without provocation he sprang forward, launching himself bodily into the midst of the women, striking out furiously in all directions.

Members of the crowd rushed forward to pull Broshears and the women apart, but not before two of the sisters had sustained minor bruises. Broshears did not stay for any further discussion but was quickly ushered through the crowd by a little group of henchmen.

Crowd reaction was divided. Some of those present called the women "sick bitches" and accused them of "spoiling our parade." Most of the bystanders seemed shocked, however, and many called him a "fascist pig."

Afterwards, one of the San Jose sisters told *Gay Sunshine* that "we only came up here to develop some solidarity with our gay brothers." Asked if the parade seemed male-dominated, one woman replied, "Oh god, is it ever!"

The Gay Sunshine Collective, which editorially criticized the parade as sexist and male-chauvinist in our June issue, has issued the following statement . . . :

"Never has the distance between the so-called leadership of the Bay Area gay movement and the rank and file been more apparent than in this incident. The male chauvinism demonstrated by the parade organizers is too obvious to require any further comment. We are disgusted by the Rev. Broshears' conduct and we would remind him that all the parades in the world will produce no sexual liberation as long as men persist in this sort of behavior towards women. We have long believed that this parade was dominated by a bankrupt "leadership" thoroughly out of touch with its constituency. This physical assault on gay sisters confirms our opinion. . . .

"We call upon the sponsoring organizations to repudiate Broshears' sexist behavior and to issue an immediate apology to the sisters from San Jose. We also call upon our gay sisters and brothers to stop acquiescing in the state of affairs which presently exists in the Bay Area gay liberation struggle. If we continue to remain passive, we deserve to be under the leadership of this bunch of male-chauvinist Machiavellians with their paper organizations and authoritarian neuroses."

DOCUMENT 195

"Chicago Parade Draws Wide Support"

The Advocate, 19 July 1972, 19

A variegated procession of an estimated 950 midwestern Gays led off Chicago's third Gay Pride Week. The parade probably attracted the widest—if not the most numerous—participation yet from the local gay community.

The march, in unseasonably cool 60° sunshine, went three miles from the gay Belmont Rocks lakefront stretch down Broadway and Clark Street, through the heart of the midwest's largest single concentration of gay residents.

The paraders ended the late afternoon June 25 celebration with a rally in Lincoln Park featuring speeches by activists Barbara Gittings and Michael McConnell from the Task Force on Gay Liberation of the American Library Association. . . .

More lesbians than ever before joined this year's parade, most under the banner of the Chicago Lesbian Liberation (formerly Gay Women's Caucus).

Cars and marchers from Minneapolis, Indianapolis, and other midwestern cities, including a large contingent from Milwaukee's new Gay Underground and the Gay People's Union, also took part.

An assortment of Chicago groups ranging from the local Dignity chapter to the Gay Women's Caucus and Youth Against War and Fascism joined in.

There were even a clown and a black Cadillac limousine, bicycles and motorcycles, as well as cars decorated by local bars, businesses, and gay organizations. . . .

The Civic Center Plaza rally focused on issues of equal opportunity in employment, housing, and public services and accommodations. . . .

A secondary focus of the civic center rally had been a protest against lack of coverage of gay news by the Chicago news media. That lack continued to characterize this year's gay week, though not as unremittingly as in the past.

No daily newspaper or television station mentioned the parade, but radio stations—WBBM, WCFL, and WIND—gave the parade and Gay Pride Week some coverage. . . .

DOCUMENT 196

Richard A. Frank, "Turnout Exceeds Expectations"

Gay Alternative, July 1972, 1, 2[1]

Encouraged by pleasant temperatures and sunny skies, large crowds of both spectators and participants turned out for Philadelphia's first Gay Pride March. The turnout, estimated by police to be 10,000 (including upwards of 3000 marchers), greatly surprised both marchers and police. Lieut. George Fencl of the Civil Disobedience Squad noted that the march was the largest recent demonstration in Philadelphia, and that even he was surprised by the size of the crowds.

Members of several Philadelphia gay activist groups took part, these including Gay Activists Alliance, the city's largest such group, Homophile Action League, Radicalesbians, Temple Gay Liberation Front, Metropolitan Community Church, and the Church of the Beloved Disciple. Also present were representatives from various out of town gay groups.

The marchers assembled at Rittenhouse Square for a rally at 2PM, with cheers, chants, and songs led by Barbara Gittings, a prominent figure in Philadelphia's Gay Liberation movement, and others. About 45 minutes later the parade began, the marchers proceeding to Chestnut St., and thence, to Independence Mall.

Large crowds of curious onlookers lined the way, at times standing six or more deep. They came from all parts of the city, their curiosity piqued by numerous radio announcements, posters, and newspaper coverage. Many of the crowd followed the marchers down to the Mall, swelling the crowd to about 10,000. . . .

Several marchers wore masks and paper chains to symbolize the oppression gay people suffer and the masked double life many feel compelled to live. These were removed and put into a coffin at the Mall to symbolize liberation from oppression, fear, and guilt. Indeed, this was a major theme of the march, as the chants and placards pointed out.

"Say it loud, I'm gay and I'm proud!"

"Two-four-six-eight / gay is just as good as straight!"

"I am neither ashamed nor afraid."

"We're marching to liberate everyone," said one female marcher, "mostly the closet gays who are afraid to march, but the straights, too."

"Whether we march with masks or not, we all know that gay is good, it's right, positive, healthy, natural, and moral," said Barbara Gittings. "We no longer are listening to those who say otherwise.... This march may not be a revolution, but it certainly is a revelation." . . .

DOCUMENT 197
Gerald Hansen, "Color, Joy in San Francisco"
The Advocate, 18 July 1973, 3, 24

A joyous parade climaxed Gay Pride Week in the San Francisco Bay area—and was noted for several surprises.

Parade officials report that the number of participants and spectators was approximately the same as last year—an estimated 40,000. Approximately 2000 persons actually marched or appeared on floats. Others who walked the route considered both estimates as wild exaggerations.

The major surprise of the day occurred after the parade. Nearly 3000 persons packed the picnic at Marx Meadows. Most observers of the gay scene had speculated beforehand that the picnic in Golden Gate Park would attract only a small turnout.

By contrast, a 4PM count at the Festival for Gay Liberation sponsored by the Rev. Ray Broshears showed 186 persons observing the entertainment. Mr. Broshears had expected an attendance of at least 5000.

The most elaborate float in the parade was presented by the Angels of Light. It featured 10 costumed members aboard a long flat-bed truck engaged in guerilla theatre. The vehicle was draped in colorful paper flowers. Firecrackers popped occasionally. . . .

A giant pink fox stood atop a float sponsored by a bar called the Fickle Fox.

Folsom Street Barracks entered another much-noticed float which featured a bathtub with several attractive numbers around it apparently clad only in towels.

Receiving lots of loud cheers was Paul Brown of the Naked Grape bar who wore, significantly, only a few grapes on his otherwise nude and well-proportioned torso. . . .

The parade attracted a moderate number of spectators in the financial district where it began on a warm afternoon under sunny skies. A large number of tourists gathered at Union Square and Powell Street where San Francisco's venerable cable cars cross.

Onlookers thinned out as the parade proceeded away from the Downtown area. . . .

DOCUMENT 198
Randy Wicker, "Gays Pour through New York"
The Advocate, 18 July 1973, 3, 5

A mighty river of gay marchers flooded Manhattan with gay pride June 24.

A slow-moving torrent of gay people in their thousands poured through Manhattan from Central Park to Greenwich Village under smiling skies in the 4th Annual Christopher Street Liberation Day Parade.

The triumphant procession, at times stretching 15 blocks, took nearly four hours to cover the 60-block parade route.

Where previous parades had ended in Central Park, this one assembled on West 60th through 63rd Streets off Central Park West. From there, marchers proceeded south on Central Park West to Columbus Circle, along Central Park South to 7th Avenue, down 7th Avenue through Times Square to Christopher Street in the Village, then eastward past the long-closed Stonewall Inn to Washington Square Park. Crowds of onlookers lined the route.

Paraders filled half of 7th Avenue's four lanes. The *New York Times* estimated 600 to 900 persons per block where the parade stretched for 15 blocks, or a total active participation of 9000 to 13,500 persons. March organizers claimed 12,000 to 20,000 participants. Police, doggedly conservative, estimated 3000 marchers. . . .

This year's march was more colorful than those of previous years. About half its bulk was made up of groups from various bars. Contingents from gay organizations, churches, counseling centers, and even some parents of Gays, made up the rest.

A large contingent of lesbians led by an all-woman marching band brought up the rear of the parade. But gay women comprised only about 20 per cent of this year's turnout, compared to nearly half of last year's parade.

At Washington Square Park, three and a half hours of speeches and entertainment were presented from an elaborate professional stage erected in front of the Washington Square Arch. The booming sound system could be heard clearly over two blocks away.

The rally itself was marred by a confused and bitter wrangle over crossdressing and the rights of transvestites, which also produced a brief scuffle between parade marshals and transvestites during the latter stages of the march. . . .

At 7th Avenue and 25th Street, Ray "Sylvia" Rivera and a confederate, holding up a "Street Transvestite Action Revolutionaries" banner, tried to force their way in front of the parade.

[Chief Marshal Jean] DeVente tried to persuade them to get back behind the lead banner but ended up in a scuffle with Rivera, along with several other marshals. Two of the marshals had their throats bruised and bloodied and their clothing torn in the melee, which temporarily halted the parade, before police intervened.

Officers asked if the parade leaders wanted Rivera arrested. Several of the CSLD Coordinating Committee members present said "yes," but [Grand Marshal John Paul] Hudson insisted on not pressing charges. During the conference with police, Rivera complicated matters by snatching off the glasses of Walt Doran, one of the marchers, which he hurled to the pavement and broke. Doran then told police, "Arrest him!"

"We don't want to make the arrest," one officer told Hudson, "but this guy whose glasses were broken is pressing us." Meanwhile, other officers trailed halfheartedly after the sequined jump-suited Rivera as he retreated through the crowd.

"Please don't," Hudson pleaded, finally getting Doran to agree.

The march then proceeded, with Rivera back in the procession.

At Washington Square, paraders swarmed into the park and quickly filled the block-square area.

Barbara Gittings' keynote address noted that over two decades ago the first Mattachine group had organized in Los Angeles behind drawn shades in a locked apartment, with a lookout posted, because they believed discussing homosexuality might get them arrested.

"But today," she said, "we've shown them. No longer can they laugh and talk about us as if we were a tribe of 300 people on a Polynesian island 6000 miles away." . . .

Dissension erupted again during the introduction of Elena Reed, a black singer who was one of at least three straight entertainers appearing. Sylvia Rivera, who Hudson said had been causing a "commotion" behind the stage, broke through marshals and onto the platform, where he grabbed the microphone. He was dragged off, and Reed soon had the crowd jumping and dancing to her rendition of "Holding Hands."

Rivera then was allowed to speak "to avoid further trouble," said Hudson. "We had the makings of a riot behind the platform. One guy took a swing at me, and I had to have him arrested."

Rivera shrieked that he had been beaten up and raped in jail and called for revolution. "We've put up with enough shit.... What do you people do for your brothers and sisters in jail? Nothing!"

Rivera's harangue drew angry mutterings from some in the crowd, and a plea for tolerance from [Master of Ceremonies Vito] Russo. He then introduced a pair of female impersonators in 1890's costume, Billie and Tiffany, and said Jean O'Leary of the newly formed Lesbian Feminist Liberation group would be allowed to read a statement after they appeared.

O'Leary said bitterly that she was being allowed to speak only because "one person, a man, makes a ruckus." In her statement, she attacked men who "impersonate women for reasons of entertainment and profit," saying they "insult women."

The statement drew angry shouts and hisses from many in the largely male audience, and again Russo called for tolerance.

O'Leary was followed by Queens Liberation Front leader Lee Brewster in full drag.

"I apologize for this outburst, but I can't sit and let my people be insulted," he said. He reminded his listeners that "the day you're celebrating was a result of what drag queens did at the Stonewall. You go to bars because of what we did for you, and these bitches tell us to quit being ourselves. Screw you, gay liberation."

Tension began to lift as more singers appeared, though Ellen Green, a heterosexual, set off some protests by singing, "Met a man today, had a cup of tea; he desired me."

An unexpected appearance by superstar Bette Midler, in jeans and a white shirt with a bright red sweater, really got things going again.

"I heard a little bit on the radio, and it sounded like you were beating each other up down here," Midler told the crowd, and then broke into her theme song, "You've got to have friends." . . .

DOCUMENT 199

Don Dunfee, "3000 Brave Heat for Chicago Pride Parade"

The Advocate, 18 July 1973, 6, 19

A huge crowd braved super hot weather here June 24 for a Gay Pride Parade which will be talked about for a long time here.

By the time the parade wound its way from the Loop to Lincoln Park, the crowd numbered over 3000, which was easily three times greater than last year's turnout. . . .

For some reason, the Chicago Establishment came through beautifully with police help, and they even provided one of the Chicago Fire Boats—just off Belmont Rocks, of course—streaming pink and green water sprays over 100 feet into the air. . . .

The parade was led by two dedicated members of the group carrying a large banner and followed by a sound truck alternating John Phillip Souza with slogans.

This reporter was in the first car, shared by the Up North Restaurant; Pat Townson, of the Free Spirit Fellowship; and Tom Erwin, past president of Mattachine Midwest.

Dugan's Bistro, a new bar which just celebrated its grand opening, was right behind us with two antique Rolls Royces, one a 1931 Phaeton convertible, packed with people and decorated with dozens of yellow balloons.

The Knight Out bar's float was a little red streetcar, reminiscent of those which Chicago used to have.

The woman president of the local chapter of Heterosexuals for Sexual Freedom was among the riders on the streetcar.

The most unusual float, from the Gold Coast leather bar, was a huge black leather boot with chains, carrying over a dozen of the "leather set." The "boot" was preceded by a 1929 Model A Form, driven by the Gold Coast's version of "Bonnie and Clyde."

The recent winner of the Trip Lounge's "Mr. Trip" contest was there, driving his convertible.

Also marching were the Milwaukee Gay Peoples Union; the Gay People's Alliance from Illinois State University, Bloomington; the Gay Alliance from Springfield; and other Illinois groups—which included all of the current organizations in Chicago, such as teachers, priests, lesbians, medical students, law students, social workers, and Workers for Better Legislation Action. . . .

The *Chicago Sun-Times*, the only paper which covered the event from the Windy City's big four, noted that Gays were angry at everybody, including Ann Landers, Mayor Daley, Alderman Dick Simpson, the *Chicago Tribune*, and President Nixon.

DOCUMENT 200

Dan Sherbo, "The Alternative Rap"

Gay Alternative, ca. Aug. 1973 (no. 5), 3

Sunday June 24 was Gay Pride Day.

Twenty thousand gay people gathered under the warm sun in New York's Washington Square, relaxing from the forty-block long march, passing joints, wildly applauding Bette Midler on stage to come back for an encore.

Thousands more in cities throughout the country were holding Gay Pride festivities of their own, experiencing the joy and freedom of the afternoon.

Sunday June 24, in New Orleans, a crowd of people were celebrating at the Upstairs Lounge, a gay bar in the city's French Quarter. Laughing, drinking beer, gathering around the baby grand to sing; much like any other Sunday afternoon.

But suddenly, a fire was seen on the bottom steps of the stairway; and seconds later the stairs were engulfed in flames. Fifty or twenty persons were able to escape through the back room, but many more never got the chance. The fire swept into the bar with an explosion that instantly turned the room into a flaming inferno, engulfing the men and the woman trapped inside.

Twenty-nine persons were found dead in the building, their bodies crushed against each other in a frantic effort to escape out the front windows, some charred beyond recognition. Three others died a week later. And eight more are still hospitalized.

Reaction to the tragic fire from the press, police and other straight authorities has been minimal; most responses have been either negative or silent. The Upstairs was a widely-known gay bar in New Orleans, one that supported and worked with the gay community as few bars do; yet only one of that city's papers spoke of it as a "homosexual" establishment. The others avoided any mention of that fact, or that the victims were gay. News coverage was brief, and quickly died out after a couple of days.

The police and fire departments of New Orleans were as unconcerned over the fire as the news media, for investigations as to the cause of the holocaust have been practically non-existent. Arson evidence, a can of lighter fluid, was found by the Upstairs management in the stairwell of the bar, where witnesses say the fire began. Yet the city fire department claims the evidence is not official. As for the New Orleans Police department, the chief of detectives Maj. Henry Morris seemed to do little more than call the bar a "hangout for thieves and homosexuals," shrugging off the lives of thirty-two men and women burned to death that afternoon as if they were vermin to be rid of anyway. Because they were gay. Or were presumed to be gay.

The tragedy that occurred in New Orleans has a lot to teach us as a community of gay people. About what the community actually is, about how we stand in the eyes of the straight world, about where our gay love for each other is at.

We can come out and celebrate in the streets all we want, but we are still regarded by straight society as undesirables and degenerates. We can put aside the oppression of the nine-to-five world for an evening in a gay bar, but the danger of heterosexist hate will still be there. We may be as proud as hell of being gay, but until we stop the oppression that's being laid on us, all that pride won't do us any good. Because, like our brothers and sisters who died in the New Orleans fire, we are considered to be just more of those goddamn faggots and dykes.

ACKNOWLEDGMENTS

My first thanks go out to Stonewall historians Donn Teal, Martin Duberman, and David Carter, whose works provided the foundations for mine. I am also grateful to Marty for providing access to his research materials at the New York Public Library and David for helpful conversations, generous sharing, and detailed comments on my introduction.

At NYU Press, Eric Zinner and Dolma Ombadykow were enthusiastic supporters of this project and expert guides through the publication process. Thanks also to Timothy Stewart-Winter and the other NYU Press reviewer of the manuscript, to Jorge Olivares and Lisa Arellano for their helpful comments on the introduction, and to production director Martin Coleman, copy editor Dan Geist, and indexer Cameron Duder for their excellent work.

At San Francisco State University, I received generous financial support through the research funds associated with the Jamie and Phyllis Pasker Chair of U.S. History. My research assistants at San Francisco State—Mario Burrus, Mike Hephner, Matthew Mackay, and Eric Noble—completed outstanding work on this project.

The libraries and archives that helped me produce this book are referenced in the introduction, but I would also like to acknowledge the assistance of the librarians at San Francisco State and Colby College (especially Margaret Ericson, Karen Gillum, Marilyn Pukkila, Gabe Stowe, and Laine Thielstrom). I am also grateful for the valuable help of Jessica Bomarito at Cengage; Peggy Glahn and Jeff Moyer at Reveal Digital; Tal Nadan at the New York Public Library; Alex Barrows, Daniel Bau, Joanna Black, and Patricia Delara at the GLBT Historical Society in San Francisco; John Anderies and Bob Skiba at the John J. Wilcox, Jr. Archives in Philadelphia; William Holden at the History Project in Boston; Caitlin McCarthy at the LGBT Community Center National History Archive in New York; Loni Shibuyama at the ONE Archives in Los Angeles; and Alan Miller at the Canadian Lesbian and Gay Archives.

In working on this book, I received generous assistance from a variety of friends, collaborators, colleagues, comrades, and heroes. They include the individuals listed in the copyright acknowledgements, along with Tyler Alpern, Tracy Baim, Anna Battista, Carla Blumberg, Darius Bost, Michal Brody, Michael Bronski, Robert Cherry, Gary Chichester, Philip Clark, John D'Emilio, Dallas Denny, Aaron Devor, Mary Elings, Jeff Escoffier, Bruce Eves, Chris Freeman, Josh Alan Friedman, Marcia Gallo, Paul Havern, Emily Hobson, Karla Jay, David Johnson, Gerard Koskovich, Molly Ladd-Taylor, Ian Lekus, Martin Meeker, Margaret Olin, Alex Paul, Joey Plaster, Claire Potter, David Reichard,

Tim Retzloff, Robert Ridinger, Randall Sell, Timothy Stewart-Winter, Whitney Strub, Susan Stryker, Ashley West, Lara Wilson, and Chris Woods.

My final thanks and eternal gratitude go to Jorge Olivares. I completed this book during a year marked by the pain and heartache of family loss, but Jorge still found it possible to listen, advise, read, and edit. He spent countless hours with me in libraries and archives, usually focusing more on my research than on his. More importantly, he continues to love and be loved by me, which brings me immeasurable happiness and joy.

ACKNOWLEDGMENTS

COPYRIGHT ACKNOWLEDGMENTS

Homophile Youth Movement and *The New York Hymnal* courtesy of the
Craig Rodwell Papers, Manuscripts and Archives Division, The New York
Public Library, Astor, Lenox, and Tilden Foundations.

International Guild Guide courtesy of Angela Grimmer.

Janus Society Newsletter courtesy of Marjorie L. McCann and Edward M.
Weber.

Journal of Sex Research courtesy of Mary Ann Muller and Taylor and
Francis.

The Ladder courtesy of Kendra Mon.

Lavender Woman by Elandria V. Henderson courtesy of Elandria V.
Henderson.

Lesbian Tide courtesy of Lynn H. Ballen.

The Los Angeles Advocate courtesy of Here Publishing Inc.

Los Angeles Free Press courtesy of Steven Finger and *LosAngelesFreePress.
com.*

Mattachine Midwest and *Mattachine Midwest Newsletter* by William B. Kelley courtesy of Chen K. Ooi.

Mattachine Midwest and *Mattachine Midwest Newsletter* courtesy of David
L. Stienecker.

Mattachine Society of New York and *Mattachine Society of New York Newsletter, Mattachine Society of New York Insider*, and *Mattachine Times*
courtesy of Richard Leitsch.

Mattachine Society of Washington and *The Insider: Newsletter of the Mattachine Society of Washington* courtesy of Paul Kuntzler.

National Guardian courtesy of Karen Gellen.

New York City Gay Scene Guide courtesy of Richard Leitsch.

New York Daily News courtesy of Daily News, L.P. (New York) © 1969.

New York Post, 28 June 1969, courtesy of New York Post © 1969 (PARS International Corporation). All rights reserved. Used by permission and protected by the Copyright Laws of the United States. The printing, copying,
redistribution, or retransmission of this content without express written
permission is prohibited.

New York Post, 8 July 1969, courtesy of Jay Levin.

New York Times courtesy of the New York Times, 29 June, 30 June, and 3
July 1969 © 1969 (PARS International Corporation). All rights reserved.
Used by permission and protected by the Copyright Laws of the United
States. The printing, copying, redistribution, or retransmission of this con-
tent without express written permission is prohibited.

ONE magazine courtesy of ONE Archives at the University of Southern California Libraries.

Out of the Closets: Voices of Gay Liberation, edited by Karla Jay and Allen
Young, courtesy of Allen Young.

Philadelphia Free Press courtesy of Robert J. Ingram (and for material by Ki-
yoshi Kuromiya courtesy of Ronda Goldfein, Jane Shull, and J.D. Davids).

Rat by Martha A. Shelley ("Gay Is Good") courtesy of Martha A. Shelley.

Rat ("Queen Power: Fags against Pigs in Stonewall Bust") courtesy of Jeffrey Shero (author of the forthcoming book *Rat Subterranean News: Insights from the Underground*).

San Francisco Free Press by Carl Wittman courtesy of Allan K. Troxler.

Tangents courtesy of Christopher Todd White and the Tangent Group.

Transvestia courtesy of the University of Victoria Libraries Special Collections & University Archives.

Vanguard courtesy of Keith St. Clare.

Vector courtesy of Larry Littlejohn.

Village Voice courtesy of the *Village Voice* (Wright Media). Copyrighted 1966–69, 262816:0418AT.

APPENDIX

Suggestions for Additional Reading

For recommendations of additional primary sources that relate to the texts reprinted in *The Stonewall Riots: A Documentary History*, readers are encouraged to consult the book's online supplementary guide. The suggestions below, which focus mostly on secondary sources, are organized into nine categories, though many works could have been included under multiple headings. Note that the individual items are organized by date of publication, which is meant to highlight the development of scholarship over time. The categories are as follows: (1) Stonewall Riots, (2) LGBT history and Stonewall (published 1980–1999 and 2000–2018), (3) primary source collections, (4) books from the early 1970s, (5) oral histories, (6) autobiographies, (7) bars and policing (Northeast, West, Midwest, South, national), (8) LGBT movements (Northeast; West; Midwest; South; psychology, psychiatry, and religion; left and labor politics; race and people of color; lesbians and lesbian feminism; gender and trans; marriage, family, and reproduction; national; transnational), (9) LGBT media.

For studies of the Stonewall Riots, see Donn Teal, *The Gay Militants: How Gay Liberation Began in America, 1969–1971* (New York: Stein and Day, 1971); Martin Duberman, *Stonewall* (New York: Dutton, 1993); Martin Manalansan, "In the Shadows of Stonewall: Examining Gay Transnational Politics and the Diasporic Dilemma," *GLQ* 2, no. 4 (1995): 425–438; Scott Bravmann, *Queer Fictions of the Past: History, Culture, and Difference* (New York: Cambridge University Press, 1997), 68–96; David Carter, *Stonewall: The Riots That Sparked the Gay Revolution* (New York: St. Martin's, 2004); Elizabeth A. Armstrong and Suzanna M. Crage, "Movements and Memory: The Making of the Stonewall Myth," *American Sociological Review* 71, no. 5 (2006): 724–751; Jesi Gan, "'Still at the Back of the Bus': Sylvia Rivera's Struggle," *Centro Journal* 19, no. 1 (Spring 2007): 124–139; Nicola Field, "'They've Lost That Wounded Look': Stonewall and the Struggle for LGBT+ Rights," *Critical and Radical Social Work* 6, no. 1 (Mar. 2018): 35–50.

For books on LGBT history with significant discussions of the Stonewall Riots (published 1980–1999), see Toby Marotta, *The Politics of Homosexuality* (Boston: Houghton Mifflin, 1981); John D'Emilio, *Sexual Politics, Sexual Communities* (Chicago: University of Chicago Press, 1983); Barry D. Adam, *The Rise of a Gay and Lesbian Movement* (New York: Twayne, 1987); Margaret Cruikshank, *The Gay and Lesbian Liberation Movement* (New York: Routledge, 1992); John D'Emilio, *Making Trouble: Essays on Gay History, Politics, and the University*

(New York: Routledge, 1992); Leslie Feinberg, *Transgender Liberation: A Movement Whose Time Has Come* (New York: World View Forum, 1992); Kevin Jennings, ed., *Becoming Visible: A Reader in Gay and Lesbian History for High School and College Students* (Boston: Allyson, 1994); Neil Miller, *Out of the Past: Gay and Lesbian History from 1869 to the Present* (New York: Vintage, 1995); Charles Kaiser, *The Gay Metropolis, 1940–1996* (Boston: Houghton Mifflin, 1997); John Loughery, *The Other Side of Silence* (New York: Holt, 1998); Molly McGarry and Fred Wasserman, *Becoming Visible: An Illustrated History of Lesbian and Gay Life in Twentieth-Century America* (New York: Penguin, 1998); Leila J. Rupp, *A Desired Past: A Short History of Same-Sex Love in America* (Chicago: University of Chicago Press, 1999); David Clendinen and Adam Nagourney, *Out for Good* (New York: Simon & Schuster, 1999).

For books on LGBT history with significant discussion of the Stonewall Riots (published 2000–2018), see John D'Emilio, William B. Turner, and Urvashi Vaid, eds., *Creating Change: Sexuality, Public Policy, and Civil Rights* (New York: St. Martin's, 2000); John D'Emilio, *The World Turned: Essays on Gay History, Politics, and Culture* (Durham, NC: Duke University Press, 2002); Susan Stryker and Stephen Whittle, eds., *The Transgender Studies Reader*, vol. 1 (New York: Routledge, 2006); Susan Stryker, *Transgender History* (Berkeley, CA: Seal, 2008, 2017); Vicki L. Eaklor, *Queer America: A GLBT History of the 20th Century* (Westport, CT: Greenwood, 2008); Sherry Wolf, *Sexuality and Socialism: History, Politics, and Theory of LGBT Liberation* (Chicago: Haymarket, 2009); Michael Bronski, *A Queer History of the United States* (Boston: Beacon, 2011); Allan Bérubé, *My Desire for History: Essays in Gay, Community, and Labor History* (Chapel Hill: University of North Carolina Press, 2011); Marc Stein, *Rethinking the Gay and Lesbian Movement* (New York: Routledge, 2012); Linda Hirshman, *Victory* (New York: Harper, 2012); Susan Stryker and Aren Aizura, eds., *The Transgender Studies Reader*, vol. 2 (New York: Routledge, 2013); John D'Emilio, *In a New Century: Essays on Queer History, Politics, and Community Life* (Madison: University of Wisconsin Press, 2014); Leila Rupp and Susan Freeman, eds., *Understanding and Teaching U.S. Lesbian, Gay, Bisexual, and Transgender History* (Madison: University of Wisconsin Press, 2014); Susan Ferentinos, *Interpreting LGBT History at Museums and Historic Sites* (Lanham, MD: Rowman & Littlefield, 2014); Lillian Faderman, *The Gay Revolution* (New York: Simon & Schuster, 2015); Megan Springate, ed., *LGBTQ America* (Washington, D.C.: National Park Service, 2016); Don Romesburg, ed., *The Routledge History of Queer America* (New York: Routledge, 2018).

For primary source collections, see Jonathan Ned Katz, *Gay American History* (New York: Crowell, 1976); Michal Brody, ed., *Are We There Yet? A Continuing History of Lavender Woman* (Iowa City: Aunt Lute, 1985); Winston Leyland, ed., *Gay Roots: Twenty Years of Gay Sunshine* (San Francisco: Gay Sunshine, 1991); Winston Leyland, ed., *Gay Roots: An Anthology of Gay History, Sex, Politics and Culture* (San Francisco: Gay Sunshine, 1993); Mark

Blasius and Shane Phelan, eds., *We Are Everywhere: A Historical Sourcebook on Gay and Lesbian Politics* (New York: Routledge, 1997); Jim Kepner, *Rough News—Daring Views: 1950s' Pioneer Gay Press Journalism* (New York: Haworth, 1998); Robert Ridinger, ed., *Historic Speeches and Rhetoric for Gay and Lesbian Rights* (New York: Harrington Park, 2004); Tommi Avicolli Mecca, ed., *Smash the Church, Smash the State!: The Early Years of Gay Liberation* (San Francisco: City Lights, 2009); Craig Loftin, ed., *Letters to ONE: Gay and Lesbian Voices from the 1950s and 1960s* (Albany: SUNY Press, 2012); Michael G. Long, ed., *Gay Is Good: The Life and Letters of Gay Rights Pioneer Franklin Kameny* (Syracuse, NY: Syracuse University Press, 2014).

For books on LGBT activism published in the early 1970s, see Robin Morgan, ed., *Sisterhood Is Powerful* (New York: Random House, 1970); Dennis Altman, *Homosexual: Oppression and Liberation* (New York: Outerbridge & Dienstfrey, 1971); Arthur Bell, *Dancing the Gay Lib Blues: A Year in the Homosexual Liberation Movement* (New York: Simon & Schuster, 1971); Karla Jay and Allen Young, *Out of the Closets: Voices of Gay Liberation* (New York: Douglas, 1972); Del Martin and Phyllis Lyon, *Lesbian/Woman* (San Francisco: Glide, 1972); Sidney Abbott and Barbara Love, *Sappho Was a Right-On Woman* (New York: Stein and Day, 1972); Kay Tobin and Randy Wicker, *The Gay Crusaders* (New York: Paperback Library, 1972); Laud Humphreys, *Out of the Closets* (Englewood Cliffs, NJ: Prentice-Hall, 1972); John Francis Hunter, *The Gay Insider* (New York: Stonehill, 1972); Lige Clark and Jack Nichols, *I Have More Fun with You than Anybody* (New York: St. Martin's, 1972); Jill Johnston, *Lesbian Nation: The Feminist Solution* (New York: Simon & Schuster, 1973); Jeanne Córdova, *It's a Nasty Affair* (New Way, 1974).

For oral history works, see Eric Marcus, *Making History: The Struggle for Gay and Lesbian Equal Rights* (New York: HarperCollins, 1992); James T. Sears, *Lonely Hunters: An Oral History of Lesbian and Gay Southern Life, 1948–1968* (Boulder, CO: Westview, 1997); Eric Wat, *The Making of a Gay Asian Community: An Oral History of Pre-AIDS Los Angeles* (Lanham, MD: Rowman & Littlefield, 2001); Paul D. Cain, *Leading the Parade: Conversations with America's Most Influential Lesbians and Gay Men* (Lanham, MD: Scarecrow, 2002); Horacio N. Roque Ramírez, "My Community, My History, My Practice," *Oral History Review* 29, no. 2 (Summer/Fall 2002): 87–91; Jack Drescher and J. P. Merlino, eds., *American Psychiatry and Homosexuality: An Oral History* (New York: Routledge, 2007); E. Patrick Johnson, *Sweet Tea: Black Gay Men of the South* (Chapel Hill: University of North Carolina Press, 2008); Twin Cities GLBT Oral History Project, *Queer Twin Cities* (Minneapolis: University of Minnesota Press, 2010); Nan Alamilla Boyd and Horacio N. Roque Ramírez, eds., *Bodies of Evidence: The Practice of Queer Oral History* (New York: Oxford University Press, 2012); Elspeth Brown, "Trans/Feminist Oral History: Current Projects," *Transgender Studies Quarterly* 2, no. 4 (Nov. 2015).

For later autobiographical works that address LGBT activism in the 1960s and 1970s, see Dennis Altman, *Coming Out in the Seventies* (Sydney: Wild and Wooley, 1980); Cherríe Moraga and Gloria Anzaldúa, eds., *This Bridge Called My Back: Writings by Radical Women of Color* (Watertown, MA: Persephone, 1981); Audre Lorde, *Zami: A New Spelling of My Name* (Trumansburg, NY: Crossing, 1982); Barbara Smith, ed., *Home Girls: A Black Feminist Anthology* (New York: Kitchen Table, 1983); Anita Cornwell, *Black Lesbian in White America* (Tallahassee, FL: Naiad, 1983); Audre Lorde, *Sister Outsider* (Freedom, CA: Cross Press, 1984); Joseph Beam, ed., *In the Life: A Black Gay Anthology* (Boston: Alyson, 1986); Joan Nestle, *A Restricted Country* (Ithaca, NY: Firebrand, 1987); Jeanne Córdova, *Kicking the Habit: A Lesbian Nun Story* (Los Angeles: Multiple Dimensions, 1990); Essex Hemphill, ed., *Brother to Brother: New Writing by Black Gay Men* (Boston: Alyson, 1991); Martin Duberman, *Cures: A Gay Man's Odyssey* (New York: Dutton, 1991); Martin Duberman, *Mid-Life Queer, 1971–1982* (New York: Scribner, 1996); Jill Johnston, *Admission Accomplished: The Lesbian Nation Years (1970–75)* (London: Serpent's Tail, 1998); Leslie Feinberg, *Trans Liberation: Beyond Pink or Blue* (Boston: Beacon, 1998); Karla Jay, *Tales of the Lavender Menace: A Memoir of Liberation* (New York: Basic, 1999); Jack Nichols, *The Tomcat Chronicles: Erotic Adventures of a Gay Liberation Pioneer* (New York: Routledge, 2004); Gale Chester Whittington, *Beyond Normal: The Birth of Gay Pride* (Bangor, ME: Booklocker.com, 2010); Jeanne Córdova, *When We Were Outlaws: A Memoir of Love and Revolution* (Midway, FL: Spinsters, 2011); Kate Bornstein, *A Queer and Pleasant Danger* (Boston: Beacon, 2013); Mark Segal, *And Then I Danced: Traveling the Road to LGBT Equality* (Brooklyn: Akashic, 2015); Allen Young, *Left, Gay & Green: A Writer's Life* (CreateSpace, 2018).

On LGBT bars and anti-LGBT policing in the 1960s and 1970s (Northeast), see Elizabeth Lapovsky Kennedy and Madeline D. Davis, *Boots of Leather, Slippers of Gold: The History of a Lesbian Community* (New York: Routledge, 1993); Esther Newton, *Cherry Grove, Fire Island: Sixty Years in America's First Gay and Lesbian Town* (Boston: Beacon, 1993); Marc Stein, *City of Sisterly and Brotherly Loves: Lesbian and Gay Philadelphia, 1945–1972* (Chicago: University of Chicago Press, 2000); Marc Stein, "Rizzo's Raiders, Beaten Beats, and Coffeehouse Culture in 1950s Philadelphia," in *Modern American Queer History: Essays in Representation, Lived Experience, and Public Policy*, ed. Allida M. Black (Philadelphia: Temple University Press, 2001), 155–180; Samuel Delany, *Times Square Red, Times Square Blue* (New York: New York University Press, 2001); Bryant Simon, "New York Avenue: The Life and Death of Gay Spaces in Atlantic City, New Jersey, 1920–1990," *Journal of Urban History* 28, no. 3 (Mar. 2002): 300–327; Phillip Crawford, *The Mafia and the Gays* (CreateSpace, 2015).

On LGBT bars and anti-LGBT policing in the 1960s and 1970s (West), see John D'Emilio, "Gay Politics, Gay Community: San Francisco's Experience," *Socialist Review* (Jan. 1981): 77–104; Katie Gilmartin, "'We Weren't Bar People': Middle-Class Lesbian Identities and Cultural Spaces," *GLQ* 3, no. 1 (1996): 1–51; Gayle S. Rubin, "The Miracle Mile: South of Market and

Gay Male Leather, 1962–1997," in *Reclaiming San Francisco: History, Politics, Culture*, ed. James Brook, Chris Carlsson, and Nancy Joyce Peters (San Francisco: City Lights, 1998), 247–272; Nan Alamilla Boyd, *Wide Open Town: A History of Queer San Francisco to 1965* (Berkeley: University of California Press, 2003); Christopher Agee, "Gayola: Police Professionalization and the Politics of San Francisco's Gay Bars, 1950–1968," *Journal of the History of Sexuality* 15, no. 3 (Sept. 2006): 462–489; Lillian Faderman and Stuart Timmons, *Gay L.A.: A History of Sexual Outlaws, Power Politics, and Lipstick Lesbians* (Berkeley: University of California Press, 2006); Whitney Strub, "The Clearly Obscene and the Queerly Obscene: Heteronormativity and Obscenity in Cold War Los Angeles," *American Quarterly* 60, no. 2 (June 2008): 373–398; Christopher Agee, *The Streets of San Francisco: Policing and the Creation of a Cosmopolitan Liberal Politics, 1950–1972* (Chicago: University of Chicago Press, 2014); Emily K. Hobson, "Policing Gay L.A.: Mapping Racial Divides in the Homophile Era, 1950–1967," in *The Rising Tide of Color: Race, State Violence, and Radical Movements across the Pacific*, ed. Moon-Ho Jung (Seattle: University of Washington Press, 2014), 188–212; Jared Leighton, "'All of Us Are Unapprehended Felons': Gay Liberation, the Black Panther Party, and Intercommunal Efforts against Police Brutality in the Bay Area," *Journal of Social History* (Jan. 2018), doi: 10.1093/jsh/shx119.

On LGBT bars and anti-LGBT policing in the 1960s and 1970s (Midwest), see Rochella Thorpe, "'A House Where Queers Go': African-American Lesbian Nightlife in Detroit, 1940–1975," in *Inventing Lesbian Cultures in America*, ed. Ellen Lewin (Boston: Beacon, 1996), 40–61; Tim Retzloff, "Seer or Queer?: Postwar Fascination with Detroit's Prophet Jones," *GLQ* 8, no. 3 (2002): 271–296; Anne Enke, *Finding the Movement: Sexuality, Contested Space, and Feminist Activism* (Durham, NC: Duke University Press, 2007); St. Sukie de la Croix, *Chicago Whispers: A History of LGBT Chicago before Stonewall* (Madison: University of Wisconsin Press, 2012); Timothy Stewart-Winter, "The Law and Order Origins of Urban Gay Politics," *Journal of Urban History* 41, no. 5 (Sept. 2015): 825–835; Timothy Stewart-Winter, "Queer Law and Order: Sex, Criminality, and Policing in the Late Twentieth-Century United States," *Journal of American History* 102, no. 1 (June 2015): 61–72; Timothy Stewart-Winter, *Queer Clout: Chicago and the Rise of Gay Politics* (Philadelphia: University of Pennsylvania Press, 2016).

On LGBT bars and anti-LGBT policing in the 1960s and 1970s (South), see John Howard, *Carryin' On in the Lesbian and Gay South* (New York: New York University Press, 1997); John Howard, *Men Like That: A Southern Queer History* (Chicago: University of Chicago Press, 1999); Karen L. Graves, *And They Were Wonderful Teachers: Florida's Purge of Gay and Lesbian Teachers* (Urbana: University of Illinois Press, 2009); Stacy Braukman, *Communists and Perverts under the Palms: The Johns Committee in Florida, 1956–1965* (Gainesville: University Press of Florida, 2012); Genny Beemyn, *A Queer Capital: A History of Gay Life in Washington, D.C.* (New York: Routledge, 2014).

On LGBT bars and anti-LGBT policing in the 1960s and 1970s (national), see Joan Nestle, ed., *The Persistent Desire: A Femme-Butch Reader* (Boston: Alyson, 1992); Brett Beemyn, ed., *Creating A Place for Ourselves* (New York: Routledge, 1997); William N. Eskridge Jr., *Gaylaw: Challenging the Apartheid of the Closet* (Cambridge, MA: Harvard University Press, 1999); David K. Johnson, *Lavender Scare: The Cold War Persecution of Gays and Lesbians in the Federal Government* (Chicago: University of Chicago Press, 2004); John D'Emilio, *Lost Prophet: The Life and Times of Bayard Rustin* (Chicago: University of Chicago Press, 2004); William N. Eskridge Jr., *Dishonorable Passions: Sodomy Laws in America, 1861–2003* (New York: Viking, 2008); Thaddeus Russell, "The Color of Discipline: Civil Rights and Black Sexuality," *American Quarterly* 60, no. 1 (2008): 101–128; Douglas M. Charles, "From Subversion to Obscenity: The FBI's Investigations of the Early Homophile Movement in the United States, 1953–1958," *Journal of the History of Sexuality* 19, no. 2 (May 2010): 262–287; Margot Canaday, *The Straight State: Sexuality and Citizenship in Twentieth-Century America* (Princeton, NJ: Princeton University Press, 2011); Whitney Strub, *Perversion for Profit: The Politics of Pornography and the Rise of the New Right* (New York: Columbia University Press, 2011); Douglas Charles, "Communist and Homosexual: The FBI, Harry Hay, and the Secret Side of the Lavender Scare, 1943–1961," *American Communist History* 11, no. 1 (Apr. 2012): 101–124; Christina Hanhardt, *Safe Space: Gay Neighborhood History and the Politics of Violence* (Durham, NC: Duke University Press, 2013); Simon Hall, "Americanism, Un-Americanism, and the Gay Rights Movement," *Journal of American Studies* 47, no. 2 (Nov. 2013): 1109–1130; Douglas Charles, *Hoover's War on Gays: Exposing the FBI's "Sex Deviates" Program* (Lawrence: University Press of Kansas, 2015); Springate, ed., *LGBTQ America* (2016); Douglas Charles, "'A Source of Great Embarrassment to the Bureau': Gay Activist Jack Nichols, His FBI Agent Father, and the Mattachine Society of Washington," *Historian* 79, no. 3 (Fall 2017): 504–522; Romesburg, ed., *The Routledge History* (2018).

For studies of the LGBT movement from 1950 to 1973 (Northeast), see Marotta, *The Politics of Homosexuality* (1981); Marc Stein, "Sex Politics in the City of Sisterly and Brotherly Loves," *Radical History Review*, no. 59 (Spring 1994): 60–92; Terence Kissack, "Freaking Fag Revolutionaries: New York's Gay Liberation Front, 1969–1971," *Radical History Review* 62 (Spring 1995): 104–134; Marc Stein, "'Birthplace of the Nation': Imagining Lesbian and Gay Communities in Philadelphia, 1969–70," in *Creating a Place for Ourselves*, ed. Brett Beemyn (New York: Routledge, 1997), 253–288; History Project, *Improper Bostonians: Lesbian and Gay History from the Puritans to Playland* (Boston: Beacon, 1998); Stein, *City of Sisterly and Brotherly Loves* (2000); Brett Beemyn, "The Silence Is Broken: A History of the First Lesbian, Gay, and Bisexual College Student Groups," *Journal of the History of Sexuality* 12, no. 2 (Apr. 2003): 205–223; Karen Christel Krahulik, *Provincetown: From Pilgrim Landing to Gay Resort* (New York: New York University Press, 2005); David

Eisenbach, *Gay Power: An American Revolution* (New York: Carroll & Graf, 2006); Richard Meyer, "*Gay Power* Circa 1970: Visual Strategies for Sexual Revolution," *GLQ* 12, no. 3 (2006): 441–464; Gan, "'Still at the Back of the Bus'" (2007); Stephan L. Cohen, *The Gay Liberation Youth Movement in New York: "An Army of Lovers Cannot Fail"* (New York: Routledge, 2008); Kevin J. Mumford, "The Trouble with Gay Rights: Race and the Politics of Sexual Orientation in Philadelphia, 1969–1982," *Journal of American History* 98, no. 1 (Jun. 2011): 49–72; *Street Transvestite Action Revolutionaries: Survival, Revolt, and Queer Antagonist Struggles* (Untorelli, 2013); Tracy Baim, *Barbara Gittings: Gay Pioneer* (Chicago: Prairie Avenue Productions, 2015); Susan Stryker, "Radical Queen: An Interview with Tommi Avicolli Mecca," *Transgender Studies Quarterly* 3, nos. 1–2 (May 2016).

For studies of the LGBT movement from 1950 to 1973 (West), see D'Emilio, "Gay Politics" (1981); Manuel Castells, *The City and the Grassroots: A Cross-Cultural Theory of Urban Social Movements* (Berkeley: University of California Press, 1983); Stuart Timmons, *The Trouble with Harry Hay: Founder of the Modern Gay Movement* (Boston: Alyson, 1990); Harry Hay, *Radically Gay: Gay Liberation in the Words of Its Founder*, ed. Will Roscoe (Boston: Beacon, 1996); Susan Stryker and Jim Van Buskirk, *Gay by the Bay: A History of Queer Culture in the San Francisco Bay Area* (San Francisco: Chronicle, 1996); Members of the Gay and Lesbian Historical Society of Northern California, "MTF Transgender Activism in the Tenderloin and Beyond, 1966–1975," *GLQ* 4, no. 2 (1998): 349–372; Michael R. Gorman, *The Empress Is a Man: Stories from the Life of José Sarria* (New York: Haworth, 1998); Martin Meeker, "Behind the Mask of Respectability: Reconsidering the Mattachine Society and Male Homophile Practice, 1950s and 1960s," *Journal of the History of Sexuality* 10, no. 1 (Jan. 2001): 78–116; Moira Rachel Kenney, *Mapping Gay L.A.: The Intersection of Place and Politics* (Philadelphia: Temple University Press, 2001); Elizabeth A. Armstrong, *Forging Gay Identities: Organizing Sexuality in San Francisco, 1950–1994* (Chicago: University of Chicago Press, 2002); Gary Atkins, *Gay Seattle: Stories of Exile and Belonging* (Seattle: University of Washington Press, 2003); Boyd, *Wide Open Town* (2003); Peter Boag, "'Does Portland Need a Homophile Society?': Gay Culture and Activism in the Rose City between World War II and Stonewall," *Oregon Historical Quarterly* 105, no. 1 (Spring 2004): 6–39; James T. Sears, *Behind the Mask of Mattachine: The Hal Call Chronicles and the Early Movement for Homosexual Emancipation* (New York: Haworth, 2006); Martin Meeker, *Contacts Desired: Gay and Lesbian Communications and Community, 1940s–1970s* (Chicago: University of Chicago Press, 2006); Faderman and Timmons, *Gay L.A.* (2006); Daniel Hurewitz, *Bohemian Los Angeles and the Making of Modern Politics* (Berkeley: University of California Press, 2007); Robert Self, "Sex in the City: The Politics of Sexual Liberalism in Los Angeles, 1963–79," *Gender & History* 20, no. 2 (Aug. 2008): 288–311; Josh Sides, *Erotic City: Sexual Revolutions and the Making of Modern San Francisco* (New York: Oxford University Press, 2009);

C. Todd White, *Pre-Gay L.A.: A Social History of the Movement for Homosexual Rights* (Urbana: University of Illinois Press, 2009); Jonathan Bell, "'To Strive for Economic and Social Justice': Welfare, Sexuality, and Liberal Politics in San Francisco in the 1960s," *Journal of Policy History* 22, no. 2 (Apr. 2010): 193–225; David A. Reichard, "'We Can't Hide and They Are Wrong': The Society for Homosexual Freedom and the Struggle for Recognition at Sacramento State College, 1969–1971," *Law and History Review* 28, no. 3 (Aug. 2010): 629–674; J. Todd Ormsbee, *The Meaning of Gay: Interaction, Publicity, and Community among Homosexual Men in 1960s San Francisco* (Lanham, MD: Rowman & Littlefield, 2010); Nan Alamilla Boyd, "San Francisco's Castro District: From Gay Liberation to Tourist Destination," *Journal of Tourism and Cultural Change* 9, no. 2 (Sept. 2011): 228–239; Betty Luther Hillman, "'The Most Profoundly Revolutionary Act a Homosexual Can Engage In': Drag and the Politics of Gender Presentation in the San Francisco Gay Liberation Movement, 1964–1972," *Journal of the History of Sexuality* 20, no. 1 (Jan. 2011): 153–181; Jonathan Bell, *California Crucible: The Forging of Modern American Liberalism* (Philadelphia: University of Pennsylvania Press, 2012); David Reichard, "Animating Ephemera through Oral History: Interpreting Visual Traces of California Gay College Student Organizing from the 1970s," *Oral History Review* 39, no. 1 (Winter 2012): 37–60; Katherine Turk, "'Our Militancy Is in Our Openness': Gay Employment Rights Activism in California and the Question of Sexual Orientation in Sex Equality Law," *Law & History Review* 31, no. 2 (May 2013): 423–469; Ian Baldwin, "Rethinking the 'Era of Limits': Equitable Housing, Gay Liberation, and the Opening of the American Family in Greater Los Angeles during the Long 1970s," *California History* 91, no. 3 (Fall 2014): 42–59; Emily Hobson, *Lavender and Red: Liberation and Solidarity in the Gay and Lesbian Left* (Berkeley: University of California Press, 2016).

For studies of the LGBT movement from 1950 to 1973 (Midwest), see Beth Bailey, *Sex in the Heartland* (Cambridge, MA: Harvard University Press, 1999); John D. Poling, "Standing Up for Gay Rights," *Chicago History* 33 (Spring 2005): 4–17; Enke, *Finding the Movement* (2007); Twin Cities GLBT Oral History Project, *Queer Twin Cities* (2010); Stewart Van Cleve, *Land of 10,000 Loves: A History of Queer Minnesota* (Minneapolis: University of Minnesota Press, 2012); De la Croix, *Chicago Whispers* (2012); Stewart-Winter, "The Law and Order Origins" (2015); Stewart-Winter, "Queer Law and Order" (2015); Andrea Rottmann, "God Loves Them as They Are," *Wisconsin Magazine of History* 99, no. 2 (Winter 2015): 2–13; Kevin Scharlau, "Navigating Change in the Homophile Heartland: Kansas City's Phoenix Society and the Early Gay Rights Movement, 1966–1971," *Missouri Historical Review* 109, no. 4 (July 2015): 234–253; Scott Seyforth, "'In People's Faces for Lesbian and Gay Rights': Stories of Activism in Madison, Wisconsin, 1970 to 1990," *Oral History Review* 43, no. 1 (Winter 2016): 81–97; Stewart-Winter, *Queer Clout* (2016).

For studies of the LGBT movement from 1950 to 1973 (South), see Daneel Buring, *Lesbian and Gay Memphis: Building Communities behind the Magnolia Curtain* (New York: Garland, 1997); Howard, *Men Like That* (1999); James T. Sears, *Rebels, Rubyfruit, and Rhinestones: Queering Space in the Stonewall South* (New Brunswick, NJ: Rutgers University Press, 2001); Johnson, *The Lavender Scare* (2004); Brock Thompson, *The Un-natural State: Arkansas and the Queer South* (Fayetteville: University of Arkansas Press, 2010); Catherine Fosl, "'It Could Be Dangerous!': Gay Liberation and Gay Marriage in Louisville, Kentucky, 1970," *Ohio Valley History* 12, no. 1 (Spring 2012): 45–64; Beemyn, *A Queer Capital* (2014); Kent Peacock, "Race, the Homosexual, and the Mattachine Society of Washington, 1961–1970," *Journal of the History of Sexuality* 25, no. 2 (May 2016): 267–296.

For studies of the LGBT movement from 1950 to 1973 (psychology, psychiatry, and religion), see Ronald Bayer, *Homosexuality and American Psychiatry: The Politics of Diagnosis* (New York: Basic, 1981); Melissa Wilcox, "Of Markets and Missions: The Early History of the Universal Fellowship of Metropolitan Community Churches," *Religion and American Culture* 11, no. 1 (2001): 83–108; Heather Rachelle White, "Proclaiming Liberation: The Historical Roots of LGBT Religious Organizing, 1946–1976," *Nova Religio* 11, no. 4 (2008): 102–119; Heather White, *Reforming Sodom: Protestants and the Rise of Gay Rights* (Chapel Hill: University of North Carolina Press, 2015); Jack Drescher, "Out of DSM: Depathologizing Homosexuality," *Behavioral Sciences* 5, no. 4 (2015): 565–575; James McCartin, "The Church and Gay Liberation: The Case of John McNeill," *U.S. Catholic Historian* 34, no. 1 (Winter 2016): 125–141; Abram Lewis, "'We Are Certain of Our Own Insanity': Antipsychiatry and the Gay Liberation Movement, 1968–1980," *Journal of the History of Sexuality* 25, no. 2 (Jan. 2016): 83–113; Gillian Frank, Bethany Moreton, and Heather White, eds., *Devotions and Desires: Histories of Sexuality and Religion in the Twentieth-Century United States* (Chapel Hill: University of North Carolina Press, 2018).

For studies of the LGBT movement from 1950 to 1973 (left and labor politics), see Justin David Suran, "Coming Out against the War: Antimilitarism and the Politicization of Homosexuality in the Era of Vietnam," *American Quarterly* 53, no. 3 (Sept. 2001): 452–488; Ian Lekus, "Queer Harvests: Homosexuality, the U.S. New Left, and the Venceremos Brigades to Cuba," *Radical History Review* 89 (Spring 2004): 57–91; Christopher Phelps, "A Neglected Document on Socialism and Sex," *Journal of the History of Sexuality* 16, no. 1 (Jan. 2007), 1–13; Regina Kunzel, "Lessons in Being Gay: Queer Encounters in Gay and Lesbian Prison Activism," *Radical History Review*, no. 100 (Winter 2008): 10–37; Christopher Phelps, "On Socialism and Sex: An Introduction," *New Politics* 12, no. 1 (Summer 2008); "Symposium on Gays and the Left (Part I), *New Politics* 12, no. 1 (Summer 2008); "Symposium on Gays and the Left (Part II)," *New Politics* 12, no. 2 (Winter 2009); Charles, "Communist and Homosexual" (2012); Christopher Phelps, "The Closet in the Party:

The Young Socialist Alliance, the Socialist Workers Party, and Homosexuality, 1962–1970," *Labor* 10, no. 4 (Winter 2013): 11–38; Phil Tiemeyer, *Plane Queer: Labor, Sexuality, and AIDS in the History of Male Flight Attendants* (Berkeley: University of California Press, 2013); Melinda Chateauvert, *Sex Workers Unite: A History of the Movement from Stonewall to SlutWalk* (Boston: Beacon, 2014); Miriam Frank, *Out in the Union: A Labor History of Queer America* (Philadelphia: Temple University Press, 2014).

For studies of the LGBT movement from 1950 to 1973 (race and people of color), see Delroy Constantine-Simms, ed., *The Greatest Taboo: Homosexuality in Black Communities* (Los Angeles: Alyson, 2000); E. Patrick Johnson and Mae G. Henderson, *Black Queer Studies: A Critical Anthology* (Durham, NC: Duke University Press, 2005); Tim Retzloff, "Eliding Trans Latino/a Queer Experience in U.S. LGBT History: José Sarria and Sylvia Rivera Reexamined," *Centro Journal* 19, no. 1 (2007): 140–161; Kevin Mumford, *Not Straight, Not White: Black Gay Men from the March on Washington to the AIDS Crisis* (Chapel Hill: University of North Carolina Press, 2016); Leighton, "'All of Us Are Unapprehended Felons'" (2018).

For studies of the LGBT movement from 1950 to 1973 (lesbians and lesbian feminism), see Deborah Goleman Wolf, *The Lesbian Community* (Berkeley: University of California Press, 1980); Moraga and Anzaldúa, eds., *This Bridge Called My Back* (1981); Cornwell, *Black Lesbian in White America* (1983); Smith, ed., *Home Girls* (1983); Lorde, *Sister Outsider* (1984); Alice Echols, *Daring to Be Bad: Radical Feminism in America, 1967–1976* (Minneapolis: University of Minnesota Press, 1989); Lillian Faderman, *Odd Girls and Twilight Lovers: A History of Lesbian Life in Twentieth-Century America* (New York: Columbia University Press, 1991); Trisha Franzen, "Differences and Identities: Feminism and the Albuquerque Lesbian Community," *Signs* 18, no. 4 (1993): 891–906; Verta Taylor and Leila J. Rupp, "Women's Culture and Lesbian Feminist Activism: A Reconsideration of Cultural Feminism," *Signs* 19, no. 1 (Autumn 1993): 32–61; Lisa Duggan, *Sex Wars: Sexual Dissent and Political Culture* (New York: Routledge, 1995); Arlene Stein, *Sex and Sensibility: Stories of a Lesbian Generation* (Berkeley: University of California Press, 1997); Stein, *City of Sisterly and Brotherly Loves* (2000); Jane Gerhard, *Desiring Revolution: Second-Wave Feminism and the Rewriting of American Sexual Thought, 1920 to 1982* (New York: Columbia University Press, 2001); Linda Garber, *Identity Poetics: Race, Class, and the Lesbian-Feminist Roots of Queer Theory* (New York: Columbia University Press, 2001); Anne M. Valk, "Living a Feminist Lifestyle: The Intersection of Theory and Action in a Lesbian Feminist Collective," *Feminist Studies* 28, no. 2 (Summer 2002): 303–332; Trinity A. Ordona, "Asian Lesbians in San Francisco: Struggles to Create a Safe Space, 1970s–1980s," in *Asian/Pacific Islander American Women: A Historical Anthology*, ed. Shirley Hune and Gail M. Nomura (New York: New York University Press, 2003), 319–334; Marcia M. Gallo, *Different Daughters: A History of the Daughters of Bilitis and the Rise of the Lesbian Rights Movement*

(New York: Carroll & Graf, 2006); Estelle B. Freedman, *Feminism, Sexuality, and Politics* (Chapel Hill: University of North Carolina Press, 2006); Enke, *Finding the Movement* (2007); Stephanie Gilmore and Elizabeth Kaminsky, "A Part and Apart: Lesbian and Straight Activists Negotiate Identity in a Second-Wave Organization," *Journal of the History of Sexuality* 16, no. 2 (Jan. 2007): 95–113; Heather Murray, "Free for All Lesbians: Lesbian Cultural Production and Consumption in the United States during the 1970s," *Journal of the History of Sexuality* 16, no. 2 (May 2007): 251–275; Joanne Passett, *Sex Variant Woman: The Life of Jeannette Howard Foster* (Philadelphia: Da Capo, 2008); Stephanie Gilmore, *Groundswell: Grassroots Feminist Activism in Postwar America* (New York: Routledge, 2012); Raewyn Connell, "Transsexual Women and Feminist Thought: Toward New Understanding and New Politics," *Signs* 37, no. 4 (Summer 2012): 857–881; Betty Luther Hillman, "'The Clothes I Wear Help Me to Know My Own Power': The Politics of Gender Presentation in the Era of Women's Liberation," *Frontiers* 34, no. 2 (2013): 155–185; Susan Stryker, "Lesbian Generations—Transsexual...Lesbian...Feminist...," *Feminist Studies* 39, no. 2 (Summer 2013): 375–383; Beemyn, *A Queer Capital* (2014); Heather Murray, "'This Is 1975, Not 1875': Despair and Longings in Women's Letters to Cambridge Lesbian Liberation and Daughters of Bilitis Counselor Julie Lee in the 1970s," *Journal of the History of Sexuality* 23, no. 1 (Jan. 2014): 96–122; Emily Thuma, "Against the 'Prison/Psychiatric State': Anti-violence Feminisms and the Politics of Confinement in the 1970s," *Feminist Formations* 26, no. 2 (2014): 26–51; Kath Browne, Marta Olasik, and Julie Podmore, "Reclaiming Lesbian Feminisms: Beginning Discussions on Communities, Geographies and Politics," *Women's Studies International Forum* 56 (May 2016): 113–123; Emma Heaney, "Women-Identified Women: Trans Women in 1970s Lesbian Feminist Organizing," *Transgender Studies Quarterly* 3, nos. 1–2 (May 2016); Cristan Williams, "Radical Inclusion: Recounting the Trans Inclusive History of Radical Feminism," *Transgender Studies Quarterly* 3, nos. 1–2 (May 2016); Talia Bettcher, "A Conversation with Jeanne Córdova," *Transgender Studies Quarterly* 3, nos. 1–2 (May 2016); Sue Katz, "Working Class Dykes: Class Conflict in the Lesbian/Feminist Movements in the 1970s," *Sixties* 10, no. 2 (Dec. 2017): 281–289.

For studies of the LGBT movement from 1950 to 1973 (gender and trans), see Joanne Meyerowitz, *How Sex Changed: A History of Transsexuality in the United States* (Cambridge, MA: Harvard University Press, 2003); Aaron H. Devor and Nicholas Matte, "ONE Inc. and Reed Erickson: The Uneasy Collaboration of Gay and Trans Activism, 1964–2003," *GLQ* 10, no. 2 (2004): 179–209; Craig M. Loftin, "Unacceptable Mannerisms: Gender Anxieties, Homosexual Activism, and Swish in the United States, 1945–1965," *Journal of Social History* 40, no. 3 (Spring 2007): 577–596; Aaron Devor and Nicholas Matte, "Building a Better World for Trans People: Reed Erickson and the Erickson Educational Foundation," *International Journal of Transgenderism* 10, no. 1 (Spring 2007): 47–68; Stryker, *Transgender History* (2008); Susan Stryker,

"Transgender History, Homonormativity, and Disciplinarity," *Radical History Review*, no. 100 (Winter 2008): 144–157.

For studies of the LGBT movement from 1950 to 1973 (marriage, family, and reproduction), see Daniel Rivers, "'In the Best Interests of the Child': Lesbian and Gay Parenting Custody Cases, 1967–1985," *Journal of Social History* 43, no. 4 (Summer 2010): 917–943; Heather Murray, *Not in This Family: Gays and the Meaning of Kinship in Postwar North America* (Philadelphia: University of Pennsylvania Press, 2010); Greta Rensenbrink, "Parthenogenesis and Lesbian Separatism: Regenerating Women's Community through Virgin Birth in the United States in the 1970s and 1980s," *Journal of the History of Sexuality* 19, no. 2 (May 2010): 288–316; Lauren Jae Gutterman, "'The House on the Borderland': Lesbian Desire, Marriage, and the Household, 1950–1979," *Journal of Social History* 46, no. 1 (Fall 2012): 1–22; Robert Self, *All in the Family: The Realignment of American Democracy since the 1960s* (New York: Hill & Wang, 2012); Daniel Rivers, *Radical Relations: Lesbian Mothers, Gay Fathers, and Their Children in the United States since World War II* (Chapel Hill: University of North Carolina Press, 2013); Katie Batza, "From Sperm Runners to Sperm Banks: Lesbians, Assisted Conception, and Challenging the Fertility Industry, 1971–1983," *Journal of Women's History* 28, no. 2 (Summer 2016): 82–102; Stephen Vider, "Lesbian and Gay Marriage and Romantic Adjustment in the 1950s and 1960s United States," *Gender & History* 29, no. 3 (Nov. 2017): 693–715; Elise Chenier, "Love-Politics: Lesbian Wedding Practices in Canada and the United States from the 1920s to the 1970s," *Journal of the History of Sexuality* 27, no. 2 (May 2018): 294–321.

For studies of the LGBT movement from 1950 to 1973 (national), see D'Emilio, *Sexual Politics* (1983); Adam, *The Rise* (1987); D'Emilio, *Making Trouble* (1992); Cruikshank, *The Gay and Lesbian Liberation Movement* (1992); Miller, *Out of the Past* (1995); Loughery, *The Other Side* (1998); James V. Carmichael, ed., *Daring to Find Our Names* (Westport, CT: Greenwood, 1998); Robert W. Bailey, *Gay Politics, Urban Politics: Identity and Economics in the Urban Setting* (New York: Columbia University Press, 1999); Clendinen and Nagourney, *Out for Good* (1999); Joyce Murdoch and Deb Price, *Courting Justice: Gay Men and Lesbians v. the Supreme Court* (New York: Basic, 2001); Black, ed., *Modern American Queer History* (2001); Vern L. Bullough, ed., *Before Stonewall: Activists for Gay and Lesbian Rights in Historical Context* (New York: Haworth, 2002); D'Emilio, *The World Turned* (2002); Cain, *Leading the Parade* (2002); Henry Abelove, *Deep Gossip* (Minneapolis: University of Minnesota Press, 2003); J. Louis Campbell, *Jack Nichols, Gay Pioneer: "Have You Heard My Message?"* (New York: Haworth, 2007); Eaklor, *Queer America* (2008); Regina Kunzel, *Criminal Intimacy: Prison and the Uneven History of Modern American Sexuality* (Chicago: University of Chicago Press, 2008); Simon Hall, "The American Gay Rights Movement and Patriotic Protest," *Journal of the History of Sexuality* 19, no. 3 (Sept. 2010): 536–562; Charles, "From Subversion to Obscenity" (2010); Marc Stein, *Sexual*

Injustice: Supreme Court Decisions from Griswold to Roe (Chapel Hill: University of North Carolina Press, 2010); Craig Loftin, *Masked Voices: Gay Men and Lesbians in Cold War America* (Albany: SUNY Press, 2012); Stein, *Rethinking* (2012); Hirshman, *Victory* (2012); Hall, "Americanism" (2013); Whitney Strub, "'Challenging the Anti-pleasure League': Physique Pictorial and the Cultivation of Gay Politics," in *Modern Print Activism in the United States*, ed. Rachel Schreiber (Burlington, VT: Ashgate, 2013), 161–77; Marc Stein, "Canonizing Homophile Sexual Respectability: Archives, History, and Memory," *Radical History Review*, no. 120 (Fall 2014): 52–73; D'Emilio, *In a New Century* (2014); Faderman, *The Gay Revolution* (2015); Stephen Vider, "'The Ultimate Extension of Gay Community': Communal Living and Gay Liberation in the 1970s," *Gender & History* 27, no. 3 (Nov. 2015): 865–881; Melissa Adler, "'Let's Not Homosexualize the Library Stacks': Liberating Gays in the Library Catalog," *Journal of the History of Sexuality* 24, no. 3 (Sept. 2015): 478–507; Scott de Groot, "'A Curse on Those Who Need Heroes?': Genealogical Appropriation and the Historical Horizons of Gay Liberation, 1969–1975," *Left History* 19, no. 1 (Spring 2015): 25–55; Charles, *Hoover's War* (2015); Whitney Strub, "The Homophile Is a Sexual Being: Wallace de Ortega Maxey's Pulp Theology and Gay Activism," *Journal of the History of Sexuality* 25, no. 2 (May 2016): 323–353; Jim Downs, *Stand by Me: The Forgotten History of Gay Liberation* (New York: Basic, 2016); Springate, ed., *LGBTQ America* (2016); Jeffrey Escoffier, "Sex in the Seventies: Gay Porn Cinema as an Archive for the History of American Sexuality," *Journal of the History of Sexuality* 26, no. 1 (Jan. 2017): 88–113; Charles, "'A Source of Great Embarrassment'" (2017); Catherine Batza, *Before AIDS: Gay Health Politics in the 1970s* (Philadelphia: University of Pennsylvania Press, 2018); Romesburg, ed., *The Routledge History of Queer America* (2018); David Johnson, *Buying Gay* (New York: Columbia University Press, 2019).

For studies of the LGBT movement from 1950 to 1973 (transnational), see David S. Churchill, "Transnationalism and Homophile Political Culture in the Postwar Decades," *GLQ* 15, no. 1 (2009): 31–66; Leila J. Rupp, "The Persistence of Transnational Organizing: The Case of the Homophile Movement," *American Historical Review* 116, no. 4 (Oct. 2011): 1014–1039; Víctor Macías-González, "Transnationalism and the Development of Domesticity in Mexico City's Homophile Community, 1920–1960," *Gender History* 23, no. 3 (Oct. 2014): 519–544; Marc Stein, ed., "U.S. Homophile Internationalism," *Journal of Homosexuality* 64, no. 7 (Apr. 2017).

For studies of LGBT media, see Roger Streitmatter, *Unspeakable: The Rise of the Gay and Lesbian Press in America* (Boston: Faber, 1995); Edward Alwood, *Straight News: Gays, Lesbians, and the News Media* (New York: Columbia University Press, 1996); Larry Gross and James D. Woods, eds., *The Columbia Reader on Lesbians and Gay Men in Media, Society, and Politics* (New York: Columbia University Press, 1999); Steven Capsuto, *Alternate Channels: The Uncensored Story of Gay and Lesbian Images on Radio and Television* (New

York: Ballantine, 2000); Meeker, *Contacts Desired* (2006); David K. Johnson, "Physique Pioneers: The Politics of 1960s Consumer Culture," *Journal of Social History* 43, no. 4 (Summer 2010): 867–892; Robert Hill, "'We Share a Sacred Secret': Gender, Domesticity, and Containment in Transvestia's Histories and Letters from Crossdressers and Their Wives," *Journal of Social History* 44, no. 2 (Spring 2011): 729–750; Kevin Allen Leonard, "Containing 'Perversion': African Americans and Same-Sex Desire in Cold War Los Angeles," *Journal of the History of Sexuality* 20, no. 3 (Sept. 2011): 545–567; Loftin, ed., *Letters to ONE* (2012); Tracy Baim, ed., *Gay Press, Gay Power: The Growth of LGBT Community Newspapers in America* (Chicago: Prairie Avenue Productions, 2012); Strub, "'Challenging the Anti-pleasure League'" (2013); Stein, "Canonizing" (2014); Elyse Vigiletti, "Normalizing the 'Variant' in *The Ladder*, America's Second Lesbian Magazine, 1956–1963," *Frontiers* 36, no. 2 (2015): 47–71; Edward Alwood, "The Role of Public Relations in the Gay Rights Movement, 1950–1969," *Journalism History* 41, no. 1 (Spring 2015): 11–20; Marcia Gallo, *"No One Helped": Kitty Genovese and the Myth of Urban Apathy* (Ithaca, NY: Cornell University Press, 2015); Johnson, *Buying Gay* (2019).

NOTES

Introduction

1 For a discussion of LGBTQ terminology, see Marc Stein, *Rethinking the Gay and Lesbian Movement* (New York: Routledge, 2012), 5–9. In this book, I use "LGBT" or "LGBTQ" to signal my inclusive intentions and align myself with today's preferred language, but there are times when I use "gay" as an all-inclusive term because this was commonly done (even by lesbians, bisexuals, and trans people) in the period addressed by this book. As for my use of "riots," some argue that the term should be avoided because of its negative, irrational, and violent connotations. I use it because it was a favored term at the time, but also because I do not agree that riots by oppressed peoples should be interpreted as necessarily negative or invariably irrational. I also refer to the Stonewall rebellion, revolt, and uprising.

2 See "Inaugural Address by President Barack Obama," White House, Office of the Press Secretary, 21 Jan. 2013, https://obamawhitehouse.archives.gov.

3 The account that follows is based on the documents reprinted and cited in part 2, as well as Martin Duberman, *Stonewall* (New York: Dutton, 1993); David Carter, Andrew Scott Dolkart, Gale Harris, and Jay Shockley, *Stonewall*, National Historical Landmark Nomination, 1999, www.nps.gov; David Carter, *An Analytical Collation of Accounts of and Documents Concerning the Stonewall Riots Recorded in the Year 1969* (2002; unpublished but shared with me by Carter); David Carter, *Stonewall: The Riots That Sparked the Gay Revolution* (New York: St. Martin's, 2004); New York City Landmarks Preservation Commission, "Stonewall Inn," 23 June 2015, http://s-media.nyc.gov.

4 Barack Obama, "Presidential Proclamation—Establishment of the Stonewall National Monument," 24 June 2016, https://obamawhitehouse.archives.gov.

5 Donn Teal, *The Gay Militants: How Gay Liberation Began in America, 1969–1971* (New York: Stein and Day, 1971); Duberman, *Stonewall*; Carter, *Stonewall*; Stein, *Rethinking*, 79–114; Ann Bausum, *Stonewall: Breaking Out in the Fight for Gay Rights* (New York: Viking, 2016); Tristan Poehlmann, *The Stonewall Riots: The Fight for LGBT Rights* (Minneapolis: Abdo, 2017).

6 For the police reports, see http://outhistory.org/exhibits/show/stonewall-riot-police-reports.

7 For oral history projects, see Eric Marcus, *Making History* (New York: Harper-Collins, 1992) and the *Making Gay History* podcast at http://makinggayhistory.com; the LGBTQ History Digital Collaboratory Oral History Hub, http://lgbtqdigitalcollaboratory.org/oral-history-hub; Stonewall: Activism and Identity—Oral Histories and Archive, https://stonewallhistory.omeka.net/collections/show/stonewall—actvism-and-identit; and a new Stonewall oral history project commissioned by the National Park Service and coordinated by the Lower East Side Tenement Museum and the Lesbian, Gay, Bisexual & Transgender Community Center in New York City.

8 See the works cited in note 5 and Don Romesburg, ed., *The Routledge History of Queer America* (New York: Routledge, 2018).

9   Randy Wicker, "The Stonewall Myth: Lies about Gay Liberation," *GAY*, 9 Apr. 1973, 4–5. See also Price Dickenson [Dick Leitsch], "What Is 'Gay Power'?," *Mattachine Society of New York Newsletter*, Sept. 1969, 1–2; Jim Kepner, "When Did Gay Militancy Begin," *Advocate*, 23 Dec. 1971, 2, 10.

10 John D'Emilio, *Sexual Politics, Sexual Communities* (Chicago: University of Chicago Press, 1983). See also Toby Marotta, *The Politics of Homosexuality* (Boston: Houghton Mifflin, 1981).

11 See, for example, Mark Gabrish Conlan, "It Didn't All Start at Stonewall!," 20 Jan. 2012, *Zenger's News Magazine* (blog), http://zengersmag.blogspot.com. Philadelphians have made similar claims based on early gay rights demonstrations at Independence Hall; see Marc Stein, "Recalling Dewey's Sit-In," *Philadelphia Gay News*, 29 Apr. 2005, 10, 22–23.

12 Elizabeth Lapovsky Kennedy and Madeline Davis, *Boots of Leather* (New York: Routledge, 1993); George Chauncey, *Gay New York* (New York: Basic, 1994). See also Nan Alamilla Boyd, *Wide Open Town* (Berkeley: University of California Press, 2003).

13 Boyd, *Wide Open Town*, 108–147, 200–236.

14 Lizabeth Cohen, *A Consumers' Republic* (New York: Knopf, 2003); David Johnson, *Buying Gay* (New York: Columbia University Press, 2019).

15 While D'Emilio's and Marotta's books, cited in note 10, emphasized the influence of the homophile movement, they also highlighted the importance of social movement radicalization in the second half of the 1960s, which later scholars have also explored.

16 Don Jackson, "Reflections on the N.Y. Riots," *Los Angeles Advocate*, Oct. 1969, 11, 33. See also Don Jackson, "L.A. Gay Riots Threatened," *Los Angeles Free Press*, 15 May 1970, 16, 18. Jackson likely was referring to the contested theories commonly attributed to James C. Davies, "Toward a Theory of Revolution," *American Sociological Review* 27, no. 1 (Feb. 1962): 5–19, and later proposed as an explanation for the Watts Rebellion.

17 Eric Pace, "Policemen Forbidden to Entrap Homosexuals to Make Arrests," *New York Times*, 11 May 1966, 36; "No Public Complaints Reported since NY Gay Harassment Ended," *Los Angeles Advocate*, July 1968, 2.

18 New York State Penal Law 40.05 (1967); *Matter of Kerma Restaurant Corporation v. Liquor Authority*, 21 N.Y.2d 11 (New York Court of Appeals, 7 Dec. 1967).

19 Webster Schott, "Civil Rights and the Homosexual: A 4-Million Minority Asks for Equal Rights," *New York Times Magazine*, 12 Nov. 1967, 44–45, 49–54, 59; Charles Alverson, "A Minority's Plea: U.S. Homosexuals Gain in Trying to Persuade Society to Accept Them," *Wall Street Journal*, 17 Jul. 1968, 1, 23.

20 "City Lifts Job Curbs for Homosexuals," *New York Times*, 9 May 1969, 1, 23. For earlier moves, see "New York City Hiring Policy," *Mattachine Society of New York Newsletter*, Jan. 1967, 1.

21 "Male Nudes Not Obscene; DSI Acquitted on 29 Charges," *Los Angeles Advocate*, Sept. 1967, 1.

22 Anthony Lewis, "Commons Adopts a Bill to Modify Penalty for Adult Homosexuality," *New York Times*, 5 July 1967, 1, 5.

23 Jack Foster, "Police OK Full Drag," *Los Angeles Advocate*, Feb. 1969, 1.

24 Lyn Pedersen, "Connecticut Passes Sex Reform Law," *Los Angeles Advocate*, Aug. 1969, 1, 3.

25 "Pickets Win," *Los Angeles Advocate*, Aug. 1969, 6, 35.

26 "Cross Currents," *Ladder*, Oct. 1969, 29–30, 32. The Canadian law received royal assent on 27 June.

27 Julie Smith, "Choosing the Gay Way of Life," *San Francisco Chronicle (SFC)*, 30 June 1969, 22; Julie Smith, "How Does Girl Meet Girl?," *SFC*, 1 July 1969, 17; "The Tenderloin—A Gay Subculture," *SFC*, 1 July 1969, 17; Julie Smith, "Homophile Gay-Is-Good Movement," *SFC*, 2 July 1969, 22; *Norton v. Macy*, 417 F.2d 1161 (D.C. Cir. 1969).

28 Richard Reeves, "Marchi Defeats Lindsay in G.O.P. Primary," *New York Times*, 18 June 1969, 1, 24. Lindsay eventually won as the Liberal Party candidate.

29 "New Chief Justice Bad News for Gays," *Los Angeles Advocate*, Aug. 1969, 1, 12.

30 "Grim Reapings—Coast to Coast," *Mattachine Society of New York Newsletter*, June 1969, 6.

31 "Professor's Wife Vows to Avenge Husband's Death," *Berkeley Barb*, 27 June 1969, 11; "S.I.R. Seeks End to Cops in Toilets," *Berkeley Barb*, 27 June 1969, 11; "Widow Asks for $1,290,000," *Berkeley Barb*, 4 July 1969, 11.

32 For inventories and assessments of LGBT "progress," see Marc Stein, "Law and Politics: 'Crooked and Perverse' Narratives of LGBT Progress," in *The Routledge History of Queer America*, ed. Don Romesburg (New York: Routledge, 2018), 315–330; Martin Duberman, *Has the Gay Movement Failed?* (Berkeley: University of California Press, 2018).

Chapter 1. Gay Bars and Antigay Policing

1 Vincenz was a member of the Mattachine Society of Washington (D.C.). *Eastern Mattachine Magazine* was published by the Mattachine Societies of New York and Washington (D.C.).

2 Polak was president of the Philadelphia-based Janus Society and editor of the organization's magazine *Drum*, which referred to itself as the "gay *Playboy*."

3 Lahusen was a Philadelphia-based homophile activist, writer, and photographer and the partner of Barbara Gittings, who edited *The Ladder* from 1963 to 1966. *The Ladder* was published by the Daughters of Bilitis (DOB), a national lesbian organization based in San Francisco.

4 The Council on Religion and the Homosexual was a San Francisco–based organization that included religious leaders and homophile representatives; similar councils were established later in other cities. *ONE*, published in Los Angeles, was the oldest U.S. homophile magazine.

5 *The Los Angeles Advocate* was founded in 1967 and published by PRIDE (Personal Rights in Defense and Education), a local homophile organization.

6 Bello (a Cuban American immigrant) and Friedman were partners and co-editors of the newsletter published by the Philadelphia chapter of the Daughters of Bilitis.

7 In 1968, PRIDE sold *The Los Angeles Advocate* to Richard Mitch (pseudonym Dick Michaels) and Bill Rau (pseudonym Bill Rand).

8 The Mattachine Society of New York was founded as a chapter of the California-based Mattachine Society, but became autonomous in the early 1960s, when the national organization was restructured.

9 Leitsch was president, executive director, and newsletter editor of the Mattachine Society of New York, using the pseudonym Price Dickinson for the latter.

10 Wicker, born Charles Hayden, was the founder and leader of the Homosexual League of New York.

11 Williams, the African American leader of Citizens Alert, was the pastor of Glide Memorial Church in San Francisco and a founder of the Council on Religion and the Homosexual.

12 *The New York Hymnal* was published and edited by Craig Rodwell, founder of New York's Oscar Wilde Memorial Bookshop and leader of Homophile Youth

Movement in Neighborhoods (HYMN). Rodwell wrote much of the newsletter's uncredited material.

13 Richard Inman was the founder and president of the Mattachine Society of Florida.

Chapter 2. Activist Agendas and Visions before Stonewall

1 *Mattachine Review* was published by the San Francisco–based Mattachine Society and edited by Harold Call, who probably wrote this column.

2 Kameny was the co-founder and former president of the Mattachine Society of Washington.

3 Jaffy was research director of the Daughters of Bilitis.

4 East Coast Homophile Organizations was a federation of the Mattachine Societies of New York and Washington (D.C.), the Janus Society of Philadelphia, and the New York chapter of the Daughters of Bilitis.

5 Legg was the long-time editor of *ONE*.

6 The introductory comments appeared in the original.

7 This text was based on Polak's August 1966 address at the Second National Planning Conference of Homophile Organizations in San Francisco.

8 Beardemphl was president of the San Francisco–based Society for Individual Rights, which published *Vector*.

9 This text was based on Beardemphl's August 1966 speech at the DOB national convention in San Francisco.

10 The North American Conference of Homophile Organizations (NACHO) adopted the "Homosexual Bill of Rights" at its August 1968 convention in Chicago; more than one hundred delegates representing twenty-six organizations attended.

11 Shirley Willer was the former president of DOB's New York chapter and president of the national DOB. This text was based on Willer's August 1966 address at the Second National Planning Conference of Homophile Organizations in San Francisco.

12 Martin was a founder and former president of DOB, the former editor of *The Ladder*, and a founding board member of the Council on Religion and the Homosexual in San Francisco.

13 Marat was the president of Vanguard, which was based in San Francisco's Tenderloin. The name was presumably a pseudonym; Jean-Paul Marat was an eighteenth-century French revolutionary. This text was based on Marat's August 1966 address at the Second National Planning Conference of Homophile Organizations in San Francisco. *Cruise News* was published by Guy Strait in San Francisco; its name was based on the name of the magazine *U.S. News & World Report*.

14 *Transvestia*, based in Los Angeles, was founded and edited by Virginia Prince and published by Chevalier Publications.

15 Susanna Valenti, also known as Tito, was a Cuban American immigrant, a regular columnist for *Transvestia*, and co-founder of Casa Susanna, a trans retreat in upstate New York.

16 This statement was adopted by the Western Regional Planning Conference at its April 1967 meeting in Los Angeles, which was attended by representatives of more than sixteen homophile groups.

17 The Erickson Educational Foundation, founded in 1964 by Reed Erickson, was based in Baton Rouge, Louisiana; it supported research on homosexuality and transsexualism.

18 For early references to gay power, see "Attorney Hallinan Advocates 'Gay Power,'" *Vector*, Nov. 1966, 1; Cindy Claire Lewis, "Gay Power," *Vector*, July 1967, 21; "U.S. Capital Turns on to Gay Power," *Los Angeles Advocate*, Sept. 1967, 1. See also A. Cecil Williams, "On Getting and Using Power," *Vector*, Jan. 1965, 4, 9, 10.

19 Laurence was the new editor of *Vector* when he wrote this column; he was removed from his position shortly thereafter.

20 *Berkeley Barb* was an underground weekly newspaper based in Berkeley, California.

Chapter 3. Political Protests before Stonewall

1 There were additional White House demonstrations on 29 May and 23 October 1965.

2 On the July Fourth Independence Hall demonstrations, 1965–69, see the documentary film *Gay Pioneers*, dir. Glenn Holsten (2001).

3 There was an additional demonstration at the State Department on 28 August 1965.

4 The CRH also joined other groups in a demonstration at the August/September 1966 California State Fair in Sacramento after fair organizers withdrew permission for homophile activists to sponsor an informational booth.

5 This report, produced six years after the events it describes and published in the program of San Francisco's 1972 gay pride parade, is the earliest known documentary record of Compton's Cafeteria Riots. See the documentary film *Screaming Queens*, dir. Victor Silverman and Susan Stryker (2005).

6 The *Village Voice* was an alternative newsweekly published in Greenwich Village.

7 Don Slater was an early member of the Mattachine Society in Los Angeles, a founder and former editor of *ONE* magazine, the editor of *Tangents* (published by former *ONE* editors while they pursued unsuccessful litigation to regain control of *ONE*), and the leader of the Committee to Fight Exclusion of Homosexuals from the Armed Forces.

8 *Homosexual Citizen* was published by the Mattachine Society of Washington and edited by Lily Hansen (Lilli Vincenz).

9 There also were July Fourth Annual Reminders at Independence Hall in 1967, 1968, and 1969.

10 Several months before this demonstration, on 2 July the Mattachine Society of New York organized a protest and boycott of the *Brooklyn Heights Press*.

11 This issue was dated January 1967, but the contents suggest that it was not published until June.

12 Other sources indicate that the February Black Cat demonstration was part of a coordinated set of Los Angeles neighborhood protests against "police lawlessness" and especially police mistreatment of African Americans, Mexican Americans, and youth.

13 Other sources indicate that Lady Java was African American.

14 This text was part of a four-page handout used at a demonstration at the Columbia University College of Physicians and Surgeons. Lawrence Kolb was chairman of Columbia's Department of Psychiatry, director of the New York State Psychiatric Institute, and president of the American Psychiatric Association.

15 On 30 April, the protests against States Steamship Company spread to the company's Los Angeles office.

16 Denaro was rehired after CHF demonstrations on 17, 24, and 25 May. CHF also participated in International Grape Boycott Day demonstrations at Safeway grocery stores on 10 May 1969.

Chapter 4. The Stonewall Inn

1   The *International Guild Guide* was published annually beginning in the early 1960s. Guild Press, founded by H. Lynn Womack, was a major producer of gay-oriented books, magazines, and photographs, which were distributed by the Guild Book Service. The excerpts reprinted here are the listings for Greenwich Village and do not include the listings for other Manhattan neighborhoods and other New York City boroughs; telephone numbers have been removed.

2   There was a separate listing for "The Stonewall" in the Manhattan section, which preceded the Manhattan/Greenwich Village section; its location was listed as "Sheridan Square West" and its hours as 10 p.m. to 6 a.m. (page 55).

3   This guide, which presented itself as a second volume, was edited by Jerome Taylor and published by Apollo Book Company, a bookstore located at 48 East 21st Street. The 1968 *Catalog of Copyright Entries* lists Mattachine Book Service as the copyright registrant. The excerpts reprinted here are the listings for Manhattan bars, baths, parks, and private clubs; there were other sections for clothing shops, restaurants, other boroughs, and nearby regions; telephone numbers have been removed.

4   Bush was an actor and writer, best known for co-authoring the play *De Sade Illustrated* (1969), acting in *Depraved!* (1967) and *The Naked Witch* (1967), and writing the screenplay for three films: *Compass Rose* (1967), *Kiss Me, Kiss Me, Kiss Me!* (1968), and *Barbara* (1970).

5   *Hymnal* also published a bar column that occasionally referenced the Stonewall. One column noted, "Dancing continues strong in the Village as the *Stone Wall* (on Christopher Street near Sheridan Square) continues operating amid rumors of closing. Usually crowded and cruisy, it caters to a young crowd who seem to spend all their time perfecting their dancing." See Carl Lee, "It's What's Happening," *New York Hymnal*, Mar. 1968, 3. Another stated, "What's happening around town can be summed up in one word: raids. Police attention has reportedly been paid to *Stonewall, Candy Store, Second Floor, Telstar* and *McGregor's*. The last closed after seven police visits in one week. The raids have nothing to do with the fact that the bars are gay, but because they are operating illegally— overcrowding, lack of proper licenses, etc." See Carl Lee, "It's What's Happening," *New York Hymnal*, Apr. 1968, 2. A third observed, "The Stone Wall (W. Christopher St.) is still in operation, unfortunately. Hoping to save their declining business, the Mafia management instituted 'go-go boys' on platforms. As was to be expected, the 'go-go boys' look and dance more like hootchy-kootchy dancers in the Casbah. This 'new' look along with the filthy john, the high prices and the goons assure that the Stone Wall remains the tackiest joint in town." See Carl Lee, "It's What's Happening," *New York Hymnal*, June 1968, 2.

Chapter 5. The Stonewall Riots

1   For other early coverage, see "N.Y. Homosexuals Protest Raids," *Washington Post*, 1 July 1969, E2; Leo Laurence, "Gays Get Panther OK," *Berkeley Tribe*, 25 July 1969, 7; William B. Kelley, "Riot, Tree-Cutting Mark NYC Gay Scene," *Mattachine Midwest Newsletter*, July 1969, 7; Bobbie Huff, "N.Y. Po-lice Scream at Queens," *Magpie*, Aug. 1969, 14; Editorial, *Tangents*, Aug. 1969, 2; "Tangents," *Tangents*, Aug. 1969, 14–15; "The Birth of Gay Power," *Daughters of Bilitis New York Newsletter*, Sept. 1969, 1–2; "Homophile News Fronts," *Vector*, Oct. 1969, 4; Nancy L. Ross, "Homosexual Revolution," *Washington Post*, 25 Oct. 1969, C1-C2; "Policing the Third Sex," *Newsweek*, 27 Oct. 1969, 76–77; Christopher Cory, "The

Homosexual: Newly Visible, Newly Understood," *Time*, 31 Oct. 1969, 56–67; Charles P. Thorp, letter to the editor, *Los Angeles Advocate*, Nov. 1969, 20; Tom Burke, "The New Homosexuality," *Esquire*, Dec. 1969, 178, 304–318. Several secondary sources cite "Cop Injured: 5 Seized in Village," *New York Post*, 3 July 1969, which can be found in Craig Rodwell's Papers (Box 10) at the New York Public Library, but the article does not appear on the *Post* microfilms that I have examined. The clipping in Rodwell's papers has a handwritten reference to the *Post* and looks like a *Post* article. Some newspapers in this era printed multiple editions each day; this article may have appeared in some but not other editions.

2 The *New York Daily News* published two versions of this article on 29 June 1969.

3 In the September *Mattachine Society of New York Newsletter* (p. 2), Leitsch noted that "The Hairpin Drop" was originally distributed as a leaflet; he described it as a "wildly amusing account of the first part of the Christopher Street Riots" and claimed that it was "the first detailed account available, having beaten the newspapers to the full story." It was later revised and published as Dick Leitsch, "Police Raid on N.Y. Club Sets Off First Gay Riot," *Los Angeles Advocate*, Sept. 1969, 3, 11–12.

4 *Rat*, also called *Rat Subterranean News*, was an underground newspaper based in New York.

5 There was an additional letter by John Thomas of Queens, New York.

6 *National Guardian* was a New York–based weekly newspaper with left politics.

7 Poland (originally named John Jefferson Poland) was one of the founders of the Sexual Freedom League, lived in the Bay Area, and referred to himself as bisexual.

8 *Berkeley Tribe* was an underground weekly newspaper based in Berkeley, California.

9 Nichols was the co-founder of the Mattachine Society of Washington (D.C.). *Screw* was a New York–based pornographic weekly newspaper edited by Al Goldstein. "Pampered Perverts" appeared in Lige and Jack's "Homosexual Citizen" column in *Screw*. The article was later revised and published as Lige and Jack, "Remember the Stonewall!," *GAY*, 29 June 1970, 5; *GAY* was published by Four Swords, Inc. (owned by Goldstein and Jim Buckley) and edited by Clarke and Nichols.

10 In the same issue, on page 18, "D.D.'s New York" observed, "GAY POWER seems to be the newest cry in the city as a result of the Stonewall bust—and lest we forget, it took the swishy, fem queens to start the ball rolling. I'm all for it as long as the movement is disciplined, organized and done within the law. I don't want my bleached head busted and I don't want my fans' heads split open, either." On page 19, "Boys out of Jail" noted, "Those who were at the special meeting on July 16 at St. John's-in-the-Village will remember that we took up a collection, which totaled $105.00, to try to get two boys out of jail who had been arrested during the rioting. Dick Leitsch turned the money over to one of our lawyers, who then took the necessary steps to get the two out on bail. They still have to stand trial, but at least they are out of jail and will be defended by Mattachine lawyers."

11 The Homophile Action League, whose newsletter was edited by Bello and Friedman, was the Philadelphia-based successor to that city's chapter of the Daughters of Bilitis.

12 *The Insider* was edited by Eva Freund and Richard Schaefers. The epigraph was taken from *Marat/Sade*, the shortened title of a 1963 play by Peter Weiss and a 1967 film by Peter Brook and Adrian Mitchell. I thank David Carter for calling this article to my attention.

Chapter 6. Activist Agendas and Visions after Stonewall

1 The original GLF was based in New York, but autonomous GLFs soon formed in other places, in and beyond the United States. This introduction appeared in the original.

2 The North American Conference of Homophile Organizations met in Kansas City in August 1969; fourteen organizations were represented. *Gay Power* was a New York–based biweekly newspaper; founded and edited by John Heys, it began publication in September 1969.

3 The original GAA, formed by disaffected GLF members who wanted to focus more exclusively on gay issues, was based in New York, but autonomous GAAs soon formed in other places.

4 Wittman was a former member of the national council of Students for a Democratic Society and a member of the San Francisco–based Committee for Homosexual Freedom. The *San Francisco Free Press* was an alternative newspaper. This text is often misdated as 1970 because the newspaper issue in which it appeared was dated December 22–January 7, 1970. Some sources suggest that Wittman wrote and circulated early drafts of this text before the Stonewall Riots.

5 Martha Shelley (originally Altman) was a former president of the New York chapter of the Daughters of Bilitis and a founding member of New York's GLF and GLF Women (a GLF caucus).

6 Kuromiya, who was Japanese American, was a former member of Students for a Democratic Society and a founder and leader of Philadelphia's GLF. *Philadelphia Free Press* was an alternative newspaper.

7 The original Radicalesbians was based in New York, but autonomous Radicalesbians groups formed in other places. The New York group, which initially called itself the Lavender Menace, formed in 1970 and included disaffected members of GLF and other gay, lesbian, and feminist groups. This manifesto was distributed at the Second Congress to United Women in New York and published in GLF's newspaper, *Come Out!*

8 The Lesbian Workshop was predominantly white; many participants were members of Radicalesbians in New York. The convention was organized by the Black Panther Party and held in Philadelphia.

9 Martin, introduced in chapter 2, redirected her activism around this time to focus on the National Organization for Women. Toward the end of 1970, *The Los Angeles Advocate* was renamed *The Advocate*.

10 Cornwell was a member of Philadelphia Radicalesbians.

11 This is the text of a speech delivered at a Los Angeles rally sponsored by the Women's National Abortion Action Campaign on 13 February 1973 (after the U.S. Supreme Court ruling in *Roe v. Wade*). Córdova was an immigrant from Germany with Mexican and Irish parents. She was a former president of the Los Angeles chapter of the Daughters of Bilitis, editor of *Lesbian Tide* magazine, and principal organizer of the 1973 National Lesbian Conference in Los Angeles. Founded by GLF Detroit in 1970, *Gay Liberator* was published by an independent collective after GLF Detroit dissolved in 1971.

12 *Gay Dealer* was a special issue of *Plain Dealer*, an alternative newspaper in Philadelphia.

13 *Drag*, subtitled *A Magazine about the Transvestite*, was published in New York by Queens Publications and edited by Lee Brewster; it began publication in 1971. Brewster was the founder of Queens, which renamed itself Queens Liberation Front after the Stonewall Riots.

14 Rivera was born and raised in New York; her family of origin was from Puerto Rico and Venezuela. She was a former member of GLF, a member of GAA, and co-founder of Street Transvestite Action Revolutionaries (originally called Street Transvestites for Gay Power).

15 Marsha Johnson, who was African American, was a founding member of GLF and Street Transvestite Action Revolutionaries (originally called Street Transvestites for Gay Power). *Out of the Closets* was an anthology of writings on gay liberation.

16 Newton was the co-founder and minister of defense of the Black Panther Party.

17 The Male Homosexual Workshop was multiracial; many of its participants were GLF activists and members of GLF caucuses for people of color. The convention was organized by the Black Panther Party and held in Philadelphia in September 1970.

18 Third World Gay Revolution was established in 1970 as a caucus for people of color in New York's GLF; groups with similar names later formed in other cities, including Chicago and Detroit.

Chapter 7. Political Protests after Stonewall

1 *Gay Flames*, subtitled *A Bulletin of the Homofire Movement*, was founded in 1970 by a group of radical GLF men in New York.

2 *Ain't I a Woman*, subtitled *A Midwest Newspaper of Women's Liberation*, was founded in 1970 by the Iowa City Women's Liberation Front.

3 *Lesbian Feminist* was the newsletter of Lesbian Feminist Liberation in New York.

4 *Gay Activist* was the newsletter of GAA in New York.

Chapter 8. Pride Marches and Parades

1 *Gay Alternative* was a Philadelphia-based periodical.

INDEX

on injustices against homosexuals, 33–34, 90–91; Mardi Gras New Year's Ball, 31–32; and political protests, 95, 104–105, 325n4; press conference about Charles Socarides, 103–104

counterculture, 7, 10, 12, 66–67, 83, 84, 153, 167–168, 180, 189, 191, 196, 213, 214, 253; influence on LGBT activism, 56, 187. *See also* Angels of Light; Cockettes; Ginsberg, Allen

Cromey, Robert W., 90–91, 104

Cronkite, Walter, 235–236

cross-dressers. *See* drag and drag queens; queens; Queens Liberation Front; Street Transvestite Action Revolutionaries (STAR); transvestites and transvestism

cross-gender impersonation, statutes and ordinances prohibiting, 13, 51, 98, 99, 101, 165, 213, 240–241, 242

Cruise News & World Report, 74, 91, 324n13

Crumly, Charles, 35–36

Cuba, 86, 228

Cubans and Cuban Americans, 86. *See also* Bello, Ada; Ruiz, Hiram; Valenti, Susanna

dances, 35, 189, 214, 229–230, 247, 282; balls, 206, 213, 240–241; gay pride, 286

d'Arcangelo, Angelo. *See* Bush, Josef

Daughters of Bilitis: and Charles Socarides, 103–104; and Citizens Alert, 46; critique of gay organizations, 72–73; demonstrations, 95, 227, 239, 249, 254, 266, 278, 279–280; and East Coast Homophile Organizations, 324n4; emergence and history of, 9, 187, 323n3, 324n3; Los Angeles chapter, 328n11; membership in the Council on Religion and the Homosexual, 31; New York chapter, 65, 227, 239, 282, 328n5; Philadelphia chapter, 323n6, 327n11; relationship with North American Conference of Homophile Organizations, 205; relationship with Radicalesbians and Gay Liberation Front, 200; relationship with transvestites, 214; and San Francisco civil rights ordinance, 261; and women's liberation, 249–250. *See also* Córdova, Jeanne; Eppenger, Ernestine; Gittings, Barbara; Homophile Action League; Jaffy, Florence; *Ladder, The*; Lahusen, Kay; Martin, Del; Shelley, Martha; Willer, Shirley

Daughters of Bilitis Philadelphia Newsletter, 36, 73, 323n6

Davies, Diana (photographer), ii

Davies, James C., 322n16

Davis, Kate (*Stonewall Uprising* film), 6

decriminalization. *See* cross-gender impersonation, statutes and ordinances prohibiting; sodomy

DeLarverie, Stormé, 17

Democratic Party, 13, 242, 269, 270–271, 288. *See also* Brown, Willie; Feinstein, Dianne; Kennedy, Robert; Koch, Ed

Denaro, Frank, 109, 325n16

Detroit, 281, 328n11, 329n18

Dewey's restaurant (Philadelphia), sit-in at, 10, 87–88

Di Brienza, Ronnie, 153–156

Dick Cavett Show, 234

Dickinson, Price. *See* Leitsch, Dick

disease/illness, homosexuality as, 7, 16, 61, 71, 211, 213, 219, 233; declassification of homosexuality as, 20, 274–275. *See also* health; psychiatry and psychology

disorderly conduct, charge of, 27, 32, 36–37, 44, 45–46, 88, 127, 129, 137, 254–255, 257, 286

Drag (magazine), 212–213, 242, 281, 328n13

drag and drag queens, 3, 32, 79, 92–93, 98, 99, 101, 214, 242, 260, 272–273; and drag balls, 206, 213, 240–241; performances, 11, 114, 206; and pride parades, 281, 288, 295–296; and the Stonewall Riots, 138, 156–157, 169, 175, 176, 179. *See also* cross-gender impersonation, statutes and ordinances prohibiting; *Drag* (magazine); Johnson, Marsha P.; queens; Queens Liberation Front; Rivera, Sylvia Lee; Street Transvestite Action Revolutionaries (STAR); transvestites and transvestism

drugs, 2, 3, 11, 95, 165, 177, 253

Drum, 14, 29, 66, 87, 323n2

Duberman, Martin *(Stonewall)*, 6, 20

Dunfee, Don, 297

East Coast Homophile Organizations, 87, 91, 324n4; July Fourth demonstration flier, 62–63

East Lansing, Michigan, 261

East Village Other, 153–156, 178

Eastern Mattachine Magazine, 28, 45, 60, 61, 89, 323n1

Eastern Regional Conference of Homophile Organizations, 226, 277

Eckstein, Ernestine. *See* Eppenger, Ernestine

Efland, Howard, 14, 43, 256

electoral politics and elections, 3, 7, 14, 16, 85, 159–160, 166, 174, 182, 225, 266, 271–272. *See also* Democratic Party; Republican Party

Electric Circus (New York), 167–168

Emmerich, Roland (*Stonewall* film), 6

employment discrimination, 69, 70, 86, 97, 104–105, 109, 221, 226, 221, 267, 292; and New York fair employment legislation, 241, 248, 259–260, 265–266, 282; and San Francisco civil rights ordinance, 261; and United States Civil Service Commission, 10, 13, 89, 264–265. *See also* States Steamship Company; Tower Records

England and Wales: decriminalization of consensual same-sex sex in, 13; homophile movement in, 57

trans and transgender, 1, 2, 3, 7, 17, 18–19, 23. *See also* Brewster, Lee G.; butches; Compton's Cafeteria; Dewey's restaurant; drag and drag queens; Johnson, Marsha P.; Prince, Virginia; queens; Queens Liberation Front; Rivera, Sylvia Lee; transsexuals; *Transvestia*; transvestites and transvestism

transsexuals, 9, 44–45, 51, 56, 71, 80–81, 145–146, 164–165, 211–212, 324n17; patrons of the Stonewall Inn, 3. *See also* Erickson, Reed; Key, Douglas; Prince, Virginia

Transvestia, 77, 324nn14–15

transvestites and transvestism, 77–78, 79–80, 246, 260, 295, 328n13; and activism, 211–214; and Black Cat bar raid, 99; and Compton's Cafeteria, 92–93; identification as gay, 18; and marriage, 79–80, 214; patrons of the Stonewall Inn, 3; and prostitution, 165; and statutes and ordinances prohibiting cross-gender impersonation, 13, 51, 98, 99, 101, 165, 213, 240–241, 242. See also *Drag*; drag and drag queens; Johnson, Marsha P.; Prince, Virginia; queens; Queens Liberation Front; Rivera, Sylvia Lee; Street Transvestite Action Revolutionaries (STAR); *Transvestia*

Truscott, Lucian IV, 138–143, *140–141*

unions, 84, 107, 236, 239, 244, 246, 325n16
United Nations, protests at, 10, 86
United States Civil Service Commission, protest at, 10, 13, 89, 264–265
UpStairs Lounge fire (New Orleans), 20, 298

Valenti, Susanna, 77–78, 324n15
Van Ronk, Dave, 5, 127, 128, 129, 138, 139, 144–145
Vanguard (magazine), 75–76, 95–96
Vanguard (San Francisco), 9, 74–75, 91–92, 95–96, 324n13
Vector, 68, 78, 82, 104, 107, 231, 289, 324n8, 325n19. *See also* Society for Individual Rights
Verra, Anthony, 128
Vietnam and Vietnamese people, 170; National Liberation Front in, 187; oppression of Viet-

namese people, 188, 194. *See also* Vietnam War

Vietnam War, 83, 170, 187, 188, 248; escalation in, 13; opposition to, 16, 190, 238, 244; protests against, 12, 238–239. *See also* Vietnam and Vietnamese people

Village Voice, 6, 20, 93, 126, 138–146, *140, 141, 146,* 158–161, 164, 167, 171, 179–181, 227, 229–230, 325n6

Viñales, Diego, 255–256

Vincenz, Lilli (Lily Hansen), 28–29, 323n1, 325n8

Walters, Barbara, 234
Warren, Earl, 14
Washington, D.C., 89, 226, 239, 247–248, 254. See also *Eastern Mattachine Magazine*; *Homosexual Citizen; Insider, The*; Kameny, Franklin E.; Mattachine Society of Washington, D.C.; Nichols, John Richard; Pentagon; United States Civil Service Commission; Vincenz, Lilli; White House; Zephyr Restaurant
Watts Rebellion, 12, 64–65, 67, 322n16
weddings, same-sex. *See* marriage
Weiser, Joel, 2
Weiser, Kelly, 279–280
West Germany, 13
Western Regional Planning Conference of Homophile Organizations, 78–79, 324n16
White House, 10, 66, 86, 95, 271, 325n1
Whittington, Gale, 107, 232, 236
Wicker, Randolfe (Randy), 8, 45–46, 165–166, 167–168, 233, 287–288, 294–296, 323n10
Willer, Shirley, 71–72, 104, 324n11
Williams, A. Cecil, 46, 83, 323n11
Williams, Cathy, 251
Williams, Lois, 46
Williams, Stan, 285
Wittman, Carl, 191–197, 328n4

Yukon (Los Angeles), 37–31
Yurman, Cary, 265–266

Zephyr Restaurant (Washington, D.C.), 247–248

ABOUT THE AUTHOR

Marc Stein is an award-winning historian who has authored three critically acclaimed scholarly books, edited a three-volume encyclopedia on LGBT history, and published a large set of short works and online exhibits aimed at general audiences. His first monograph, *City of Sisterly and Brotherly Loves: Lesbian and Gay Philadelphia, 1945–1972* (2000), was the first book-length study of gay and lesbian history in a major U.S. city. He then served as the editor in chief of the *Encyclopedia of LGBT History in America* (2003), which won four major awards for reference works. More recently, he published *Sexual Injustice: Supreme Court Decisions from Griswold to Roe* (2010), which was selected as a *Choice* Outstanding Academic Title, and *Rethinking the Gay and Lesbian Movement* (2012), which is taught in a large number of courses. Stein has chaired both the Committee on LGBT History (affiliated with the American Historical Association) and the Committee on the Status of LGBTQ Historians and Histories (a standing committee of the Organization of American Historians). He is a former coordinating editor of the Boston-based *Gay Community News*; a member of the board of directors and national advisory board of the GLBT Historical Society in San Francisco; an advisory board member of the John Wilcox Archives at the William Way LGBT Community Center in Philadelphia; a contributing editor for the *OutHistory* website; and a contributor to *OutHistory*, the *Notches* blog, the *History News Network*, and the *UNC Press Blog*. He has taught at the University of Pennsylvania, Bryn Mawr College, Colby College, and York University; since 2014 he has been the Jamie and Phyllis Pasker Professor of History at San Francisco State University.